Implementing to Cash Process in SAP

An end-to-end guide to understanding the OTC process and its integration with SAP CRM, SAP APO, SAP TMS, and SAP LES

Chandrakant Agarwal

BIRMINGHAM—MUMBAI

Implementing Order to Cash Process in SAP

Group Product Manager: Aaron Lazar

Publishing Product Manager: Kushal Dave

Senior Editor: Rohit Singh

Content Development Editor: Vaishali Ramkumar

Technical Editor: Rashmi Subhash Choudhari

Copy Editor: Safis Editing

Project Coordinator: Deeksha Thakkar

Proofreader: Safis Editing

Indexer: Pratik Shirodkar

Production Designer: Prashant Ghare

First published: April 2021

Production reference: 1140421

Published by Packt Publishing Ltd.

Livery Place

35 Livery Street

Birmingham

B3 2PB, UK.

ISBN 978-1-80107-610-4

www.packt.com

Writing a book on implementing the Order to Cash process in SAP was an eventful journey as it took a considerable amount of time and effort to complete. I would like to acknowledge all my friends and colleagues with whom I have been associated during my SAP career till now, and while implementing SAP Order to Cash solutions in various projects. I would like to extend my thanks to my mentors who have helped me to gain knowledge at each phase of my projects and who have given me the opportunity to lead projects in the customer and supply chain domains.

I would like to acknowledge the contributors from SAP Help and **SAP Community Network (SCN)** who helped me to understand and resolve critical issues. This book would not have been possible without me contributing to SAP Help and SCN. My special thanks to the whole Packt Publishing team, especially the production team, and Vaishali Ramkumar, in particular, for helping me to bring this book together.

I would like to thank my parents; without their blessings, this book would not have been possible. I would like to first and foremost thank my loving and patient wife, Pallavi, and both of my sons, Divyang and Arjun, for their continued support, patience, and encouragement throughout the long process of writing. My wife and kids have sacrificed a lot during this journey and their unconditional support was the driver for me to write and finish this book.

Last but not the least; this book is dedicated to the memory of my late brother, Ravi Agarwal.

Contributors

About the author

Chandrakant Agarwal primarily works within the customer and supply chain domains as an architect, and has 18 years of SAP experience, ranging from SAP project implementation to SAP upgrade projects to SAP rollout projects. He has had exposure to global assignments in customer-facing roles, ranging from business consulting, solution implementation, rollouts, and production support/development to quality assurance.

He is a certified SAP CRM and SAP ERP MM consultant, with advanced business knowledge of Order to Cash processes. Chandrakant has implementation experience in SAP CRM Marketing, Sales, and Service, SAP APO (DP, SNP, and GATP), SAP TMS, and SAP LES. He has also worked on SAP cloud technologies, including Sales Cloud, SAP Ariba, and SAP IBP, and UI technologies such as SAP Fiori. He has led multiple projects that span across different areas, including SAP CRM, SCM, and TMS, as well as across different regions, such as Asia, Europe, and America.

About the reviewer

Murtaza Kapadia primarily works within the customer relationship management domain as a solutions architect, with over 15 years of SAP experience ranging from SAP project implementation and upgrades to rollout projects. Murtaza has implementation experience in SAP CRM Sales, Service, and Marketing, SAP ECC, and ISU. He has led multiple projects with various end clients globally in Asia and Europe and currently works in America. His technical expertise (over 10 years of hands-on experience) includes SAP-ABAP, ABAP on HANA, BSP, and Python programming.

Table of Contents

3

Master Data in SAP APO

4

Master Data in SAP TMS

5

Master Data in SAP LES

6

Basic Functions in a Sales Document

7

Sales Document Processing in SAP CRM

8

Order Fulfillment with SAP APO

9

Transportation Requirements in SAP TMS

10

Transportation Planning and Freight Order Management in SAP TMS

11

Logistics Execution in SAP LES

12

Customer Billing

13
Analytics

Other Books You May Enjoy

Index

Preface

SAP has extended the functionalities in SAP **Customer Relationship Management (CRM)**, SAP **Advanced Planning and Optimization (APO)**, and SAP **Transportation Management System (TMS)** beyond those available within SAP **Enterprise Central Component (ECC)**. With this book, you'll not only cover the Order to Cash process with SAP ECC, but also with SAP CRM, SAP APO, SAP TMS, and SAP **Logistics Execution System (LES)**, exploring their key functionalities and configuration.

Using different SAP systems in an integrated manner to gain maximum benefits in the running of your business is made possible by this book. The book covers how to effectively implement Order to Cash processes with SAP CRM, SAP APO, SAP TMS, SAP LES, and SAP ECC.

With this book, readers will follow a step-by-step implementation of the various techniques involved in the integration touchpoints of different systems to optimize the complete Order to Cash process with mySAP Business Suite. This will help you to implement mySAP Business Suite and understand the shortcomings in your existing SAP ECC environment. The book starts with an introduction to the UI technologies in SAP systems followed by the chapters on master data covering different SAP environments. From there, this book will take you to the Order to Cash cycle, including order management in SAP CRM, order fulfillment in SAP APO, transportation planning in SAP TMS, logistics execution in SAP LES, and billing in SAP ECC.

By the end of this SAP book, you will have a thorough understanding of how different SAP systems work together with the Order to Cash process in SAP.

Who this book is for

This book is for SAP consultants, subject-matter experts, solutions architects, and key users of SAP with end-to-end knowledge of Order to Cash business processes. Customers operating SAP CRM, SAP APO, SAP TMS, and SAP LES as part of their daily operations will also benefit from this book by understanding their key capabilities and integration touchpoints. Working knowledge of SAP ECC, SAP CRM, SAP APO, SAP TMS, and SAP LES is required before getting started with this book.

What this book covers

Chapter 1, Introduction to the Order to Cash Cycle, offers an overview of the Order to Cash process with SAP CRM, SAP APO, SAP TM, and SAP ECC-LES functions and its architectural view. This chapter provides the reader with knowledge on how SAP systems are integrated to fulfill the Order to Cash process. You will also learn about the UI technologies used in these systems.

Chapter 2, Master Data in SAP CRM, covers the topic of master data in SAP CRM, including organization management, business partners, products, pricing, vendors, and plants. It also covers the configuration required to set up the master data in SAP CRM, including replication from SAP ECC to SAP CRM. The key takeaway from this chapter is understanding the significance of master data usage in SAP CRM.

Chapter 3, Master Data in SAP APO, covers master data in SAP APO, including locations, products, and resources. This chapter covers the setup of master data in SAP APO, including how to replicate data from SAP ECC to SAP APO. The key takeaway from this chapter is understanding the significance of master data usage in SAP APO.

Chapter 4, Master Data in SAP TMS, covers master data in SAP TMS, including organization management, business partners, products, transportation networks, and resources. This chapter covers the setup of master data in SAP TMS, including how to replicate the data from SAP ECC to SAP TMS. The key takeaway from this chapter is understanding the significance of master data usage in SAP TMS.

Chapter 5, Master Data in SAP LES, covers the setup of warehouse master data that is required during picking, including warehouse structure, storage types, storage sections, storage bins, and quants. This chapter covers the setup of the warehouse master, including its configuration in SAP LES. The key takeaway from this chapter is understanding the significance of the warehouse master data setup required in order to pick, pack, and ship products to customers.

Chapter 6, Basic Functions in Sales Documents, teaches the foundations of business transactions in the SAP CRM system. It covers the basic functions, including the structure of sales transactions, partner processing, text management, date management, status management, credit management, and actions.

Chapter 7, Sales Document Processing in SAP CRM, covers sales transaction processing, its key concepts, and how to configure these transactions in SAP CRM as per your business needs. Sales document processing in SAP CRM allows companies to perform sales transactions with the customer. This chapter helps readers to understand the extent of sales document processing, including sales contracts, sales quotations, and sales orders.

Chapter 8, Order Fulfillment with SAP APO, provides information on how to fulfill orders based on customer-requested dates. This chapter helps readers to understand true **global available-to-promise** (**GATP**) and how to provide accurate product availability and substitution possibilities with the SAP APO system. Key takeaways within this chapter are understanding and building the order fulfillment capabilities with configuration setup in the SAP APO environment.

Chapter 9, Transportation Requirements in SAP TMS, covers the transportation requirement processes and its integration with the SAP ECC system. This chapter covers the complete functionality around how transportation requirements are realized in SAP TMS. The transportation process starts with the request for transportation services and this chapter provides an understanding of different transportation requirement options, including order-based and delivery-based transportation requirements.

Chapter 10, Transportation Planning and Freight Order Management in SAP TMS, teaches you about the transportation planning processes and freight order management in SAP TMS. This chapter covers the planning constraints and key concepts around the freight order document, including its configuration. You will also learn the concepts of carrier selection and tendering processes within this chapter.

Chapter 11, Logistics Execution in SAP LES, covers the freight order integration with shipment documents in SAP ECC, along with shipment processing and posting goods issues. You will also learn the concept of transportation charge management and how to settle freight with the carrier in this chapter. The key takeaway here is understanding how shipment execution takes place and the steps required to pick, pack, and ship the products.

Chapter 12, Customer Billing, covers processing bills in the SAP ECC system. It teaches you about different billing document types, methods of billing, their functions, and the configuration required to set up billing document types. Key takeaways in this chapter are understanding how billing documents are processed after the freight settlement steps.

Chapter 13, Analytics, covers high-level reporting capabilities in SAP CRM and SAP TMS, including how to measure the accuracy of the Order to Cash cycle. You will also understand the concepts involved with the HANA Sidecar approach in the SAP environment and how you can leverage the reporting capabilities with HANA Sidecar.

To get the most out of this book

Working knowledge of SAP ECC, SAP CRM, SAP APO, SAP TMS, and SAP LES is required before getting started with this book. You will be following a step-by-step implementation of the various techniques involved in the integration of different systems to optimize the complete Order to Cash process with mySAP Business Suite.

Download the color images

We also provide a PDF file that has color images of the screenshots/diagrams used in this book. You can download it here: `https://static.packt-cdn.com/downloads/9781801076104_ColorImages.pdf`.

Conventions used

There are a number of text conventions used throughout this book.

`Code in text`: Indicates code words in text, database table names, folder names, filenames, file extensions, pathnames, dummy URLs, user input, and Twitter handles. Here is an example: "You can use any partner functions based on your requirements; the most commonly used are `Sold-To Party`, `Ship-To Party`, `Bill-To Party`, and `Payer`."

Bold: Indicates a new term, an important word, or words that you see on screen. For example, words in menus or dialog boxes appear in the text like this. Here is an example: "If the **Block** field on the partner function configuration is active, it blocks the source partner from being determined when the partner determination takes place."

> **Tips or important notes**
> Appear like this.

Get in touch

Feedback from our readers is always welcome.

General feedback: If you have questions about any aspect of this book, mention the book title in the subject of your message and email us at `customercare@packtpub.com`.

Errata: Although we have taken every care to ensure the accuracy of our content, mistakes do happen. If you have found a mistake in this book, we would be grateful if you would report this to us. Please visit www.packtpub.com/support/errata, selecting your book, clicking on the Errata Submission Form link, and entering the details.

Piracy: If you come across any illegal copies of our works in any form on the internet, we would be grateful if you would provide us with the location address or website name. Please contact us at copyright@packt.com with a link to the material.

If you are interested in becoming an author: If there is a topic that you have expertise in and you are interested in either writing or contributing to a book, please visit authors.packtpub.com.

Reviews

Please leave a review. Once you have read and used this book, why not leave a review on the site that you purchased it from? Potential readers can then see and use your unbiased opinion to make purchase decisions, we at Packt can understand what you think about our products, and our authors can see your feedback on their book. Thank you!

For more information about Packt, please visit packt.com.

1
Introduction to the Order to Cash Cycle

The **Order to Cash (O2C)** cycle in SAP supports businesses involved in handling and receiving orders from customers, including planning and shipping items to customers and processing payments. In essence, the O2C process is the process of receiving and managing customer sales orders. In this chapter, we'll provide an overview of processing the O2C cycle in SAP and its integration with the SAP business suite, which includes **SAP Customer Relationship Management (SAP CRM)**, **SAP Advanced Planner and Optimizer (SAP APO)**, **SAP Transportation Management System (SAP TMS)**, and **SAP Logistics Execution System (SAP LES)**. In addition, we'll learn about how a business can integrate these systems when they're implementing the Order to Cash cycle with SAP. In this chapter, you will learn the benefits of running your Order to Cash cycle with CRM, APO, TMS, and LES. Later in this chapter, you'll find further information about the Order to Cash process flow and the user interface technologies that are used by SAP CRM and SAP TMS.

The following topics will be covered in this chapter:

- Understanding order to cash with CRM, APO, TMS, and LES
- Getting to know UI technologies

By the end of this chapter, you will understand the significance of integrating different SAP systems such as CRM, APO, TMS, and LES within the Order to Cash process. You will also learn about the UI technologies that are used in these systems.

Understanding order to cash with CRM, APO, TMS, and LES

The Order to Cash business process is important to any company when it comes to satisfying their customer needs. Order to Cash impacts the complete supply chain of the business if it's not run efficiently. Another impacted area is the cash flow; any delay in receiving payment from the customer can impact the cash flow of any business. Therefore, considering these factors, it is imperative to effectively and efficiently run this process by eliminating inefficiencies across the entire business.

Within SAP, you can implement the Order to Cash process within the **Sales and Distribution (SD)** module if your business doesn't require advanced features from SAP CRM, SAP APO, and SAP TMS. Running the Order to Cash cycle with these SAP business suites helps you leverage advanced features in each system. To implement these systems with the Order to Cash cycle, you should have a good understanding of how to integrate these systems. This section will provide you with an overview of each of these elements. You will discover and understand each element of this cycle in more detail as we move along with the chapters in this book.

Understanding sales

The Order to Cash cycle begins with a customer calling and placing an order. When it comes to the sales process, it is split into pre-sales activities and sales order processing. Pre-sales activities include generating and targeting leads, creating opportunities for these leads, and converting these leads into customers. Once the leads have been converted into customers, the sales representatives can create a contract or a quotation for them.

When a customer starts buying products, the customer service representative will initiate creating the sales order, that can reference quotation or a sales contract. All these pre-sales activities and sales order processes are executed in the SAP CRM environment. *Chapter 7, Sales Document Processing in SAP CRM*, will cover pre-sales activities such as quotation and sales contract processing, as well as sales order processing, its functionality, and how to set up its configuration.

Understanding order fulfillment

When placing a sales order, the system checks if the product that's been ordered is available and whether the company will be able to deliver the product based on the customer's delivery date. The sales order provides the request date, and the system runs a product availability check. Based on this product availability check, the system provides the best date for when the product can be delivered to the customer. This product availability check has various options that can be executed in SAP APO.

Chapter 8, Order Fulfillment with SAP APO, will look at the different product availability options, such as basic product availability checks and advanced product availability checks, in SAP APO.

Understanding transportation planning and shipment creation

Once the product availability check has been executed in SAP APO, the next step is to execute the transportation planning, carrier selection, and tendering process and initiate the shipment creation process. SAP provides an optimizer that helps evaluate various transportation constraints and resource capacities before providing optimal transportation dates.

Various activities of transportation planning including the carrier selection and tendering process, its functionality, and profile set up all are done in the SAP TMS system. *Chapter 10, Transportation Planning and Freight Order Management in SAP TM,* covers how to plan and create transportation and shipment creation triggers within SAP TMS.

Understanding shipping

Once transportation planning and shipment creation have been completed, shipping activities such as picking the product, packing it, loading it, and shipping it out from the warehouse are executed in SAP LES. As soon as the product is shipped out from the warehouse, the customer is notified that the product has been shipped and is provided with tracking information.

Chapter 11, Logistics Execution in SAP LES, covers key functions such as the stock pick and stock putaway strategies within SAP LES, including initiating freight settlement for the carrier invoicing in SAP TMS.

Understanding customer billing

As soon as the goods have been shipped out of the warehouse, the system generates a billing document. This billing document is sent to the customer to process the account receivables. Once the customer has paid for the goods they've ordered, the account receivables are updated, showing the payment that was received by the customer.

Chapter 12, Billing Processing in SAP ECC, covers the key billing functionality in SAP ECC, including understanding different billing document types, their functionality, and their configuration details.

Understanding the order to cash process flow

If you have a good understanding of how SAP business suites integrate, you can automate the Order to Cash process, which results in improved customer service and reduced errors. This leads to greater customer satisfaction and maximizing your profits.

The following diagram shows the Order to Cash cycle process flow with SAP CRM, SAP APO, SAP TMS, and SAP ECC:

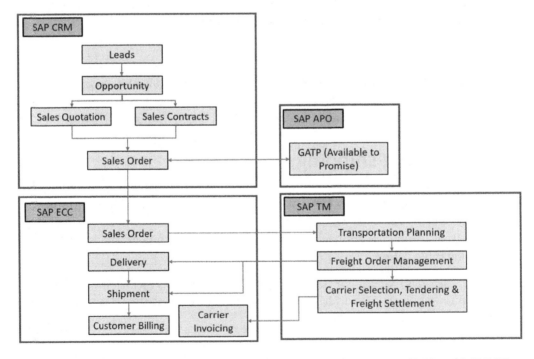

Figure 1.1 – The Order to Cash process flow with SAP CRM, SAP APO, SAP TMS, and SAP ECC

The following steps are what happens in the Order to Cash process flow:

1. The lead places an inquiry and shows interest in buying goods from the company.

2. The sales representative creates an opportunity for the lead and goes on to the opportunity life cycle with that lead.

3. The leads are converted into customers as the lead confirms that they're buying the goods from the company.

4. The sales representative creates a sales quotation or sales contract based on certain terms and conditions between the buyer and the seller. These transactions are created in SAP CRM.

5. The customer calls and confirms the date when they would like to buy the goods from the seller.

6. The customer service representative places a sales order and applies a sales contract or quotation price in SAP CRM.

AVAIL. TO PROMISE (ATP)

7. When creating the sales order, the system undergoes an ATP check based on the requested delivery date on the sales order. A product availability check is done in SAP APO. *ADV. PLANNING & OPTIMIZATION (APO)*

8. The sales order is confirmed on the date when the product is available. The sales order is then saved in SAP CRM. Once the sales order has been saved, the order is replicated to SAP ECC. *ENTERPRISE CENTRAL COMPONENT (ECC)*

9. The sales order that was replicated in SAP ECC is also replicated to SAP TM for transportation planning. *TRANSPORT MGMT SYSTEM (TMS)*

10. SAP TMS executes the transportation planning process and a freight order is created. Carrier selection takes place in the freight order and the tendering process is executed.

11. The carrier confirms the pickup date and the seller awards the tender to the carrier.

12. A delivery and shipment proposal is sent from SAP TMS to SAP ECC.

13. The shipment process of picking, packing, and loading is initiated in SAP ECC.

14. The delivery process executes the goods issue from the warehouse in SAP ECC.

15. Once the goods have been issued and the products have been shipped out from the warehouse, a customer billing document is generated in SAP ECC. Billing confirmation is triggered and the customer receives the billing document.

16. Separately, the freight settlement document is created to settle the invoice for the carrier.

prospect lifecycle | lead opportunity lifecycle | customer lifecycle

The process flow described here will be covered in detail throughout this book. We will cover each function, including master data and how to configure it in each of the SAP business suites, including SAP CRM, SAP APO, SAP TMS, and SAP ECC. Before we look at these functions, let's understand the **user interface** (**UI**) that's used in SAP CRM and SAP TMS.

Getting to know UI technologies

UI technologies play a vital role in connecting the business user to the system. The UI defines how well the system provides easy-to-use navigation to business users. Likewise, SAP provides a web UI in both SAP CRM and SAP TMS that helps with ease of usage for business users. Additional UI capabilities with SAP Fiori have taken the UI to the next level for business users as they can launch reports with SAP Fiori. Let's go through the web UI technologies within SAP CRM and SAP TMS and then cover the key UI concepts with SAP Fiori. *SAP FIORI*

Understanding the SAP CRM WebClient UI

The SAP **CRM** tool allows us to easily access a transaction while spending a minimal amount of time navigating various screens or transactions. The traditional way of accessing different transactions within SAP systems is by using a **Graphical User Interface** (**GUI**), which requires any business user to key in different transaction codes to access those transactions. It is a bit cumbersome to remember and access transaction codes. Therefore, SAP has introduced the WebClient UI, which is a web UI that allows users with different roles in the organization to use and navigate different transactions very easily, without the need to remember any transaction codes. The WebClient UI is a role-based user interface and is designed for business users with different roles such as marketing, sales, and service.

> **Note**
> The SAP CRM WebClient UI is not meant for external users and is not exposed outside the organization's firewall. External users are internet users who can log in via B2B or B2C portal and can be part of the SAP Commerce Cloud solution.

Understanding the WebClient UI framework

The WebClient UI framework provides an overall view of the SAP CRM web application. The framework is designed to suit business user needs and configure/customize the application with limited effort and less complexity. The SAP CRM WebClient UI framework boosts a business user's tailored needs and increases their productivity.

The UI framework is surrounded by different key UI functions, as follows:

- User interface configuration

- Business role configuration

- User experience/productivity

- Development tools

- Extensibility

The CRM WebClient UI screen is divided into three areas, as shown here:

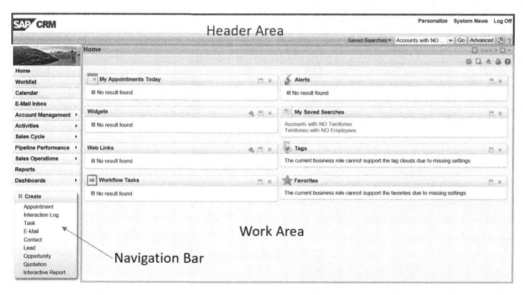

Figure 1.2 – WebClient UI screen

Let's take a look at the different parts of the WebClient UI screen:

- **Header Area**: This consists of the message bar, logo area, saved searches, personalization, work area title, and the page history within a **Back** button.

- **Navigation Bar**: This consists of work centers, including **Home**, **Worklist**, **Calendar**, **E-Mail Inbox**, and direct links to create transactions.

- **Work Area**: This consists of different views within the component and different page types; that is, the work center page, overview page, edit page, and search page.

The SAP CRM WebClient UI is a **Business Server Pages (BSP)** application that is divided into different layers: the presentation layer, the business layer, and the business engine.

This can be seen in the following diagram:

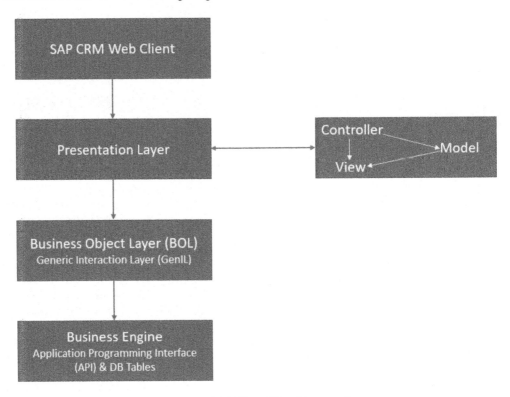

Figure 1.3 – WebClient UI architecture flow

The presentation layer is based on the MVC concept in that it receives a request from a user and sends it to the controller. The request is passed from the controller to the model, which is connected to the business layer. The business logic is not written in the presentation layer and it is recommended that you write the business logic on the CRM backend.

The business layer consists of the **Business Object Layer** (**BOL**) and **GenIL**. The BOL consists of a business object, which doesn't store any data but passes data from the presentation layer to GenIL. GenIL handles the data transfer between the CRM database and the BOL. It triggers the API (business logic) so that it gets the required data to the BOL from the CRM database.

The business engine consists of the business logic; that is, the APIs for CRM business objects.

SAP provides a WebClient UI Component Workbench, which acts as a UI development tool for developing UI components within the WebClient UI framework. UI components are different for different objects and can be accessed via the `BSP_WD_CMPWB` transaction code in SAP CRM.

Now that we have gone through the SAP CRM Web Client UI concept and its architecture flow, let's learn about business roles.

Understanding business roles

SAP CRM provides a role-based WebClient user interface for users based on their day-to-day work at any organization. Multiple standard business roles are based on business user functionality. The whole concept of the WebClient UI is to provide ease of access to the transactions that users work on daily, and also to give them the benefit of a web user interface.

Business roles within SAP CRM are designed based on the users working in each of the CRM core functions, such as marketing, sales, and service.

One of the business roles that SAP has provided for the call center application is an **Interaction Center Agent** (**IC_AGENT**) business role. This is widely used in call centers wherein the customer calls a customer service agent and the application has softphone capabilities that help with taking calls, transferring the calls to the right agent, and much more.

Let's go through a business role example for Sales and IC Agents. Based on your business needs, you can change the business role to suit your business requirements. SAP recommends copying the standard business role and making further changes based on your specific needs:

- **Sales Professional**: This business role allows business users to process and create quotations, sales contracts, and sales orders. Having defined the sales cycle, the organization takes advantage of this business role to create the sales transaction. Here is a screenshot of the Sales Professional business role:

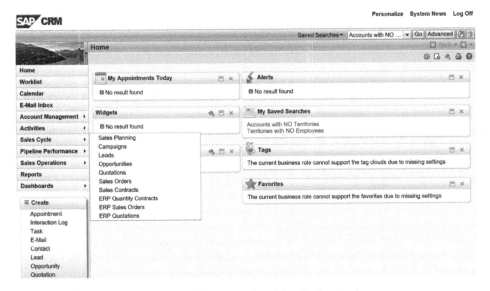

Figure 1.4 – Business role – Sales Professional

The sales life cycle may differ from organization to organization; SAP has provided a **Sales Professional** business role that covers **Sales Planning**, **Campaigns**, **Leads**, **Opportunities**, **Quotations**, **Sales Contracts**, and **Sales Orders**. Sales Operations has many more functions that are included in the Sales Professional business role. SAP recommends copying the Sales Professional business role and making changes based on your business needs.

- **Interaction Center Agent**: The Interaction Center Agent business role allows business users to carry out call center activities when a call is received by the customer service representative. Every company is unique in satisfying its customer needs. You can change the Interaction Center business role based on your specific needs by copying the standard business role. Many companies working through the call center application would add the sales cycle work center, which would enable customer services to create the sales contract, quotation, and sales orders. This business user role is also called Interaction Center Sales (**IC_SALES**).

Interaction Center Sales covers a wide range of functionality that a customer sales representative does as part of their-day to-day work. Sales is an important function for any organization. To remain in the market and to overcome today's tough competition, companies have to be aggressive in the marketing and sales departments. Most companies cover **Account Identification**, **Sales Cycle** (Leads, Opportunity Quote, Contract, and Sales Order), **Complaints**, **Agent Inbox**, **Product Search**, and **Report Work Center** with the IC Agent role.

Whenever calls come in, the system creates an interaction record on the system. Any activities or transactions that are carried out during the call are attached in the activity clipboard of the interaction record transaction, which provides good reporting information on what activities were executed during that call:

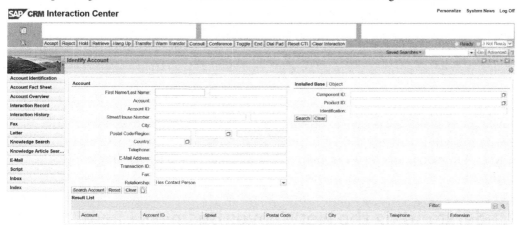

Figure 1.5 – Business role – Interaction Center

Interaction Center is a core SAP CRM application that connects to the customer via multiple channels, such as phone, fax, email, chat, and so on. The customer calls the agent to place a new order or to express their grievances regarding a product they've bought. Interaction Center effectively and efficiently manages customers to help resolve customer issues and support both agents and managers who are involved in the interaction. Interaction Center allows agents to manage both inbound and outbound communication. Communication can by be either email, phone, fax, or chat.

The following screenshot shows the SAP CRM Interaction Center WebClient layout, with the key Interaction Center features highlighted:

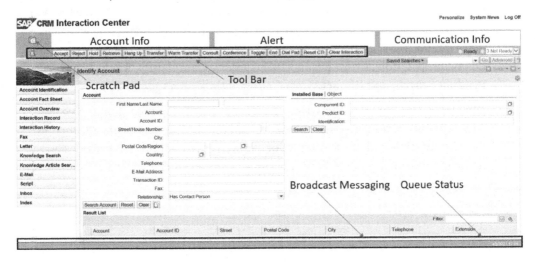

Figure 1.6 – Interaction Center WebClient layout

SAP's Interaction Center navigation bar profile can be configured to suit your business needs, including marketing, sales, or service functions. Now that we have covered the SAP CRM UI functions and their capabilities; let's understand the UI capabilities of SAP TMS.

Understanding the NetWeaver Business Client

Like SAP CRM, business users in SAP TMS use **NetWeaver Business Client (NWBC)** as their UI and do not use SAP GUI to execute their day-to-day activities. With NWBC, business users do not need to remember transaction codes and can use the menu structure to navigate and launch business transactions. SAP NWBC renders the Web Dynpro and SAP GUI transactions. Within NWBC, you can move seamlessly between Web Dynpro and SAP GUI transactions, which is efficient and provides more ease of use and a better user experience.

The following is a screenshot of SAP NWBC; it shows menu folders and various applications:

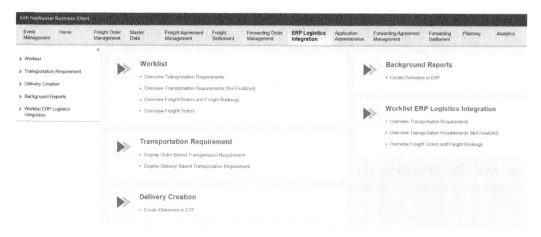

Figure 1.7 – SAP NWBC

User can log into NWBC via SAP GUI by entering an NWBC transaction code. This will launch a standard browser showing a list of the roles that have been assigned to the user. The user selects the role to log into the application. This method is generally used by the administrator. Browser-based NWBC is used by external users, which includes carriers. The carrier can log into the SAP TM system in their standard browser to respond to the tender. The carrier can also log in to the Collaboration Portal to support the collaborative business processes.

Business users generally use the client-installed version of NWBC, which is the most preferred way of using SAP TM.

Understanding user-specific roles in TM

SAP TM provides roles and authorization based on business users and their day-to-day work at any organization. Multiple standard roles are based on business user functionality. Logically, the roles of the transportation function can be split into four different parties; that is, the shipper, freight forwarder, carrier, and customer:

- The shipper is an organization that manages the production of goods and informs TM to deliver the goods to the customer.

- The freight forwarder organizes and arranges the transportation. They can also work through the custom clearance activities.

- The carrier is responsible for physically shipping the goods from the seller to the customer.

- The customer is responsible for taking possession of the goods that have been physically shipped by the carrier in the transportation network.

When it comes to segregating duties, the roles within TM can be divided into transportation planner, transportation dispatcher, and transportation charge clerk. In TM, you can assign these roles to users so that they see the relevant menu when they log into NWBC. Roles contain authorization so that the user can access and execute functions based on their roles. The authorization and profile details are stored in SAP's backend system. Within TM, three main authorization objects are controlled via roles: the user's **personal objects worklist** (**POWL**) access, object access authorization, and user-specific layouts and visibility of certain fields.

The role maintenance within SAP TM is similar to the role maintenance in any other SAP system. A PFCG transaction is used to maintain the roles, authorization, and profiles within SAP TM.

SAP TM provides standard roles based on business user functions, as follows:

- Transportation planner: /SCMTMS/PLANNER

- Capacity manager: /SCMTMS/CAPACITY_MANAGER

- Dispatcher: /SCMTMS/DISPATCHER

- Booking specialist: /SCMTMS/BOOKING_AGENT

- Carrier settlement specialist: /SCMTMS/CARRIER_SETTLEMENT_SP

- Freight contract specialist: /SCMTMS/FREIGHT_CONTRACT_SPEC

- Process administrator: /SCMTMS/PROCESS_ADMINISTRATOR

- Transportation manager: /SCMTMS/TRANSPORTATION_MGR_V2

Now that we have looked at NWBC and user roles in SAP TMS, let's understand the high-level SAP Fiori architecture.

Understanding the Fiori UI architecture

SAP Fiori provides a next-generation user experience for business users across different streams within the SAP environment.

It fundamentally reduces the user interface's complexity and allows for ease of use. The Fiori concept is also based on user roles and business processes. SAP Fiori is a collection of apps that represent the new user experience of SAP. It ensures that both employees and managers have a consistent, coherent, simple, and intuitive user experience across multiple devices.

There are three types of SAP Fiori apps; namely, transactional apps, factsheet apps, and analytical apps. Transactional apps can run on any database, including SAP HANA, whereas factsheet and analytical apps can only run on SAP HANA databases.

The following diagram shows an architecture overview of SAP Fiori, which requires SAP Fiori apps to be installed on the frontend server:

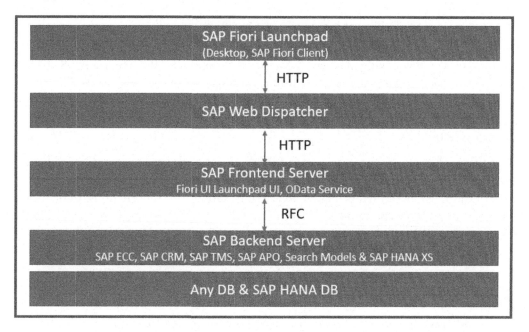

Figure 1.8 – SAP Fiori architecture

SAP Fiori apps consist of a frontend component and a backend component. The frontend component is the user interface, while the backend component is the OData service that connects to the SAP Business Suite Backend via the **SAP NetWeaver Gateway**.

SAP UI components for SAP Fiori and SAP NetWeaver Gateway are deployed on the same server; the UI component is a SAP Fiori product that needs to be installed on the NetWeaver application server, ABAP. SAP Fiori runs on desktop, smartphones, and tablets. To run SAP Fiori apps, the client (for example, a browser) should be compatible with HTML5. The information flows from the client to the SAP NetWeaver Gateway via OData and then connects to the backend Business Suite.

Install the SAP Fiori UI components and SAP NetWeaver Gateway, and ensure they are compatible with the SAP backend version before you use and implement SAP Fiori for SAP CRM, SAP ECC, or SAP TMS.

SAP Fiori can be used in conjunction with SAP CRM, SAP ECC, and SAP TMS to provide a great user experience and helps increase productivity. SAP Fiori provides a transactional app that supports SAP CRM, SAP ECC, and SAP TMS functionalities.

Summary

In this chapter, we provided a high-level overview of the Order to Cash process by covering sales, order fulfilment, transportation planning and shipment creation, and shipping and customer billing. We also looked at and understood the Order to Cash process and its integration touchpoints.

We then provided you with an overview of the UI technologies that are used in SAP CRM and TMS, as well as their ease of usage for business users. We reviewed the architecture of the SAP Fiori UI and how its UI capabilities can be used with SAP Business Suite. This will help you visualize these UI capabilities as we cover the business processes around Order to Cash.

Now that we have looked at the context of the Order to Cash processes and the systems involved with the integration touchpoints, let's deep dive into the master data topics of each of the SAP environments that are followed by Order to Cash functions. In the next chapter, we will learn about master data in SAP CRM; you will learn about the master data elements that are needed to create a sales order in SAP CRM and the configuration that's required for these master data elements to be set up.

Further reading

- Additional information on the SAP CRM, SAP TMS, and SAP ECC Fiori apps can be found at the following Fiori Apps Library link: https://fioriappslibrary.hana.ondemand.com/sap/fix/externalViewer/#.

2
Master Data in SAP CRM

Master data forms the basis of all order to cash transactions; it drives the business functionality. Accurate master data drives the success of any project implementation. Having incorrect master data set up leads to project delays and inaccuracy in the implementation of business requirements. Therefore, it is very important to understand the data aspect and the settings required in SAP systems to run the order to cash cycle successfully. So, you should have a good understanding of these data elements, including how they work and how they impact downstream processes. In this chapter, we will focus on the master data setup and configuration in SAP CRM.

SAP ECC is the originating system for most master data that then replicates to the CRM, APO, and TM systems. We will cover data relevant to sales transaction order fulfillment in this chapter.

Here is a list of the topics to be covered in this chapter:

- ECC master data – client of record
- CRM master data elements and their concepts
- Business partner master data
- Product master data

- Pricing overview
- Vendors
- Plant settings

By the end of this chapter, you will be well versed in the master data setup required in SAP CRM to process sales transactions successfully.

ECC master data – client of record

Master data is the most critical data setup for the order to cash process to run smoothly. Before covering master data in SAP CRM, SAP APO, and SAP TMS, it is important to understand that the SAP ECC system is the client of record for most of the master data that propagates to SAP CRM, SAP APO, and SAP TMS. The following screenshot shows different master data initiating from an SAP ECC system and replicated into SAP CRM, SAP APO, and SAP TMS:

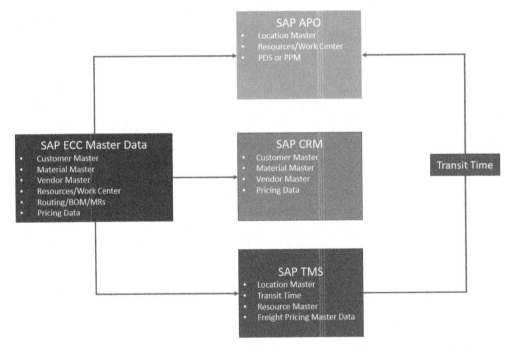

Figure 2.1 – SAP ECC master data propagation to SAP CRM, SAP APO, and SAP TMS

The transit time from SAP TMS is replicated to SAP APO. Note that there is no standard integration of the transit time to replicate between SAP TMS and SAP APO, but it could be customized if you are working with these SAP ecosystems together. Next, we'll examine the master data elements.

CRM master data elements and their concepts

The key master data elements required to execute sales transactions in SAP CRM are organization data, business partners, products, and pricing. Vendors are also replicated from SAP ECC to SAP CRM as business partners. CRM doesn't have inventory; therefore, it doesn't have the concept of a plant as in the SAP ECC system. Let's review CRM master data and concepts around each of these master data elements, starting with organization management.

Organization management overview

One of the first steps when setting up a system with master data is setting up the organization model. The organization model should be set up based on the organization structure requirements based on the project's needs.

The organization structure in CRM is the master data, whereas the organization structure in ECC is a part of the configuration. The maintenance of the organization structure is different in CRM than in ECC. CRM organization structure is more flexible as you can add org units.

ECC organization determination is based on the customer master; that is, if the customer is extended to a different sales org, these sales orgs will be shown as an option when creating a sales order. In CRM, the org determination is based on the org profile assigned to the transaction.

The organization structure in CRM is more flexible and easily maintainable. You can have different organization structures for sales and service business functions within the same organization. A sales org within CRM is mapped to an ECC org unit. Additionally, you can maintain a sales and service org for sales org units or you can create a sales org based on the ECC org structure and create the service org structure based on the service scenarios in CRM.

Explanations of organizational data in the CRM system are as follows:

- **Sales organization**: The organization unit responsible for selling a product based on certain terms and conditions is termed as the sales organization. In CRM, organization units are created and are mapped to the ECC sales organization within the **Function** tab of the org master data.

- **Distribution channel**: A distribution channel is a channel or medium through which materials or services are delivered to the customer. The assignment of the distribution channel within CRM is similar to the sales org. Organization units that are created in CRM are mapped to a distribution channel and division within the **Function** tab of the org master data.

- **Division**: The division is the product line of business within an organization. Multiple product lines can fall into multiple divisions and each product line corresponds to each division.

- **Sales office**: The sales office is defined based on the geographical location of the organization and a company creates the sales office based on the territory they want to sell their product. A sales office within the CRM org structure is assigned to a sales org. The business partner and other attributes, such as postal code, can be assigned to the sales office independent of the sales org.

- **Sales group**: The number of people working within a sales office is divided into groups and those are called sales groups.

- **Sales district**: A sales district can be assigned to the org unit attributes within the CRM org structure and can be copied to the transaction from the org structure.

- **Service organization**: A service organization owns an entity and is comparable to a sales organization in a sales scenario. It is responsible for processing service transactions such as service order/confirmation, service contracts, and so on.

Division usage in SAP CRM

A division is part of a sales area and one of the key pieces of information in sales transactions that helps in reporting a specific line of business. It is also represented as the line of business in a sales transaction. Some businesses may have a requirement to use a dummy division if they aren't using a division as part of their sales area. In that case, the division entered on the sales order is a dummy division mostly represented by 00 and this also ensures the transactions are free of error. Here are the division usage options available in SAP CRM:

- **CRM Division Not Active**: If you want to use a dummy division in your business transaction, you must activate the **Division not active** field. If you are not working with divisions in CRM, then activate this field and add an R/3 dummy division. Please note that the divisions entered in R/3 dummy divisions should exist in the ECC system. For example, if the value of an R/3 dummy division is 00 and the **Division not active** checkbox is activated, then the order created in CRM will be replicated to ECC with division 00 as the header and line items.

- **Header Div. Active**: An organization working with multiple product lines is recommended to keep the header division active and the division will be determined based on the determination rule. If this is active, then the header division on the CRM sales order is replicated to ECC. For example, if the order division at the order header is 07 in CRM, the order replicated to ECC will consist of 07 as the header division and will be copied to the items as well. If the material is assigned with a different division than in the sales order header, the line item on the sales order will have a division from the product master.

Here is the configuration menu path to configure the use of a division within SAP CRM: **SPRO | CRM | Master Data | Organizational Management | Division Settings | Define Use of Division and Dummy Division**

Organization data setup

The steps to maintain the org structure in the SAP CRM system are discussed next.

Step 1 – maintaining number ranges for an org structure

You define the number range for the org structure in this step. The following is the configuration menu path to define the number range **SPRO | CRM | Master Data | Organization Management | Number Range Maintenance | Maintain Number Range**

A subgroup is defined where the first two characters specify the plan version and the last two specify the object type. $$$$ is the default setting. SAP recommends using an internal number range for the org unit. The next screenshot shows **Subgroup** with the internal and external number range assignment:

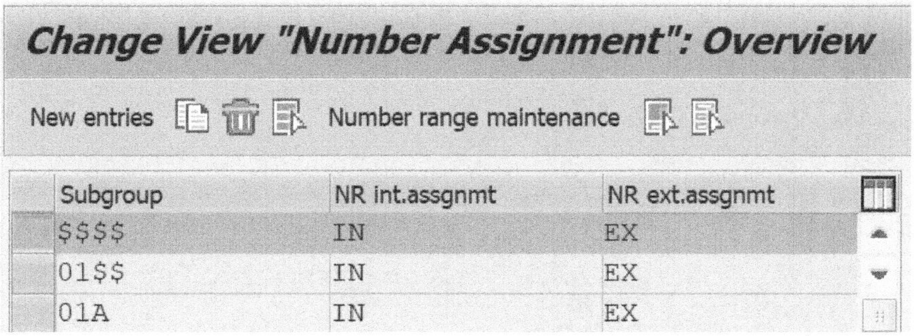

Change View "Number Assignment": Overview		
New entries 📋 🗑 📑 Number range maintenance 📑 📑		
Subgroup	NR int.assgnmt	NR ext.assgnmt
$$$$	IN	EX
01$$	IN	EX
01A	IN	EX

Figure 2.2 – Subgroup number assignment

The next screenshot shows the actual number range assignment to the subgroup. Here you can mark the number range to be external or internally determined by the system:

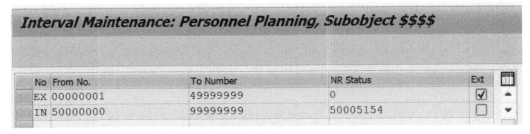

No	From No.	To Number	NR Status	Ext	
EX	00000001	49999999	0	☑	
IN	50000000	99999999	50005154	☐	

Figure 2.3 – Organization number range maintenance

> **Note**
>
> To add your own number range, please add the entry based on plan version + object type and click **Number Range Maintenance** to add the number range based on your business requirements.

Step 2 – maintaining number ranges for an org business partner

First, we need to create number ranges for the org business partner, using transaction code BUCF.

Then, we need to define **Grouping** and assign a number range. This is done using the following menu path: **SPRO | Cross-Application Components | SAP Business Partner | Basic Settings | Number Ranges and Groupings | Define Grouping and Assign Number Ranges**

The following screenshot shows defining the business partner grouping for an organization and assigning a number range to the grouping:

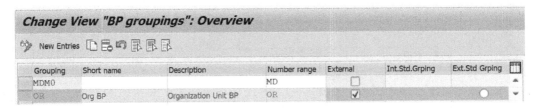

Change View "BP groupings": Overview

New Entries

Grouping	Short name	Description	Number range	External	Int.Std.Grping	Ext.Std Grping	
MDM0			MD	☐			
OR	Org BP	Organization Unit BP	OR	☑		○	

Figure 2.4 – Defining and assigning a number range to the business partner grouping

You can use either an internal or external number range based on your business requirements. To keep the number same between business partner and the organization number within organization model; you need to maintain the parameter for **HRALX Group, PNUMB** as 3 within **Set up Integration with HR** under **Integration Business Partner-Employee** in CRM configuration.

Step 3 – converting an org model to represent multiple assignments in SAP ECC

If you are using the ECC backend system with multiple assignments, then it is recommended to convert the org model into multiple assignments in CRM. Once this report is executed, you cannot go back to the standard backend integration version. Therefore, before running this report, you can first run it in test mode.

Multiple distribution channels and divisions can be assigned to the org units (sales organization, sales office, and sales group) with this report: **SPRO | CRM | Master Data | Organizational Management | Data Transfer | Convert Organization Model to Represent Multiple Assignments in SAP ECC**

Once you execute the report, you will see the option shown in the next screenshot. You can also run it in test mode. To run the report in test mode, hit **Test** to test the program:

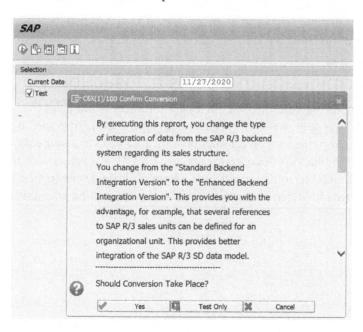

Figure 2.5 – Converting an org model to represent multiple assignments in SAP ECC

The current date will default to the date of the program run. Execute it. The log display will show you a list of the org units converted to the enhanced version.

Step 4 – organizational structure download

Run the `CRMC_R3_ORG_GENERATE` report to download the ECC org structure and create the same organization structure in CRM: **SPRO | CRM | Master Data | Organizational Management | Data Transfer | Copy SAP ECC Sales Structure**

Select **R/3 Org Structure** listed in the upper portion of the screen under **R/3 Organization Structures** and hit the **Generate Selected Lines** button. This step will generate the organization structure within CRM, which can be seen in the lower portion of the screen. You can also see the status of the generated organization structure in CRM, whether it is generated successfully or not. Once the generated structure shows successfully generated, save the organization structure. The org structure will create on saving.

You can also create service skill groups as an org unit in the CRM org structure if you are working with a service organization and the service structure is separate from the sales structure. This can be created manually with transaction code `PPOSA_CRM`. Under the org unit, you can create positions and a holder and add attributes to the org unit based on your specific business needs. Make sure to activate the **Obj Permitted in Determination** checkbox for the organization to determine any CRM transactions. Run the `HRBCI_ATTRIBUTES_BUFFER_UPDATE` program to clear the org buffer. It is recommended to run the report during business off-hours as this report deletes the tables and rebuilds them.

Org determination in a sales transaction

A sales organization captures the sales in a sales transaction and helps the business to identify the revenue generated in a specific sales organization. Therefore, it is of the utmost importance to determine the correct sales organization in a sales transaction. There are two ways to determine the sales organization in an SAP CRM sales order, that is, with an organization model determination rule or a responsibilities determination rule. Detailed configuration steps for determining the org in a sales transaction are mentioned here.

Rule type responsibilities

Rule type responsibilities are determined based on the org unit assigned to the responsibility. For example, if region R1 is assigned to sales org unit S1 and you want to determine the organization on the transaction based on this specific region, then a rule will be created to assign the business partner (Sold to Party) to region R1. When the transaction is created for Sold to Party, sales org S1 will be determined on the sales order based on region R1 assigned to sales org S1. The attributes within this rule are defined directly in the rule container. Therefore, even if the org model is set up, the attributes need not be linked to the org model. The configuration path to configure a rule and assign it to the org data determination is as follows: **SPRO | CRM | Master Data | Organizational Management | Organizational Data Determination | Wizard for Organizational Data Determination | Create Determination Rule of the Responsibility Type**

Once an org determination rule is created, the rule is assigned to the org data profile. The configuration path is as follows: **SPRO | CRM | Master Data | Organizational Management | Organizational Data Determination | Wizard for Organizational Data Determination | Change Rules and Profiles | Maintain Organizational Data Profile**

The following screenshot shows the organizational data profile that a determination rule is assigned to:

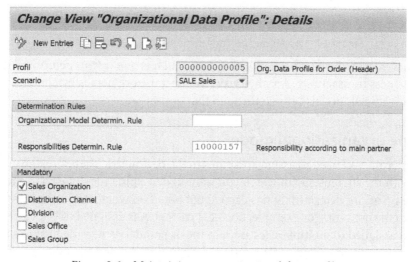

Figure 2.6 – Maintaining an organizational data profile

Assign the org data profile to the transaction type as shown:

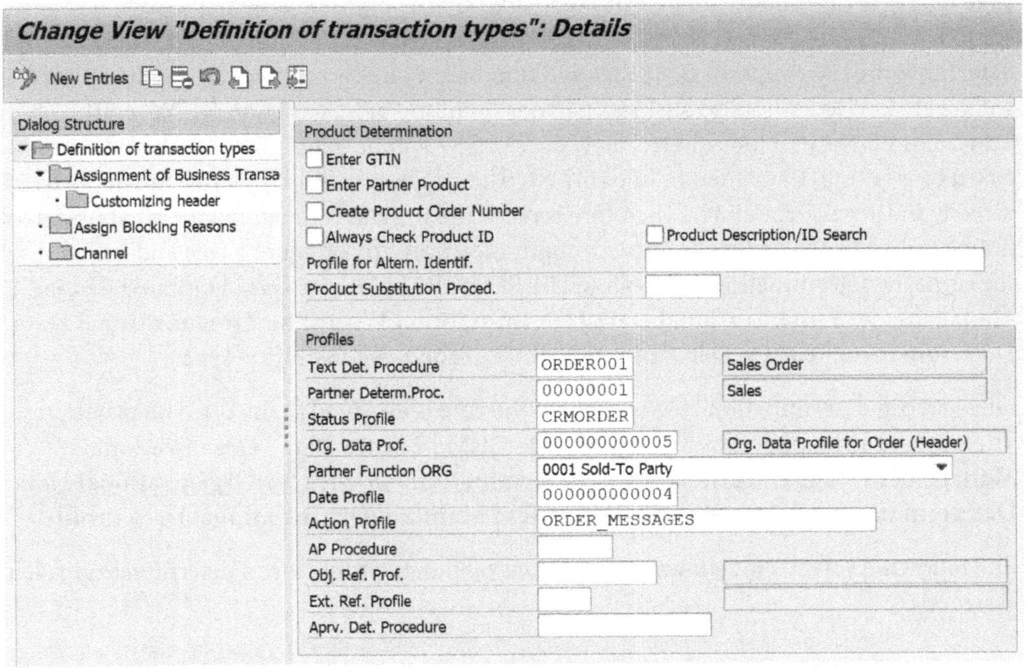

Figure 2.7 – Assigning the org data profile to the transaction type

Now we have covered rule type responsibilities, which is one way to determine the org data in business transactions. Another way to determine org data is by configuring a rule type organizational model. Let's go through that option.

Rule type organizational model

Within this rule, you need to assign attributes to the org model. Therefore, the org model is set up with the attributes with which you want to determine the org data in the business transaction. The org determination is carried out based on what attribute values you have assigned to the org unit. For example, business partner A is assigned to sales group SG1 and SG1 is assigned to multiple sales areas in the org model. When the business transaction is created for business partner A, the system determines SG1 and the sales org, distribution, and division linked to SG1 in the org model. It is necessary to activate the **Object Permitted for Scenario** flag for org data determination in the transaction to be successful.

The steps to configure a rule and assign it to the org data determination are as follows:

1. Like the configuration done for the rule type responsibilities, create a determination rule for the rule type organization model. In this step, you select the attributes from the wizard and assign these attributes to the org model: **SPRO | CRM | Master Data | Organizational Management | Organizational Data Determination | Wizard for Organizational Data Determination | Create Determination Rule from Organizational Model**

2. Once the rule is generated, assign the rule to the org data profile. Assign this rule to the org data profile as outlined in the following path: **SPRO | CRM | Master Data | Organizational Management | Organizational Data Determination | Wizard for Organizational Data Determination | Change Rules and Profiles | Maintain Organizational Data Profile**

   The following screenshot shows org determination rule being assigned to the org data profile:

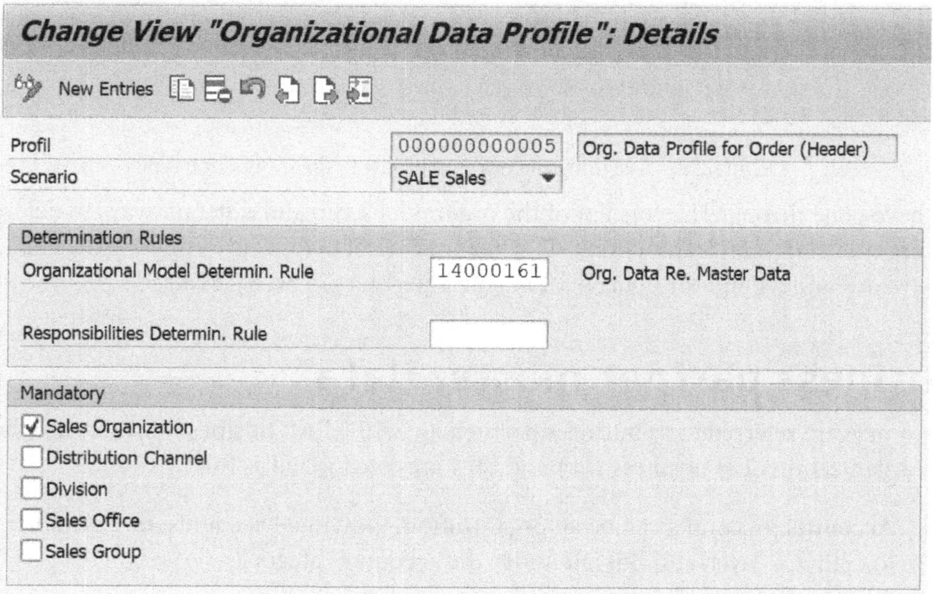

Figure 2.8 – Assigning an org determination rule to the org data profile

3. The final step is to assign the org data profile to the transaction type as shown:

Change View "Definition of transaction types": Details

New Entries

Dialog Structure	Product Determination	
▼ Definition of transaction types	☐ Enter GTIN	
▼ Assignment of Business Transa	☐ Enter Partner Product	
• Customizing header	☐ Create Product Order Number	
• Assign Blocking Reasons	☐ Always Check Product ID	☐ Product Description/ID Search
• Channel	Profile for Altern. Identif.	
	Product Substitution Proced.	

Profiles		
Text Det. Procedure	ORDER001	Sales Order
Partner Determ.Proc.	00000001	Sales
Status Profile	CRMORDER	
Org. Data Prof.	00000000005	Org. Data Profile for Order (Header)
Partner Function ORG	0001 Sold-To Party	▼
Date Profile	000000000004	
Action Profile	ORDER_MESSAGES	
AP Procedure		
Obj. Ref. Prof.		
Ext. Ref. Profile		
Aprv. Det. Procedure		

Figure 2.9 – Assigning the org data profile to the transaction type

We have gone through the concept of the org model setup and different ways to determine the org model in sales transactions. Our next master data topic is business partners. Let's review and understand the concept of business partners in SAP CRM.

Business partner master data

Customers are referred to as business partners in SAP CRM. Business partners are those that organization does business with and they are categorized as follows:

- **Accounts**: Accounts can be an organization, individual accounts, or a group. Sold to, Ship to, Payer, and Bill fall under the accounts category.

- **Contacts**: Account contacts are people assigned to the accounts. These are maintained as a relationship to the accounts.

- **Employee**: Employees are also people, and are the members of the company that are responsible for any interactions with the accounts.

A business partner consists of general data and sales area data. The data in most business scenarios needs to be in sync from ECC to CRM. In most SAP implementations, ECC is the client of the record that propagates to CRM, APO, and TM:

- **General data**: This includes information such as address, identification, control of where the tax information resides, classification (information about account group mapping and the business partner, marking whether it is a competitor, prospect, consumer, or customer), and status.

- **Sales area data**: This includes data on sales, shipping, billing, and pricing. It is specific to the sales area (sales org, distribution channel, and division).

Business partner concepts

The concept of a business partner in CRM is different from accounts in SAP ECC. You need to assign a grouping, that is, a number range, manually when creating a business partner in CRM. Roles are assigned to the business partner and these can be Sold to, Ship to, Bill to, and so on. The following sections look at these in detail.

Business partner roles

Business partner roles classify the business partner in business terms. This means every business partner has a specific role; for example, a business partner can have the Sold to, Ship to, Bill to, or Payer role (and so on). Each of these roles also controls the view of the business partner web UI. Some business partner roles show specific views that are different from other roles; for example, a competitor role has views that normal business roles such as Sold to and Ship to don't have.

It also derives the classification of the customer whether the business partner is a consumer, customer, prospect, competitor, or rented address. The business partner role is used for classification purposes during data exchange with SAP ECC.

Business partner relationship

The business partner relationship specifies the connections between two partners. A business partner relationship has business partner relationship categories that describe the kind of relationship between two partners, for example, *Is a contact person of* or *Is a Bill to party of*. Basically, the business partner relationship category describes the characteristics of the business partner relationship. You can also set a validity period for a business partner relationship.

Business partner functions

Like ECC customer masters, CRM has business partners with general data consisting of the address, identification, control, classification, payment transaction, long text, marketing attributes, status, and factsheets. This screenshot shows a business partner example in SAP CRM that shows various tabs:

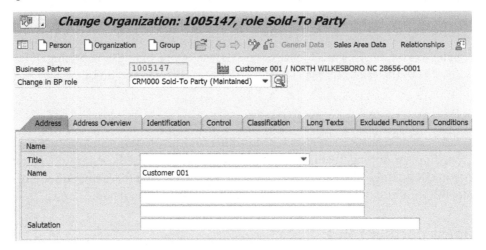

Figure 2.10 – A business partner with the Sold to Party role

The following points look at these tabs in detail:

- **Address**: Address data within a business partner is maintained when creating the business partner in SAP CRM. The address maintained in ECC is replicated to SAP CRM. You can have multiple addresses based on the address usage; for example, standard addresses of a Sold to can have a different billing address and delivery address. If only one address is maintained in the customer master data, then that is referred to as the standard address.

- **Identification**: Identification data within a business partner gives the company the ability to key in some industry-specific information, identification numbers, that is, linking the ECC customer master data to the CRM customer master data based on ID type, and tax information. In the case of vertical industry standards where you are required to have GLNs, they are maintained in the account master. This can be keyed in the **Location 1** and **Location 2** number fields within the **Identification** tab, which helps to determine the account based on GLNs.

  Tax classification and tax number data can be stored in the **Identification** tab of the business partner. This is data that is required to determine how business partners are to be taxed. The tax classification corresponds to the ECC tax classification used in the customer master records.

- **Control**: Control information in the business partner consists of control parameters, that is, business partner type, authorization group, and print format.
The authorization group is used to stipulate which business partners a user is allowed to process. Control data also gives information on the business hours, such as goods receiving hours. Goods receiving hours are assigned with the factory calendar, which has the number of weekdays that the Ship to party can receive products.

- **Payment transaction**: **Payment transaction** allows the organization to maintain the bank details and payment card information. When a transaction is processed for a customer, the payment card information on the transaction is populated based on the data fed in the customer master.

- **Classification**: Classification information shows you whether the account is a competitor, consumer, customer, or prospect. If the PIDE transaction settings in ECC have the account group mapped to the classification customer for a specific CRM customer grouping, then the customer check is activated in the **Classification** tab.

- **Long Texts**: Long texts are customer text IDs that can be populated on the transaction for a given specific customer.

- **Status**: A customer's status information is populated in the **Status** tab. A customer can be archived, centrally locked, or not released. Based on the customer status, you can either use this customer to process any transaction or not. Any status related to a transaction blocking reason, delivery blocking reason, or billing blocking reason is showed on the business transaction if the customer master data has any of these statuses populated.

To define blocking reasons you customize in CRM under the path **Master Data | Business Partner | Status Management | Define Blocking Reasons**.

The life cycle stages signify the different stages of a business partner. Different stages may entail the customer being a lead at the starting stage, then the lead turns into an opportunity, and then the lead is converted into a customer. Once a customer is created in SAP, sales transactions are created for this customer to perform sales.

As we have gone through the business partner functions; let us now understand the business partner employee and its distribution from ECC into CRM in our next section.

Role Employee for HR Integration in CRM

An employee is a business partner that is a person within an organization. This is an internal business partner with a business partner category person. You can establish a relationship between a customer and an organization employee. You can create a business partner employee in SAP CRM or you can integrate an employee within HR in ECC and load it to CRM.

You can distribute your existing internal employee records by **Application Link Enabling (ALE)** from the HR application components in the ECC system to CRM.

If you configure the settings in CRM under Integration Business Partner – Employee, the system creates an employee in CRM from the distributed HR master data, that is, business partners with the employee role and *Is employee of* relationship between these business partners and your organization.

Duplicate checks for the Accounts and Contacts

You can activate duplicate checks for accounts and contacts in SAP CRM. The duplicate check is not activated by default. Once the duplicate check is activated, the duplicate business partner is shown as a popup and you can either discard the new business partner creation or merge it with another account.

You activate duplicate checking in customizing under **SPRO | SAP NetWeaver | Application Server | Basis Services | Address Management | Duplicate Check | Activate Duplicate Check and Determine Limit for BAPIs**.

Make sure that the duplicate check has been activated for both index pools (tables BUT000 and BUT052):

Change View "Customizing settings for logical search pools": Overview

Table	Field	Index active	Threshold BAPIs	Logical search pool name
BUT000	PARTNER	✓	80.0	SAP Business Partner
BUT052	ADDRNUMBER	✓	80.0	Contact Person Relationships (SAP Business Part
KNA1	ADRNR	✓	80.0	Customers, suppliers and commercial organizatic

Figure 2.11 – Activating duplicate checks and determining the limit for BAPIs

You can add a **Threshold BAPIs** value, as shown in *Figure 2.11*, if 80% of the data of the new partner creation matches an existing business partner in the system; in that case, the user will receive a duplicate check popup.

Pre-requisite steps to replicate customers from ECC to CRM

First, we need to define business partner number ranges in SAP CRM:

1. In the SAP CRM menu, go to the BUCF transaction.

2. Choose **Change Intervals**.

3. Click on **Add Intervals** to add the number range shown in the following screenshot:

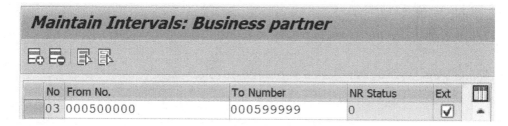

Figure 2.12 – Adding business partner intervals

4. You can maintain number ranges the same as they are maintained in ECC (transaction code OVZC), marking them as an external number range.

Next, we need to assign number ranges to business partner groupings (SAP CRM):

1. Go to **SPRO | Cross-Application Components | SAP Business Partner | Business Partner | Basic Settings | Number Ranges and Groupings | Define Groupings and Assign Number Ranges**.

2. Choose **New Entries** and add an entry as follows for **Sold-To**, **Ship-To**, **Bill-To**, **Payer**, and other partners per your business needs, and then assign a number range to the groupings based on the same number ranges in ECC:

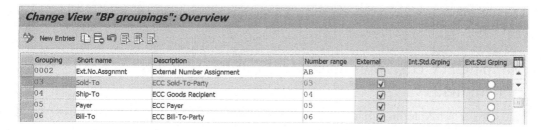

Figure 2.13 – Maintaining business partner groupings

Now we have to assign ECC account groups to CRM business partner groupings (SAP ECC). For each of the SAP ECC account groups, define a mapping to a CRM business partner classification and grouping. The steps are as follows:

1. Access the activity using the PIDE transaction.

2. For each account group, specify the classification (CRM customer) and the grouping (that is, number ranges).

3. In the dialog, choose **ECC | CRM: Assign Account Group to BP Classification**.

4. Choose **New entries**.

5. Enter the following values based on your business requirements:

Change View "R/3->CRM: Assign Account Grp. to BP Classification": Over

New Entries

Dialog Structure	Account group	Name	Classification	Grou...	Exte...
• CRM->R/3: Assign BP Classificatic	0001	Sold-to party	B	03	☑
• R/3->CRM: Assign Account Grp. t	0002	Goods recipient	B	04	☑
	0003	Payer	B	05	☑
	0004	Bill-to party	B	06	☑
	0012	Hierarchy Node	B	07	☑

Figure 2.14 – PIDE – R/3→CRM Assign Account Group to BP Classification

Business partner roles within SAP CRM don't map to the ECC account groups automatically. Therefore, mapping ECC account groups to the Sold-To, Ship-To, Bill-To, and Payer CRM roles must be done programmatically.

Customers loaded from ECC to CRM are loaded as **Sold-To party** for any account groups in ECC. Therefore, it is necessary to map the account groups to the business partner roles as specified in **SAP Note 914437** – Pre-assigning business partner roles during download from account group. The standard **business transaction event** (**BTE**) that maps ECC account groups to CRM business partner roles needs to be enhanced using a custom user exit.

Mapping ECC customer master data standard fields to CRM custom fields

The steps required to map fields from ECC customer master data to CRM business partner master data are as follows:

1. Create a custom field on the customer master data based on your requirements through the AET tool. This will add the custom fields to the BUT000 table.

2. In ECC, access transaction code SE11 and enter BSS_CENTI as the structure name. Double-click on **CI_CUST** and create a structure called CI_CUST by adding the custom fields that were added in the CRM business partner using AET. Please make sure to have it added in ECC with the same sequence that was added in CRM.

3. Repeat the same steps for the BSS_CENTIX structure. Double-click on **CI_CUST_X** and create a CI_CUST_X structure by adding the custom fields that were added in the CRM business partner using AET. Use the GB_BAPIUPD component type.

4. Modify the code to map the fields as a copy of FM SAMPLE_FCTMODULE_DE_EIOUT in ECC.

5. Create a customer product entry in TBE24, and then assign it to the DE_EIOUT event with the new **function module** (**FM**) created (copy of FM SAMPLE_FCTMODULE_DE_EIOUT) in the TBE34 table.

Adding additional fields to customer adapter objects

You can add additional fields to a customer adaptor object via transaction SM30, accessing the SMOFFILFLD table and maintaining the entries. Once you add the entries, save them.

Maintaining the adapter settings

The steps to maintain filters before downloading the customer and customer relationship are as follows:

1. Go to transaction R3AC1.

2. Select the **CUSTOMER_MAIN** business object and choose **details**.

3. Go to the **Filter Settings** tab.

4. In the **Source Site Name** field, choose the site (OLTP).

5. Maintain the filter settings based on your business requirements.

6. Save your settings.

7. Hit the **Filter Sync (R/3)** button to synchronize your filter settings.

With this step, you have maintained the adapter settings by adding a filter. Filters are fields or attributes with a filter value that you can mark as inclusive or exclusive and download the customer from SAP ECC to SAP CRM. For example, if you want to exclude a customer of a certain account group, you would exclude it while setting the customer adapter object.

Customer master data replication

Once you have completed all the pre-requisite steps, you can start loading a customer from ECC to CRM. To replicate a customer, follow these steps:

1. Go to the SAP CRM menu and access transaction R3AS, as shown in the following screenshot:

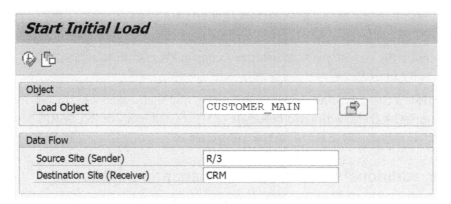

Figure 2.15 – Customer master initial load

2. In the **Load Object** field, enter CUSTOMER_MAIN.

3. In the **Source Site** field, enter OLTP, and in the **Destination Site** field, enter CRM.

4. To run the replication, choose **Execute** (*F8*).

5. Confirm the next screen's message by clicking **Continue**.

Monitoring the replication status (SAP CRM)

You can monitor the replication status via transaction R3AM1. The replication is complete if the object is marked with the **Done** status. If there are any problems during replication, you can access transaction code SMW01 to get details of the error.

We have now gone through the business partner concept and its configuration to replicate it from SAP ECC to the SAP CRM system. Our next focus is the **Product Master Data (PRD)**, its concept and how we replicate it into SAP CRM.

Product master data

Products are the goods or services that are sold by an organization to customers. A product drives most of the key functionality on the order line item. It consists of different data elements; that is, the basic data is applicable across different functions whereas sales area data is specific to sales. Some attributes can be plant-specific and some can consist of conditions with a price. Any business-relevant data related to the products is stored in the product master and drives the complete order to cash process.

The product type in SAP CRM describes the basic characteristics of a product. There are different types of products in SAP CRM but the most relevant product types in sales transactions are of the **Material** and **Service** types.

You can control deactivating the product types based on your business requirements by going to **SPRO | Cross-Application Components | SAP Product | Settings for Product Type | Deactivate Product Types**.

A technological overview of product master data in SAP CRM is as follows.

Attributes and set types

Set types are the group of fields (attributes) that are assigned to a category. Based on your business scenario, you can create your own set types and attributes. A hierarchy consists of categories and categories consist of set types and attributes. Some standard set types are assigned to the MAT_ base hierarchy, which is inherited by the next level of hierarchies, for example, MAT_HAWA and MAT_FERT.

Categories and hierarchy

A product hierarchy consists of multiple categories and can be created based on your business requirements. Lower-level categories inherit set types from higher-level categories. R3PRODSTYP is the default base hierarchy.

A product can be assigned to only one category within the same hierarchy and set types can be assigned to more than one category within the same hierarchy that belongs to a particular product type, for example, material. The same set type cannot be assigned to a different hierarchy of the material product type.

To download the product hierarchy, run the DNL_CUST_PROD1 customizing adaptor object load. This loads the product hierarchy from SAP ECC to SAP CRM.

The following diagram shows a diagrammatic representation of the **Hierarchy**, **Category**, **Set Type**, and **Attribute** flow:

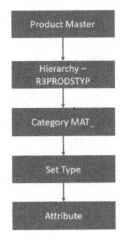

Figure 2.16 – Hierarchy, Category, Set Type, and Attribute flow

You create the attribute and set the type via **SAP Menu | Master Data | Product | COMM_ATTRSET - Maintain Set Types and Attributes**. *Figure 2.17* shows an example of an attribute. You assign a value range to attributes while maintaining the attributes:

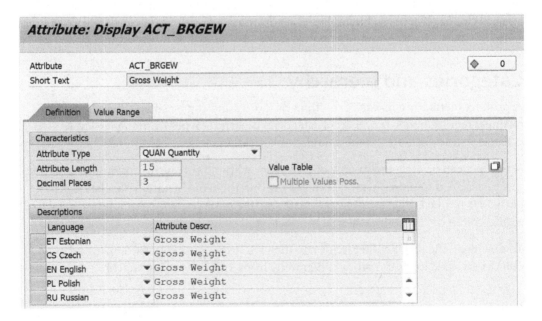

Figure 2.17 – Defining attributes

The next screenshot shows an example of a set type. A set type has attributes and can be org-dependent. If an attribute is marked as Business Warehouse-relevant, a data source is created for the set type automatically. You also need to mark the set type as **Material**, **Service**, **Financing**, or **Warranty**. You can also add fields to the UI product view and create UI configurations for set types:

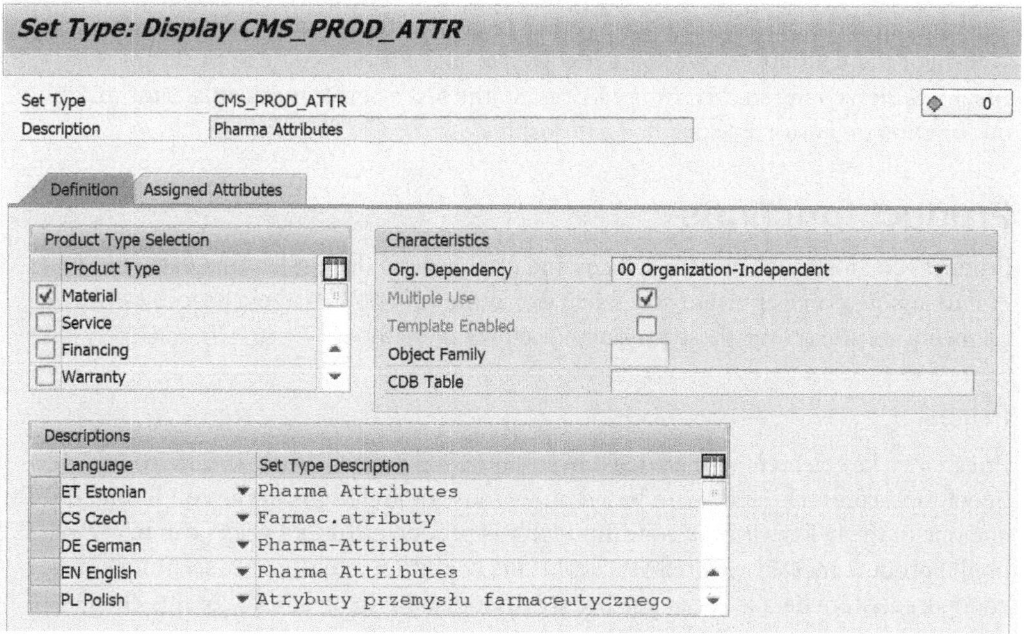

Figure 2.18 – Defining the set type

We have now covered the maintenance of attributes and set types that can be created for the product master and covered the sequential connection of the hierarchy, category, set type, and attribute. Let's now understand relationships within the product master.

Relationships

Products can have relationships maintained in the PRD and those can be accessories, warranties, customer material information records, vendors, components, customers, and so on. The data stored in the relationship of the product master is essentially used in CRM business transactions. There is no customer material information record as separate master data like in the SAP ECC system. The customer material information is a part of the product master relationship. Customer material information can be maintained in the CRM product master relationship and a customer material information record can be loaded via the CUST_MAT_INFO middleware adapter object from ECC to CRM. The customer/distribution chain relationship is updated with the customer material information record from ECC.

The accessories relationship can be used to assign additional products that can be used as a part of product proposals in a transaction. The **Customers** tab in the product master relationship corresponds to the customer material number. This can be maintained in the product master. Similarly, the **Vendors** tab in the relationship corresponds to the vendor material number.

Customer-specific relationship types can be defined with the Easy Enhancement Workbench and additional steps are involved to make these visible in the CRM web client UI. Please refer to *SAP Note 1139562* in the SAP service marketplace for more information on customer-specific relationships.

Product functions

Product functions such as prices, taxes, material general data, sales area data, and units of measure play an important role when executing different business processes. The following sections cover these product functions in detail.

Prices

Prices are a key element and are used in business transactions such as sales orders, quotations, contracts, and so on based on various combinations in the condition tables, and one of the fields within a condition table is product. Product prices can be viewed on the product master within SAP CRM if the condition maintenance techniques are configured. More details about pricing are discussed in the next topic of this chapter, which gives you an overall idea of the functionality of pricing and how it works within a business transaction.

If you want to use the pricing functionality in the product master, you must assign product-specific condition tables and types to the appropriate condition group in customizing path for **Customer Relationship Management**, by choosing **Master Data | Conditions and Condition Technique | Condition Technique: Basics | Create Maintenance Group**.

If you want to use the pricing functionality in the product master, you must assign the condition group to the SAP CRM application in customizing path for **Customer Relationship Management**, by choosing **Master Data | Products | Special Settings for Sales Operations | Assign Condition Group to Application CRM**.

If you want to view details of the price calculation, you must enter the PRC_CALC_TRACE user parameter and the X parameter value in your user preferences (transaction SU3).

Taxes

You can view whether a product is taxed in the product master. By assigning a sales tax to a product, you determine how the product is taxed. The details in the tax assignment block are country, region, tax type, and tax group.

Units of measure

You can maintain **Base Unit**, **Sales Unit**, **Delivery Unit**, and **Alternate Unit of Measures** in SAP CRM as you do in the ECC system. When creating a sales transaction, the **Sales Unit of measure** is populated by default and if the sales unit of measure is not maintained, then the base unit of measure defaults on the sales transaction.

You can only use base units of measure that have been defined in customizing path in **CRM SPRO | SAP Web Application Server | General Settings | Check Units of Measurement**.

Sales area data

Sales area data within the product master is shown on the **Sales and Distribution** tab and contains information specific to sales. You can have multiple sales areas assigned to a product and each of the sales area information on the **Sales and Distribution** tab can be different. The concept is the same as in the ECC system. When creating a product in SAP CRM, you can assign the sales area manually, whereas if a product is replicated from the ECC system, the data cannot be changed manually. If you want to change an ECC-replicated product, then you need to maintain the set type for the product type in the **BAdI: Allow Changes to Product Data** configuration.

Product groups and sales groupings, such as volume rebate groups, are maintained in the sales area data. Two set types assigned to the sales area data are CRMM_PR_SALESA (**Sales: Control Fields, Quantities**) and CRMM_PR_SALESG (**Sales: Groupings**). You can also enter product sales text that can be determined on the sales order if required based on the text determination procedure.

Material data

Material data of the product is applied at the material level, meaning this data is not dependent on the sales area data or purchasing data. This is similar to the basic data of the material master in the ECC system. Material data consists of **Basic Data for Materials**, **Base Units of Measure**, **Global Trade Item Number**, and **Basic text**.

The division is maintained in the basic data in CRM whereas in ECC, the material has the division at the sales area level. A division is an attribute in organizational management. If a header division is not used in your system, the division exists only at the item level and is derived from the product data. You specify in **Customizing** whether a header division is to be used.

The **General Item Category** group is defined to determine the item category on the sales transaction, for example, NORM.

Global Trade Item Number is used to identify products in CRM business transactions. This can be used as a product determination on sales transactions. The **Global Trade Item Number** (**GTIN**) is a 14-digit number that includes various EAN/UCC numbering structures and is used to uniquely identify a product worldwide.

Status management

The status within the product master controls whether you can use the product in a business transaction, whether it is locked, deleted, and so on. The following system statuses are predefined in various central SAP tables for the PRD object type and cannot be changed:

- **Locked**
- **Can Be Archived**
- **To Archive**
- **Archived**
- **Deleted**

You can also configure the user status, but it doesn't have any effect on the standard functionality.

Products download

In order to download products successfully, there are pre-requisite steps to download customizing objects for categories and hierarchy. Once the customizing objects are loaded successfully, the following steps need to be carried out before loading the products from ECC to CRM.

Defining number ranges for materials (SAP CRM)

The material number range setting is different from the customer master and it doesn't require a number range definition for replicating materials from the R/3 system to the CRM system. This means that if the categories within the material product type are not assigned to any of the groups containing a number range, then the system will take the number from the R/3 system and automatically create products with the same number in the CRM system. To avoid duplicate numbers when creating materials in both the CRM and ECC systems, it is imperative that the number ranges for materials in the CRM system and the R/3 system do not overlap.

To define the product number range, follow this menu path, **Cross-Application Components | SAP Product | Settings for Product Type | Number Assignment | Define Number Ranges**, for the **Material** product type. This will present the following screen:

Maintain Intervals: Prod. Type Material

No	From No.	To Number	NR Status	Ext	
01	00000000000000000001	00000000000000099999	581	☐	▲
02	00000000000000999999	00000000000099999999	1001158	☐	▼

Figure 2.19 – Defining number ranges for the Material product type

Maintaining number range groups (SAP CRM)

You can assign a number range and group the category IDs within the configuration path mentioned to configure the number ranges. This will be based on your business scenario and what category ID you need to assign to what number range.

The following screenshot shows the number range maintenance for the material product type wherein you can define the number range interval:

Range Maintenance: Prod. Type Material

Groups   Groups   Change documents

Intervals	Intervals	NR Status

Figure 2.20 – Maintaining groups

You can assign a number range to maintained groups and then assign material types to the group. When creating products, the numbers assigned to the material are taken from the group, as shown in *Figure 2.21*:

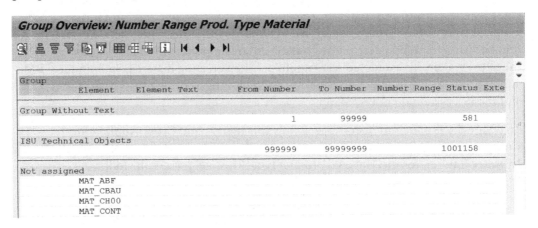

Figure 2.21 – Group overview

Defining item category groups (SAP CRM)

To avoid any failure of material load from ECC to CRM, it is necessary to sync the item category group configuration from ECC to CRM. Follow the given path to configure an item category group: **SPRO | Customer Relationship Management | Transactions | Basic Settings | Define Item Category Group**

Once you are done with the preceding configuration, you maintain the master data adaptor object setting as stated here:

1. Go to transaction R3AC1 and select the **MATERIAL** business object, and then choose **Details** (F2).

2. Go to the **Filter Settings** tab.

3. In the **Source Site Name** field, choose the site (OLTP).

4. Maintain the filter settings based on your business requirements and save your settings.

Replicating products (SAP CRM)

Once you are done with setting up the Material adaptor object, the next step is to replicate the material from SAP ECC to SAP CRM. The steps to execute the material load are as follows:

1. Go to the SAP CRM menu, and then to transaction R3AS.

2. In the **Load Object** field, enter MATERIAL.

3. In the **Source Site** field, enter OLTP, and in the **Destination Site** field, enter CRM:

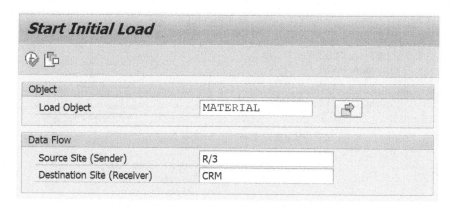

Figure 2.22 – Material initial load

4. To run the replication, choose **Execute** (*F8*).

5. Confirm the next screen message by choosing **Continue**.

Monitoring the replication status (SAP CRM)

After initiating the material load, you monitor the load via transaction R3AM1. In the **Object Name** field, enter the MATERIAL downloaded object to get the download status of this object. The replication is complete if all objects have the status **Done**.

We have covered the concept of PRD, its various functions, and the replication steps from SAP ECC to SAP CRM. Now that we are well versed in the concept of PRD in the SAP CRM system, let's continue with the pricing concept and see how it works with business transactions.

Pricing overview

Pricing in SAP CRM is carried out in business transactions such as quotations, sales orders, contracts, or service processes. Based on the company's requirements, a pricing procedure is created that comprises different condition types, for example, **List Price**, **Discounts**, **Freight Charges**, **Rebate condition** (if applicable), and **Surcharge**. While creating a business transaction, the system uses the condition techniques to determine the correct price for the product. Pricing information in SAP CRM can be downloaded from the ECC system or can be created in CRM directly:

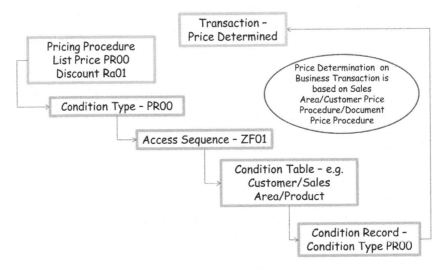

Figure 2.23 – Price determination in CRM sales transactions

This diagram shows the flow logic of price determination in the SAP CRM system. The pricing procedure is assigned with condition types; condition types are assigned with an access sequence; an access sequence has condition tables, and you create the condition record for the condition table defined in the **Customizing**. Price determination in business transactions is based on the sales area, the document pricing procedure assigned to the transaction type, and the customer pricing procedure assigned to the customer master. Let's review the configuration steps to understand how to determine the pricing procedure in business transactions.

Pricing procedure determination

Pricing procedure is determined based on sales area (sales org, distribution channel, and div), customer pricing procedure, and document pricing procedure. The pricing procedure comprises a list of condition types and subtotals based on the business requirements. Routines can be assigned to each of the condition types based on business logic.

The next screenshot shows a pricing procedure determination configuration and the path to configure is **SPRO | CRM | Basic Functions | Pricing | Pricing in the Business Transaction | Determine Pricing Procedures**:

New Entries: Overview of Added Entries

Determination of Pricing Procedure

Sales Organization ID	Dis. Chan.	Division	Doc. Pric....	C.	Procedure
1000	00	99	A	1	0CRM01

Figure 2.24 – Pricing procedure determination

Before creating or determining our pricing procedure, condition types, access sequences, and condition tables should be configured or loaded from ECC based on your business requirements. Let's review this setup:

- **Condition types**: Condition types are the actual price, discounts, surcharges, and so on in the business document. Condition types can be determined automatically, or they can be entered manually. For automatic determination of the condition type, an access sequence should be assigned to it. A condition type can be a group condition, header condition, or item condition.

- **Access sequences**: The access sequence determines the sequence of the condition tables that determines the condition record for a specific condition type.

- **Condition tables**: A condition table consists of a list of fields that determines the correct condition type based on the access sequence. An SAP-delivered condition table ranges from *0* to *500* and a customer-specific table ranges from *501* to *999*.

- **Condition records**: These are entries or records based on the condition table and fields. The actual price, discounts, and surcharge are entered in the condition records for a specific period. These are either loaded from ECC or can be maintained directly in CRM.

There are specific steps required to load customer-specific condition records and the maintenance of the condition records in CRM.

Downloading the pricing procedure and condition types

The steps to download the pricing procedure and condition records are as follows.

Defining ECC fields in CRM

To download the condition records, the fields within condition tables in CRM should be in sync with ECC condition tables, meaning if there are certain fields that are not available in CRM, those should be added to load the condition records successfully.

If the ECC fields are not present in the CND_MAPT_ACS_REM structure, they should be added into the CND_MAPT_ACS_REM_CUST structure.

Defining customer-specific fields in the CRM field catalog

A customer-specific field should be added to the field catalog within CRM. These are the list of fields that are going to be accessed to determine the price and once added to the field catalog, they are available in the communication structure of CRM_COND_COM_BADI.

The menu path is **Customer Relationship Management | Basic Functions | Pricing | Define Pricing Related Settings | Define Field Catalog**.

The following screenshot shows the field catalog wherein you can define additional fields you want to add to determine the prices on the sales transaction. The fields that you create for the condition table should be available in this field catalog:

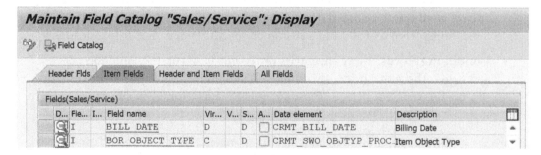

Figure 2.25 – CRM field catalog

Defining a mapping of fields between CRM and ECC

To map standard fields, SAP has provided the CND_MAPC_CNV_FLM table, wherein you will find the field mapping between CRM and ECC for standard fields with the conversion function module assigned if needed. To maintain the field mapping for custom fields, the CND_MAPM_CNV_FLM table should have the entry of the field mapping as previously and this can be added via the V_CND_MAP_CNVFLD view.

The following screenshot shows an example for the **Process_Type** field, which is maintained in the CND_MAPM_CNV_FLM table:

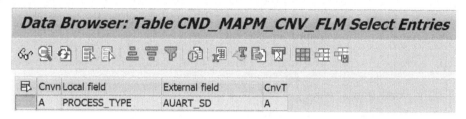

Figure 2.26 – The CND_MAPM_CNV_FLM table maintained with Process_Type

Download the customizing object to sync the condition tables and pricing procedure between ECC and CRM.

Once the condition tables with custom fields are created in CRM, you can load the condition tables from ECC to CRM before loading the actual condition records. A pre-requisite step is to open the CRM client so that the custom field and condition tables are replicated correctly. This is done by following these steps:

1. From the SAP CRM menu, go to transaction R3AS and fill in the **Load Object** field with the DNL_CUST_CNDALL entry.

2. In the **Source Site** field, enter OLTP, and in the **Destination Site** field, enter CRM:

Start Initial Load

Object	
Load Object	DNL_CUST_CNDALL

Data Flow	
Source Site (Sender)	R/3
Destination Site (Receiver)	CRM

Figure 2.27 – Downloading pricing customizing objects

3. To run the replication, choose **Execute** (*F8*).

4. Confirm the next screen message by clicking **Continue**.

Access transaction code R3AM1 to confirm that the customizing load ran successfully. Verify that all the pricing procedures, access sequences, condition types, and condition tables are generated corrected after the download.

Creating condition tables

After the pricing customizing object is downloaded successfully, the next step is to create the condition adaptor objects for the condition tables and then load the condition records by running these condition adaptor objects one by one.

The steps to create the condition adaptor objects for the condition tables are as follows:

1. Go to transaction R3AC5.

2. Create adapter objects for the following condition tables (if the adapter object for the condition table doesn't exist as standard) as a copy of a standard object, say, DNL_COND_A621:

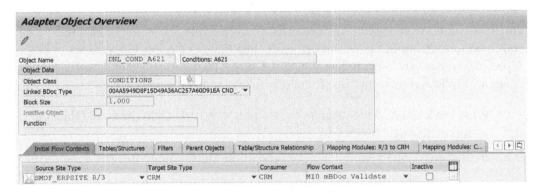

Figure 2.28 – Condition adaptor object

Downloading condition records

The steps to execute the condition record download are as follows:

1. Go to transaction R3AS.

2. In the **Load Object** field, enter ZDNL_COND_A621.

3. In the **Source Site** field, enter OLTP, and in the **Destination Site**, enter CRM.

4. To run the replication, choose **Execute** (*F8*).

5. Confirm the next screen message by choosing **Continue**.

Repeat these steps for all the condition adaptor objects to load all the condition records. Once the condition records are loaded and the pricing configuration is completed, the price determination will happen on the CRM business transactions.

The concept of pricing routines in SAP CRM using IPC

The SAP **Internet Pricing and Configurator** (**IPC**) is used in CRM to calculate the price of any business transactions, for example, quotations, orders, or contracts. IPC is used in any CRM application, whether it is a Web Channel or Interaction Center application. The routines created in CRM are developed in Java and are assigned to the condition type within a pricing procedure. Downloading the pricing customization takes care of assigning a routine to a condition type if pricing is loaded from ECC.

Once you have carried out all the previous activities, if there are certain custom routines that you have implemented in ECC and you want to create the same routine in CRM, then you need to follow the next steps.

To create a new custom routine, you must have a Java project created in the Eclipse environment. You can refer to the steps on how to download, create your own custom routine, and upload the pricing routine to the SAP CRM environment. This is mentioned in *OSS Note 809820 – User exit concept for pricing*. You can access the SAP OSS note via the service marketplace (`service.sap.com`). Based on your environment setup, you can also use NWDI.

Pre-requisites

Pricing a user exit should be compiled with J2SE 1.4.x and it is important that the compiled class files are compatible with JDK version 1.4. The VMC Java environment of SAP BASIS 7.00 does support 1.4 class files and libraries.

You download the routine and upload the JAR file via the `/SAPCND/UE_DEV` transaction.

Creating PRC_UE_CUSTOMER.jar to upload the user exit

After implementing the specific pricing logic based on the business requirement, you upload the pricing routine to the SAP environment. JAR files are generated through Eclipse, which you upload in the /SAPCND/UE_DEV transaction code. This is shown in the next screenshot:

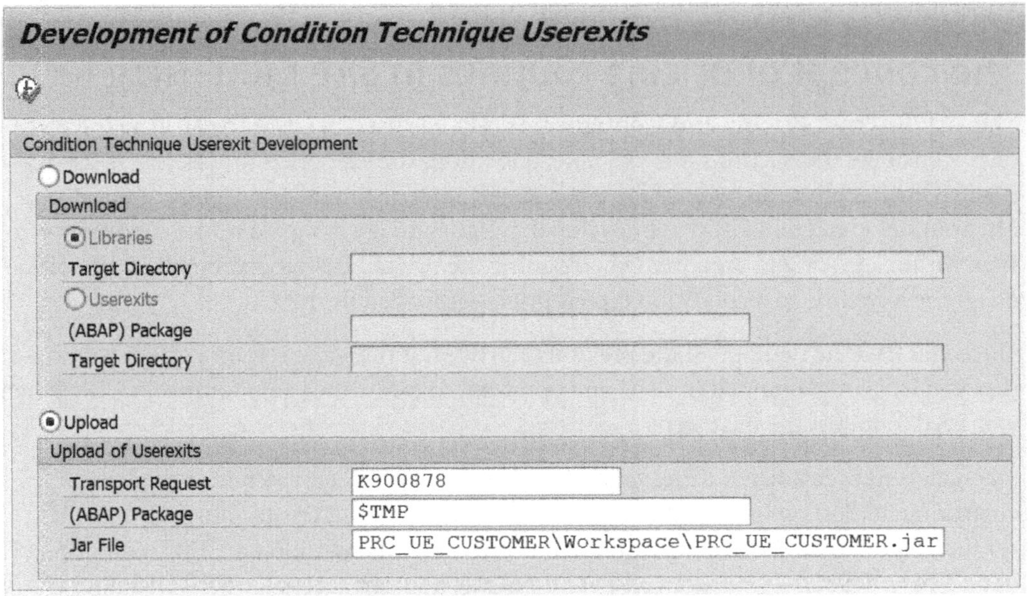

Figure 2.29 – Uploading a user exit JAR file

Once the user exits are loaded to the SAP system, it is a time to register the routine and the attributes if required in the configuration as mentioned in the following sections.

Overview of different user exit types

The next screenshot shows the different user exit types for usage PR (pricing). These need to be configured based on your requirement and the routines added to the pricing procedure. The transaction code to configure the user exit types is /SAPCND/UEASS.

Any rules based on the user exit type should be added as an implementation and formula. This is shown in the following screenshot, where you can see there are different user exit types:

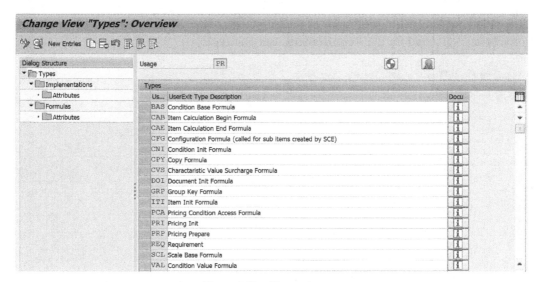

Figure 2.30 – User exit types

These user exit types are **Condition Base Formula**, **Requirement, Condition Value Formula**, and so on. Each of these user exit types can be assigned with implementations and formulas and associated attributes:

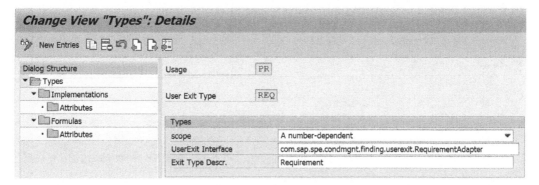

Figure 2.31 – User exit type details

On the detail screen of each user exit type, the **Scope** field and **User Exit Interface** exist. Options within the **Scope** field are A number-dependent, B One unique-implementation, or C Multiple-Implementations.

Registering an implementation

Once you have identified which routine belongs to which user exit type, you will need to register an implementation within this step. Here is an example of the REQ user exit type and the attributes assigned to the implementation that is required in the user exit.

The following screenshot shows one of the examples of the **DEPARTURE_CTY** user exit type being registered for the **Requirement** user exit type:

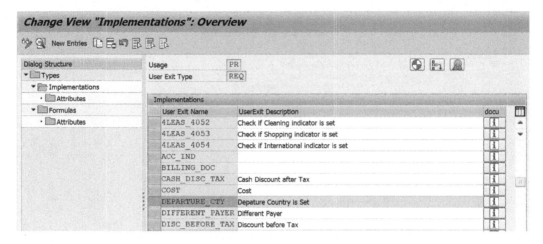

Figure 2.32 – REQ user exit type implementations

The next screenshot shows the attribute assigned to the user exit type named **DEPARTURE_CTY**. This attribute is passed via a pricing communication structure to VMC to calculate the prices on the sales transaction line item:

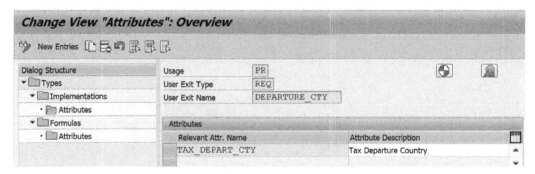

Figure 2.33 – User exit attributes

Assigning implementations to a formula

After defining the implementation for the user exit type, the next step is to assign the formula. The customer formula extends from *600* to *999* and the number is the same as what is being assigned in the pricing procedure. Each user exit type must have a formula number assigned to it as shown:

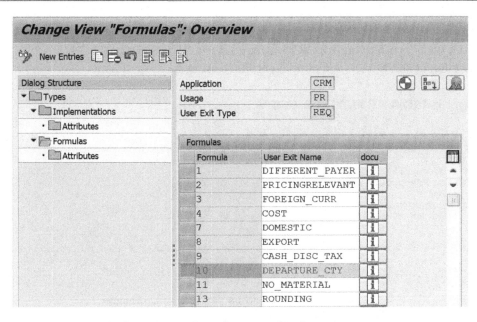

Figure 2.34 – Formulas assigned to the user exit

Attributes assigned

The next screenshot shows tax departure city as one of the attributes assigned that is used to determine the price for the condition type:

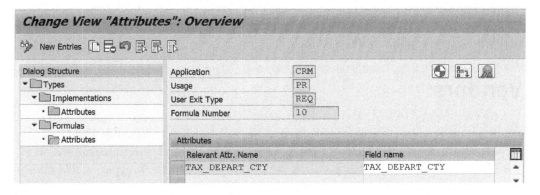

Figure 2.35 – Attributes assigned to the formula

After going through all the configuration steps, it is necessary to reset VMC (transaction code SM53) and run the IPC_DET_CLEAR_CUST_BUFFER IPC buffer program to make your changes effective. In the CRM SMOFPARSFA table, you can control the pricing redetermination in ECC for CRM orders by adding the entry for PRICINGTYPE with the pricing indicator, for example, pricing indicator G is set for reprising tax in ECC when the sales orders are replicated from CRM to ECC.

Verifying routines loaded to SAP CRM

You can verify routines in SAP CRM that are loaded via /SAPCND/UE_DEV. Access transaction code VMCJDB and double-click on **dbsources** as highlighted:

```
Program RSVMCRT_MINI_DEBUGGER

Available commands: activate per double click or enter at command line below
        attach  step  stepup  next  cont  help  checkpoints  source  dbsources  classes

Available connections:
        No open connections.

Command output for: help
        attach <port>                — connect to an VM listening for port
        exit                         — exit debugger

        dbsources                    — list Java source files located in the database
        source [source file]         — list Java source files reachable per source path
                                       or display source file content
```

Figure 2.36 – Virtual machine container mini debugger

You will see the list of the routines you have uploaded to the SAP CRM system under the list of Java source files located in the database. Double-click on one of the routines to view the Java source file.

We have covered the pricing master data concept, that is, the configuration to determine the price on the business transaction, configuration required to communicate pricing to the **Virtual Machine (VM)** container, and download pricing from SAP ECC to SAP CRM. Now that we have covered business partners, products, and pricing, let's continue to understand how vendors work in SAP CRM.

Vendors

Vendors are created in ECC and can be loaded to CRM based on your business requirements. Vendors are an integral part of the order to cash transaction when it comes to third-party sales orders. When products are not available in the organization's warehouse, then the sourcing is executed via a third-party vendor. In typical CRM sales order scenarios, a customer service representative might need vendor information if it is a third-party sales order and therefore it becomes imperative to determine the correct vendor on the CRM sales order. For vendor determination, you need to load vendors into the CRM system. In CRM, these vendors are created as a business partner in the **BBP000-Vendor** role when downloaded from ECC.

Downloading vendors

Downloading vendors from ECC to CRM requires some pre-requisite steps, which are stated as follows.

CRM settings

The following steps are performed in CRM settings:

1. Activate the VEND_MWX_CREATE_MAIN_BDOC function. In transaction SM31, the CRMC_BUT_CALL_FU table for the business partner outbound of business partner objects and the VEND_MWX_CREATE_MAIN_BDOC function must be active.

2. Activate the VEND_MAIN and VENDOR_MAIN adaptor objects. In transaction R3AC1, the VEND_MAIN and VENDOR_MAIN adapter objects must be active. A filter for each role of role category vendor must be set for the VEND_MAIN object.

3. Create a subscription for vendors in SMOEAC. In transaction SMOEAC (admin console), there will be a subscription for the **All Vendors** publication to the ECC system (site). For example, you can specify All Vendors (MESG) as the subscription's name:

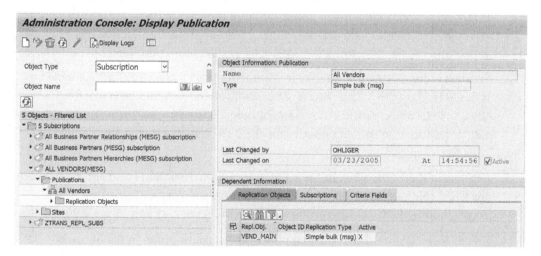

Figure 2.37 – Vendor subscription in SMOEAC

4. Creation of Business Partner Grouping for Vendors: In this step the business partner grouping for vendors is created by activating the external grouping and assigning the **Number range** to the grouping. The **Number range** should be same as the ECC vendor number range.

Figure 2.38 shows the activation of external grouping and the **Number range** getting assigned to grouping:

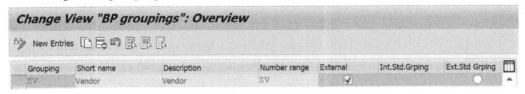

Figure 2.38 – Vendor business partner grouping

SAP ECC settings

Like the settings and the steps executed in SAP CRM to set up vendors, you need to execute the settings in the SAP ECC system. These are as follows:

1. Activate PI_BP_PROXY_BAPI_VENDOR: Within transaction SM31, the COM_BUPA_CALL_FU table for R/3 object inbound processing (time R3OBI) of vendor records (object VEND), the PI_BP_PROXY_BAPI_VENDOR function must be active, and the PI_BP_PROXY_BAPI_CUST_VEND function must not be active.

2. Settings in the CRMSUBTAB table: In transaction SM31, the CRMSUBTAB table for user CRM, the COM_VEND_MAIN_INBOUND function should be active for the VEND_MAIN object of the BUPA class for upload. The PI_BP_VENDOR_MAIN_EXTRACT function should be active for the VENDOR_MAIN object of the VEND class for download.

3. Settings in the PIDV table: In the PIDV transaction, maintain the mapping between the CRM role categories for vendors (usually role category BBP000) and the corresponding ECC account group as shown in *Figure 2.39* and *Figure 2.40*.

   The next screenshot shows the mapping of the account group to the business partner role category from R/3 to CRM, that is, the data flow from SAP ECC to SAP CRM:

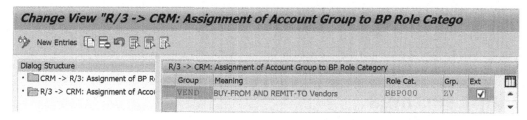

Figure 2.39 – Assignment of the account group to the business partner role category

The next screenshot shows the mapping of the business partner role category to the account group from CRM to R/3, that is, the data flow from SAP CRM to SAP ECC:

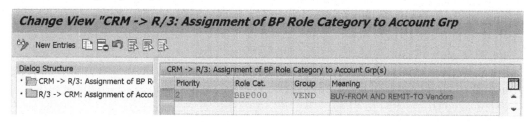

Figure 2.40 – Assignment of the business partner role category to the account group

By default, **Business Documents (BDOCS)** of the VEND_MAIN type are sent in the SAP CRM system for all CRM business partners as soon as you activate the distribution function in the CRM_BUT_CALL_FU table for VEND_MWX_CREATE_MAIN_BDOC. This is a mandatory step to load the vendors in CRM.

Vendor download in CRM – R3AS

After all the previous activities, vendors are downloaded using the R3AS transaction in CRM:

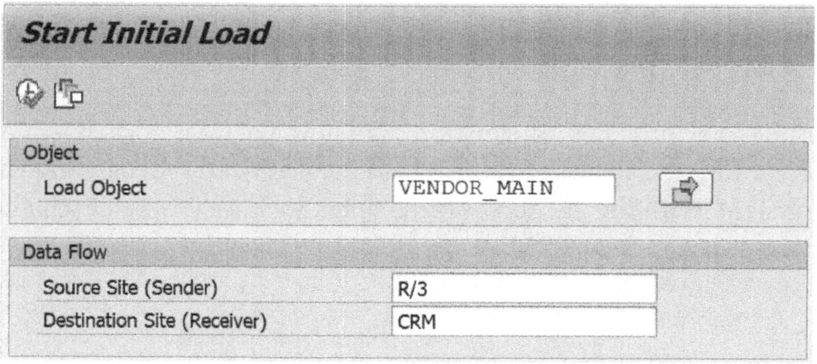

Start Initial Load	
Object	
Load Object	VENDOR_MAIN
Data Flow	
Source Site (Sender)	R/3
Destination Site (Receiver)	CRM

Figure 2.41 – Vendor initial load via R3AS

Now that we have covered the concept of the vendor master and understood the exact settings required to download the vendor from SAP ECC to SAP CRM, our next topic is plant settings and the concept of how to utilize a plant as a business partner in SAP CRM.

Plant settings

The concept of a plant doesn't exist in SAP CRM as there is no inventory maintained in the SAP CRM system. Inventory management is executed in the SAP ECC system. A plant is maintained as a business partner in SAP CRM. A plant is the logistical organizational unit where the products are manufactured and stored. An availability check of any product is based on the plant wherein the ATP check happens, and the transfer of requirement occurs from CRM to APO. For the system to use the number range of the plant when downloading the plant, the internal standard grouping should be activated against the plant grouping entry. Also, CRM doesn't have storage locations and a shipping point. The storage location and shipping points are determined in ECC when the orders are replicated from CRM to ECC.

Within CRM, a plant is created as a business partner and is mapped to the plant in ECC or APO based on where the availability check happens. The plant business partner is termed as location mapping to plant in ECC or APO in the CRMM_LOCMAP table. You can download a plant by executing the following steps:

1. Create number ranges for the plant – transaction code BUCF.

2. Define a grouping and assign number ranges using the following menu path: **SPRO | Cross-Application Components | SAP Business Partner | Basic Settings | Number Ranges and Groupings | Define Grouping and Assign Number Ranges**.

3. Run transaction R3AS for the DNL_PLANT object.

These steps will create the business partner with the role plant and will map the location to the plant in ECC or APO in the CRMM_LOCMAP table.

The plant setting topic provides information as to how a plant is created as a business partner in SAP CRM; the adaptor object to load the plant and the mapping table updating in the CRM system. With this section of the chapter, we have covered each and every element of master data in SAP CRM.

Summary

In this chapter, we went through SAP CRM master data: the organizational model, business partners, products, pricing, plants, and vendors. This chapter forms the basis of the sales process within SAP CRM and it is necessary before understanding transaction processing in SAP CRM. With this chapter, you have got a good understanding of how to set up master data and configure the system to replicate data from the SAP ECC system to CRM.

Organization data, business partners, and products form the basis of all transactions. Any issue with this data has an impact downstream and causes hindrance to the order to cash cycle. This chapter gave appropriate information to minimize and reduces risk related to master data and to make sure you understand the details around the setup.

This chapter also built a foundation for the remaining chapters in this book. The next chapter is about master data in SAP APO, where we will cover the master data including location, plant, and resource master that plays a role in the order fulfillment process while business transactions are processed in the SAP CRM system.

Further reading

- Additional information related to CRM organizational management can be found in the SAP Help documentation at `https://help.sap.com/viewer/b90203d3616f482ebd9776775ac722d8/7.0.4.15/en-US/9e0682c5fb4744fe95cc4e7b669d67bb.html`.

- Information on the concept of the business partner and details can also be found at `https://help.sap.com/viewer/b90203d3616f482ebd9776775ac722d8/7.0.4.15/en-US/48b3d5a903d0356be10000000a421937.html`.

3
Master Data in SAP APO

Master data in SAP APO forms the basis of the fulfillment process. The data in SAP APO is critical to performing the ATP/product allocation check. Having incorrect master data leads to incorrect ATP checks or errors on sales orders. Therefore, it is very important to understand the data aspect and the settings required in the SAP APO system in order to run the cash cycle successfully. Having said that, you should have a good understanding of how these data elements work in SAP APO. In this chapter, we will focus on master data setup and configuration in SAP APO.

Note that master data related to product allocation data and scheduling master data will be covered in *Chapter 8, Order Fulfillment in SAP APO*.

The topics to be covered in this chapter are as follows:

- Introduction to master data in SAP APO
- Location master data concepts in SAP APO
- Product master data in SAP APO
- Resource master data in SAP APO
- Transferring master data from the SAP ECC system to SAP APO

By the end of this chapter, you will understand the significance of master data usage in SAP APO.

Introduction to master data in SAP APO

Master data in SAP APO is a key element similar to master data in SAP ECC. To perform ATP checks in SAP APO, it is important that master data such as customer, product, and plant information is accurately set up. In most cases, ECC is the client of record and the master data is replicated from ECC to APO. In this section, we will explore these data elements in SAP APO and the mechanisms for replicating customer, plant, product, and resources from SAP ECC to SAP APO.

Figure 3.1 represents an overview of each of the master data elements applicable within APO and the relevance of each of these data elements to different SAP APO functionalities:

APO Functionality	Corresponding Master Data
Demand (DP)	Characteristics Value Combo (CVC) Product
Sales (ATP)	Product Location (Customer, Plant, and Vendor)
Transport (TP/VS)	Product Location (Customer, Plant, and Vendor) Resources Transportation Lanes
Distribution (SNP)	Product Location (Customer, Plant, and Vendor) Resources Transportation Lanes
Production (SNP and PP/DS)	Product Location (Customer, Plant, and Vendor) Resources PPM/PDS
Procurement (SNP and PP/DS)	Product Location (Customer, Plant, and Vendor) Resources Transportation Lanes Procurement Relationship

Figure 3.1 – Master data relevance for each SAP APO function

Figure 3.2 presents the ECC master data corresponding to APO master data:

ECC Master Data	APO Master Data
Plant	Location
Customer	Location
Vendor	Location
Material	Products
Work Center/Resources	Resources
Routing/BOM/Master Recipe	PPM or PDS

Figure 3.2 – ECC master data corresponding to SAP APO master data

As we have gone through the list of the master data objects in the SAP APO system and their relevance to SAP ECC, let's explore each master data element in the SAP APO system, starting with location master data.

Location master data concepts in SAP APO

Unlike in SAP ECC, location in SAP APO represents different data objects. In SAP ECC, the plant, the customer, and the vendor are completely different objects. On the other hand, in SAP APO these are represented as location types – for example, `Production Plant`, `Distribution Center`, `Shipping Point`, `Customer`, `Vendor`, and so on. *Figure 3.3* shows location master data screen with different location types:

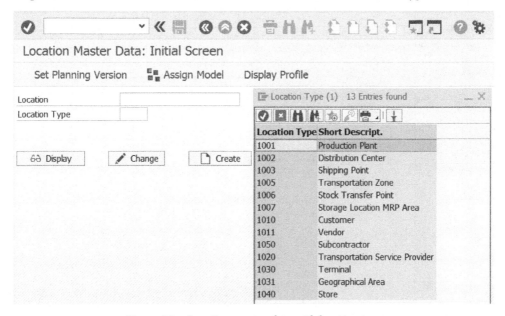

Figure 3.3 – Location master data with location type

> **Important Note**
>
> There should be a unique code for each of these location types. In the case
> of any number range overlaps for objects with different location types, SAP
> provides the user exit APOCF001 to concatenate a suffix or prefix for the code.

Location is the central organization unit, which holds information about business
partners, addresses, calendar, resources, transportation data, and ATP. Every location
includes address information wherein the address data is stored. The following screenshot
shows the **Address** tab information from the location master data:

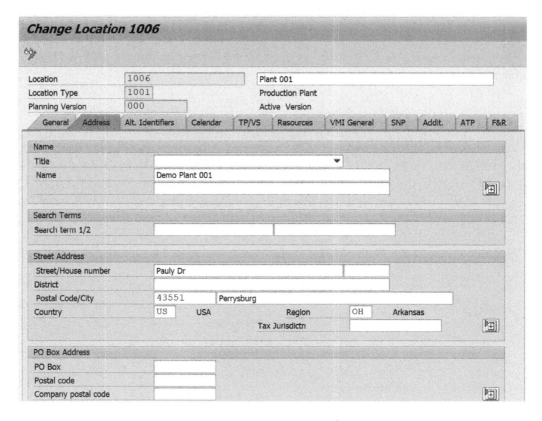

Figure 3.4 – Location master data

> **Note**
>
> The most relevant data in the location master data that needs to be set up for the order to cash cycle to run successfully is calendar information, which is used to determine the hours of operation for the plant. Tabs such as **TP/VS** and **Resources** are part of transportation planning, which is covered in *Chapter 4, Master Data in SAP TMS*, whereas other tabs, such as **VMI General**, **SNP**, and **F&R** are not relevant to the order to cash process.

The calendar plays an important role in identifying plant operation hours during an ATP check on the sales order. Within the calendar master data, you maintain a period wherein you can define the hours of operations. There are different calendars that can be assigned to locations: production, warehouse, shipping, receiving, and planning. The calendar is maintained in the /SAPAPO/CALENDAR transaction. An ATP check on the sales order considers the shipping calendar and performs backward/forward scheduling based on the location hours of operations and the periods defined in the calendar for a particular location. *Figure 3.5* shows an example of the location master data page wherein the shipping calendar is assigned:

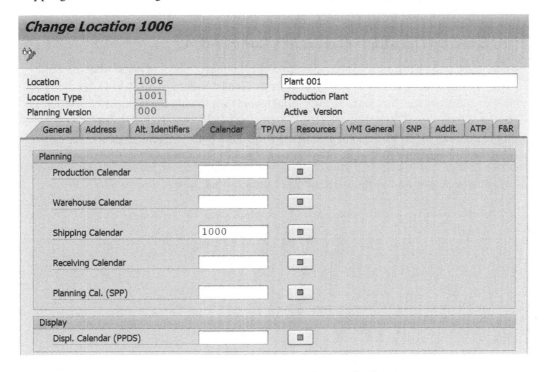

Figure 3.5 – Location master data – Calendar

The SAP ECC vendor, customer, and plants are converted to APO locations with the location type plant, customer, and vendor.

From `BAdI SMOD_APOCF001`, SAP has provided (via the `IF_EX_SMOD_APOCF001` interface) the `EXIT _/SAPAPO/SAPLCIF_LOC_001` method to modify location inbound data to SAP APO.

> **Important Note**
>
> Location is stored in the `/SAPAPO/LOC` table and the location mapping between ECC and APO is stored in `/SAPAPO/LOCMAP`. The entries between the `/SAPAPO/LOC` and `/SAPAPO/LOCMAP` tables should always match. If there are any inconsistencies, then SAP has provided a `/SAPAPO/CHECK_LOC` report to correct those inconsistencies.

Now that we have gone through the location master data, and the significance of the calendar in backward/forward scheduling during an ATP check on the sales order, let's continue with learning about product master data in SAP APO.

Product master data in SAP APO

Products are used within the system to represent the materials or services that are sold by any organization. Attributes within the product master data in SAP APO can be global or location-specific. Data at the global level is applicable for all locations, whereas data specific to a location applies to that location only. The material master in SAP ECC is replicated to SAP APO, and various fields within the SAP ECC material master are mapped to the corresponding product master data in SAP APO.

The following figure shows different views of the product master data in SAP APO:

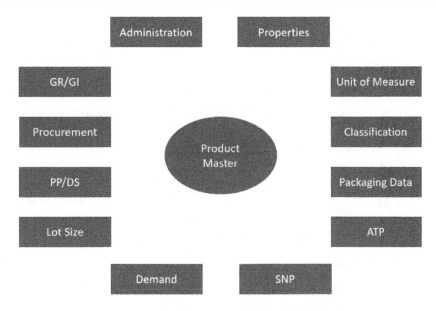

Figure 3.6 – Product master views

Let's discuss the various product functions shown in the previous diagram:

- **Administration**: Within **Administration**, you can assign a planner to the location product. This is at the location level. A planner here could be a material planner, who works on resolving any material availability issues for a specific sales order.

- **Properties**: This is the general data applicable for all locations. It consists of the material group, the product hierarchy, the transportation group, weights and measurements, and shelf life. It also shows the **business system group** (**BSG**).

- **Unit of Measure (UoM)**: As in SAP ECC, UoM consists of the base and alternate units of measurements with different UoM conversions. The UoMs are replicated from ECC to APO. UoM is also global data, applicable for all locations.

- **Classification**: This is global data, as in SAP ECC. Classification data is replicated from ECC to APO. This data is primarily used in demand planning and characteristics-based planning.

- **Packaging Data**: The data in this tab includes the packaging instructions of the product. Again, this is at the global level.

- **Storage**: This data is primarily used in extended warehouse management. It consists of the basic data around the warehouse product group, storage condition, item category group, product freight group, and more.

- **ATP**: The information in this tab is the most important for ATP to work correctly when a sales order is placed in the SAP CRM system (the same is true for SAP ECC sales orders as well). Allocation procedures can be maintained globally or by location to determine product allocation during sales order entry. The check mode is replicated from ECC to APO. The check mode is the requirement class assigned to the strategy group in SAP ECC. The checking horizon in the APO product master is the replenishment lead time from the MRP 3 view in the SAP ECC system. The ATP group is the available check in the SAP ECC material master MRP 3 view. This helps in determining the scope of a check during an ATP check on the sales order. To replicate the ATP data correctly from SAP ECC to SAP APO; it is important to transfer ATP customization from SAP ECC to SAP APO. The integration model setup is required for ATP customization import from ECC to APO.

- **SNP**: The **SNP 1** and **SNP 2** tabs in the product master are relevant for **supply network planning (SNP)**. The data here has the SNP profiles required for SNP.

- **Demand**: The **Demand** tab is relevant for **Production Planning** and **Detailed Scheduling (PP/DS)**. This includes data around requirements, consumption, and pegging. You can define fixed or dynamic pegging in this tab. The strategy group, consumption mode, and dependent requirement settings are replicated from the MRP 3 view of the material master to the **Demand** tab in SAP APO.

- **Lot size**: Just like **Demand**, lot size is relevant for PP/DS. The data in this tab includes stock data, for example, data on safety stock, reorder points, max stock levels, and so on. Lot size data from the MRP 1 view of the ECC material master is replicated to the **Lot size** tab of the product master in SAP APO.

- **PP/DS**: PP/DS is used in production planning and detailed scheduling. This tab has planning procedure, procurement planning, and horizons data mainly used in PP/DS.

- **Procurement**: The information in the procurement tab is related to external procurement. The procurement type and planned delivery time are replicated from the MRP 2 view of the ECC master data to the procurement tab of the SAP APO product master data.

- **GR/GI**: This tab has information around processing times, costs, and loading group data. The information in this field is also replicated from the ECC material master data.

We have now covered the product master data and understood each function within the product master in the SAP APO system. Let's now review resource master data in SAP APO at a high level. Although resource master data is not used during an ATP check at the time of sales order processing, it is important to understanding the concepts of resource master data as we will delve into it in more detail in *Chapter 4*, *Master Data in SAP TMS*.

Resource master data

Resources in SAP APO are used in SNP, PP/DS, and TP/VS. Using the resource master data to check warehouse capacities with TP/VS is not in the scope of this book. Using the resource master data to check various capacities using SAP TMS for transportation planning will be covered in *Chapter 4*, *Master Data in SAP TMS*. The work center and associated capacities are replicated to SAP APO as resources. Resources in SAP APO have capacities and working times defined for machines, means of transport, and warehouses. There are four different types of resource categories: `Production`, `Transportation`, `Warehouse`, and `Handling Unit`. *Figure 3.7* shows the resource master data with all the relevant tabs used for machines, personnel, means of transport, and warehouses:

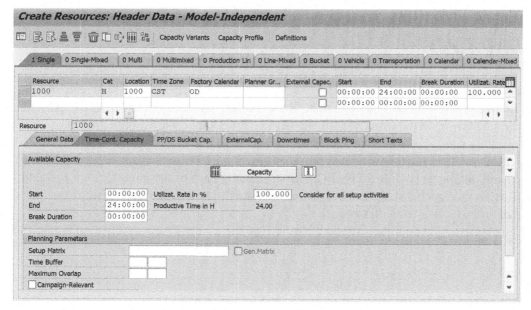

Figure 3.7 – Resource master data

There are different resource types in SAP APO master data. They are as follows:

- Single-activity and multiactivity resources

- Single-mixed and multi-mixed resources

- Bucket resources

- Line resources

- Calendar resources

- Vehicle resources

- Transportation resources

Each of these resource types has resource categories assigned to it in the resource master data.

Having covered location master data, product master data, and resource master data, the next step is to understand the replication of these datasets from the SAP ECC environment to the SAP APO environment.

Transferring master data from SAP ECC to SAP APO

Master data transfer from SAP ECC to SAP APO is done via the **Core Interface Framework (CIF)**. To run the order to cash cycle successfully, you need to create the location and product master data first. In most cases, the client of record is SAP ECC and the data is transferred from ECC to SAP APO. This is applicable for both creating and changing data. Therefore, the new data and the changed data are replicated from ECC to APO using CIF. The following diagram maps each master data element in SAP ECC to its corresponding element in SAP APO. The structure of each of these master data elements is different in each system. During the master data transfer, the core interface maps the data from ECC to APO master data:

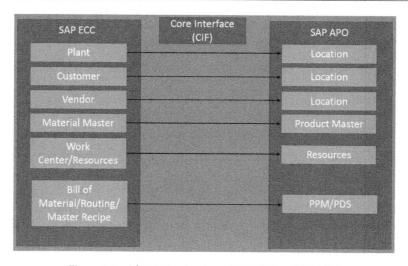

Figure 3.8 – The CIF maps from SAP ECC to SAP APO

Let's have a look at the steps that need to be performed in the system before you start the replication of data from SAP ECC to SAP APO:

1. **SM59**: Set up an RFC connection between the SAP ECC and SAP APO systems.

2. **CFC1**: Define inbound queues. This config requires a logical system, operation mode T, and Q-Type I to be added as entries.

3. **BD61**: Activate change pointers generally. This is to activate the change master data flow from SAP ECC to SAP APO.

4. **BD50**: Activate change pointers for the specific master data type. For example, activate change pointers for CIFMAT, CIFCUS, CIFVEN, and so on.

5. **CFC9**: Here you set the transfer of the master data to 2 - BTE Transfer, Immediately. BTE is a business transaction event that can be triggered immediately with this setting. This setting should be activated for customers, materials, and vendors if you want to transfer changes in real time.

6. **SMQR/SMQS**: Register inbound and outbound CIF queues in this transaction.

7. **CFC2**: This transaction helps you to activate CIF logging.

The steps to be performed on the APO side are as follows:

1. **SM59**: Set up an RFC connection between SAP ECC and SAP APO.

2. **/SAPAPO/C1**: You define a business system group in this transaction. The business system group helps you to identify the same data in SAP APO from a different backend system.

3. **/SAPAPO/C2**: You assign the logical system to the business system group in this transaction.

4. **SMQR/SMQS**: Register inbound and outbound CIF queues in this transaction.

Once these steps are complete, the next steps are to generate and activate the CIF integration model required to replicate the master data from SAP ECC to SAP APO. The steps to generate and activate the integration model are covered later.

Generally, the CIF integration model consists of two datasets:

- **Material Dependent Objects**: These are objects that are material relevant, for example, plant, MRP, ATP, planning material, customer material, and transaction data. The following screenshot shows the integration model with material-dependent objects:

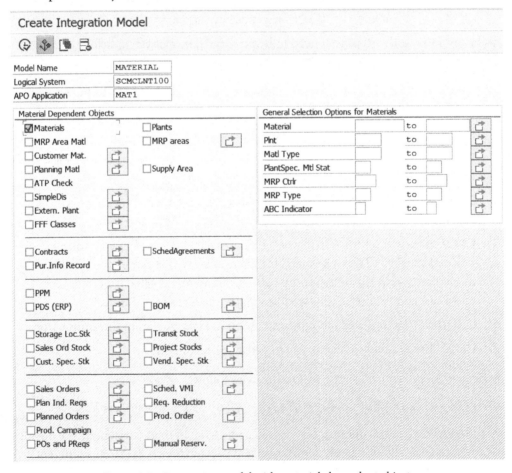

Figure 3.9 – Integration model with material-dependent objects

- **Material Independent Objects**: These are **Customer**, **Vendor**, **Shipping points**, **Work centers**, and **ATP Customizing**, as shown in the following screenshot:

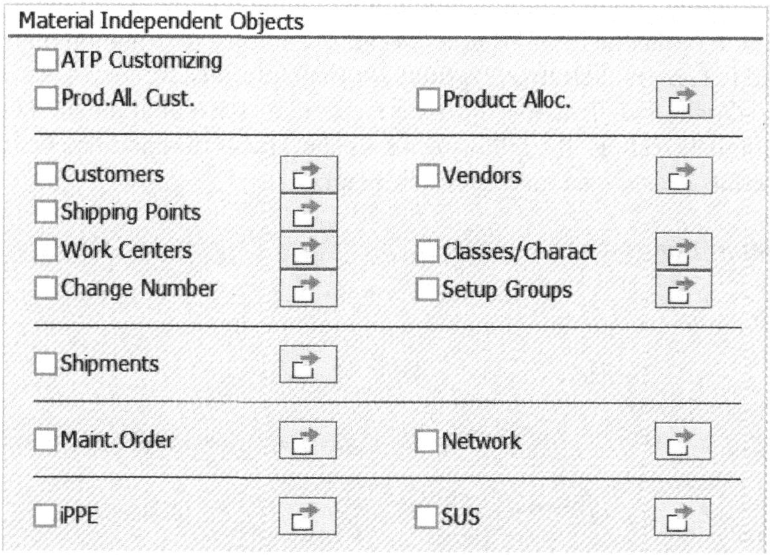

Figure 3.10 – Material Independent Objects

The transfer of master data is one way, that is, from SAP ECC to SAP APO. The changes made in the SAP APO master data don't replicate back to SAP ECC.

Creating an integration model

To create an integration model, go to transaction code CFM1 in SAP ECC and add the model name, logical system, and APO application. Select the checkbox for the master data that you want to create the integration model for. Additional information on the materials can be added to **General Selection Options for the Materials**, where you can maintain plant, material type, and plant-specific material status as some additional criteria for the integration model creation. The following screenshot shows the checkbox being activated for the **Materials** master data for the specific plant:

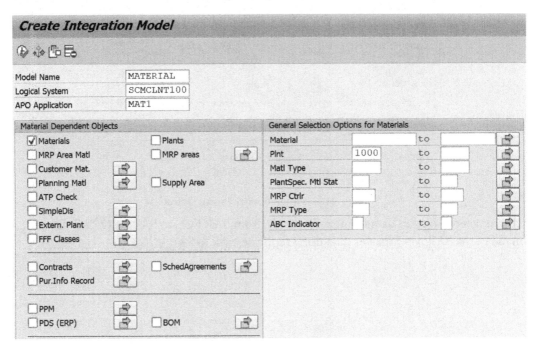

Figure 3.11 – Creating an integration model

For each of the master data objects, there is an option to create a integration model with additional restrictions. For example, in the customer master data, you can add account groups, sales orgs, and also state if you want to create a customer as a business partner, location, or both. Please see the following screenshot of creating integration model with customer criteria:

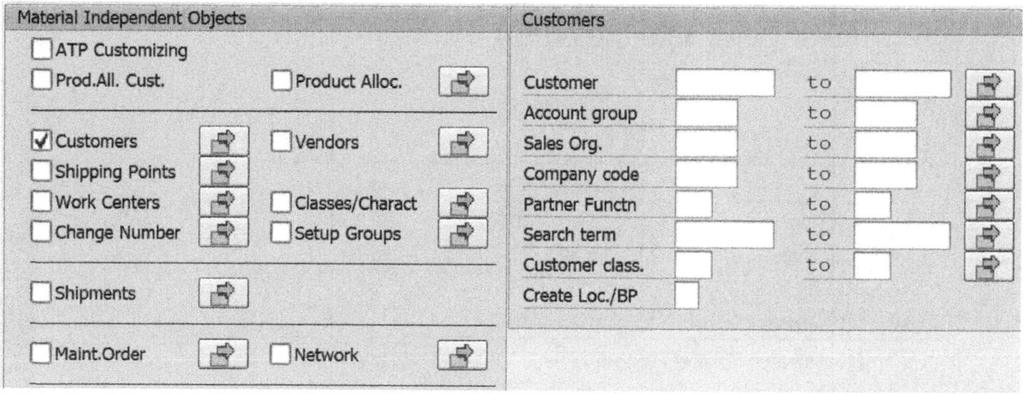

Figure 3.12 – Creating an integration model with customer criteria

Once you click on **Create the integration model**, all material for the specific plant and material type will show in the output screen, and you can view a list of all the materials. Generate the integration model in this transaction and save it.

Activating the integration model

Once the integration model is generated, the next step in replicating the data between ECC and APO is to activate the integration model. Activation of the integration model is done through CFM2. The following screenshot shows the CFM2 transaction with the required selection criteria for **Model**, **Logical System**, and **APO Application**:

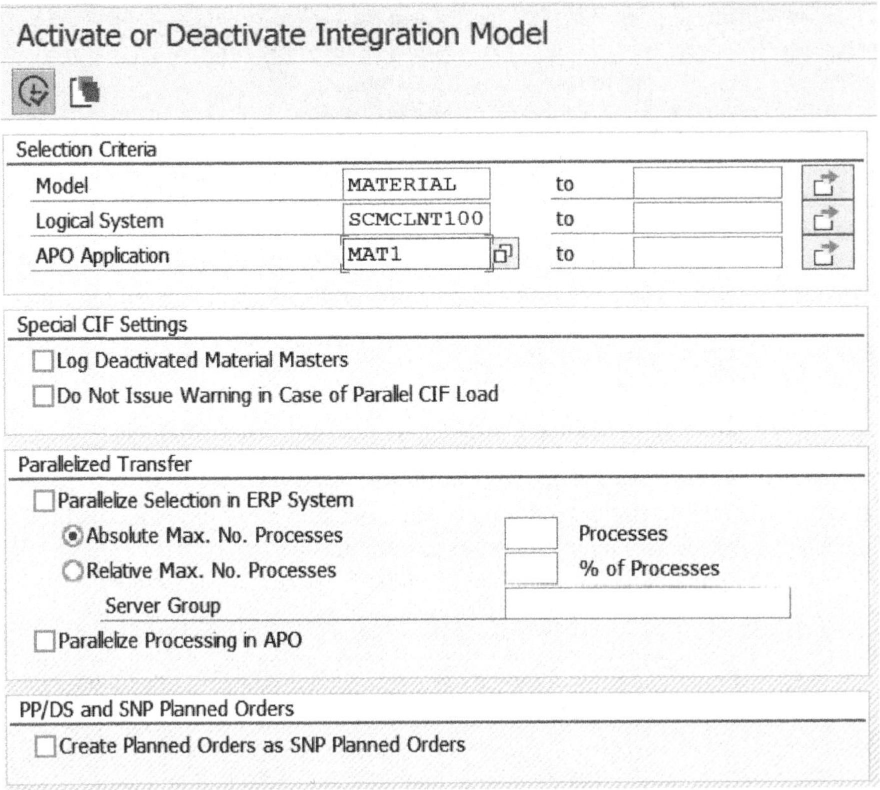

Figure 3.13 – Activating the integration model

Once you run this transaction, the output shows the version of the integration model. You can activate the new version of the integration model. This will initiate the initial transfer of the data from SAP ECC to SAP APO.

Background jobs

You can also schedule background jobs to generate and activate the CIF jobs that replicate the data from SAP ECC to SAP APO. The changes made to the master data in SAP ECC replicate to SAP APO based on the change pointers setting, described in the prerequisites setup earlier, before generating and activating the integration model.

An ongoing business could require new materials, customers, and vendors to be created on a daily basis. Therefore, most businesses schedule background jobs to generate and activate a new version of the CIF integration model on a recurring basis each day.

SAP has provided the report program **RIMODDEL** (transaction code – CFM7) to delete the inactive integration model version. This program can be scheduled in the background to delete inactive integration models. Please make sure to activate the **Select Inactive IMs only** checkbox when scheduling this program as a background job, as shown in the following screenshot:

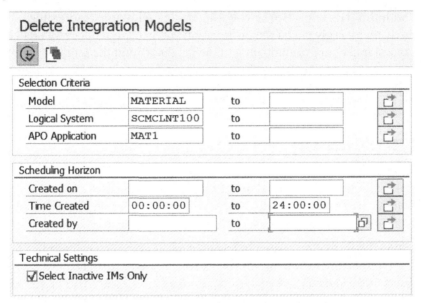

Figure 3.14 – Deleting an integration model

The **RIMODGEN** report program (transaction code – CFM1) is used to generate the integration model. Whenever a new master data record is created, this report program creates a new inactive version of the integration model. Again, this report program can be scheduled in the background to run at regular intervals.

The **RIMODAC2** report program (transaction code – CFM3) is triggered in the background to activate the new integration model version, which then replicates the master data from SAP ECC to SAP APO.

This section covered data transfer between SAP ECC and SAP APO. Now, you are well versed in the steps required to set up a CIF integration model to replicate data from SAP ECC to SAP APO.

Summary

In this chapter, we went through SAP APO master data, that is, location, product, and resource master data, and the transfer of this master data from SAP ECC to SAP APO. This chapter covered the basis of the order fulfillment process and functionality within SAP APO. With this chapter, you have gained a good understanding of how to set up master data and configure the system to replicate data from the SAP ECC system to the APO system.

Location and product data forms the basis of ATP and product allocation functionality. Any issue with this data impacts ATP checking during sales order processing in SAP CRM. This chapter has given you the information you need to reduce risk related to master data and make sure you understand the details around the setup.

The next chapter is about master data in SAP Transportation Management, where we will learn about executing transportation planning successfully.

Further reading

- Additional information related to integration using the CIF can be found in the SAP documentation at `https://help.sap.com/viewer/c95f1f0dcd9549628efa8d7d653da63e/7.0.4/en-US/4b45c95360267614e10000000a174cb4.html`.

- Additional information related to resource master data can be found in the SAP documentation at `https://help.sap.com/viewer/c95f1f0dcd9549628efa8d7d653da63e/7.0.4/en-US/9447c95360267614e10000000a174cb4.html`.

4
Master Data in SAP TMS

Master data in SAP TMS is the most important data if we wish to execute effective and successful transportation planning in SAP TMS. It forms the basis of efficiently planning the transportation and tender carrier to fulfill and ship products on time. Having incorrect master data set up will lead to incorrect transportation planning, which will result in missed deliveries and will impact the customer's shipments. Therefore, it is very important to understand the data aspect and the settings required in the SAP TMS system to run the Order to Cash cycle successfully. Having said that, you should have a good understanding of these data elements and how they work in SAP TMS. In this chapter, we will focus on the master data's setup and configuration in SAP TMS.

Note that the master data related to charge management will be covered in *Chapter 10, Transportation Planning and Freight Order Management in SAP TMS*.

The following topics will be covered in this chapter:

- TMS master data elements and its concept
- Organizational structure overview
- Business partners

- Transportation network
- Resources

By the end of this chapter, you will understand the significance of master data usage in SAP TMS. You will have also learned about some of the aspects around the configurations required to set up the master data in these systems, including their replication steps.

TMS master data elements and its concept

Similar to SAP CRM and SAP APO, SAP TMS requires master data to process the transportation planning and propose delivery/shipments for the SAP ECC system, which allows you to ship an order for a particular customer. In this chapter, we will learn about the master data that's required in SAP TMS to plan for goods to be transported. This includes organization data and general master data, products and business partners, the transportation network, and resources.

The following diagram shows the ECC master data and its equivalent data in SAP TMS. The data replication between the two systems is done using the Core Interface, similar to SAP APO:

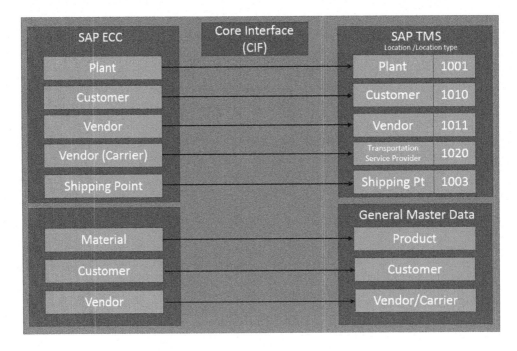

Figure 4.1 – ECC master data and its equivalent data in SAP TMS

As we can see, the plant, customer, vendor, and shipping point from SAP ECC are mapped to the location master in SAP TMS. The location master has a location type that corresponds to the type of master data in SAP ECC. The SAP ECC material master is created as a product master in SAP TMS, whereas the customer master and vendor master from SAP ECC are created as business partners.

Now that we have gone through the master data elements and their mappings between SAP ECC and SAP TMS, let's deep dive into the master data objects. In the next section, we will provide an organizational structure overview of SAP TMS.

Organizational structure overview

The organization structure in TMS is similar to the org structure in CRM but different from the SAP ECC system. The org unit in TMS is flexible and is modeled to structure individual staff assignment to org units. You can also trigger the workflow based on these staff assignments to the org model and assign the task to whoever is involved in this workflow. One of the first steps when setting up the system with the master data is setting up the organization model. The organization model should be set up based on the organization structure requirements for the project's needs.

Within ECC, the sales org is assigned to the company code. This assignment is used for invoicing and settlement. In TMS, company code is not needed to assign the sales org as there is no accounting settlement implication in SAP TMS. The SAP TMS organization structure is divided into different org structure elements, as follows:

- Company code
- Sales organization
- Purchasing organization
- Planning and execution group

The organizational structure within SAP TMS is shown in the following diagram:

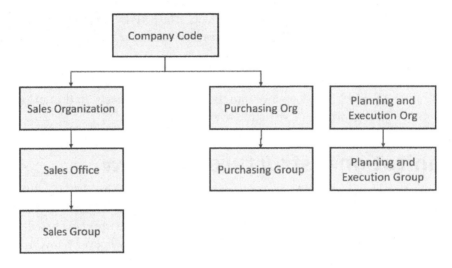

Figure 4.2 – Organization structure in SAP TMS

SAP TMS has org units with the following org unit functions:

- Sales
- Purchasing
- Planning and Execution
- Company
- Corporate
- Forwarding House

These unit functions are also shown in the following screenshot:

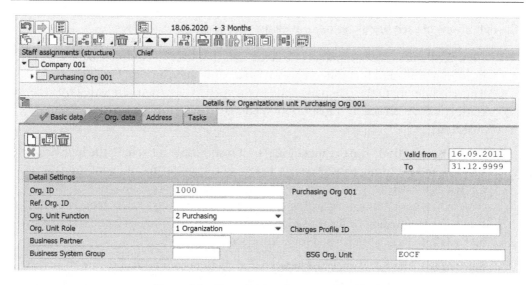

Figure 4.3 – Organizational units in SAP TMS

The organizational structure in SAP TMS is comprised of org unit and position. You can assign the holder (employee/user) to the position. The option of creating an org unit and position is shown in the following screenshot:

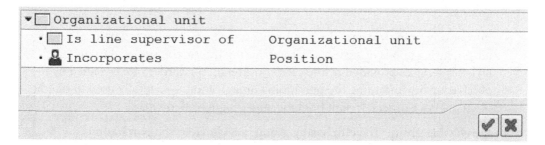

Figure 4.4 – Creating an org unit and position in SAP TMS

Org units could have an org unit function regarding sales, purchasing, or planning and execution, whereas the org unit role for these functions could be an organization, office, or group. You can assign a position to the org unit, such as approvers, and also assign the user to that position. In SAP TMS, multiple sales organizations can be assigned to one company code, multiple sales offices can be assigned to one sales org, and multiple sales groups can be assigned to one sales office, just like in SAP ECC.

Similarly, multiple purchasing orgs can be assigned to one company code, while multiple purchasing groups can be assigned to one purchasing org. Multiple planning and execution groups can be assigned to one planning and execution organization.

The definitions of each organization unit element in TMS are as follows:

- **Company code**: The company code is the unit that holds a complete balance sheet, including profit and loss statements within a company. You assign a sales org and a purchasing org to the company code in the SAP ECC system. In SAP TMS, the company code is used in transportation charge management for invoicing and charging.

- **Sales organization**: The organizational unit responsible for selling the logistics services and executing those services based on certain terms and conditions is known as the sales organization. In SAP TMS, the sales org is generally used in forwarding quotations, forwarding orders, and forwarding settlements. The sales org in the forwarding order is used for selling transportation services, whereas in SAP ECC, the sales org is used for selling goods.

- **Sales office**: The sales office is defined based on the geographical region of an organization, and the company creates the sales office based on the territory they want to sell the product in. The sales office is assigned to the sales org. It could be a specific region; for example, east region, west region, north region, and so on.

- **Sales group**: The number of people working within the sales office is divided into groups and those are known as sales groups. The individuals are assigned to sales groups.

- **Purchasing organization**: The purchasing organization is the org unit responsible for procuring goods or services. All purchasing transactions related to the logistics services provided by the carrier or freight forwarders are executed by the purchasing organization. The purchasing organization is generally used in freight orders, service orders, freight booking, and freight settlement.

- **Purchasing group**: The purchasing group is assigned to the purchasing organization. You need a purchasing group and purchasing organization for subcontracting.

- **Planning and execution organization**: Planning and execution organization is generally used in the case of **Logistics Service Provider** (**LSP**) scenarios. Planning and executing organization structures help you plan and execute forwarding orders. You can model how the planning and execution organization can interact with the sales organization in the case of LSP.

- **Planning and execution group**: The planning and execution group is assigned to the planning and execution organization. Multiple planning and execution groups are assigned to the planning and execution organization, but one group cannot be assigned to multiple planning and execution organizations.

With that, we have gone through the core concept of the organizational model in SAP TMS, including understanding the sales org, purchasing org, and planning and execution org, along with their functionality and usage. Now, let's review how to maintain these organizations in SAP TMS.

Maintaining organization structure in TMS

You can create an organization structure in TMS by going to **SPRO | SAP Transportation Management | Transportation Management | Master Data | Organizational Management | Create Organizational Model**.

Alternatively, you can maintain the org structure using the transaction code PPOME.

Another option is to create and merge the organization structure from your source system, which could be SAP ECC or SAP APO. The following screenshot shows the **Create and Merge Organizational Hierarchy** page. This can be created by going to **SPRO | SAP Transportation Management | Transportation Management | Master Data | Organizational Management | Create and Merge Organizational Hierarchy**:

Create and Merge Organizational Hierarchy from SAP ERP or SAP SCM			
Source System			
Restrictions for Data Selection in the Source System			
Company Code		to	
Sales Organization		to	
Purchase Organization		to	
Restrictions for Data Selection in the SAP SCM System			
Company Organization		to	
Sales Organization		to	
Purchasing Organization		to	
Plng & Exec Org		to	
Forwarding House		to	

Figure 4.5 – Create and Merge Organizational Hierarchy from SAP ECC or SAP SCM

With this report, you can create and merge the org structures from SAP ECC or SAP APO. The program reads the existing structure from the source system and maps it to the org structure to be created in SAP TMS. Once executed, it creates and saves the corresponding elements in the SAP TMS organization model.

With that, we've learned how to maintain the organizational structure in SAP TMS; that is, how to create the organizational structure in TMS. Now that we understand the organizational data concept and maintenance as a whole, let's continue with our next master data topic: business partners.

Business partners

The concept of business partners in SAP CRM and SAP TMS is almost similar in nature. Customers, vendors, and carriers are referred to as business partners in SAP TMS. Business partners are those that the organization does business with, and they can be categorized as follows:

- **Business partners**: Business partners could be customers, vendors, or carriers. This is a business partner that a company has a business interest in.

- **Contacts**: Business partner contacts are people who have been assigned to the business partner. These are maintained as a relationship with the accounts. The contacts are the customer contacts, and these are external customers.

- **Employees**: Employees are also people and members of a company that are responsible for any interactions with the business partner. These are internal company employees.

Business partners have general data, including information such as address, identification, control (wherein the tax information resides), output management, status, and their relationship. The data in most business scenarios needs to be in sync from ECC to TMS. In most SAP implementations, ECC is the client of record that propagates to TMS.

Now that we have provided a brief overview of the business partners in SAP TMS, let's understand the concepts surrounding business partners.

Business partner concepts

The business partner concepts in SAP TMS are the same as those in SAP CRM. You need to assign the grouping (the number range) manually while creating the business partner in TMS. The roles are assigned to the business partner and can be either Sold-to, Ship-to, or Bill-to. Let's take a look:

- **Business Partner Roles**: Business partner roles classify the business partner in business terms. This means every business partner has a specific role; for example, a business partner can be a customer (business partner – general), contact person, employee, carrier, and so on. Some business partner roles show specific views that are different from other roles.

- **Business Partner Relationship**: A business partner relationship specifies the connections between the two partners. A business partner relationship has business partner relationship categories that describe the kind of relationship between two partners; for example, Is a contact person of, Is a Bill to party of, and so on. Basically, the business partner relationship category describes the characteristics of the business partner relationship. You can also put a validity period on the business partner relationship.

- Let's look at these in detail.

Business partner functions

Like the ECC customer master, TMS has a Business Partner master with general data consisting of **Address**, **Identification**, **Control**, **Payment Transactions**, **Status**, **Output Management**, and **Additional Texts**. The following screenshot shows the business partner example in SAP TMS:

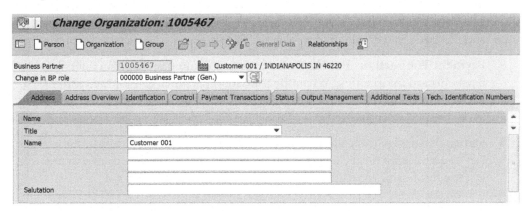

Figure 4.6 – Business partner example in SAP TMS

The preceding screenshot shows just one business partner example in SAP TMS that shows various tabs. Let's have a look at them in detail:

- **Address**: Address data within the **Business Partner** is maintained when you create the business partner in SAP TMS. The address that's maintained in ECC is replicated to SAP TMS. You can have multiple addresses based on the address' usage; for example, the standard addresses of **Sold-to** can have different billing and delivery addresses. If only one address is maintained in the customer master data, then that is referred to as a standard address.

- **Identification**: Identification data within the **Business Partner** allows the company to key in some industry-specific information and identification numbers; that is, you can link the ECC customer master to the TM customer master based on ID type and tax information. In the case of vertical industry standards, you are required to have GLN numbers maintained in the Business Partner master. This can be keyed into the **Location 1** and **Location 2** number fields within the **Identification** tab. This helps determine the business partner based on GLN numbers.

  Tax Classification and **Tax Numbers** data can be stored in the **Identification** tab of the business partner. This is data that is required to determine how business partners are to be taxed. The tax classification corresponds to the ECC tax classification that's used in customer master records.

- **Control**: Control information in the **Business Partner** master consists of control parameters such as **BP Type**, **Authorization Group**, and **Print Format**. Authorization Group is used to stipulate which business partners a user is allowed to process. Control data also provides information on business hours, such as goods receiving hours. Goods receiving hours is assigned to the factory calendar, which specifies the number of weekdays that the **Ship-to party** can receive the products.

- **Payment Transaction**: This allows the organization to maintain bank details and payment card information. When the transaction is processed for the customer, the payment card information on the transaction is populated based on the data being fed to the customer master.

- **Status**: Business partner status is populated in the **Status** tab. The business partner can be archived, centrally locked, or not released. Based on the business status, you can use this business partner to process any transaction or not.

You can define the status profile for the business partner in **Customizing for TM** by going to **Master Data | Business Partner | Status Management | Define Status Profile for User Status**.

- **Additional Texts**: You can add additional text in different languages here. You can then print this information in the documents of a specific business partner.

> **Important note**
> Contact persons and employees are created as a Person category in SAP TMS. You can create a contact person and assign it as a relationship to the main business partner.

Now that we have gone through the business partner concept and its functionality within SAP TMS, let's look at the next master data element, the product master.

Products

Products are used within the system to represent the material or services that are sold by any organization. The attributes within the product master can be global- or location-specific. The data at the global level is applicable to all locations, whereas the data specific to a location applies to that location only. The concept and maintenance of the product master in SAP TM is similar to that of SAP APO. In the case of the shipper scenario, the material from SAP ECC is replicated to SAP TM through CIF. The material master in SAP ECC is replicated to SAP TM and various fields within the SAP ECC material master are mapped to the corresponding product master in SAP TM. Any product master data that constitutes a classification or grouping of the various materials or that represents the services are generally used in LSP scenarios. This is a scenario where the company using SAP TMS is a logistics company, such as FedEx, USP, and so on.

The other scenario is the shipper scenario, wherein manufacturing is the process of managing the freight and subcontracting the transportation of goods to the logistics company. Since this book mostly covers the shipper scenario, the following information on the product master relates to the data structure that's relevant to the shipper scenario. In most cases, the client that's used to record this is SAP ECC for the shipper scenario.

Information regarding **Unit of Measure (UoM)**, weights, and volumes are very important for logistics processing as they are used to calculate shipments. For example, the given material can fit into the company's truck based on a certain volume limit. If the limit goes beyond the truck's capacity, the logistics planning has failed and requires manual intervention by the transportation planner.

The transportation group is replicated from the SAP ECC material master to the SAP TM product master. The transportation group groups products with similar transportation requirements; for example, all food products need to be refrigerated so that they can be shipped from one location to another. The loading group from ECC is also replicated to SAP TM. The loading group is used to group products that have the same loading requirements. This information resides in the **GR/GI** tab of the product master.

The following diagram demonstrates the product master views for the product master data in SAP TMS:

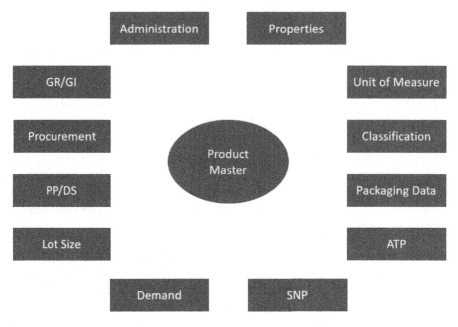

Figure 4.7 – Product master views in SAP TMS

Some of the product functions that are relevant to transportation management are as follows:

- **Administration**: Within administration, you can assign a planner to the location product. This is done at the location level. The planner can be a transportation planner that resolves transportation capacity issues and maintains the customer's requested delivery dates.

- **Properties**: Properties specifies the general data that can be applied to all locations. It consists of the material group, product hierarchy, transportation group, weights and measurements, and shelf life. It also shows the **Business System Group** (**BSG**).

- **UoM**: Like SAP ECC, the UoM in SAP TMS consists of the base and alternate UoMs with different UoM conversions. These UoMs are replicated from ECC to TMS. UoM is also global data and can be applied to all locations.

- **Packaging Data**: The data in this tab includes the packaging instructions for the product. Again, this is done at the global level.

- **Storage**: This data is primarily used in extended warehouse management. It consists of the basic data around the warehouse product group, storage condition, item category group, product freight group, and so on.

With that, we have gone through the product master data concept in SAP TMS, such as the product master data in SAP APO. With this, you understand the product master data elements and the functionality it drives within SAP TMS. Now, let's start looking at one of the main key master data concepts: the transportation network. The data setup here acts as input to the transportation planning phase.

Transportation network

The transportation network defines the optimal way to reach one location from another. Transportation can be location-specific and can be point-to-point; that is, transporting goods from location A to location B with one means of transport. Another scenario could be an intermodal, where multiple means of transport are used to ship the goods from one location to another. For example, you could be exporting goods from one country to another that's overseas, so transportation could be via roads as well as the ocean.

In this section, we will look at the locations, transportation zones, and transportation lanes that are required and important to the master data in TMS. This information helps to determine the transit time of the sales order. Additionally, network data is essential for automatic planning as it helps us choose the most appropriate carrier for the given transportation demands.

Locations

The location master concept in TMS is similar to the location master concept in SAP APO, which we defined earlier in this chapter. It represents different data objects, unlike in SAP ECC. In SAP ECC, plant, customer, and vendor are completely different objects, whereas in SAP TMS, these are represented as location types; for example, `Production Plant (1001)`, `Distribution Center (1002)`, `Shipping Point (1003)`, `Customer (1010)`, `Vendor (1011)`, and so on. The following screenshot shows a **Location** master showing different location types:

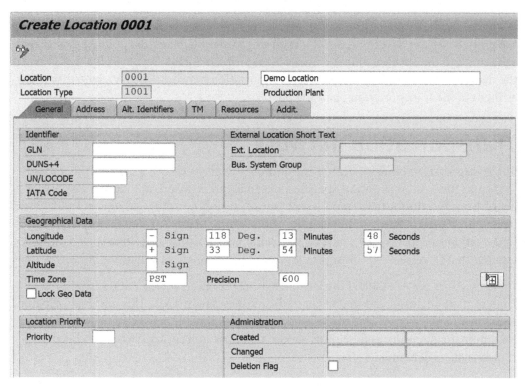

Figure 4.8 – Location master example in SAP TMS

A location is a central place or an organization unit that holds information regarding the business partner, address, calendar, resources, and transportation data. A location is a physical place where goods are picked and delivered. This location can be a transshipment location where the mode of transport can change. The details around the location master in SAP TMS are as follows:

- **General**: General data includes information around the **global location number (GLN)**, DUNS+4 (a four-character identification number), UN/LOCODE (United Nations code for trade and transport locations), and an **International Air Transport Association (IATA)** Location Identifier (a three-letter code used to identify the airport location in the airline industry). It also includes geographical data, such as latitude, longitude, and altitude information. Geographical information is populated automatically when you maintain address information.

- **Address**: Address data within the **Location** master contains the address information that's maintained for that location; for example, the customer address from ECC is replicated to the location address through CIF.

- **Alt. Identifier**: You can maintain an alternate location identifier in this tab. This is used when you want to identify a location based on a standardized or project-specific number for the location. The alt identifier can be configured by going to **SPRO | SAP Transportation Management | Transportation Management | Master Data | Transportation Network | Location | Configuration for Alternative Location Identifiers**.

- **TM**: The TM tab provides information around goods wait time. You can add the goods wait time to this tab. This also provides information for trailer handling and air cargo security. You can define the trailer handling strategy if coupling, uncoupling, or swapping the trailer is possible in this location.

- **Resources**: You can assign handling resources for loading/unloading and operating times (calendar) in this tab.

You can assign the inbound and outbound time for both the handling and calendar resources. The calendar defines the opening time of the location, whereas handling resources can further define the amount of loading and unloading that can be performed at a location. If you do not assign the inbound or outbound time in the **Resources** tab, the system assumes you have an unlimited capacity during scheduling/transportation planning. The following screenshot shows the **Resources** tab, with the handling resources and operating times assigned:

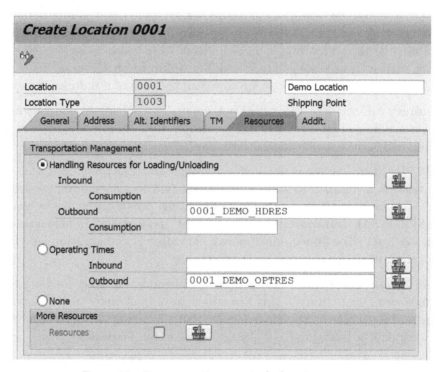

Figure 4.9 – Resource assignment in the location master

Location masters are typically CIFed from SAP ECC to SAP TMS. Like SAP APO, the location master is stored in the /SAPAPO/LOC table and the location mapping between ECC and APO is stored in /SAPAPO/LOCMAP. The entries between the /SAPAPO/LOC and /SAPAPO/LOCMAP tables should always match.

Transportation zones

Transportation zones group the location that is used to create lanes and determines the transit time required to ship the goods from one location to another. Creating lanes from one location to another location is very a intensive data maintenance process, so aggregating multiple locations and defining them as zones is the practice any business follows to determine lanes. In the case of the shipper scenario, the source location is a plant or a shipping point, while the destination location is the ship-to address of the customer. To determine the distance between these two locations, master data is needed, and this requires transportation zones to be created.

Transportation zones are used in sales order scheduling to determine the appropriate material availability date. It is also used to group multiple shipments in the case of a consolidation of orders going to the same geographical area. The different types of transportation zones are as follows:

- Postal code zone

- Direct zone

- Leg zone

- Region zone

- Mixed zone

The following screenshot shows the transportation zone maintenance screen, with one example stated for the SE_HALLEKIS zone:

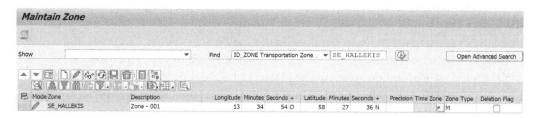

Figure 4.10 – Maintain Zone

The location is assigned to the transportation zone at the following levels:

- **Zone – Location**

- **Zone – Postal Code**

- **Zone – Region**

The following screenshot shows that the transportation zone can be created at different levels; that is, **Location, Postal Code**, and **Region**:

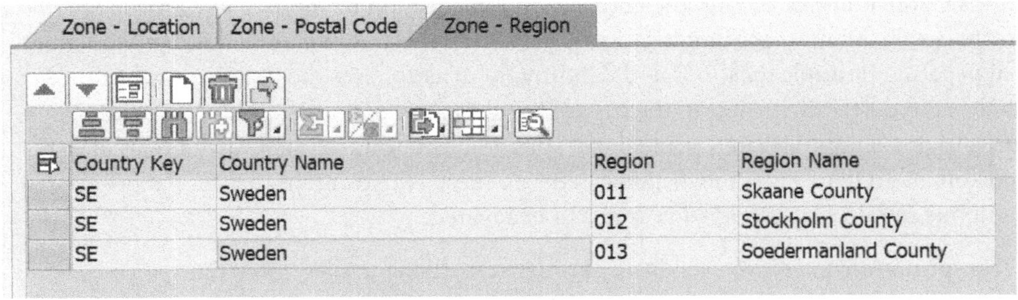
Zone - Location
Zone - Postal Code
Zone - Region
Country Key
Country Name
Region
Region Name
SE
Sweden
011
Skaane County
SE
Sweden
012
Stockholm County
SE
Sweden
013
Soedermanland County

Figure 4.11 – Transportation zone by Location, Postal Code, and Region

Let's define each of these ways you can maintain a transportation zone:

- **Zone – Location**: You can assign multiple locations to one zone.
- **Zone – Postal Code**: You can assign the postal code to the transportation zones. Within a specific location, you can cover a postal code to determine one transportation zone.
- **Zone – Region**: You can assign a region to the transportation zone; for example, the state of Ohio can be defined as a region and the transportation zone can be created at this level.

You can use any of these types of zone if the mixed zone type is selected while you're creating the transportation zone. The transportation zone doesn't have an address, so the system determines the coordinates based on the location, postal codes, or region that have been assigned to the zone. It estimates the center point of all the locations or postal codes based on the coordinates of all the locations in that zone. You can maintain the transportation zones in the master data path by going to **SAP Menu | SAP Transportation Management | Master Data | Transportation Network | Define Transportation Zones** (Tcode - `/APOTMS/ZONE`).

Now that we understand the transportation zone and how to maintain it in SAP TMS, let's cover the transportation zone hierarchies. You can maintain transportation zone hierarchies to reduce the amount of master data that needs to be maintained for each combination of source and destination locations.

Transportation zone hierarchies

Using a transportation zone to create transportation lanes and determine the transit time may also lead to humungous data. Therefore, many companies work through the transportation zone hierarchy as it helps them combine multiple transportation zones. This helps reduce the amount of master data and also provides flexibility. You can maintain the transportation hierarchies by going to **SAP Menu | SAP Transportation Management | Master Data | Transportation Network | Maintain Hierarchy** (Tcode - /SAPAPO/RELHSHOW).

Now that we understand the concept of transportation zone hierarchies; let's deep dive into how transportation lanes are maintained. This is required to determine the transit time of the sales order.

Transportation lanes

Transportation lanes control how the goods can be shipped from one location to another. They play a key role in planning transportation and sales order scheduling:

- Transportation lanes provide the duration required to ship the goods from one location to another.

- They determine the means of transport required to ship the goods from one location to another.

- They also determine the carrier required to ship the goods from one location to another.

To maintain the transportation lanes, go to **SAP Menu | SAP Transportation Management | Master Data | Transportation Network | Define Transportation Lanes**.

The following screenshot shows the transportation lane creation process:

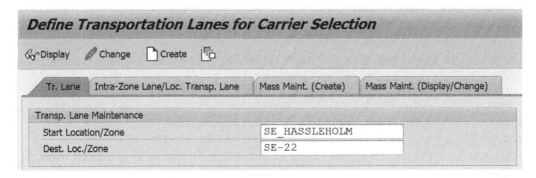

Figure 4.12 – Define Transportation Lanes for Carrier Selection

Let's look at each of the options available for this transaction:

- **Tr. Lane**: You enter a **Start Location/Zone** and **Dest. Loc./Zone** to create or change lanes. Creating lanes based on zone reduces the amount of master data compared to creating lanes based on location.

- **Intra Zone Lane/Loc. Transp. Lane**: Here, you can create a transportation lane from one location to the same location or one zone to the same zone.

- **Mass Maint. (Create)**: You can copy lanes from an existing zone to a new zone. There is an option for whether you want to update the existing lanes or not overwrite them. You can also adopt the distance and duration from the existing lane or calculate it.

- **Mass Maint. (Display/Change)**: Based on the selection criteria on this tab; that is, **Start Location/Zone** and **Dest. Loc./Zone**, you can display or change the transportation lane.

The transportation lane master data shows specific means of transport, including the distance and the duration required by the Means of Transport (MTr) to ship the goods from SE_HASSLEHOLM to SE-22. You can also assign a carrier to the lane for the specific MTr. This is shown in the following screenshot:

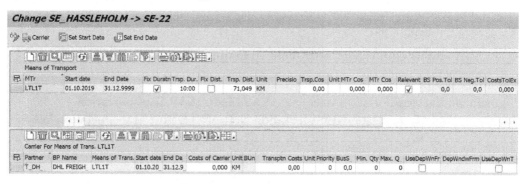

Figure 4.13 – Transportation lane details for carrier selection

For the means of transportation within the transportation lane master data, you can define a validity period and mark the duration and distance as fixed so that no duration or distance calculations happen automatically.

Precision in the lane master data indicates how you want to determine the distance and duration. Three options are available: straight-line distance (0000), geographical information system (0100), and manually maintained (1000).

Since you can assign carriers to the lanes, you can determine the **Transportation Service Provider** (**TSP**) and the cost strategy to be assigned here. Whether cost should be calculated by TCM or internally/externally is also considered during transportation planning. You can define the minimum and maximum load capacity for each carrier here too, which is also considered during transportation planning and carrier assignment.

The following screenshot shows the details around the MTr settings regarding the transportation lane's master data maintenance:

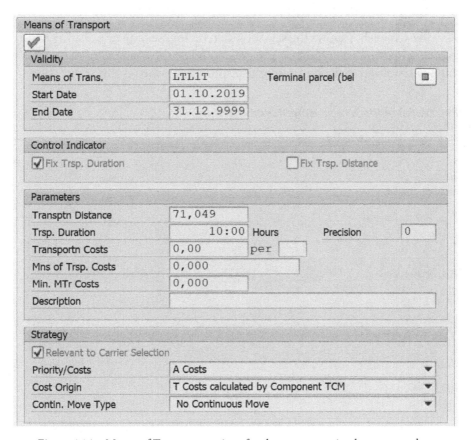

Figure 4.14 – Means of Transport settings for the transportation lane master data

With that, we've learned how transportation lanes are created, how to assign the means of transport, the settings around means of transport, assigning a carrier to each of the means of transport, and their relevant settings. Now, let's go through and understand transshipment locations.

Transshipment locations

Transshipment locations are the physical locations where the mode of transport changes; for example, loading and unloading the goods from the truck to the container, in the case of the ocean shipment. In a nutshell, the mode of transport is changed at the transshipment location where the goods are unloaded and reloaded.

You can maintain the transshipment location's assignment by going to **SAP Menu | SAP Transportation Management | Transportation Management | Master Data | Transportation Network | Define Transshipment Location Assignments**.

The following screenshot shows the selection criteria for creating or updating the transshipment location's assignment. You create/update the assignment of the transshipment location to the location or transportation zone via this transaction:

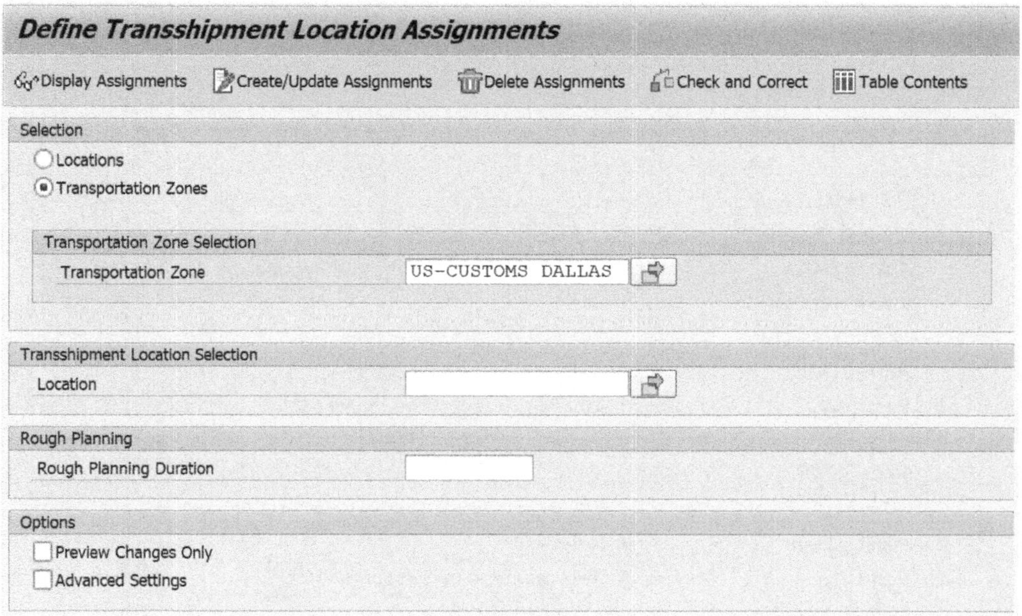

Figure 4.15 – Transshipment location assignment to the transportation zone – part I

The following screenshot shows an example of the transshipment location being assigned to a transportation zone:

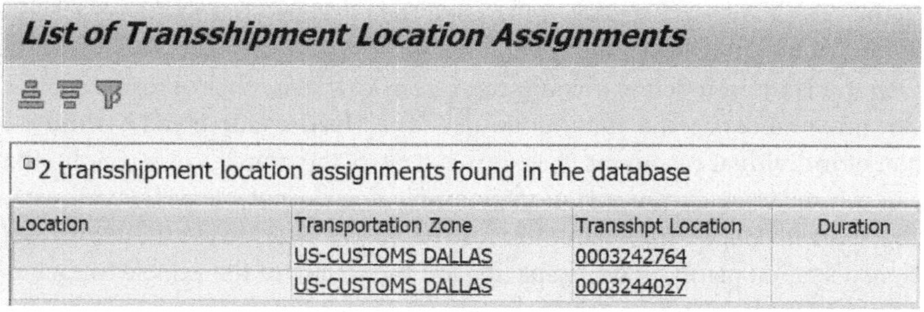

List of Transshipment Location Assignments

□2 transshipment location assignments found in the database

Location	Transportation Zone	Transshpt Location	Duration
	US-CUSTOMS DALLAS	0003242764	
	US-CUSTOMS DALLAS	0003244027	

Figure 4.16 - Transshipment location assignment to the transportation zone – part II

This section covered the concept of transshipment location and how to assign it to the transportation zone. Our next topic within the TMS master data is resources. Resources are one of the most important pieces of master data when it comes to transportation planning. Let's understand resources and the key functions of the resource master data.

Resources

Resources are critical when it comes to planning and executing the transportation requirements in SAP TMS, as it helps us ship goods from one location to another in the most optimal way. The resource master helps determine the operating hours and the capacity that the resource can handle during transportation planning. The operating hours of the location, its handling resources, and the vehicle's capacity are all considered in the resource master, and this information is very critical to planning and scheduling for transportation.

The following resources are used in transportation planning:

- **Vehicle resources**: You create a vehicle resource for the required means of transport in the vehicle resource master. You assign the resource class to the vehicle resource; that is, to say that the vehicle is a truck, railcar, trailer, airplane, and so on. Within **General Data**, you define if you want to restrict the number of resources to a certain number or make them unlimited. The **Multiresource** and **Unlimited No. of individual resources** checkboxes control the number of resources that can be used during transportation planning. You cannot use passive means of transport in conjunction with the **Multiresource** checkbox. You can also assign the transportation planning unit capacity and the weight of the vehicle to each of the resources in the **Capacity** tab of the vehicle resource master:

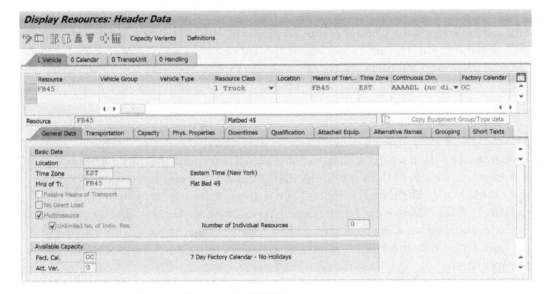

Figure 4.17 – Vehicle resource master

- **Calendar resources**: These specify the operating hours of the resource with the factory calendar assigned to it. For example, the shipping point is created as a resource master and has the calendar resource and the factory calendar assigned to it. The shipping point is from Monday to Friday, from 8 a.m. to 10 p.m. During planning and scheduling, these hours are taken into consideration and scheduling takes place based on these operating hours:

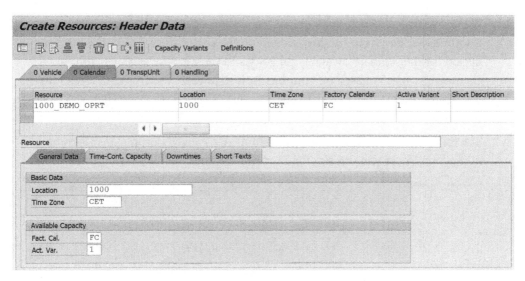

Figure 4.18 – Calendar resource master

- **Handling resources**: Handling resources specify a resource class; that is, doors, forklifts, dollies, and so on. You assign the capacity for each of the doors and also assign the capacity profile, along with the shifts on each of the doors, for example. The factory calendar is also assigned in the general data tab. In addition to the operating hours, you can go ahead one level granular with the handling unit and assign the required factory calendar based on the working hours – in this case, for doors:

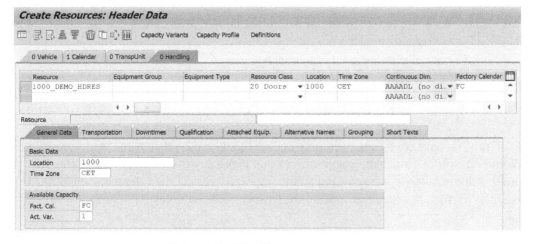

Figure 4.19 – Handling resources master

The capacity profile helps you define the available capacity for the handling unit resources per day, from the current date to the end of the resources' validity period for the standard available capacity and the capacity variants. You can change the capacity based on your business requirements. This data feeds into the transportation planning layer and acts as one of the constraints when you're slotting the trucks for shipment.

The following screenshot shows an example of a capacity profile. It shows the number of trucks you can slot for a specific day and their start/end time:

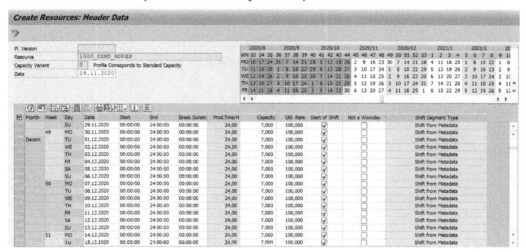

Figure 4.20 – Capacity profiling

Data integration model

The concept of the master data transfer between ECC and SAP TMS is the same as what we captured in *Chapter 3, Master Data in SAP APO*, in the *Transferring master data from ECC to SAP APO* section. SAP TMS uses the CIF integration model to replicate the master data between ECC and TMS.

With this, we have covered the resource master functionality; that is, the vehicle resources, calendar resources, and handling resources that play a key role in planning the freight order. Additionally, we have covered all the important master data elements, including the business partner, product, transportation network, and resources.

Summary

In this chapter, we went through SAP TMS master data; that is, organization structure, products, business partners, transportation networks, and resource master. The concept of master data transfer between SAP ECC and SAP TMS is the same as what we covered in *Chapter 3, Master Data in SAP APO*. This chapter provided you with a good understanding of the TMS master data that helps in successfully executing transportation planning. This chapter also helped you understand how to set up master data – primarily the transportation network and the resource master, which are important elements to understand.

Any issues with this data impacts the transportation planning and shipment processing phases. This chapter helped teach you how to minimize and reduce risks related to master data and made sure you understood the details around how they're set up.

In the next chapter, we will cover the warehouse master data in SAP ECC. We will cover the warehouse structure flow and its assignment. If you wish to effectively track your goods in a warehouse, it is imperative that you understand warehouse master data.

Further reading

- Additional information on the transportation network can be found at `https://help.sap.com/viewer/54cf405c9d9e4c96bf091967ea29d6a7/9.6.2/en-US/9c4a4bac857d446fbf51028f08401022.html`.

- Additional information on resources can be found at `https://help.sap.com/viewer/54cf405c9d9e4c96bf091967ea29d6a7/9.6.2/en-US/aa0deb63fb22457fa41c36a156f69157.html`.

5
Master Data in SAP LES

In the previous chapter, we learned how to set up master data in TMS while covering all the aspects of transportation. In this chapter, we will look at the **SAP Logistics Execution System (SAP LES)** and learn how to configure warehouse master data to achieve logistics execution. SAP LES is an integral component of the SAP ECC system and allows us to move goods both inbound and outbound. It also provides transportation functions, shipment functions, and warehouse management functions. The logistics execution within this book is achieved by **SAP LES** and not through **SAP Extended Warehouse Management (EWM)**.

In this chapter, master data comprises how to set up the warehouse master data that is required during picking, if warehouse management is active for your warehouse. Having warehouse management active helps you track your inventory efficiently. To set up the warehouse, it is important to understand how to set up the warehouse master data in SAP LES and consider the several configuration aspects. This chapter will help you understand all these aspects so that you can pick, pack, and ship items successfully. This chapter also covers concepts around lean, and full warehouse.

In this chapter, we will cover the following topics:

- Warehouse master data in LES
- Warehouse structure
- Storage type
- Storage sections
- Storage bin
- Quants
- Concept of lean and full warehouse management
- Data in material master WM views

By the end of this chapter, you will be familiar with how to set up the warehouse master data and the configuration required to activate the warehouse functionality with SAP LES.

Warehouse master data in LES

Delivery, picking, packing, and shipment processing are all part of logistics execution. Warehouse management is also part of logistics execution. The master data in this topic mostly pertains to warehouse management. For processing deliveries and shipments when working with warehouse management, master data is required. If you are looking to interface your deliveries with warehouse management, then it is important to understand what master data setup is required for warehouse management. Let us begin by understanding the warehouse structure.

Warehouse structure

A **warehouse** is a physical location where goods are inventoried. Optimizing warehouse space and keeping the product at the appropriate location within the warehouse helps you track and ship products in a timely fashion. SAP warehouse management provides an automated way of processing goods movement in a complex warehouse setup. Warehouse management is integrated with inventory management, quality management, production supply, delivery processing, and transportation. If you are not using warehouse management, then the lowest level of your inventory will be at the storage location level.

The warehouse structure assignment process can be seen in the following diagram:

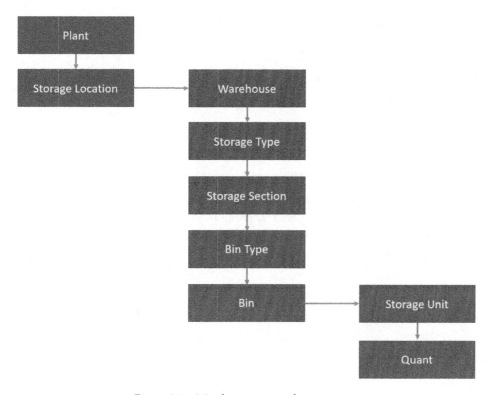

Figure 5.1 – Warehouse master data structure

The warehouse that's created by the system is assigned to the storage location; the storage type is assigned to the warehouse; the storage section is assigned to the storage type; and the storage bins are assigned to the storage sections. You assign the storage unit to the storage bin and the quant is assigned to the storage unit and storage bin.

Let's go through the configuration for defining and configuring the warehouse master data structure:

1. First, define the warehouse by going to **SPRO | Enterprise Structure | Definition | Logistics Execution | Define, copy, delete, check warehouse number**.

2. Once you've defined the warehouse, you assign the warehouse number to the plant/storage location by going to **SPRO | Enterprise Structure | Assignment | Logistics Execution | Assign warehouse number to plant/storage location**.

The following screenshot shows how to assign the warehouse number to the plant/storage location:

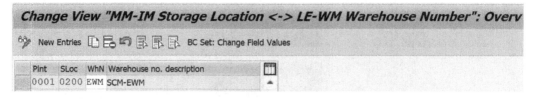

Figure 5.2 – Assigning the warehouse number to the plant/storage location

3. Once you've defined and assigned the warehouse number, you can configure the warehouse control parameters by going to **SPRO | Logistics Execution | Warehouse Management | Master Data | Define Control Parameters for Warehouse Number**:

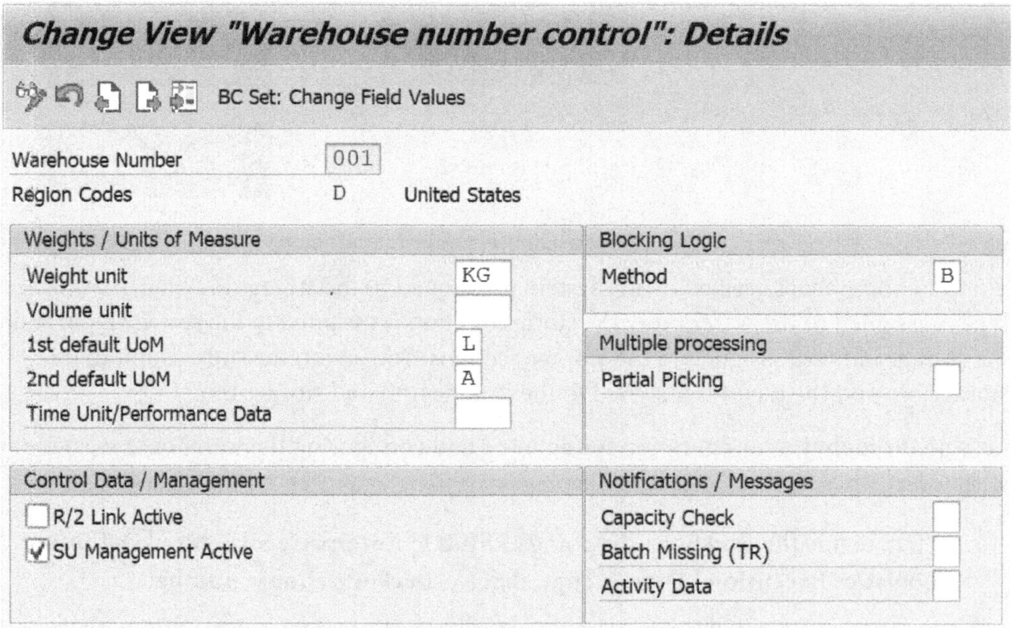

Figure 5.3 – Configuring the Control Parameters for Warehouse Number

The information in the control parameter defines **Weights/Unit of Measure** as to how the unit of measure determination takes place when you're working with the warehouse's managed location. You also have the option of activating storage unit management at the warehouse. You can do this by selecting the **SU Management Active** checkbox.

The storage unit consists of different items in a box or a pallet. These items, when combined, create a uniquely identifiable storage unit in the warehouse.

Next, we will look at how to configure the storage type.

Storage type

Storage type is the storage area in the warehouse facility. Warehouse space is divided into smaller areas that can be characterized as storage types. For example, the storage types could be bulk storage, open storage, picking area, shelf storage, high rack storage, and much more. You can create a storage type based on your business requirements. The layout of the warehouse is divided into the storage types, and these definitions of the storage type depend on your business requirements and the material's movements, depending on if the material is fast moving or slow moving.

To configure the storage type, go to **SPRO | Logistics Execution | Warehouse Management | Master Data | Define Storage Type**.

The following screenshot shows a storage type configuration that shows various configuration options for setting up the storage type:

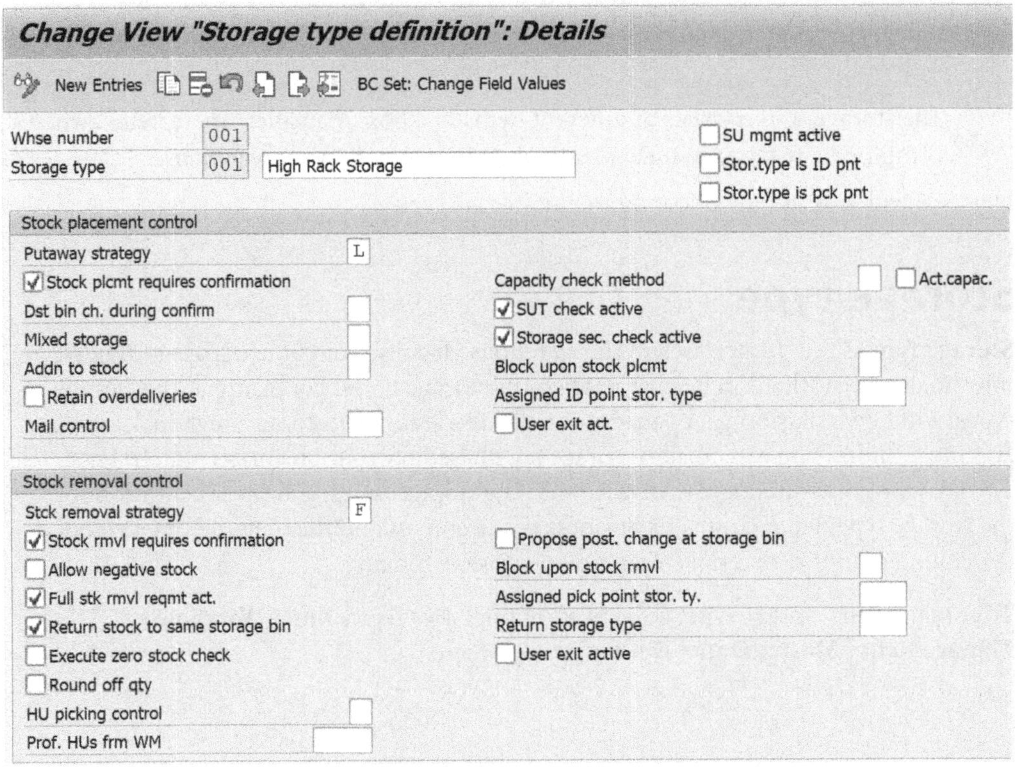

Figure 5.4 – Defining the storage type

Storage type configuration allows you to activate storage unit management. It also provides a strategy for stock placement control, which includes bulk storage, fixed bins and open storage, and stock removal control, which includes LIFO, FIFO, and the "no stock removal" strategy. Here, the configuration determines the flow of the material with respect to putting away and picking activities and the way the inventory is handled for each storage type.

Having learned about storage types, let us look into storage sections.

Storage sections

Storage type is divided into different areas known as **storage sections**. Storage sections group storage bins with similar products. You need to define a storage section for a storage type. You can have one storage section for one storage type.

To define the storage sections you can use the configuration path **SPRO | Logistics Execution | Warehouse Management | Master Data | Define Storage Sections**.

As shown in the following screenshot, a new storage section can be assigned to both the warehouse number and the storage type:

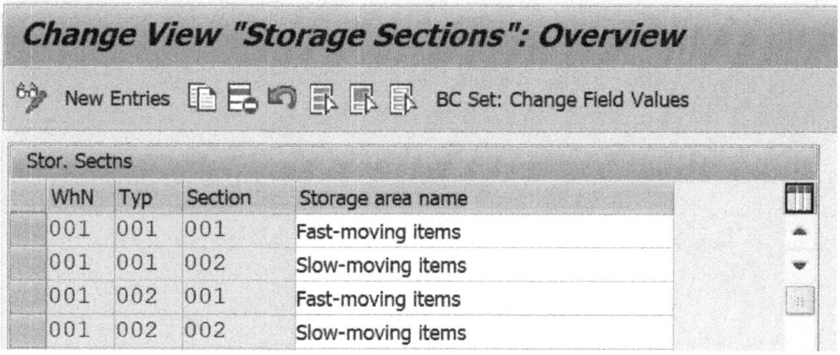
Change View "Storage Sections": Overview
New Entries
BC Set: Change Field Values
Stor. Sectns
WhN
Typ
Section
Storage area name
001 001 001 Fast-moving items
001 001 002 Slow-moving items
001 002 001 Fast-moving items
001 002 002 Slow-moving items

Figure 5.5 – Defining storage sections

Typically, one storage section is assigned to one storage type, but you can also have multiple storage sections for a storage type. It all comes down to your business requirements as to how many storage sections need to be created for your storage type. Storage sections are important for bin determination during the stock removal process.

Next we look at configuring storage bin.

Storage bin

Storage bin is a location where the goods are stored in the warehouse. It is the smallest available space unit in the warehouse where the goods are stored. The storage type can have multiple storage bins, and a storage bin is assigned to a warehouse and storage type based on its location.

The following screenshot shows the storage bin master data:

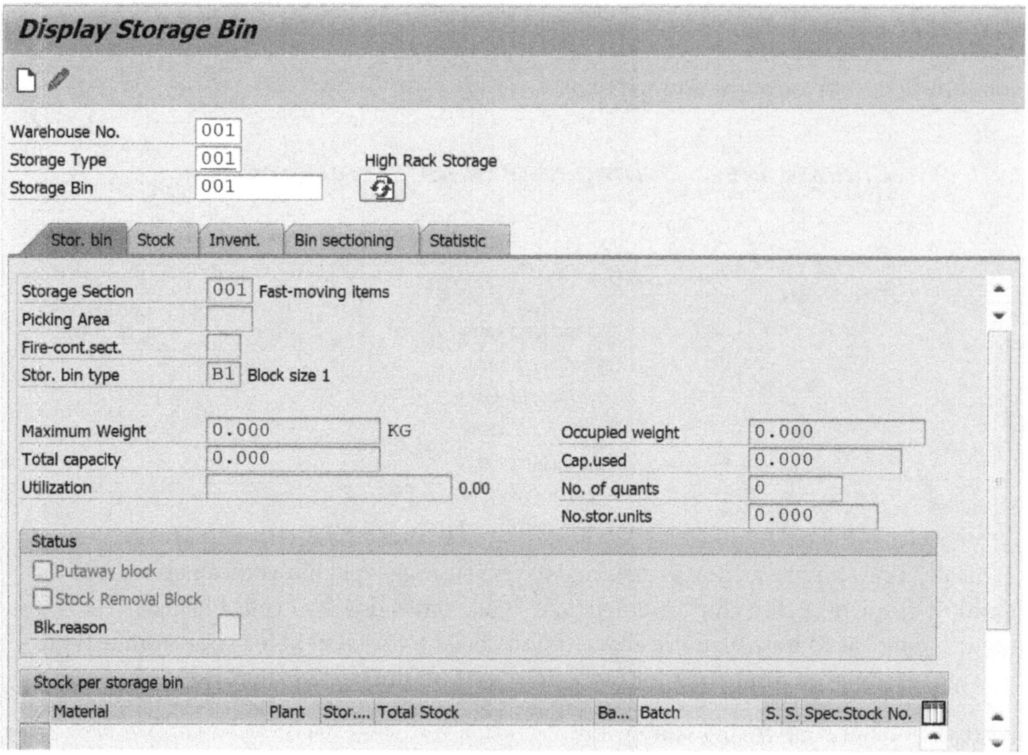

Figure 5.6 – Defining a storage bin

You can define additional characteristics in the storage bin master, such as **Storage Section**, **Picking Area**, **Stor. bin type**, **Maximum Weight**, **Total capacity**, and much more, as shown in the preceding screenshot. You can create storage bins from the SAP menu at **SAP Menu | Logistics | Logistics Execution | Master Data | Warehouse | Storage Bin | LS01N – Manually**.

In the warehouse management system, you can create storage bins automatically. For this to happen, you need to define the parameters in the storage bin structures.

The following screenshot shows the storage bin structure for automatic creation:

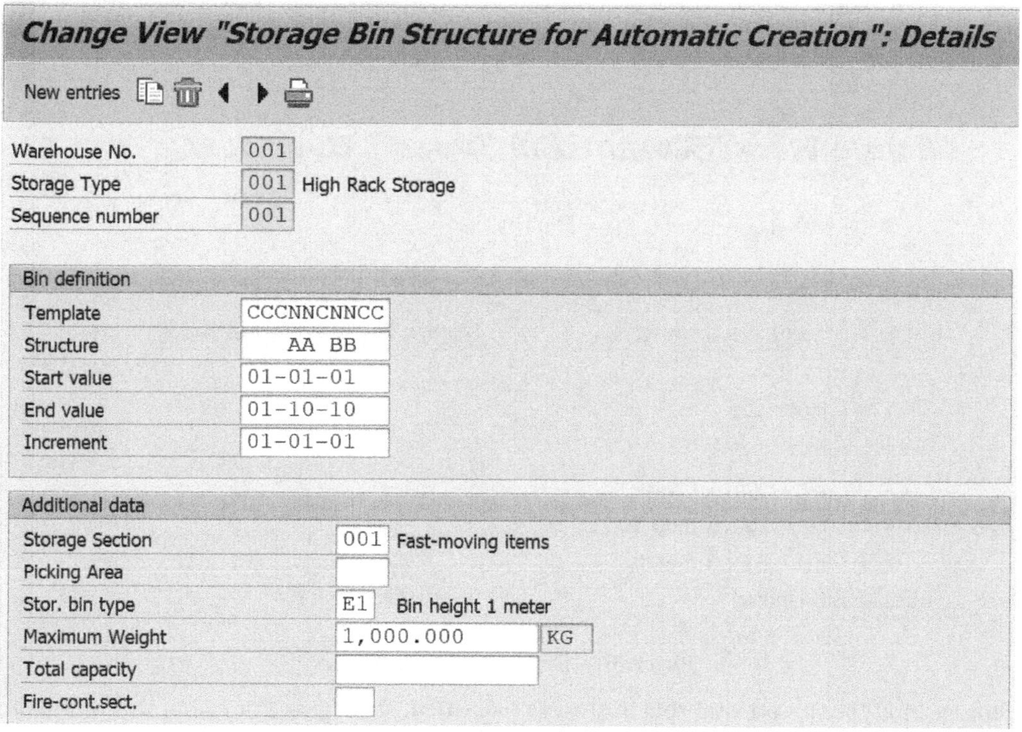

Figure 5.7 – Defining a storage bin structure for automatic creation

To create the storage bins automatically, go to **SAP Menu | Logistics | Logistics Execution | Master Data | Warehouse | Storage Bin | LS10 – Automatically**.

Storage bin creation automatically takes the template and structures of the storage bin from the storage bin structure.

Defining storage bin types

Storage bin type is a grouping for similar products within different storage bins. Multiple storage bins can be assigned to a single storage bin type.

You can configure the storage bin types by going to **SPRO | Logistics Execution | Warehouse Management | Master Data | Storage Bins | Define Storage Bin Types**.

The following screenshot shows the storage bin type configuration and the bin type that's been assigned to the warehouse:

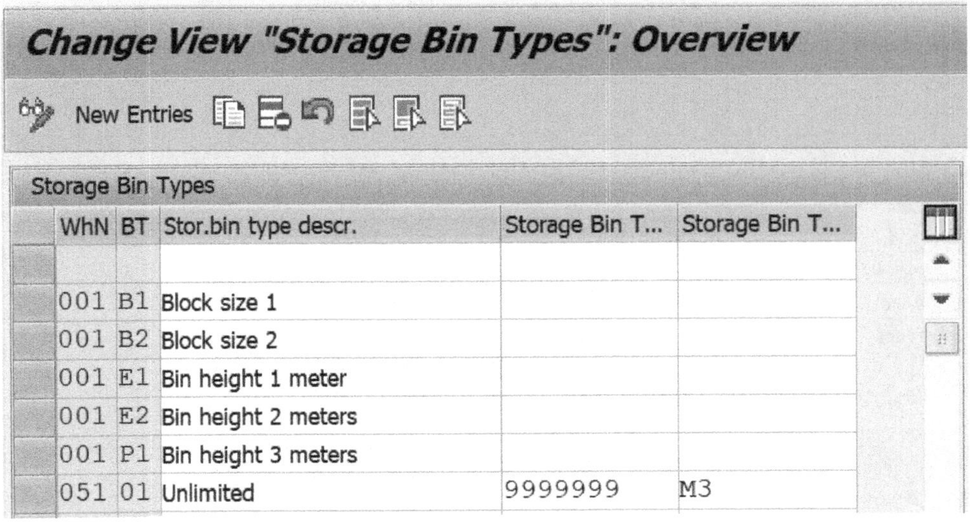

Change View "Storage Bin Types": Overview

New Entries

Storage Bin Types

WhN	BT	Stor.bin type descr.	Storage Bin T...	Storage Bin T...
001	B1	Block size 1		
001	B2	Block size 2		
001	E1	Bin height 1 meter		
001	E2	Bin height 2 meters		
001	P1	Bin height 3 meters		
051	01	Unlimited	9999999	M3

Figure 5.8 – Defining storage bin types

Storage bin types play a vital role in storage placement strategies. For example, the small, medium, and high storage bins types are assigned to the bins that are used in the stock placement and removal strategies.

Now, that we have understood about storage bin types, next we look into how to configure quants.

Quants

A **quant** is the quantity of a material within the same batch of a single storage bin. A quant with the same material but a different batch is typically stored in a different storage bin. You can add or remove the material in the quant using goods movement.

When the goods are stored in the storage bin, the system creates some quants and assigns a quant number automatically. When the material is picked completely, the system deletes the quant number. The following are parts of the quant that group the material:

- Quant identification
- Plant
- Material number

- Batch number
- Stock category
- Special stock indicator and number.

You can display a quant by going to **SAP Menu | Logistics | Logistics Execution | Internal Warehouse Processes | Bins and Stock | Display | Single Displays | LS23 – Quant**.

Now, that we have understood how to configure quants, let us now understand lean and full warehouse management.

Concept of lean and full warehouse management

Within a lean warehouse, you manage your inventory at the storage location level, whereas if you implement a full warehouse, you manage your inventory at the storage bin level.

You can create a transfer order in both scenarios using lean and full warehouses. If you do not want to update the stock at the storage bin level and you do not have a complex warehouse environment, then using lean is the other option. The lean option gives us advantages to using warehouse management through transfer order in the same way as the full warehouse management solution does.

Next, we look into the concept of material master.

Data in material master WM views

For the material to be warehouse managed, you must maintain the warehouse management data in the **material master**. Without maintaining the warehouse data in the material master, materials cannot be stored in the storage bin of the warehouse management system.

The following screenshot shows the material masters of the **Warehouse Mgmt 1** and **Warehouse Mgmt 2** views. It shows **General data** and some **Storage strategies** wherein you can update these views per your business requirements:

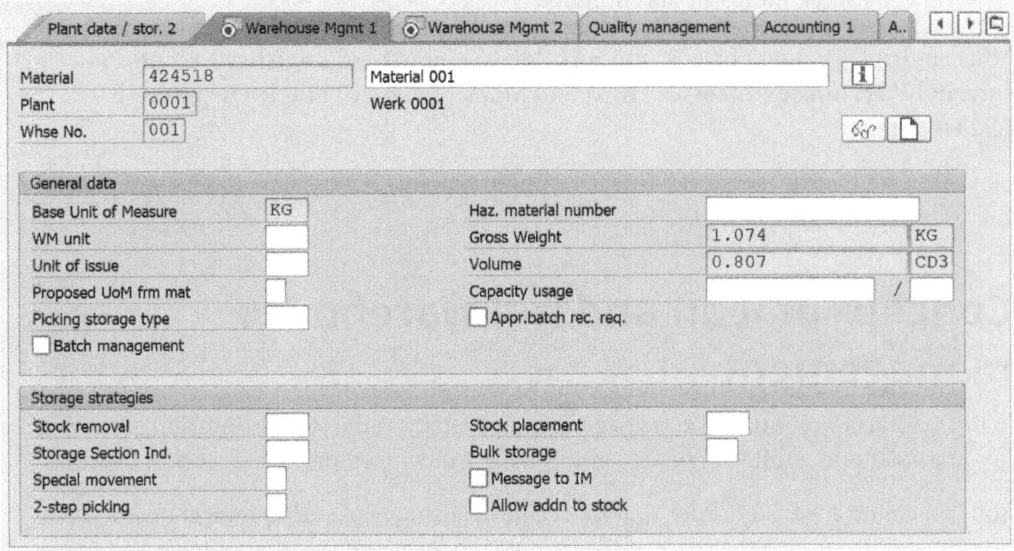

Figure 5.9 – Material master warehouse management view

The organization data within the warehouse management view is at the plant, warehouse number, and storage type level. Once you've maintained the warehouse org data, you can maintain the information around **Unit of Measure** (**UoM**) and storage strategies.

By selecting the **Batch management** checkbox, the system allows the batches to be created for the material. A hazardous material number can be assigned to the material in the **Warehouse Mgmt 1** view of the material master. This view also shows the **Gross Weight** and **Volume** properties of the material.

You can control the storage strategies in the material master **Warehouse Mgmt 1** view, wherein you can enter stock removal and stock placement strategies. You can also define if you want one-step or two-step picking in the same view.

The following screenshot shows the **Palletization data** and **Storage bin stock** information that can be filled in for the **Warehouse Mgmt 2** view of the material master:

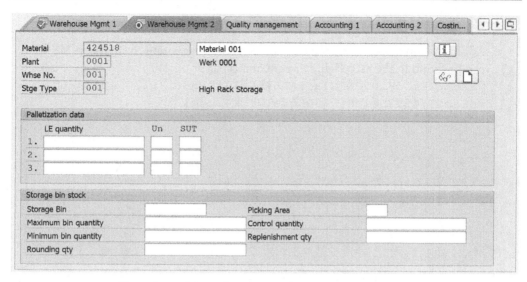

Figure 5.10 – Material master warehouse management view

Palletization data determines how the material is stored in the warehouse. It helps you determine the specific quantities to be placed in the bin. For example, let's say you have *50* cartons to be placed in stock and you specify *25* cartons in the palletization data. Here, the system will propose *2* pallets for *25* cartons each. It is possible to store the material in different ways depending on the storage unit type.

Summary

In this chapter, we look at warehouse master data and how to set up its configuration, including the warehouse's structure, storage types, storage sections, storage bins, and quants. This chapter covered the prerequisite master data required for outbound shipment when you are working with warehouse management functionality. With this chapter, you have got a good understanding of how to set up the warehouse master data and configure it within SAP LES.

Chapter 2, Master Data in SAP CRM, Chapter 3, Master Data in SAP APO, Chapter 4, Master Data in SAP TMS, and this chapter cover all the master data settings required as a prerequisite to running the order to cash cycle with CRM, SCM, TMS, and LES. These master data chapters have provided you with a good understanding of the master data requirements in **mySAP** suite ecosystems.

In the next chapter, we will cover the basic functions within sales documents in the SAP CRM system. This will provide you with the functionality and configuration required to support the sales order creation process.

Further reading

- Additional information related to **Warehouse Management Systems (WMS)** can be found in the SAP Help Documentation at `https://help.sap.com/viewer/34fc810a607e4ae5a287b6e233b8566f/6.18.15/en-US/ee8abd534f22b44ce10000000a174cb4.html`.

6
Basic Functions in Sales Document

This chapter lays the basis for understanding business transactions in **SAP Customer Relationship Management (CRM)**. Before understanding sales transactions in SAP CRM, it is imperative to understand the transaction structure and what is required to set up a transaction in SAP CRM. To have transactions that are free of error and to accommodate business needs, an understanding of the business transaction structure and its configuration is key. This chapter covers the basic functions and their structure related to sales documents in SAP CRM. It also explains the concepts of basic functions within CRM business transactions, such as quotations, contracts, and sales orders.

Here is a list of the topics covered in this chapter:

- Overview of the order to cash cycle
- Business transactions in SAP CRM

By the end of this chapter, you will understand the basics of business transactions, such as sales documents and transaction-related functions, in SAP CRM.

Overview of the order to cash cycle

The order to cash cycle helps businesses run their end-to-end sales processes when receiving customer orders. The order to cash cycle begins with sales order creation. A sales order created in SAP CRM allows businesses to carry out the selling of products or goods to the customer. Once a sales order is created in SAP CRM, delivery processing and billing is carried out to complete the whole order to cash cycle.

Figure 6.1 shows the order to cash cycle in CRM, Advanced Planner and Optimizer (APO), ERP Central Component (ECC), and Transport Management System (TMS):

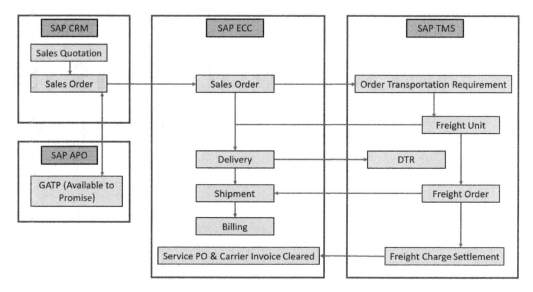

Figure 6.1 – The order to cash cycle in SAP CRM, SAP APO, SAP TMS, and SAP ERP

The steps shown in *Figure 6.1* have been elaborated here:

1. The order to cash cycle in CRM, APO, and TMS starts with sales order creation in SAP CRM.

2. An **Available to Promise (ATP)** check is carried out in the SAP APO system.

3. Once the sales order is saved in SAP CRM, the order is replicated to SAP ECC.

4. The sales order in ECC replicates to SAP TMS for transportation planning.

5. A freight unit is created, the freight order is planned, and a carrier is assigned in TMS, resulting in the delivery and shipment creation in SAP ECC to execute the transportation steps.

6. The shipment processing of picking, packing, and loading happens in SAP ECC.

7. Goods are issued in SAP ECC and the billing document is generated in SAP ECC as well.

8. Separately, the freight settlement document is created to settle the invoice for the carrier.

The following section covers the key elements of a business transaction in SAP CRM – its structure and the capability to process transactions in SAP CRM.

Business transactions in SAP CRM

SAP CRM's core functions are marketing, sales, and service. This chapter is focused on sales and the functions that are required to create sales quotations and sales orders successfully to process the whole order to cash cycle.

Figure 6.2 shows the high-level business processes in the areas of marketing, sales, and service in SAP CRM:

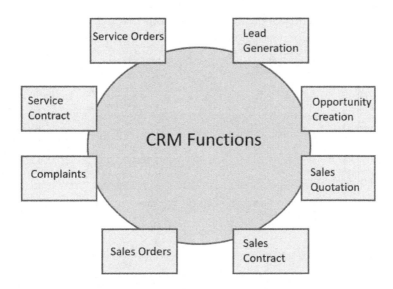

Figure 6.2 – Business processes in SAP CRM

Lead generation and opportunity creation are pre-sales processes, followed by the sales quotation, sales contract, and sales orders creation processes.

Once the product is shipped out to the customer, the customer may call back due to any product-related issues pertaining to quality, damage, being short shipped, and so on, to create a complaint.

The design and structure of business transactions

Like SAP ECC, business transactions in SAP CRM comprise header data and item data. Header data is governed by the transaction type configuration, whereas item data is governed by the item category configuration:

- **Header data**: The header data of business transactions mainly consists of organization data, business partners, text, status, actions, and so on. These functions are controlled at the transaction type level.

- **Item data**: Item data consists mainly of products and most of the functionality of an item is controlled via the item category. The functions at the item and header levels are similar; these are text, status, actions, and so on.

Figure 6.3 shows the structure of business transactions that mainly consist of header and item data:

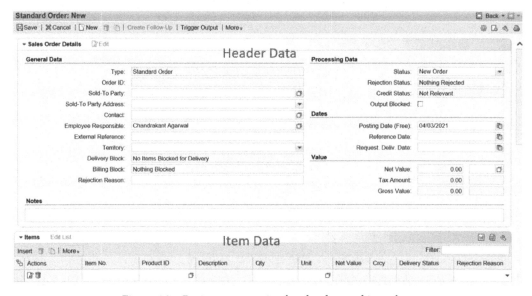

Figure 6.3 – Business transaction header data and item data

You can enter various items in the transaction such as customer orders similar to the sales order items in SAP ECC. The application in SAP CRM is a web UI application, whereas it is a GUI in SAP ECC.

Business transactions in SAP CRM are often referred to as transaction types.

Transaction types

Transaction types in SAP CRM are like document types in SAP ECC. Different sales functions, such as organization data, text, status, action, and dates, are all determined based on the sales transaction type. The product, quote, and contract determination are also configured at the transaction type level. These functions are configured based on the business requirements. You can also assign a number range, whether external or internal, to the transaction type. The figure here shows the configuration of the TA transaction type:

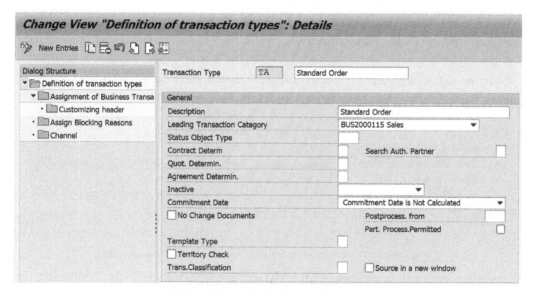

Figure 6.4 – Business transaction type

Business transaction categories

Business transaction categories are defined by SAP within SAP CRM; business transaction categories cannot be changed and correspond to business object types. *Figure 6.4* shows that **Sales** has the business transaction category BUS2000115.

A business transaction category determines how the business transactions can function at the business transaction level or the item level. It determines the following:

- The maximum allowed structure of a certain type of transaction

- Secondary transaction categories with which the transaction category can be combined, for example, sales categories combined with service categories

- The business transaction categories at the transaction level

- The item object types for the business transaction category at the item category level

Every business transaction is assigned a business transaction category. You can assign one or more business transaction categories to a business transaction, but you cannot just assign any business transaction categories to the transaction types. There can be one leading business transaction category followed by subsequent business transaction categories assigned to the transaction type.

Figure 6.5 shows a TA standard order consisting of **Sales** as a leading business transaction category followed by **Business Activity**:

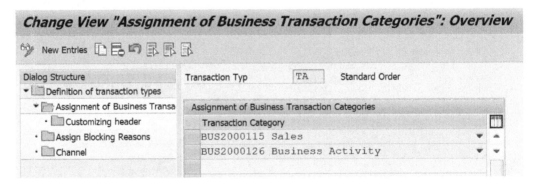

Figure 6.5 – Assignment of a leading business transaction category

The leading transaction category of a transaction type determines which customizing options are available for that transaction type. Only one specific business transaction category can be assigned to a specific item category. The assigned transaction categories define which additional functionality is available for the transaction type; for example, whether the transaction type is used for sales processes and the same transaction type will be used for service processes.

Figure 6.6 shows the details of customization at the header level for **Sales**:

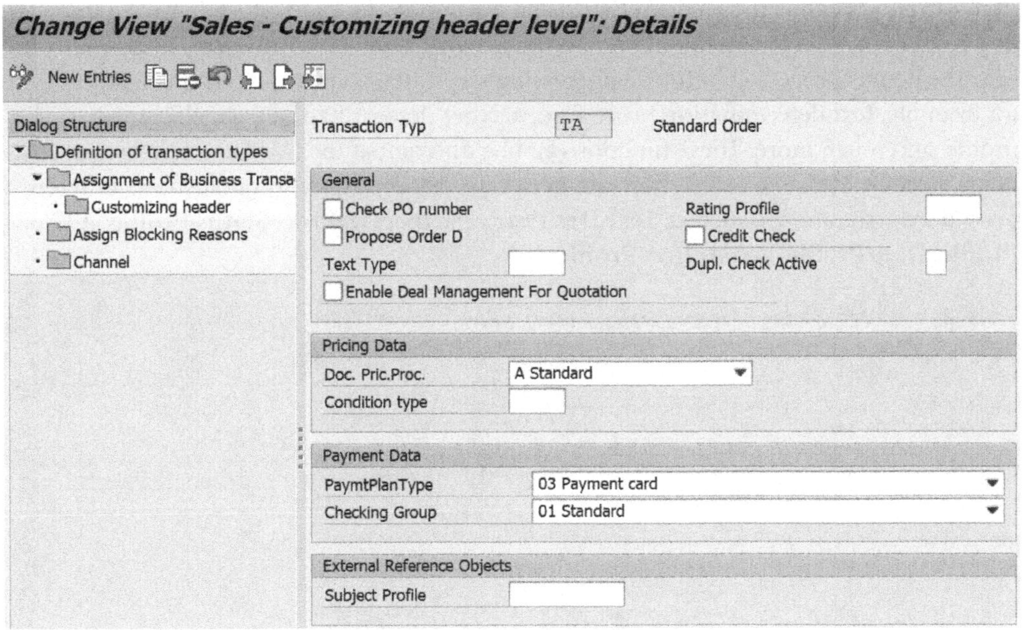

Figure 6.6 – Sales – customizing the header

You define **Doc. Pric.Proc.** to determine the pricing in sales transactions. You can also activate **Credit Check** at the transaction level. In the general data configuration, you can check for a duplicate PO number and also control whether you want to set a default current date as the PO date by activating the **Propose Order D** checkbox.

Item categories

Item categories define the characteristics and attributes of a transaction item. An item can be a sales item, a service material item, or an activity item. Item categories help determine how the item is processed in future processing steps. Item categories also have profiles, for example, text determination procedure, partner determination procedure, status profile, and much more. These functions can be different at the transaction level versus the item category level. *Figure 6.7* shows an item category configuration that shows different procedure assignments, such as **Text Det.Proc.**, **PartnerDetProc**, **Status Profile**, **ATP Profile**, **Date Profile**, and **Action Profile**:

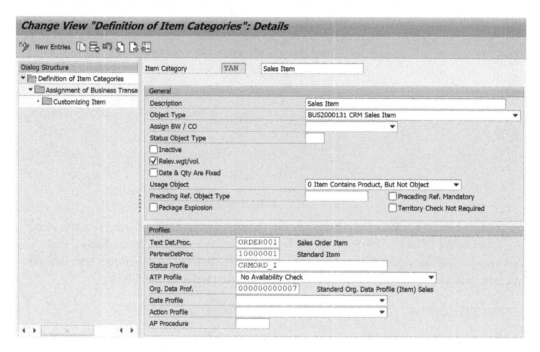

Figure 6.7 – Item category definition

Each item category is assigned an item object type that defines the context in which the item can be used (for example, sales or service processes). This context is defined by the transaction categories that are assigned to the item. There could be one, or more than one, business transaction category assigned to an item category. Only certain business transaction categories are assigned to an item category. In addition to the general settings for each item category, you need to customize the settings specifically for each business transaction category assigned to an item category.

Figure 6.8 shows business transaction categories assigned at the item category level:

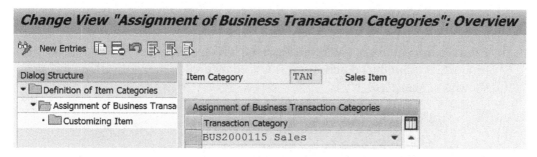

Figure 6.8 – Assignment of business transaction categories for an item category

Figure 6.9 shows a diagrammatic representation of the business transaction category assignment to the transactions type and the item category:

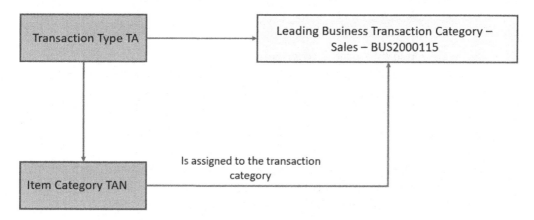

Figure 6.9 – Overview of business transaction category assignment to the transaction type and the item category

This shows the linkage of the transaction type, item category, and the business transaction categories.

Transaction types, their elements, and their functions

Transaction types consist of basic functions that are used to process business transactions. These basic functions include partner processing, text management, pricing, availability checks, actions, date management, and credit management.

These functions are discussed in detail with the configuration steps in this chapter as we go along. There are other features of business transactions that are also imperative while logging transactions within the SAP CRM system. These are stated next:

- **Product entry**: You can enter the product in the quotation and sales order via the product ID or product description. This is configured in the transaction type, as shown in *Figure 6.10*:

Product Determination	
☐ Enter GTIN	
☐ Enter Partner Product	
☐ Create Product Order Number	
☐ Always Check Product ID	☑ Product Description/ID Search
Profile for Altern. Identif.	
Product Substitution Proced.	

Figure 6.10 – Product description/ID search within a transaction type

If you have enabled any other product search capabilities, for example, product determination by **Global Trade Item Number (GTIN)**, along with the product description, the system uses your entry in the product ID field to first search for products by GTIN. If the system finds a match, it does not search by product description. However, if the system does not find a match, it continues to search for product descriptions that match your entry. You can configure and assign a product substitution procedure here; product substitution helps you substitute a product in the sales order if the product substitution master data and configuration are activated.

- **Change history**: Change history provides information about the changes done during the sales order processing. If **No Change Documents** is activated, the changes to the document aren't logged.

Here, the screenshot shows the checkbox for **No Change Documents** activated. Unchecking the checkbox will log the transaction changes. This capability is available within the transaction type configuration:

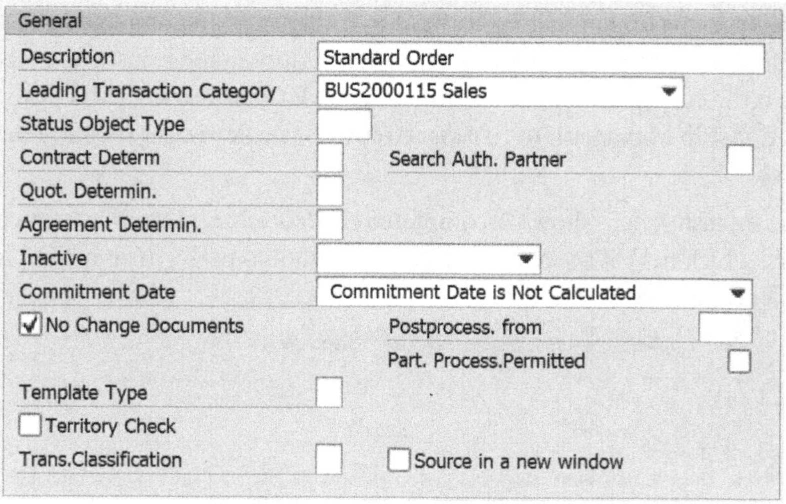

General	
Description	Standard Order
Leading Transaction Category	BUS2000115 Sales ▼
Status Object Type	
Contract Determ	☐ Search Auth. Partner ☐
Quot. Determin.	☐
Agreement Determin.	☐
Inactive	▼
Commitment Date	Commitment Date is Not Calculated ▼
☑ No Change Documents	Postprocess. from
	Part. Process.Permitted ☐
Template Type	☐
☐ Territory Check	
Trans.Classification	☐ ☐ Source in a new window

Figure 6.11 – No Change Documents within the transaction type

A general recommendation is to always uncheck the **No Change Documents** checkbox so that the system logs any changes done to the transaction by any users.

- **Follow-up transactions**: When you create a new transaction that relates to an existing transaction, you can create the new transaction as a follow-up transaction, thereby creating a relationship between the two transactions that provides additional contextual information to business users in the Transaction History assignment block. This is controlled through the copy control settings.

- **Copying of business transactions**: To save time creating a new transaction that is not a follow-up to an existing transaction, you can copy an existing transaction that contains data relevant to your new transaction. No link is created between the existing and new business transactions. To restrict the copying of a business transaction, you can control that with the Business Add-In (BAdI) copy control.

- **Incompleteness check**: An incompleteness check helps the organization to configure the transaction in a way that if there are certain fields that must be filled in the transaction, users should fill those in before saving the transaction. If those fields are empty, the transaction will be saved with errors.

To achieve this functionality, you need to configure an incompleteness determination procedure and assign the procedure to the transaction type within the configuration path shown here: **SAP Customizing IMG | Customer Relationship Management | Transactions | Basic Settings | Incompleteness Check**

This screenshot here shows **Incompleteness Procedure: Detail**, where you can define which field at the header or item level should perform an incompleteness check on the sales document:

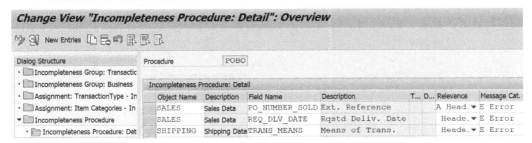

Figure 6.12 – Incompleteness procedure

Here, you can define fields in the sales order to set a warning or error message. Once configured, if any of these fields are not filled in on the sales order, the system will give either a warning or an error message based on the configuration performed in *Figure 6.12*.

Partner processing

Partner processing determines the partner in the transaction. In a sales order, partners are determined by configuring the partner determination just like the partner determination in SAP ECC. Based on the business scenario and the organization's needs, the partner determination on a business transaction can be determined automatically or the user can add partners manually. In most cases, the partners in a transaction are **Sold-To Party**, **Ship-To Party**, **Bill-To Party**, or **Payer and Delivering Plant**. Since CRM doesn't have inventory, there isn't a plant concept in CRM as there is in SAP ECC. The delivering plant is the partner and is determined in the sales order based on the configuration as per the business requirements.

The concept of partner processing and its elements

Partners in transactions are derived through specific steps in the configuration. This is shown in the diagrammatic representation in *Figure 6.13*:

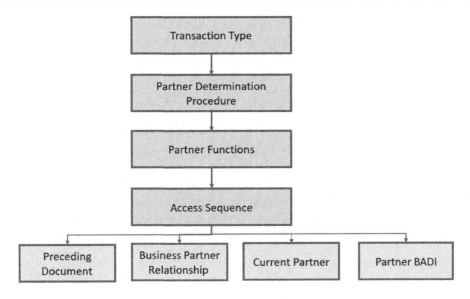

Figure 6.13 – Partner processing overview

Transaction types are assigned to the partner determination procedure and partner functions are attached to the partner determination procedure. An access sequence is assigned to the partner functions that helps determine the rules, which in turn determine partners in the sales order.

An access sequence has multiple rules, for example, determine the partner by relationship, by organization data, or by partner BADI. Here are the steps of the partner determination procedure in detail.

Step 1 – Defining partner functions and partner categories

The first step in the partner determination procedure is to define the partner function and the partner categories. Partner functions are the partners that the organization carries out business with, that is, the customer. *Figure 6.14* shows some partner functions:

Change View "Partner Functions": Overview

New Entries

Function	Text	Text	Function category		Usage		Relatshp Cat.		Block	Hide
00000001	Sold-To Party	SP	0001 Sold-To Party	▼	CRM Customer Relationship	▼	CPG001 Is the Sold-To Party	▼	☐	☐
00000002	Ship-To Party	SH	0002 Ship-To Party/Serv	▼	CRM Customer Relationship	▼	CRMH02 Is the Ship-To-Party/	▼	☐	☐
00000003	Bill-To Party	BP	0003 Bill-To Party	▼	CRM Customer Relationship	▼	CRMH04 Is the Bill-To Party	▼	☑	☐
00000004	Payer	PY	0004 Payer	▼	CRM Customer Relationship	▼	CRMH03 Is the payer of	▼	☐	☐

Figure 6.14 – Defining the partner functions

You can use any partner functions based on your requirements; the most commonly used are `Sold-To Party`, `Ship-To Party`, `Bill-To Party`, and `Payer`. Every partner function defined has a function category that is hardcoded into the system. Partner function usage can be CRM or B2B enterprise buyer.

The partner relationship category is assigned to each of the partner functions for determining the relationship of the business partner with other partners.

If the **Block** field on the partner function configuration is active, it blocks the source partner from being determined when the partner determination takes place. For example, let's say `Bill-To Party` is not activated with **Block**; then `Sold-To Party` and `Bill-To Party` will show in the popup for the bill to be determined on the sales order. In *Figure 6.14*, for `Payer`, **Block** is activated, therefore you will see that the partner payer will be set by default on the sales order without any popup for `Payer` determination.

The following is the configuration path to configure partner functions: **SPRO | Customer Relationship Management | Basic Functions | Partner Processing | Define Partner Functions**

Step 2 – Access sequences

An access sequence helps to determine the partner in the business transaction based on a search performed in a specific sequence. This sequence on partner determination is assigned in the access sequence and this access sequence is assigned to the partner function. *Figure 6.15* shows an overview of the partner function access sequence:

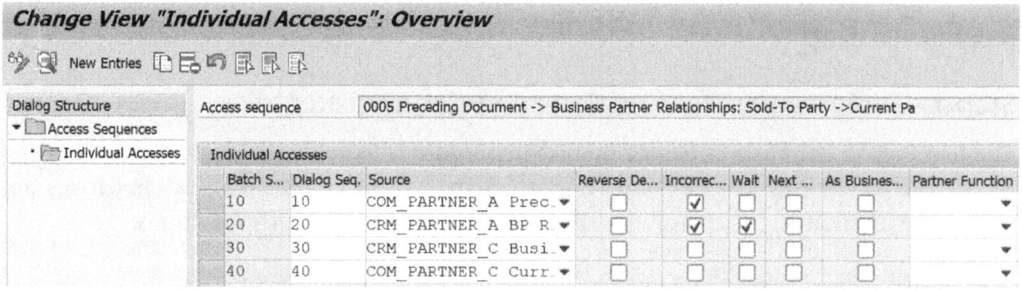

Figure 6.15 – Partner function access sequence overview

Access sequences allow the system to carry out partner determination, the process by which the system automatically finds the partners in a transaction. When you define a partner determination procedure, you can assign an access sequence to each partner function listed in the procedure. Then, when you create a transaction, the system knows how to search for partners to carry out these functions. If you do not assign an access sequence or the system cannot find partners in the sources listed, then you enter the partner manually.

Figure 6.16 shows the `0005` access sequence consisting of the `COM_PARTNER_A -` `Preceding Document`, `CRM_PARTNER_A -BP relationship by Sales Org`, `CRM_PARTNER_C -Business partner relationship`, and `COM_PARTNER_C` `-Current partner` sequences:

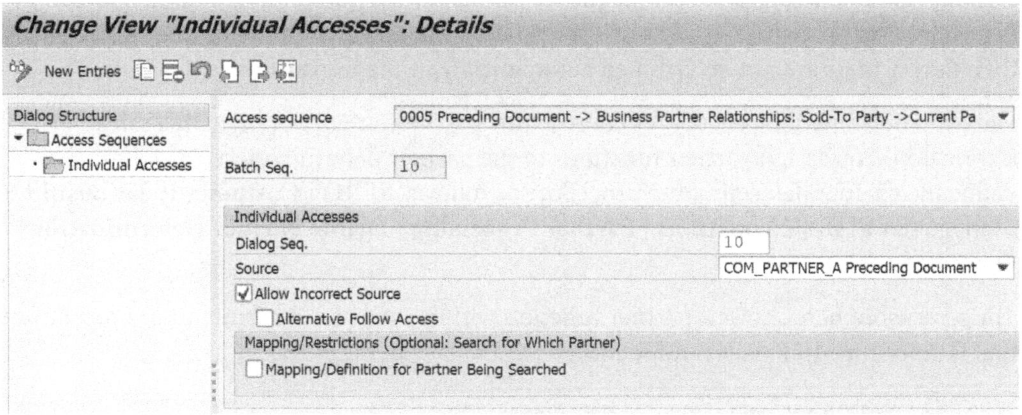

Figure 6.16 – Access sequence details with source assignment

Access sequence `0005` is assigned to the `Ship-To Party` partner function in the configuration. When creating the sales order, `Sold-To Party` is entered and `Ship-To Party` determination takes place based on the access sequence. First, it will check whether there is any preceding document, that is, whether the order is copied from the reference order. If it is not a copied order, then it will check the Sold-To relationship by sales area, meaning if the sales area on the order doesn't match the sales area of the ship to relationship, then it will jump to the next sequence, which is the business partner relationship. This is independent of the sales area and if it doesn't find a partner in the relationship, then the current partner, which is the Sold-To is a Ship-To be determined on the business transaction.

Within the access sequence, you can assign a function category, as shown in *Figure 6.17*:

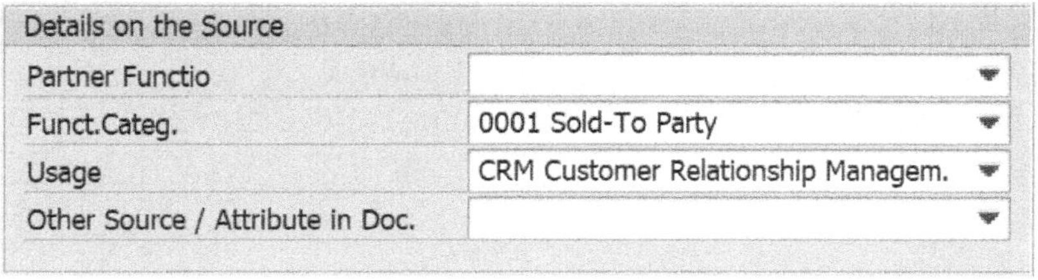

Figure 6.17 – Function category within the access sequence

This helps to determine the source partner to determine the other partner functions in the business transaction.

Step 3 – Access sequence assignment to a partner function

It is important to assign an access sequence to the partner function within the partner determination procedure. If an access sequence is not assigned to the partner function, then the partners are not determined automatically in the transaction.

Partner determination procedures control how partners are determined in a sales transaction. You assign partner functions to the partner determination procedure. You define the partner determination procedure as follows: **SPRO | Customer Relationship Management | Basic Functions | Partner Processing | Define Partner Determination Procedure**

The screenshot here shows a partner function within a partner determination procedure that is determined in a sales transaction:

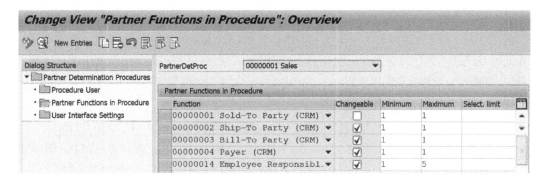

Figure 6.18 – Partner function in a transaction

Access sequence 0005 is assigned to the Ship-To Party, Bill-To Party, and Payer partner functions. Employee Responsible is assigned the 0008 access sequence, which determines the employee responsible based on the business partner assigned to the user.

Figure 6.19 shows an example of Ship-To Party with access sequence 0005, Preceding Document, and Business Partner Relationship:

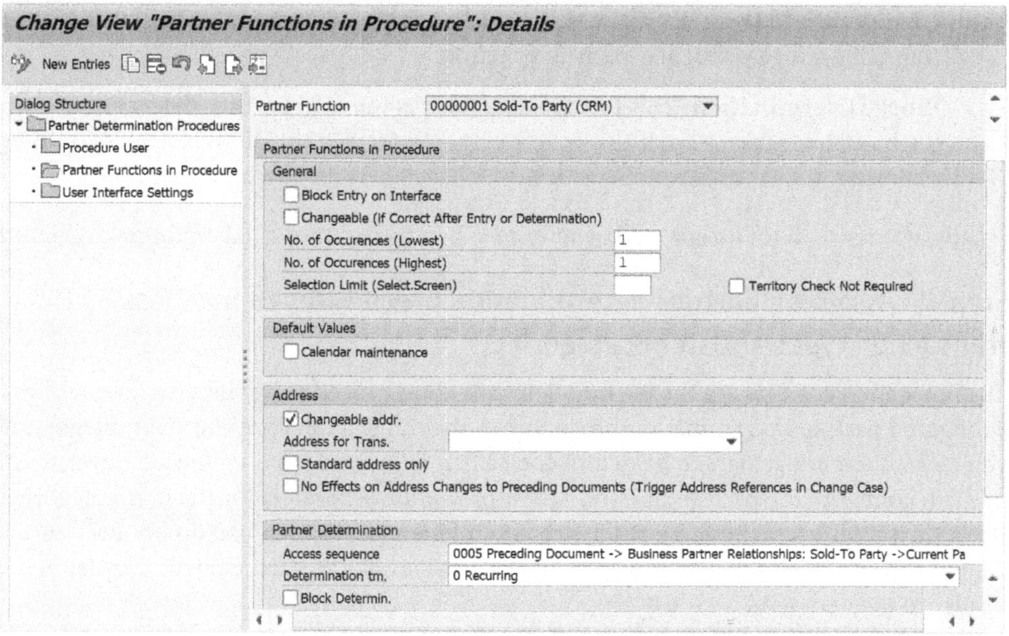

Figure 6.19 – Assigning an access sequence to a partner function

The determination of Ship-To Party is based on the access sequence assigned in this step.

The definitions around the configuration that can be done when setting up the partner determination procedure are mentioned here:

- **Block Entry on Interface**: This checkbox enables the functionality to restrict the entry of partners in the business transaction manually. You determine the partner automatically in this case if it cannot be entered manually.

- **Changeable**: This flag allows you to change the partner after the transaction is saved.

- **No. of Occurrences (Lowest)** and **(Highest)**: If you want at least one partner to be added to the partner function, then add 1 to the number of occurrences (lowest). This will make the partner function mandatory in the business transaction. For the highest number of occurrences, you can have either 1 or any number based on the number of times you need to enter the same partner function in the business transaction.

- **Changeable address**: This allows you to change the address on the business transaction for a particular partner function.

- **Block Determination**: This functionality blocks the auto partner determination on the business transaction. If this is active, then you need to add the business partner manually in the business transaction.

Finally, we move on to the last step, where we assign the partner determination procedure.

Step 4 – Assigning partner determination procedures to business transaction types and item categories

The last step in configuring the partner determination procedure is the assignment of the configured partner determination procedure to the transaction type and item category. If you have different partners to be determined at the item level from the header level, then you can configure the partner determination procedure separately for the item categories. But if the partners are the same at the header and item levels, then you do not need to configure the access sequence separately at the item level. The partners will copy from the header to the item level on the business transaction automatically.

To assign a partner determination procedure to a transaction type, follow the configuration path shown here: **SPRO | Customer Relationship Management | Transactions | Basic Settings | Define Transaction Types**

Figure 6.20 shows the partner determination procedure being assigned to the transaction type:

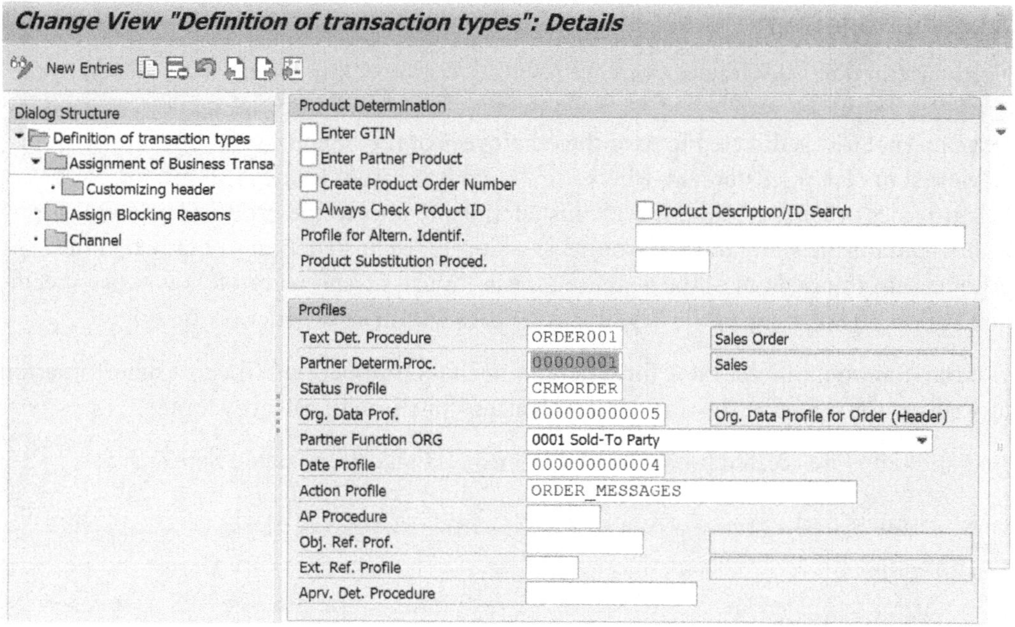

Figure 6.20 – Assigning a partner determination procedure to the transaction type

With this, we finish the partner determination procedure and now move on to data transfer.

Data transfer

In order to download partner functions from ECC to CRM, you need to map the ECC and CRM partner functions in a distribution of partner functions from ECC to CRM.

Mentioned here are the configuration steps to map a CRM partner to an ECC partner: **SPRO | Customer Relationship Management | Basic Functions | Partner Processing | Data Transfer | Distribution of Partner Functions from SAP ECC into CRM**

For the sales order partners to be replicated from CRM to ECC, you need to configure the partner function mapping with these configuration steps: **SPRO | Customer Relationship Management | Basic Functions | Partner Processing | Data Transfer | Distribution of Partner Functions from CRM into SAP ECC**

Text management

Notes captured in sales transactions are referred to as text; any information related to the customer, carrier, or warehouse is logged in text. Text can be **internal text** or **external text**. Internal text is directed toward the employees of the organization only and cannot be viewed or sent to customers, whereas external text is sent to the customer or carrier. When a sales order is created, specific instructions related to the product handling can be updated for the warehouse personnel as a warehouse instruction so that when the products are shipped out of the warehouse, warehouse personnel can follow those specific instructions. Text is one of the key functionalities within sales order processing.

You can maintain different text for different business transactions. The text determination procedure is assigned at the transaction level and/or the item category level.

Text and notes are created for several other business objects, as stated here:

- Business partners
- Products
- Product catalog
- Billing documents (header and item)

Text can be maintained in different languages. Let's understand what text objects and text types are:

- **Text objects**: A text object is used to define the connection between a business object and text ID, for example, a transaction and associated texts.
- **Text types**: Text types are unique codes that are assigned to text objects and are displayed on the business transaction, for example, `Internal Notes`, `Header note`, or `description`.

Here are the steps to configure text in SAP CRM:

1. Define text objects and text types with the following configuration path: **SPRO | Customer Relationship Management | Basic Functions | Text Management | Define Text Objects and Text Types**

The screenshot here shows where you define text objects and their associated text IDs:

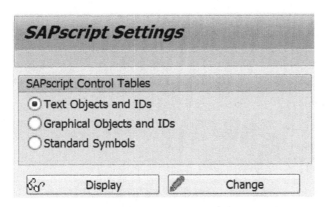

Figure 6.21 – Defining text objects and text types

Select the CRM_ORDERH text object for the header and CRM_ORDERI for the item, as shown in *Figure 6.22*:

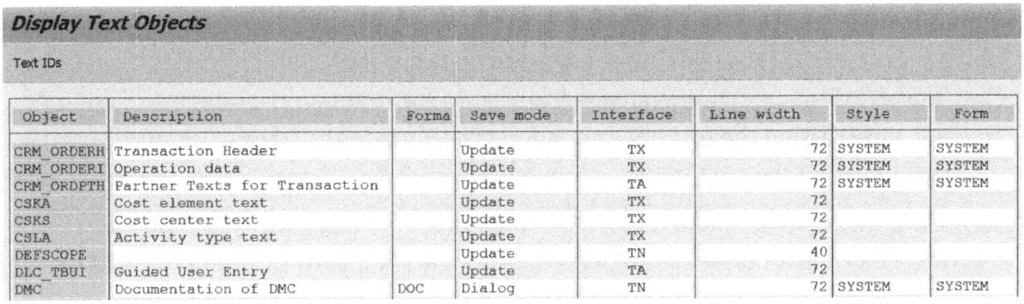

Display Text Objects

Text IDs

Object	Description	Forma	Save mode	Interface	Line width	Style	Form
CRM_ORDERH	Transaction Header		Update	TX	72	SYSTEM	SYSTEM
CRM_ORDERI	Operation data		Update	TX	72	SYSTEM	SYSTEM
CRM_ORDPTH	Partner Texts for Transaction		Update	TA	72	SYSTEM	SYSTEM
CSKA	Cost element text		Update	TX	72		
CSKS	Cost center text		Update	TX	72		
CSLA	Activity type text		Update	TX	72		
DEFSCOPE			Update	TN	40		
DLC_TBUI	Guided User Entry		Update	TA	72		
DMC	Documentation of DMC	DOC	Dialog	TN	72	SYSTEM	SYSTEM

Figure 6.22 – Defining text objects and text types

2. Create the text ID by hitting the create button based on the text ID required for your business scenario.

The screenshot here shows the creation of the text ID for the CRM_ORDERH text object wherein you can add the text ID and a description:

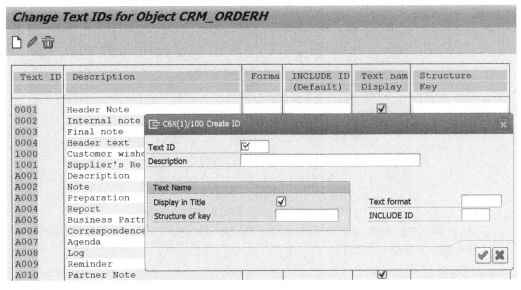

Figure 6.23 – Creating a text ID

The text ID created in this step will appear in the notes on the sales transaction when you assign the text determination procedure to the transaction type. This is mentioned in the next step.

3. Once the text object and text ID are configured, the next step is to create the text determination procedure with the configuration path shown here: **SPRO | Customer Relationship Management | Basic Functions | Text Management | Define Text Determination Procedure**

Here, you define the text determination procedure and assign the associated text ID to the text determination procedure. The following screenshot shows the text determination procedure with the text ID:

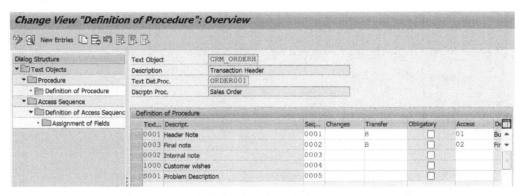

Figure 6.24 – Text object within the text determination procedure

4. Assign the text determination procedure to the text object as shown in *Figure 6.25*:

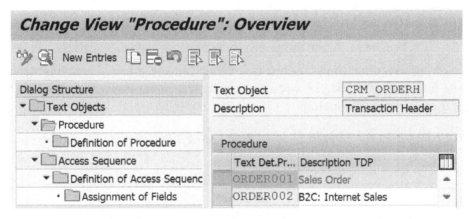

Figure 6.25 – Text determination assignment to the CRM_ORDERH text object

5. Assign the text IDs to the text determination procedure as shown in *Figure 6.26*:

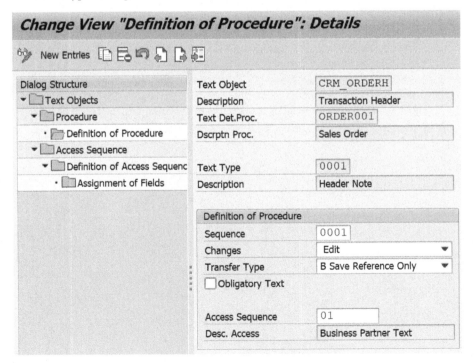

Change View "Definition of Procedure": Overview

New Entries

Dialog Structure	Text Object	CRM_ORDERH
▾ ☐ Text Objects	Description	Transaction Header
▾ ☐ Procedure	Text Det.Proc.	ORDER001
• ☐ Definition of Procedure	Dscrptn Proc.	Sales Order
▾ ☐ Access Sequence		
▾ ☐ Definition of Access Sequenc	Definition of Procedure	
• ☐ Assignment of Fields		

Definition of Procedure

Text...	Descript.	Seq...	Changes	Transfer	Obligatory	Access
0001	Header Note	0001		B	☐	01
0003	Final note	0002		B	☐	02
0002	Internal note	0003			☐	
1000	Customer wishes	0004			☐	
S001	Problem Description	0005			☐	

Figure 6.26 – Text ID assignment to the text determination procedure

The following screenshot shows the text type detail configuration and definition around changes. It also shows the access sequence, transfer type, and obligatory text, which are all part of the text type configuration:

Change View "Definition of Procedure": Details

New Entries

Dialog Structure	Text Object	CRM_ORDERH
▾ ☐ Text Objects	Description	Transaction Header
▾ ☐ Procedure	Text Det.Proc.	ORDER001
• ☐ Definition of Procedure	Dscrptn Proc.	Sales Order
▾ ☐ Access Sequence		
▾ ☐ Definition of Access Sequenc	Text Type	0001
• ☐ Assignment of Fields	Description	Header Note

Definition of Procedure

Sequence	0001
Changes	Edit ▾
Transfer Type	B Save Reference Only ▾
☐ Obligatory Text	
Access Sequence	01
Desc. Access	Business Partner Text

Figure 6.27 – Text procedure details

Here are detailed definitions of each of the fields under the text type configuration:

a) **Changes**: This field controls whether you want to allow the text to be changed by the user for the specific text ID.

b) **Transfer Type**: **Transfer Type** provides additional features by providing the **A Copy**, **B Save reference Only**, and **C Only Read Dynamically** options. If you want the text to be copied from the reference document and that text should not be changed, then you should select the A Copy option for the **Transfer Type** field. Likewise, **not yet defined** is set when there isn't any access sequence assigned to the text ID. **C Only Read Dynamically** is set when a reference text is determined via the text determination procedure. Neither the text nor the reference is saved in the case of reading the text dynamically.

c) **Obligatory Text**: This is used when you want to make the text ID mandatory for the transaction.

d) **Access Sequence**: The access sequence is assigned to the text ID; it determines the logic sequence to determine the text content in the sales order. *Figure 6.28* shows an access sequence assigned to text objects:

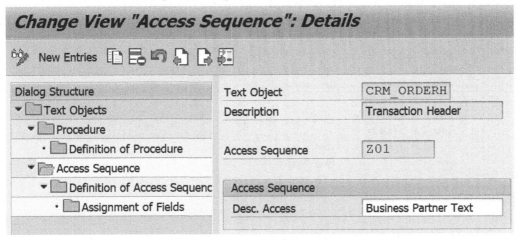

Figure 6.28 – Access sequence assigned to text objects

The following screenshot shows multiple sequences for the access sequence. The system runs through the sequence until it finds the hit:

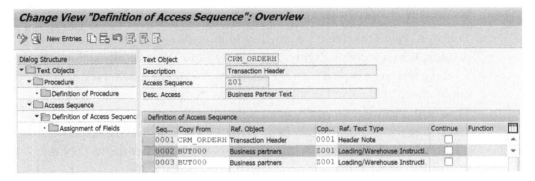

Figure 6.29 – Text access sequence with multiple sequences

The following screenshot shows an example of the **Ref Text Type** value that is going to get copied to the sales transaction:

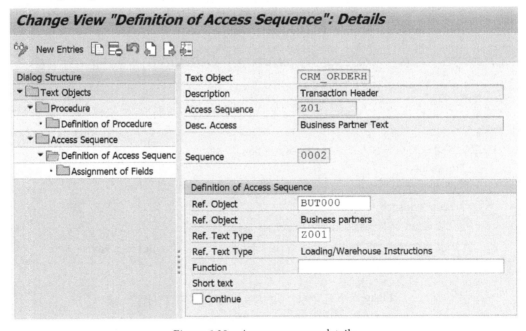

Figure 6.30 – Access sequence details

You can also assign a function module to determine the text based on your business needs. The next step explains access sequence determination logic in more detail.

e) **Desc. Access** (determination of access sequence): At this level, the source of the text is determined, that is, from which business object the text will be populated on the sales order. *Figure 6.30* shows the Z001 reference text type for the business partner, which specifies from which business object the text is going to be copied.

If the **Continue** indicator has been set, the system displays multiple texts. This function is particularly important if you require text in several languages. This will continue the text determination even if the text is found. If the standard configuration isn't enough to determine the text per your business requirements, then you can assign FM COM_TEXT_DETERMINE_TEXT to the access sequence and add the business logic to determine the text.

Assignment of the fields in the access sequence is as shown in *Figure 6.31*:

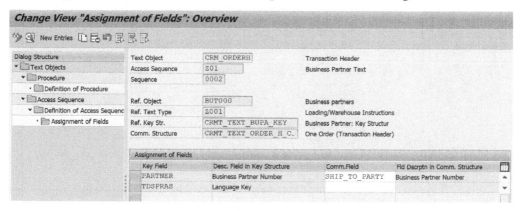

Figure 6.31 – Access sequence field assignments

The configuration shows the text being copied from Ship-To Party in the sales order.

6. This screenshot shows the text determination procedure assignment to the transaction type:

Change View "Definition of transaction types": Details

New Entries

Dialog Structure	Product Determination
▼ Definition of transaction types	☐ Enter GTIN
▼ Assignment of Business Transa	☐ Enter Partner Product
• Customizing header	☐ Create Product Order Number
• Assign Blocking Reasons	☐ Always Check Product ID ☐ Product Description/ID Search
• Channel	Profile for Altern. Identif.
	Product Substitution Proced.

Profiles

Text Det. Procedure	ORDER001	Sales Order
Partner Determ.Proc.	00000001	Sales
Status Profile	CRMORDER	
Org. Data Prof.	000000000005	Org. Data Profile for Order (Header)
Partner Function ORG	0001 Sold-To Party	▼
Date Profile	000000000004	
Action Profile	ORDER_MESSAGES	
AP Procedure		
Obj. Ref. Prof.		
Ext. Ref. Profile		
Aprv. Det. Procedure		

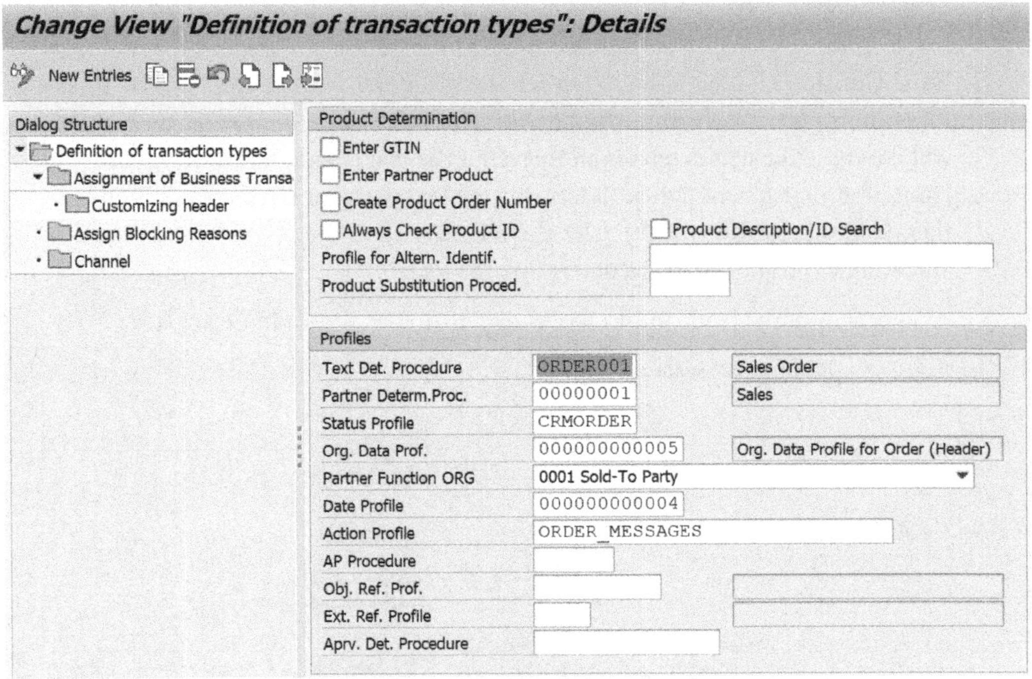

Figure 6.32 – Text determination procedure assigned to the transaction type

To assign the text determination procedure to the transaction type, go in **Customizing** for transaction types in a CRM System and choose the following: **Customer Relationship Management | Transactions | Basic Settings | Define Transaction Types**

Having gone through all the steps of text management, next let's look into date management.

Date management

Date management helps you to capture different types of dates on sales transactions. You can configure these date types as per your business requirements. One typical example of date management would be sending confirmation to customers based on the confirmed delivery dates. You can configure different date types for different scenarios. For example, if you are confirming dates based on transportation planning, then you can configure different date types to capture confirmed dates based on transportation planning dates. Otherwise, you can send confirmation based on the material availability dates. If you are confirming based on material availability on a sales order, then you can configure different date types to capture the confirmation date after transportation planning and confirm that date to the customer. It can also be used in contracts and quotations as a part of valid from and valid to dates. Dates are configured using date types, duration types, and date rules:

- **Date types** are unique identifiers that help the business understand different dates, for example, the contract start and contract end.

- **Duration type** is a timeframe between two points in time that consists of a number value and a time unit.

- **Date rules** are used for calculating times. The calculation can depend on other times, durations, and reference objects.

A reference object is used to calculate dates. Within a reference object, you can assign different objects to date types other than user or system. You can assign a business partner as an example in a reference object. The reference object is assigned to the date type and the date type can use the time zone and the factory calendar of the business partner, in this case apart from the system or the user. Similarly, you can also assign a reference object to durations. You can influence the time zone and calendar to durations like the date type. You can assign different reference objects to different date types but you can assign only one reference object to each date type.

These are the steps to configure a date profile where the configuration example includes a standard date type, the duration, and date rules:

1. Create a date profile with the configuration path mentioned here **SPRO | CRM | Basic Functions | Date Management | Define Date Profile**

The screenshot here shows the date profile for the sales order where the date profile configured is assigned to the sales transaction type:

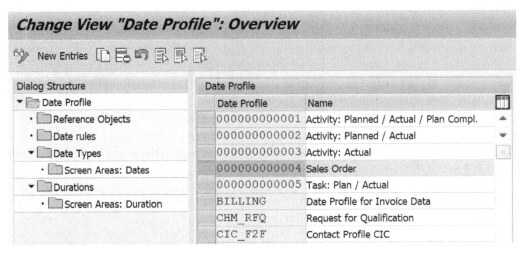

Figure 6.33 – Date profile

The **System** reference object's time zone is added to **Date Profile** and is shown in *Figure 6.34*:

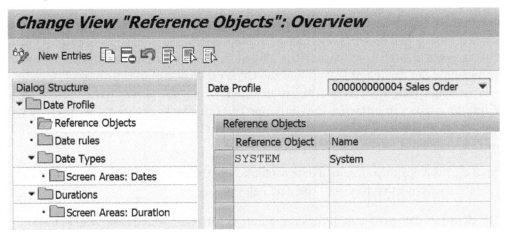

Figure 6.34 – Date profile reference objects

2. You can assign a date rule to **Date Profile** based on your business scenario. In this case, a standard date rule is assigned to the date profile, as shown in *Figure 6.35*:

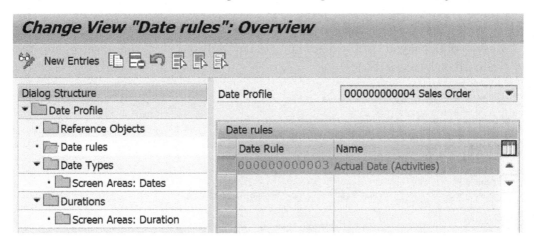

Figure 6.35 – Date profile date rule

3. Assign **Date Types** to **Date Profile** as shown in *Figure 6.36*. Double-click on **Date Types** to view the details and assign a date rule if required:

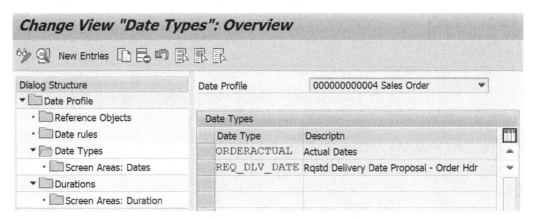

Figure 6.36 – Date Types within Date Profile

In the **Date Types** details, you have the capability to show the date in the format **Weekday**, **Date**, **Time Zone**, or **Time**. A reference object can be assigned in the date type details specifying whether the date type should take the system time zone. Within the date type, you can assign the date rule as shown in *Figure 6.37*. There is an option if you want to determine the date only once versus re-determining it based on business rules:

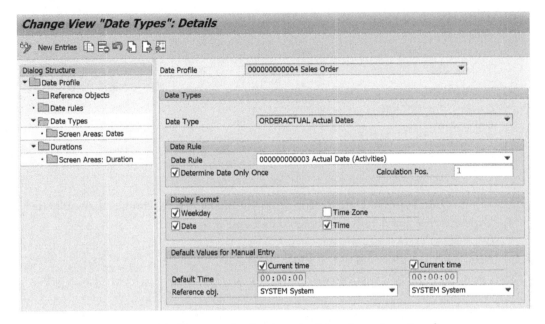

Figure 6.37 – Date type details where the date rule can be assigned

You can also define **Duration** for the date profile as shown in *Figure 6.38*:

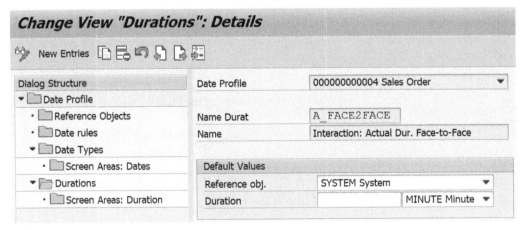

Figure 6.38 – Duration within the date profile

4. You assign the date profile to the transaction type after configuring the date profile, as shown in *Figure 6.39*:

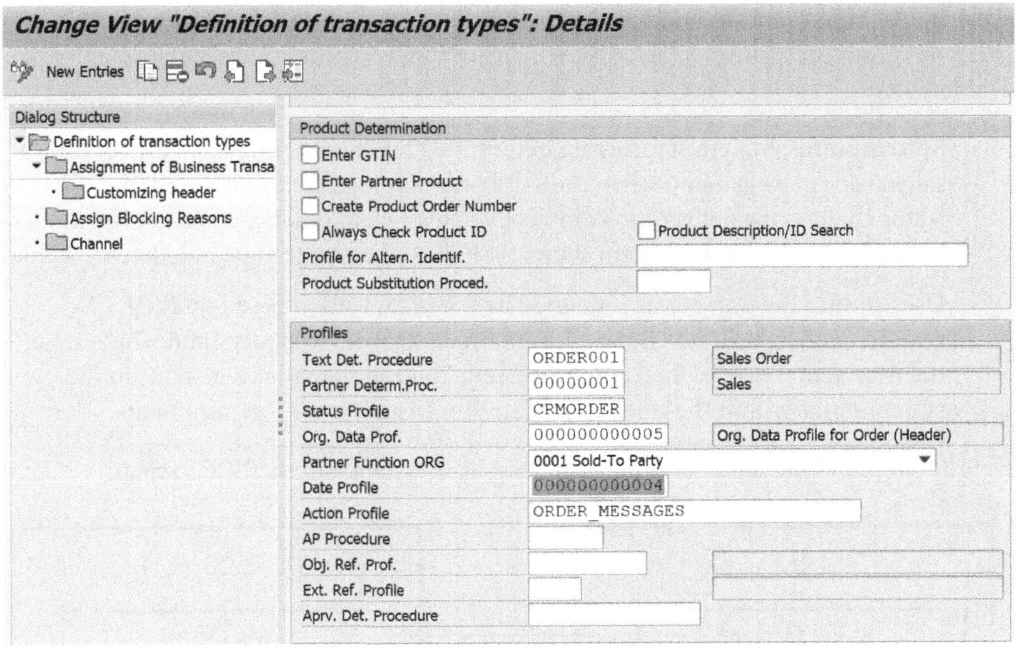

Figure 6.39 – Date profile assignment to the transaction type

The following is the Implementation Guide (IMG) path to assign a date profile to the transaction type: In **Customizing** for transaction types in a CRM System, choose **Customer Relationship Management | Transactions | Basic Settings | Define Transaction Types**.

With this, we have finished the steps for date profile configuration. Now, we will look into status management.

Status management

Status management shows the different stages of an order in the complete order to cash cycle. It is an important function in any SAP business transaction. Primarily, there are two types of statuses within SAP CRM, which are system status and user status, as detailed here:

- **System status**: System statuses are determined by the system. For example, within sales order management, when the sales order is created and delivered, the system status changes the delivery to completely delivered automatically. Similarly, when billing is processed, the system status for billing changes to fully billed.

- **User status**: The user status is defined by the organization based on their requirements. This status is used for internal purposes to understand which stage the transaction has reached and processed. You can map the user status to the system status within the status configuration based on your requirements.

Figure 6.40 shows the status flow between the CRM system and the ECC system:

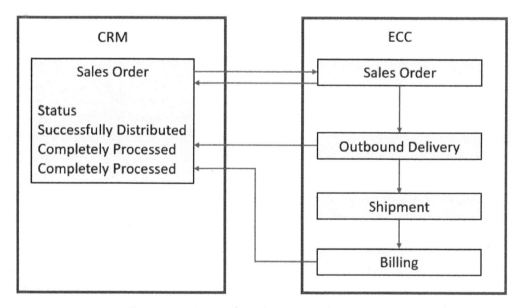

Figure 6.40 – CRM sales order status update overview

The sales order created in CRM is replicated to SAP ECC. The order status in CRM shows distributed successfully. As soon as the delivery and shipment are created in ECC, the delivery status of the line item in CRM changes to completely processed. When the billing document is generated in ECC, the billing status in CRM changes from not processed to completely processed.

The following are the steps required to configure the status in a sales order:

1. Define the status profile for the user status in SAP CRM under **Customer Relationship Management | Transactions | Status Management | Define Status Profile for User Status**.

    In this activity, you will create a status profile as per your business requirements. The statuses you configure here are shown as the user status, where the user can influence the status based on their business needs. In a status profile, you can perform the following activities:

    a) Define user statuses and assign the transaction control. You can define multiple user statuses based on your business requirements.

    b) Assign the lowest status number and highest status number to each of the user statuses. This determines the sequence in which the user status should appear in the transaction based on your business needs. This is controlled via the **Lowest status** and **Highest status** fields.

    c) An object type is assigned to the status profile.

    d) The user status is mapped to the system status, as shown in *Figure 6.41*:

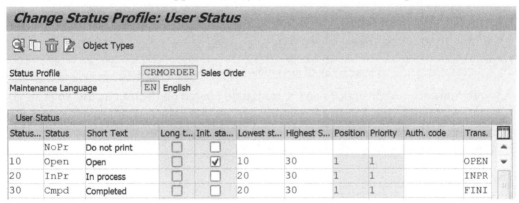

Change Status Profile: User Status

Object Types

Status Profile	CRMORDER	Sales Order
Maintenance Language	EN	English

User Status

Status...	Status	Short Text	Long t...	Init. sta...	Lowest st...	Highest S...	Position	Priority	Auth. code	Trans.
	NoPr	Do not print	☐	☐						
10	Open	Open	☐	✓	10	30	1	1		OPEN
20	InPr	In process	☐	☐	20	30	1	1		INPR
30	Cmpd	Completed	☐	☐	20	30	1	1		FINI

Figure 6.41 – Status profile – user status

Figure 6.41 shows how the Cmpd (Completed) user status is mapped to FINI. FINI is the system status of the transaction that completes the transaction. Once the transaction is completed, no further processing can be done on that transaction.

2.   Click on the object type to activate **Allowed Object Types** for the user status profile. This is shown in *Figure 6.42*, where **CRM Order Header** is activated for the object type:

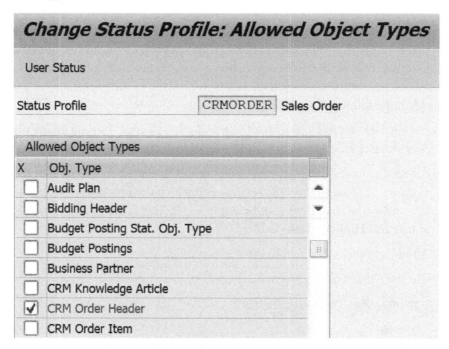

Figure 6.42 – Status profile – allowed object types

3.   To influence certain actions on the transaction based on the user status, you can access **Transaction Control** based on a certain user status, as shown in *Figure 6.43*:

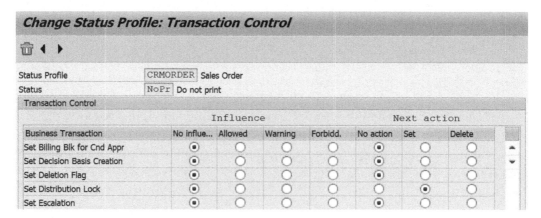

Figure 6.43 – Setting the business transaction to complete

In this example, the NoPr (Do not print) user status has an influence on the transaction to set the distribution lock. This means the order will not replicate to ECC when setting this status.

4. Once the status profile is configured, you assign the status profile to the transaction type. This is done with the IMG path mentioned here: **SPRO | Customer Relationship Management | Transactions | Basic Settings | Define Transaction Types**

Figure 6.44 shows the status profile being assigned to the transaction type:

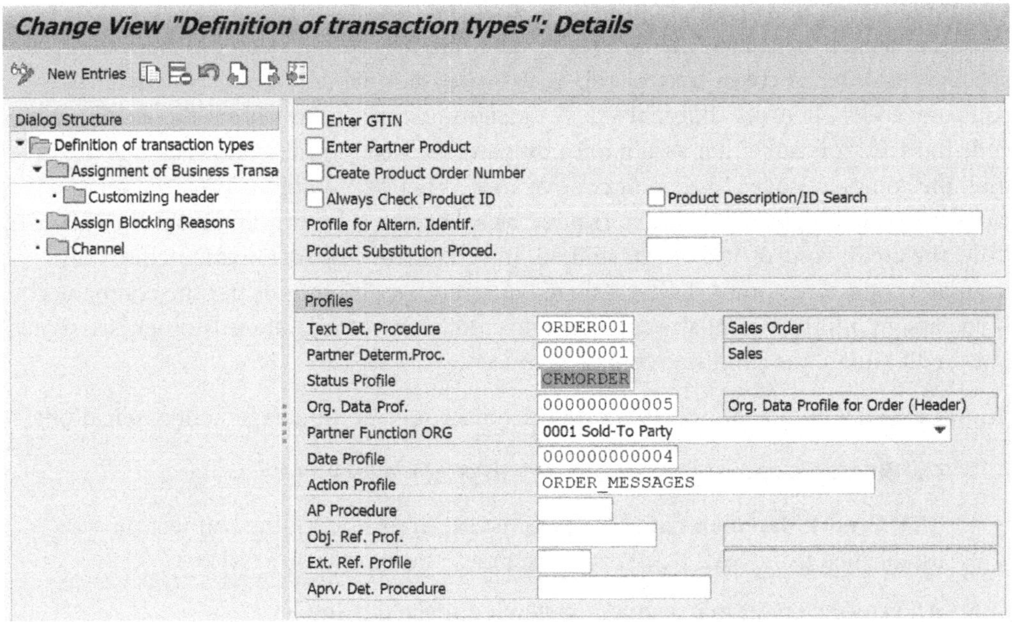

Figure 6.44 – Assigning the status profile to the transaction type

The configuration to influence the user status at the item level is the same as what is configured at the header level. The difference between the header and item levels is that the status profile is configured for the transaction type at the header level whereas the status profile is configured for the item category at the item level.

Credit management

The credit standing of the customer is determined by the credit management functionality provided by SAP. Based on the payment terms assigned to the customer, the customer needs to pay the amount or settle their account when they buy any products. It is a loss to the company if customers don't settle the account by the specified period. For this reason, SAP has introduced the **Credit Management** function, which allows companies to understand the credit rating of the customer and deliver the products only if their credit limit has not been exceeded. The order goes on credit block if the customer has not cleared their account.

Credit management helps to minimize the financial risk of any organization. A credit control area maintained in ERP determines the rules to undergo a credit check for a specific customer. A credit control area is an organizational unit that is assigned to a company code. There are different ways of assigning a credit control area to a company code in ECC. You can either assign one company code to a credit control area or assign multiple company codes to a credit control area. Whenever an order is placed for a customer, the company code is determined based on the sales org, and from the company code, the credit control area is determined. If a credit control area is assigned to one company code, a customer can be assigned different credit limits as per the company code. If you assign multiple company codes to one credit control area, the customer is assigned one credit limit across multiple company codes.

Within CRM, you can connect to one of the following credit management applications:

- **Credit Management (FI-AR-CR, SD-BF-CM)** in SAP ECC.

- **SAP Credit Management (FIN-FSCM-CR)** in SAP ECC; the connection is established using SAP NetWeaver **Exchange Infrastructure (XI)**.

- An external credit management system connected using XI.

The credit check on the sales order happens when the sales order is saved in SAP CRM. A SAP standard credit check BADI is executed on the sales order save that calls ECC to run the credit check on the customer. The result of the credit check comes back with credit OK or not OK depending on the credit standing of the customer. If the customer order goes on to a credit check, the credit team releases the credit from the sales order based on their communication with the customer on settling the balance due.

SAP provides `BAdI CRM_CREDIT_CHECK`, which controls how the system performs credit checks. For example, you can implement rules that allow Credit Management in SAP CRM to communicate with systems other than SAP Credit Management (`FIN-FSCM-CR`).

The standard system contains the following implementations:

- Implementation of rule 01, which accesses the automatic credit check in Credit Management (`FI-AR-CR`)
- Implementation of rule 02, which accesses the automatic credit check in SAP Credit Management (`FIN-FSCM-CR`)

The following are the IMG steps required to configure the credit management functionality in SAP CRM.

Step 1 - Maintaining the credit group

First, we maintain the credit group through the configuration path given here: SAP CRM under **Customer Relationship Management | Basic Functions | Credit Management | General Settings | Maintain Credit Group**

The following screenshot shows the area wherein you maintain the credit group:

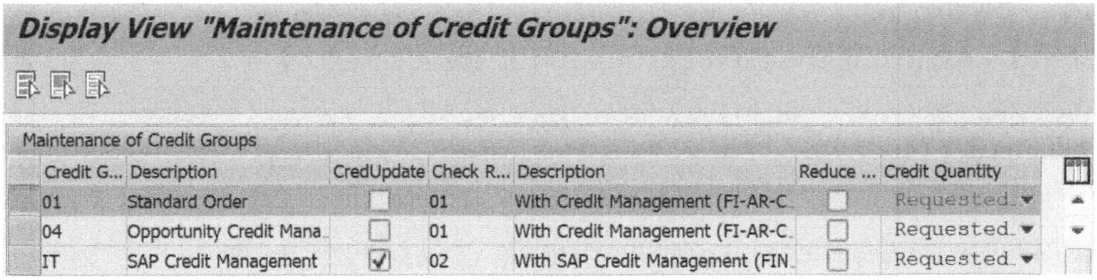

Credit G...	Description	CredUpdate	Check R...	Description	Reduce ...	Credit Quantity
01	Standard Order	☐	01	With Credit Management (FI-AR-C...	☐	Requested...
04	Opportunity Credit Mana...	☐	01	With Credit Management (FI-AR-C...	☐	Requested...
IT	SAP Credit Management	☑	02	With SAP Credit Management (FIN...	☐	Requested...

Figure 6.45 – Maintaining the credit group

Let's review some of the key configuration and the functionality within the credit group:

- **Reduce Confirmed Qty**: **Reduce Confirmed Qty** allows you to reduce the schedule line confirmed quantity when the credit check on the sales order is **Credit Not OK**. This removes the requirement of the material on the confirmed date in `MD04` since the confirmed schedule is set to `0`. Set this indicator if you want the system to carry out the following actions automatically after a negative credit check (status: **Credit check not OK**) for the corresponding items:

  a) Reduce confirmed quantity to the quantity already delivered.

  b) Block further ATP checks by setting the status to **ATP Block**.

  c) The status is displayed in the document.

  d) Do not update the corresponding credit value.

After the item has been released or another credit check has been performed with a positive result (status: **Credit check OK**), the system automatically removes the status ATP block and carries out a new ATP check in order to get the confirmed schedule line.

5. **Credit Quantity**: The **Credit Quantity** field has two options, which are **Confirmed Quantity** and **Request Quantity**. A credit check is based on the order request quantity or confirmed quantity based on the configuration set here. This indicator is used to identify the relevant quantity for the credit check. You can define the following quantities as credit-relevant for the credit check:

    a) **The requested quantity maintained in the order**: If you choose to make the requested quantity credit-relevant, it is included in the credit check regardless of the result of an ATP check.

    b) **The confirmed quantity**: If you choose to make the confirmed quantity credit-relevant, the credit check only calculates values that are based on the confirmed quantity.

Step 2 – Assigning the credit group to the item category

You assign the credit group to the item category in SAP CRM under **Customer Relationship Management | Basic Functions | Credit Management | General Settings | Assign Credit Group to Item Category**.

Here, the screenshot shows the assignment of the credit group to the item category in the item category configuration:

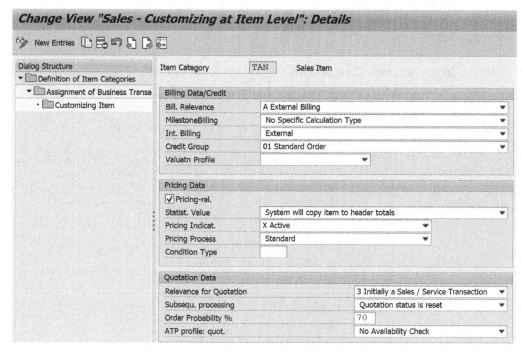

Figure 6.46 – Credit group assignment to the item category

Step 3 – Activating the credit check in the transaction

To activate the credit check follow the path in SAP CRM under **Customer Relationship Management | Basic Functions | Credit Management | General Settings | Activate Credit Check In Transaction.**

In this step, you activate the credit check for the transaction type shown in the screenshot here:

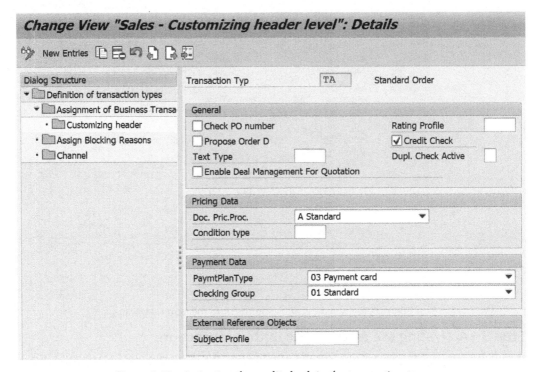

Figure 6.47 – Activating the credit check in the transaction type

Payment card processing

Payment card processing allows the organization to assign a credit card to the sales order and bill the customer based on the credit card accepted by the clearing house. Once the information regarding the credit card, CVV, and expiration date is added to the **payment method** tab, the credit card is authenticated.

On saving, the system authorizes the payment card transaction with the clearing house. The clearing house sends the information back to the SAP CRM sales order. It can be in the form of denial or approval. If approved, the order is replicated to ECC for further processing to create the delivery and invoice.

You can also encrypt the credit card so that it is shown in a masked format. This encryption is saved in the database and only authorized users can view this information. Payment card data can be encrypted in the database using the CRM_ORDER_PC_ RETROGR_ENCRYPT report. To view the payment card details, SAP has provided the B_CCSEC authorization object, which can be assigned to authorized users.

SAP has provided a **credit analyst workbench** wherein the credit team can review all sales documents with the credit block and release them through the credit workbench.

Actions

Actions are important functionality in SAP CRM; within actions, you can trigger various business functions. This can be done by triggering the workflow to initiate the next process step as per your business requirements. You can trigger an order confirmation or create a subsequent transaction with actions as per your business needs.

Actions in CRM use the **Post Processing Framework (PPF)** and are used in any business transactions for processing subsequent functions and output. Actions help to improve your business process and automate the process based on the set conditions and timelines. *Figure 6.48* shows an action overview with action profile creation and its assignment to the transaction type or item category:

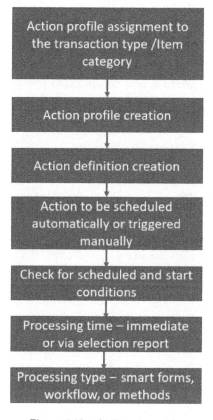

Figure 6.48 – Actions overview

The action profile has action definitions and action definitions can be configured to schedule an action automatically or manually. If an action is configured to be scheduled automatically, the conditions are checked; that is, the schedule conditions and the start conditions are checked. If the schedule and start conditions are met, the next check is the processing time and processing type. The processing time is whether the action is to be scheduled immediately or through a selection report. The processing type is whether a smart form, workflow, or method needs to be triggered. This is based on the configuration. For a sales order, it is generally the order confirmation that is configured with the smart form processing type. If you want to create a subsequent document from the sales order, for example, the activity or task creation, then the processing type is **Method**. There are around *180* actions provided by SAP for the CRM_ORDER application transaction processing.

Here are the steps to configure an action profile:

1. Define action profiles and actions with the following SAP menu path: **SPRO | Customer Relationship Management | Basic Functions | Actions | Actions in Transaction | Change Actions and Conditions | Define Action Profiles and Actions**

Figure 6.49 shows a standard action definition example for order messages:

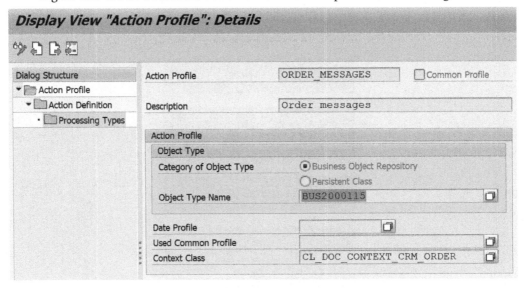

Figure 6.49 – Order messages action profile

You assign a business object type to actions regardless of whether they are order-related. In this example, it is BUS2000115. A common profile is used when you have overlapping action definition functionality for similar objects. If you want to reuse action profiles, you can set up a common profile and assign it to other profiles. This reduces the configuration effort.

An action profile has a list of action definitions that fulfill your business requirements. *Figure 6.50* shows an example of an order confirmation:

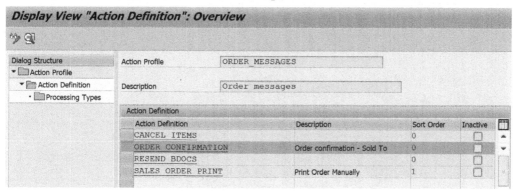

Figure 6.50 – Action definition

Within the action definition details, there are configuration options that you can activate based on your business requirements, as shown in *Figure 6.51*:

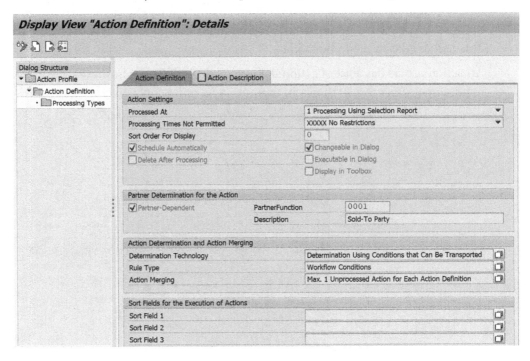

Figure 6.51 – Action definition details

The following are the action field definitions and descriptions of the usage of these fields within a business environment:

a) **Processed At**: **Processed At** helps to determine whether you would like to trigger an action when fulfilling the condition or on saving the document or trigger the action using the selection report. There are three options in the dropdown for this field: **Immediate processing**, where as soon as the start conditions are met, the action is executed; **Processing when saving document**, where on saving the transaction, the action is executed; and **Processing using selection report**, where the action is executed using the selection report. The report checks whether the start conditions are met; if so, the action is executed by using the report. This report can be scheduled at regular intervals based on business needs.

b) **Schedule Automatically**: If the indicator is set, the actions are automatically activated for processing as soon as the schedule and start conditions are met. If the action isn't configured for schedule automatically, then you can trigger actions manually.

c) **Changeable in dialog**: To change the condition and the processing parameter for each action that can be executed in the transaction, you activate the **Changeable in dialog** field.

d) **Executable in dialog**: To trigger the action manually from the action assignment block, activate the **Executable in dialog** flag within the configuration.

e) **Display in toolbar**: To display the action in the toolbar within the sales transaction, activate the **Display in toolbar** checkbox.

f) **Delete After Processing**: You can delete actions automatically when they are processed successfully. Any errors during processing the action will keep the action in the transaction and are not deleted.

g) **Partner Determination for the Action**: If the **Partner-Dependent** checkbox field is activated, you can define which partner you want to trigger the action for. In this example, the **Partner Dependent** checkbox is active, and **PartnerFunction** is set to 0001 – Sold-To Party. The action will trigger only for Sold-To Party in this case.

h) **Action Description**: Here, the action description is added and the same can be seen on the business transaction for a specific action definition.

i) **Action Merging**: In **Action Merging**, there are options for selecting the number of unprocessed actions and the number of processed actions, as shown in *Figure 6.52*:

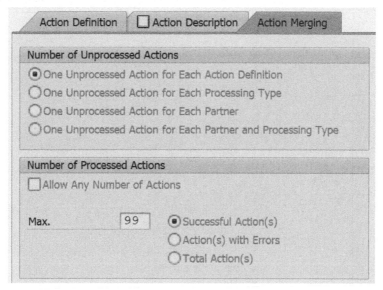

Figure 6.52 – Action Merging

j) **Number of Unprocessed Actions**: **Number of Unprocessed Actions** provides the capability to select an option for triggering unprocessed actions based on the action definition or processing type or for partners.

k) **Allow Any number of Actions**: This setting allows any number of actions to be triggered, meaning if the conditions are satisfied, the action will trigger. You can retrigger actions based on the settings defined here.

The rule type within the action determination can be a workflow or COD – Conditions Using Business AddIn; you can assign a BADI to the scheduled condition. You can use the BAdI EVAL_SCHEDCOND_PPF schedule condition or the BAdI EVAL_STARTCOND_PPF start condition.

l) **Processing Types**: There are three types of processing types that you can configure within the action definition based on your business scenarios. The types are **SAP Smart Forms**, which is used when confirmation needs to be sent to any customer, for example, fax, email, or print confirmations; **Method**, which is nothing more than a BADI implementation that can be assigned to the actions to create any subsequent transaction, for example, the creation of activities or tasks as a follow-up transaction to the sales order (EXEC_METHODCALL_PPF is the relevant BADI for a method call); or **Workflow**, which allows you to assign a workflow task that you have created via the workflow builder to the action definition.

Figure 6.53 shows the smart forms for an order confirmation:

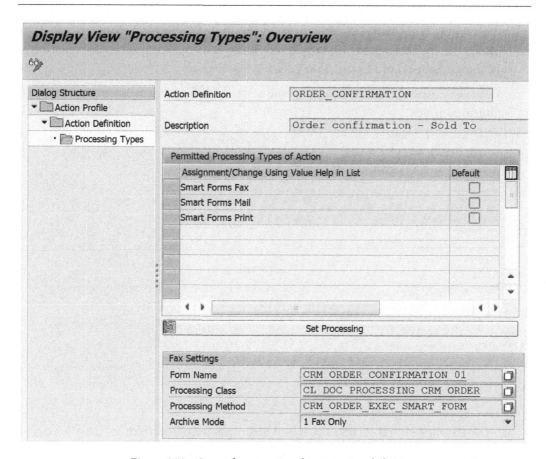

Display View "Processing Types": Overview

Dialog Structure	Action Definition	ORDER_CONFIRMATION
▼ ☐ Action Profile		
▼ ☐ Action Definition	Description	Order confirmation – Sold To
• 📁 Processing Types		

Permitted Processing Types of Action

Assignment/Change Using Value Help in List	Default	
Smart Forms Fax	☐	
Smart Forms Mail	☐	
Smart Forms Print	☐	

Set Processing

Fax Settings

Form Name	CRM_ORDER_CONFIRMATION_01
Processing Class	CL_DOC_PROCESSING_CRM_ORDER
Processing Method	CRM_ORDER_EXEC_SMART_FORM
Archive Mode	1 Fax Only

Figure 6.53 – Smart forms assigned to an action definition

Form Name, **Processing Class**, and **Processing Method** are assigned to the smart form processing type. The print program fills in the smart form based on the business logic mentioned here. You can also archive the form after triggering the confirmation based on the configuration setting for archive mode.

2. In this step, you define conditions for each action definition based on your business scenario. There are two types of conditions: schedule conditions and start conditions. The schedule condition acts as the first criteria before the next condition is met. You can schedule a condition for a business rule, for example, if this business rule is met, then the action is generated on the transaction. Once the conditions are scheduled, the next condition that the system checks is the start condition. If the start conditions are met, then the action is triggered and executed.

Here is the IMG path to configure action conditions: **SPRO | Customer Relationship Management | Basic Functions | Actions | Actions in Transaction | Change Actions and Conditions | Define Conditions**

You can create a schedule condition and start condition here based on your business needs:

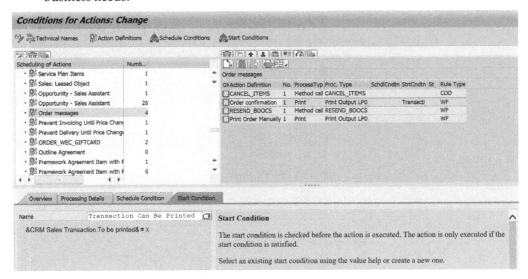

Figure 6.54 – Action conditions

3. Then, you need to configure the action determination procedure.

Once you configure the action profile, you create the action determination procedure to create the condition record in CRM. Here are the IMG steps to create a condition table: **SPRO | Customer Relationship Management | Basic Functions | Actions | Actions in Transaction | Set Up Action Profile Determination | Create Condition Tables**

Figure 6.55 shows an example of a standard SAP condition table, SAP00003, a **Transaction Type/Sold-to party** combination. You can create a new condition table based on the specific business needs:

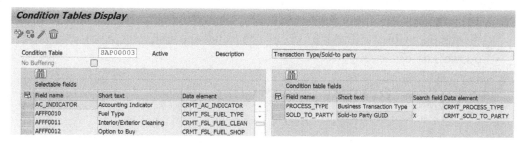

Figure 6.55 – Action condition tables

4. In this step, you create the access sequence with the IMG path mentioned next:
    **SPRO | Customer Relationship Management | Basic Functions | Actions |
    Actions in Transaction | Set Up Action Profile Determination | Create Access
    Sequence**

    Figure 6.56 shows the 0001 standard access sequence for **Sales Order**. Here,
    Application is CRM and **Usage** is AP. You assign the condition table to the access
    sequence:

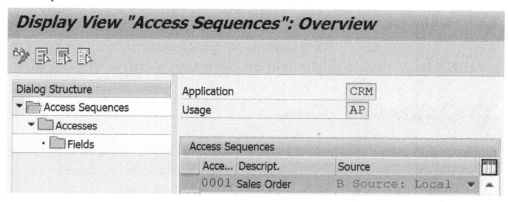

Figure 6.56 – Action access sequences. Application is CRM and Usage is AP

The following screenshot shows the tables assigned to the access sequence. It shows the standard tables and you can create new tables and assign them based on your business needs:

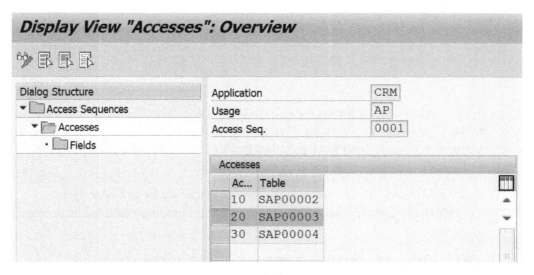

Figure 6.57 – Tables assigned to the action access sequence

Here, the screenshot shows the fields assigned to the action table. This field drives the condition record to determine the actions in the transaction:

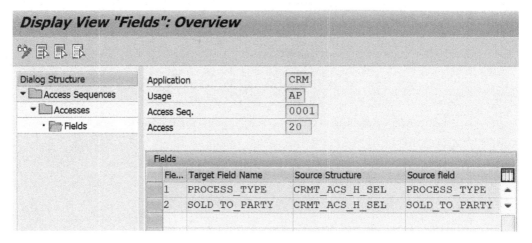

Figure 6.58 – Fields assigned to the action table

5. In this step, you create the condition type for the action procedure: **SPRO |
    Customer Relationship Management | Basic Functions | Actions | Actions in
    Transaction | Set Up Action Profile Determination | Create Condition Types**

The screenshot here shows the OACK (Order Confirmation) standard
condition type assigned with access sequence 0001:

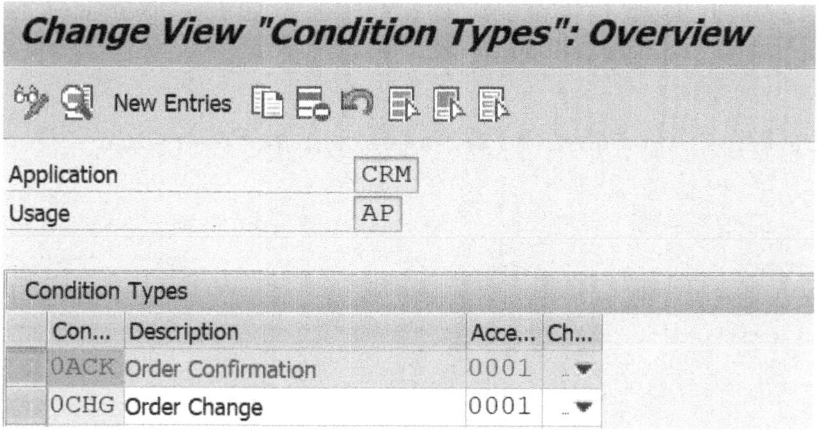

Figure 6.59 – Maintaining condition types

Figure 6.60 shows the condition type detail screen:

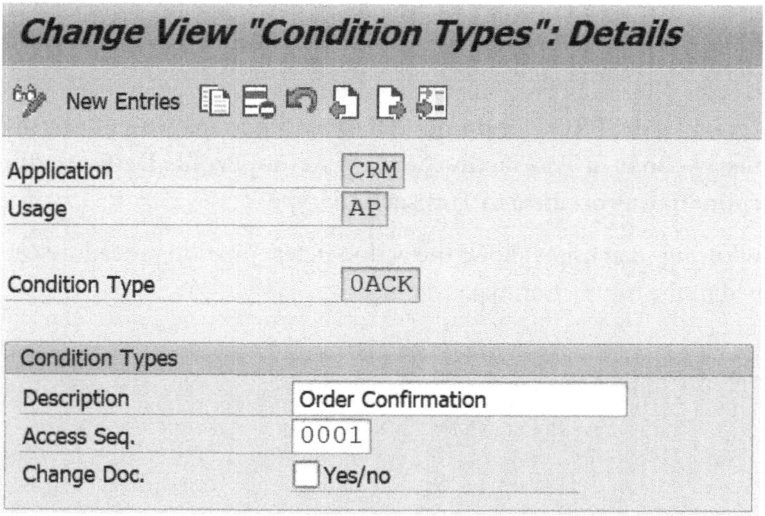

Figure 6.60 – Maintaining condition types

6. In this step, you create the action determination procedure and assign the condition type: **SPRO | Customer Relationship Management | Basic Functions | Actions | Actions in Transaction | Set Up Action Profile Determination | Define Determination Procedure**

Create an action determination procedure and assign the condition type created in the previous step to the action determination procedure. *Figure 6.61* shows the 0CRM01 standard action determination procedure assigned with the 0ACK condition type:

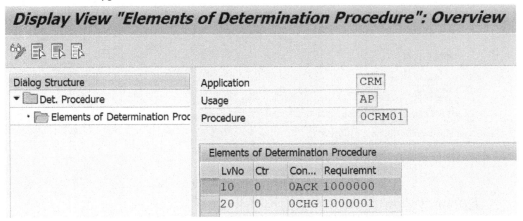

Figure 6.61 – Maintaining the action determination procedure and assigning condition types

7. In this step, you assign the action procedure created in the previous step to the transaction type: **SPRO | Customer Relationship Management | Basic Functions | Actions | Actions in Transaction | Set Up Action Profile Determination | Assign Determination Procedure to Transaction Type**

The following screenshot shows the action determination procedure getting assigned to the transaction type:

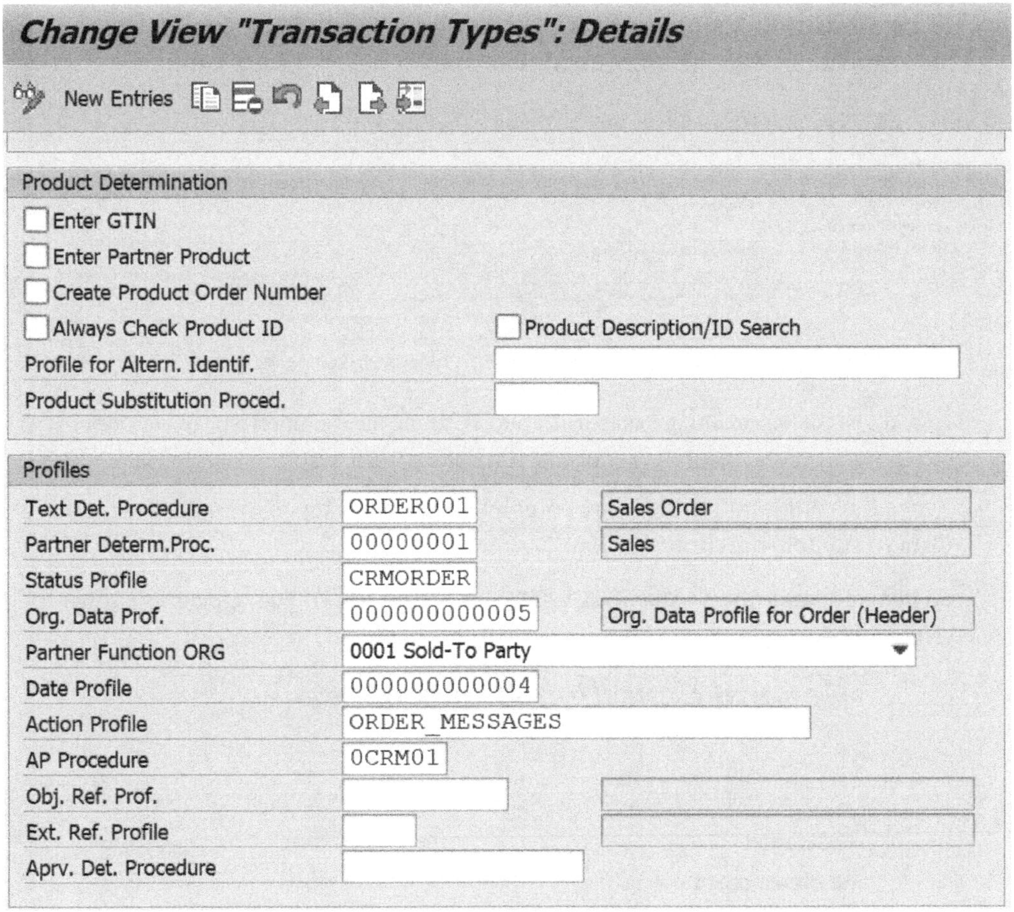

Change View "Transaction Types": Details

New Entries

Product Determination

- [ ] Enter GTIN
- [ ] Enter Partner Product
- [ ] Create Product Order Number
- [ ] Always Check Product ID   [ ] Product Description/ID Search

Profile for Altern. Identif.

Product Substitution Proced.

Profiles

Text Det. Procedure	ORDER001	Sales Order
Partner Determ.Proc.	00000001	Sales
Status Profile	CRMORDER	
Org. Data Prof.	000000000005	Org. Data Profile for Order (Header)
Partner Function ORG	0001 Sold-To Party	
Date Profile	000000000004	
Action Profile	ORDER_MESSAGES	
AP Procedure	0CRM01	
Obj. Ref. Prof.		
Ext. Ref. Profile		
Aprv. Det. Procedure		

Figure 6.62 – Assigning the action determination procedure to the transaction type

8. In this step, you configure the condition maintenance group. This step is required before you create the condition record: **SPRO | Customer Relationship Management | Basic Functions | Actions | Actions in Transaction | Set Up Master Data Maintenance for Action Profile Determination | Create Condition Maintenance Group**

Here, **Condition Maintenance** is CRM_AP and it is used for action profile determination. Add the 0ACK condition type for the AP **Usage** setting:

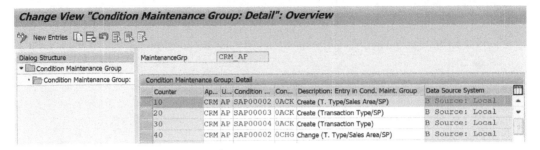

Figure 6.63 – Action condition maintenance and assigning the condition type to the CRM_AP maintenance group

9. Once the configuration steps are completed, the next step is to create the master data to support the configuration.

When you enter the TCode - /SAPCND/GCM, the screen will appear as shown in *Figure 6.64*:

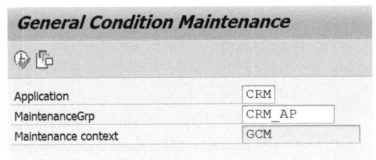

Figure 6.64 – Condition type maintenance group screen

The screenshot here shows the condition record for the 0ACK condition type:

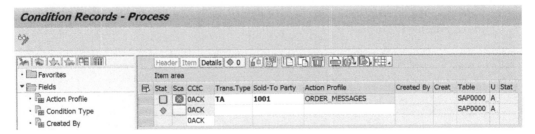

Figure 6.65 – Maintaining the action condition type

The action configuration is complete once the condition record is maintained. Now, when the order is created with the master data as mentioned in the condition record, the 0CRM01 action profile procedure is triggered. Since the action profile procedure is called, the system looks for the condition record with the 0ACK condition type. It determines the condition record and the ORDER_MESSAGES action profile is assigned to the condition record.

Action monitor

The action monitor provides you with information on actions that are in the queue or that are successfully generated. You can trigger an action for the actions that are configured using a selection report. The transaction code for the action monitor is SPPFP and the program name is RSPPFPROCESS. You can trigger a background job for the RSPPFPROCESS program with the relevant variant and trigger an action from the job. This is based on the configuration of the action definition if the action is scheduled immediately on save or via a selection report.

Summary

This chapter provided an understanding of the basic functions in business transactions, including how headers and items are connected to the transaction type and how to configure the profiles associated with a business transaction. These profiles are partner processing, text management, date management, status management, credit management, and actions. We have gone through all the pre-requisites required to create a sales transaction in the SAP CRM system, that is, covering the master data and the basic functions for the sales transactions.

With this chapter, you are now well versed with the configuration required to execute different basic functions within a sales transaction. Now, we will deep dive into the processing of these sales transactions in SAP CRM.

Our next chapter covers sales document processing in SAP CRM, which explains the significance of the sales document and is the very first step in the complete order to cash cycle.

Further reading

- Additional information on sales order basic functions can be found at https://help.sap.com/viewer/cb77bf16eae9401fb7c569c5ac3b4bb6/7.0.4.15/en-US/4582ba517e9a40bfe10000000a1553f7.html.

7
Sales Document Processing in SAP CRM

This chapter covers business transaction processing in SAP CRM. Sales document processing in SAP CRM allows a company to perform sales transactions with their customers. This chapter looks at the various sales document functions you can use to run sales transactions successfully. We'll be looking at the first step in the Order to Cash cycle, where the sales order is created and documented in the SAP CRM system before being sent to transportation planning and execution to ship the product out to the customer.

Here is a list of the topics covered in this chapter:

- Sales contracts
- Quotations
- Sales orders
- Data exchange for sales transactions from CRM to ERP systems

By the end of this chapter, you will understand sales transaction processing, including its key concepts and how to configure sales transactions in SAP CRM as per your business needs.

Sales contracts

A sales contract is an agreement between a customer and a supplier stating a specific price or discount for a specific period of time. Once the sales contract's validity period expires, the contract can no longer be used to sell the product for the contracted price. The functionality of sales contracts in SAP CRM is the same as in SAP ECC.

Sales contracts provide functionality such that a supplier can offer a lower price than the market price to extend their customer base and improve customer retention. *Figure 7.1* shows a representation of contract management in SAP CRM:

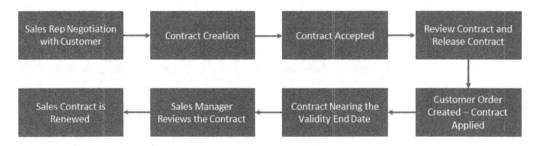

Figure 7.1 – Contract management in SAP CRM

Here are the steps involved in the sales contract management cycle in SAP CRM:

1. The sales representative negotiates a price with the customer based on certain terms and conditions for a specific period.

2. The sales representative creates a contract based on their discussion with the customer and certain terms and conditions.

3. A contract is created in SAP, consisting of quantity, value, and validity period details.

4. The customer reviews the contract and accepts it.

5. The sales manager reviews the final contract and releases the contract items.

6. The customer places an order against the contract and gets special discounts for the contract validity period.

7. The contract nears the end of its validity period.

8. The sales manager reviews the contract and connects with the customer to renew the contract.

9. The sales contract is renewed.

Having understood the sales contract management cycle, let's now learn about the functions offered by sales contracts.

Sales contract functions

A sales contract business transaction comprises header and item data, similar to a sales transaction. The transaction type controls the header data, whereas the item category controls the item data. In SAP CRM, there are two types of contract that exist: quantity contracts and value contracts:

- A **quantity contract** is an agreement that a customer will buy a certain quantity of the product for a certain validity period. The standard transaction type for a quantity contract is QCTR. You can create your own transaction by copying the standard transaction type and configuring it based on your business needs.

- A **value contract** is an agreement that a customer will buy a certain value of a product for a certain validity period. The value contract transaction type is VCTR.

Within SAP CRM, a sales contract provides the following functions:

- **Price agreement**: A price agreement is a handshake between a customer and an organization regarding a specific price for a specific product and for a specific period. These are condition records that are assigned to the contract as a part of price agreements. One prerequisite to maintain the price agreement is a condition maintenance technique, which is assigned as a condition group to the item category or the contract transaction type. You can configure price agreements for a sales contract using the following IMG path: **SPRO | CRM | Transaction | Settings for Contract | Price Agreements and Configuration**.

- **Actions in contracts**: Actions can be used in a workflow to trigger notifications for relevant parties when a contract is nearing its validity end date. You can also trigger the contract output and send it to the customer if the customer would like to review the contract before the contract item is released. These are some examples where actions could be vital for contracts. You can assign an action profile to the contract transaction type or to the item category based on business needs. You can configure actions via the following IMG path: **SPRO | CRM | Transaction | Basic Functions | Actions | Actions in Transaction | Change Actions and Conditions**.

- **Releasable products**: Products are entered at the item level within a contract. You can enter a product number or a product category in a contract transaction. These products are assigned with condition types and special pricing is assigned to them.

- **Authorized partner**: The authorized partner functionality allows you to determine a sales contract for a sales order for multiple partners. *Figure 7.2* shows the configuration option to activate authorized partners for the sales transaction type:

Figure 7.2 – Authorized Partners in Contract Search

For example, say you have **additional sold to** as an authorized partner on a sales contract; the sales order can determine the contract for this **additional sold to**. You activate this functionality by activating the authorized partner configuration in the sales transaction type area. A sales contract can be determined for the authorized partner at the partner list level or group hierarchy level; you can choose from the options **A – Authorized Partners According to Partner List**, **B – Authorized Partners According to Group Hierarchy**, or **C – Authorized Partners According to List and Hierarchy**, based on your business needs.

- **Cancellation**: You can configure a cancellation rule and cancellation reason for any contracts created in SAP CRM. You can combine cancellation rules and cancellation parties to form cancellation procedures. Cancellation completes a contract; once a contract is complete, you cannot create a release order for it. You create a cancellation rule and assign it to a cancellation procedure. The cancellation procedure is assigned to a contract transaction type. Here is the IMG path to set up a cancellation procedure: **SPRO | Customer Relationship Management | Transactions | Settings for Contracts | Cancellation**.

- **Dates in business transactions**: Date details provide the functionality to determine the validity of contracts. This is one of the most important functionalities as it allows contracts to be applied to a sales order based on the contract validity period. SAP has provided standard date rules that you can implement to determine a validity period; for example, if you want to create a contract with a contract validity period of 3 months, then you can configure the date type to be the contract end date and set it to today's date + 3 months. You configure date management here: **SPRO | CRM | Basic Functions | Date Management | Define Date Profile**.

Completion rules: Item category configuration drives the behavior of contract completion and provides different options based on your business needs. *Figure 7.3* shows a screenshot of the completion rules configuration:

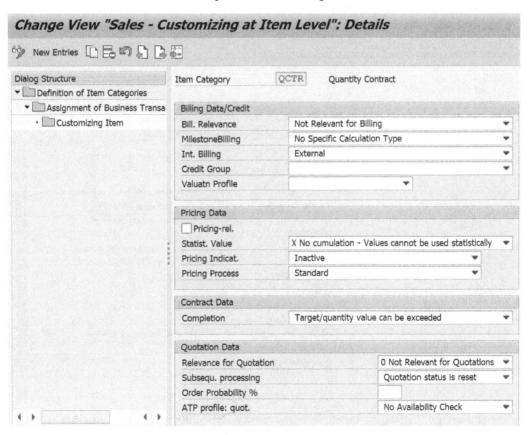

Figure 7.3 – Item Category | Contract Data | Completion

There are four options available at the item category level: (i) **Target/quantity value can be exceeded**, (ii) **A – Target/quantity value cannot be exceeded**, (iii) **B – Target/quantity value can be exceeded once**, and (iv) **C – Split release item when the target quantity exceeded**.

With this, we have covered the several functions in sales contracts. Now let's look into how we configure sales contracts.

Configuring sales contracts

The transaction structure of sales contracts is similar to that of sales orders. The following screenshot shows the configuration of the contract transaction type:

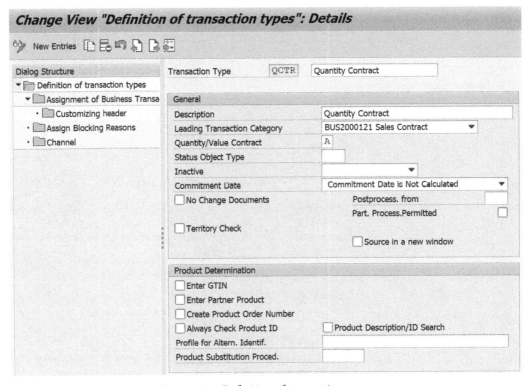

Figure 7.4 – Definition of transaction types

Here you assign the leading business transaction as **BUS2000121 Sales Contract**. You can execute product determination on a sales contract as you can with a sales order. The **Quantity/Value Contract** field specifies whether the contract is **Quantity Contract (A)**, **Value Contract (B)**, or **Quantity & Value Contract**. The example here shows the value **A**, which is for **Quantity Contract**.

Within **Profiles**, you can assign a text determination procedure wherein you can determine specific text for a sales contract and determine partners (like with sales orders) through a partner determination procedure. You can configure statuses, dates, and actions on a sales contract to assign a specific status, configure date rules to determine the validity period, and trigger action emails regarding contract closure.

Price agreement is one of the core functions in SAP sales contracts in that it determines the contract price on the release order. For this function to work, you need to assign the price agreement condition types to the sales contract. To assign a condition type as a price agreement to the sales contract, you need to assign a condition group to the contract transaction type. This enables you to add condition types to sales contracts under the **Price Agreement** tab.

A prerequisite for creating a condition maintenance group is to create a price procedure and configure its assignment to the sales area, as well as configuring the condition tables, access sequence, and condition type to make appropriate assignments. Once the pricing activities are done, then you assign these condition types to condition techniques, which form the basis for the condition group.

This screenshot shows the assignment of a condition group to the sales contract transaction type:

Profiles		
Text Det. Procedure	ORDER001	Sales Order
Partner Determ.Proc.	00000121	Customer Contract Header
Status Profile	CRMORDER	
Org. Data Prof.	00000000005	Org. Data Profile for Order (Header)
Partner Function ORG	0001 Sold-To Party	▼
Date Profile	CONT001	
Action Profile		
AP Procedure		
Cancellation Proced.		
Condition Group	ZMAINTGRP	
Authrzd Hier. Cat.		▼
Ext. Ref. Profile		

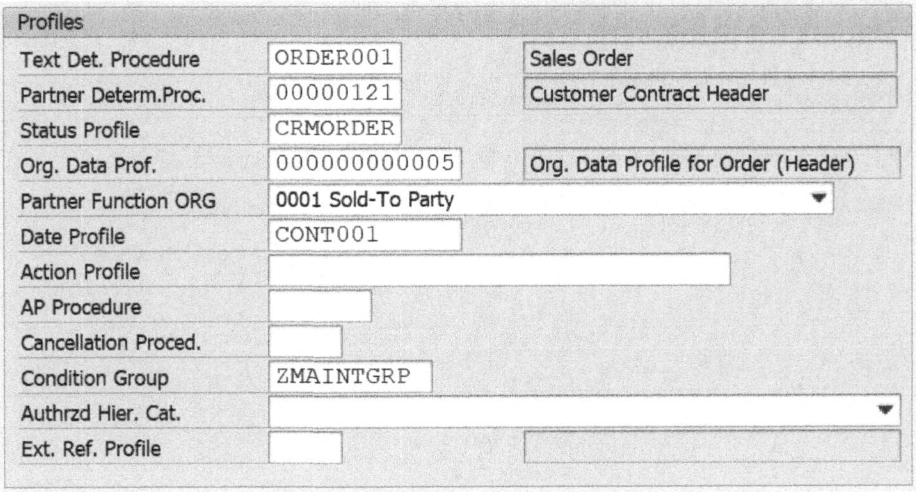

Figure 7.5 – Contract transaction profiles

The transaction type has a transaction category, as mentioned in *Chapter 6, Basic Functions in Sales Documents*. There is a limited number of transaction categories that can be assigned to a transaction type based on the type of transaction; the type can be sales transaction or service transaction. *Figure 7.6* shows the **Transaction Category** field, with the values **BUS2000115 Sales** and **BUS2000121 Sales Contract**:

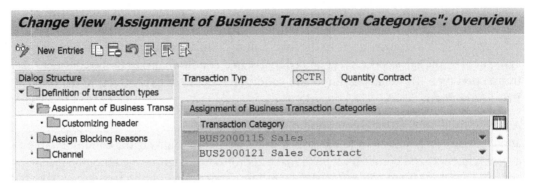

Figure 7.6 – Business transaction categories

The configuration details for sales transaction categories are shown in *Figure 7.7*:

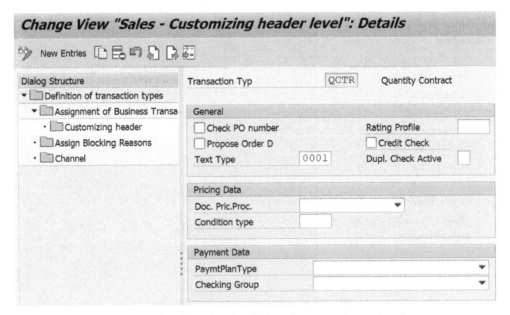

Figure 7.7 – Configuration details for sales transaction categories

You can assign a document pricing procedure here and determine the pricing procedure on the sales contract. Other sales functions can be utilized on a sales contract, such as PO checks and duplicate checks.

You determine the contracts on a sales order based on the configuration settings of the sales order transaction type, which are **No Contract Determination**, **E-Only at Item Level**: **Assign immediately if unique**, and **F-Only at Item Level**: **Always with Selection Option**. Contract determination flags do not belong at the item category level; they are only at the transaction level.

Configuring an item category

The functionality of a transaction at the item level, as opposed to the header level, can differ based on the configuration executed at the item category level. You have similar options at the item category level as you do for a sales contract, for instance, transaction type options. What it is, really, is profile configuration – for example, configuring date profiles, action profiles, partner determination procedures, and so on. You can configure item category profiles based on your business needs. The object type for the contract item category should be **BUS2000135 CRM Quantity/Value Contract Item**, as shown in *Figure 7.8*:

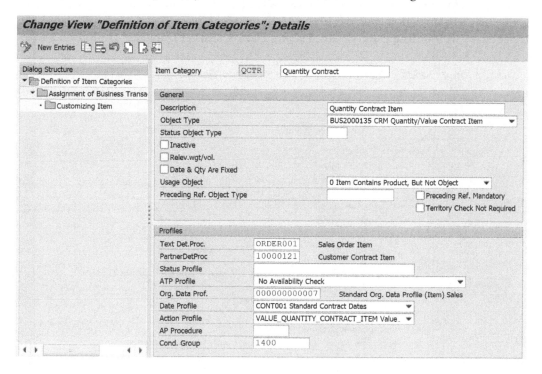

Figure 7.8 – Item category definition

Similar to the transaction type, a transaction category can also be assigned to an item category. *Figure 7.9* shows the **BUS2000115 Sales** transaction category being assigned to the QCTR item category:

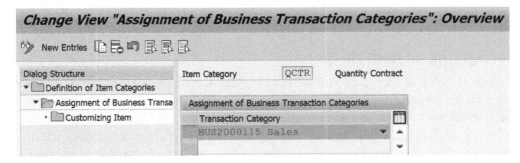

Figure 7.9 – Assignment of the business transaction categories

The most relevant data for contract item categories is pricing data and contract data to do with contract completion. *Figure 7.10* shows the details of the QCTR contract item category customized with **Billing Data/Credit**, **Pricing Data**, **Contract Data**, and **Quotation Data**:

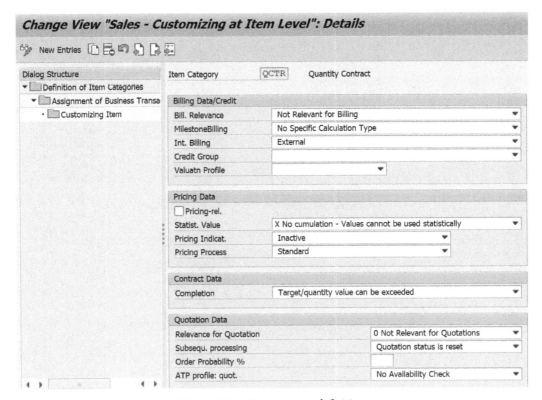

Figure 7.10 – Item category definition

Quotation data doesn't hold much significance for a contract if you are only using contract determination on a sales order.

You will need to activate pricing and configure the completion settings based on your business scenario; that is, based on whether you want to exceed the quantity when creating the release order. **Available to Promise (ATP)** is also not of much significance as most businesses do not want to activate an ATP check for a sales contract item and would be activated with the sales order. There is a configuration option to activate an ATP check on a sales contract if required.

Copy control settings at the header and item levels

To determine the contracts on a sales order, configure copy control settings at the header and item levels. *Figure 7.11* shows the copy control settings for a standard transaction:

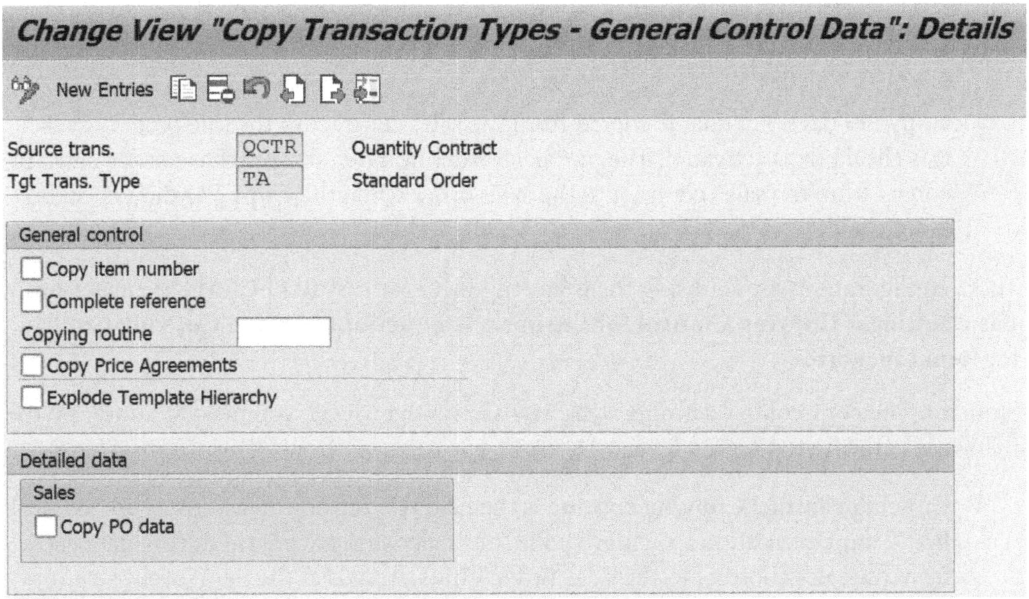

Figure 7.11 – Copy control settings

You can configure the copy control settings using the following IMG path: **SPRO | CRM | Transactions | Basic Settings | Copying Control for Business Transactions | Define Copying Control for Transaction Types**.

Here are the details on each of the fields defined in the copy control configuration area for the business transaction type:

- **Copy item number**: This will copy the item number from the sales contract to the sales order item. If this is not selected, the item number is determined automatically in the sales order based on the numbering configuration.

- **Complete reference**: This will copy all transaction information from the source to the target transaction.

- **Copying routine**: This is the field where you can assign a copy control Business Add-In (BAdI) implementation to achieve your specific business scenario during data copy from a sales contract to a sales order.

- **Copy Price Agreements**: This should be checked when you want to copy the price agreement condition type from a sales contract to a sales order at the header level.

- **Explode Template Hierarchy**: This specifies whether existing template hierarchies are to be expanded when they are copied.

- **Copy PO data**: PO data is copied from the sales contract to the sales order when this checkbox is activated. The purchase order number and purchase order date are copied from the sales contract to the sales order when the **Copy PO data** checkbox is activated.

These configurations are set using the following IMG path: **SPRO | CRM | Transactions | Basic Settings | Copying Control for Business Transactions | Define Copying Control for Item Categories**.

Similar to the copy control settings at the transaction type level, you need to configure the following at the item category level:

- **Copying routine: Copying routine** is the field where you can assign a copy control BADI implementation to achieve your specific business scenario during data copy from the sales contract to the sales order. This setting is at the item level, meaning the item data that's copied can be altered based on this routine.

- **Copy conditions**: The condition type from the sales contract is copied to the sales order when the sales contracts are determined for the sales order. **Copy conditions** triggers the functionality of copying conditions from the contract to the sales order. There are four options available with this configuration: **Do not copy conditions, D – Copy all conditions, C – Copy only manual conditions**, and **G – Copy conditions and re-determine taxes**. You can choose any one of these options based on your business needs.

- **Copy Configuration**: Here you specify whether configured products are determined or copied in follow-up transactions.

- **Fix**: This defines whether the configuration can be changed in the target transaction.

- **Generate prod.master data again**: If you tick this checkbox, all product master attributes will be regenerated again in the target transaction. For example, price reference material, UoM, and volume rebate group attributes will be copied from the contract if this checkbox is not checked; otherwise, these attributes are re-determined as product master data instead of the contracts in the target transaction.

- **Price Agreements**: **Price Agreements** should be checked when you want to copy the price agreement condition type from the sales contract to the sales order at the item level.

- **Copy Survey**: Here you specify whether a survey that is linked to the source transaction should be copied to the target transaction.

The following screenshot shows the item category copy control configuration screen:

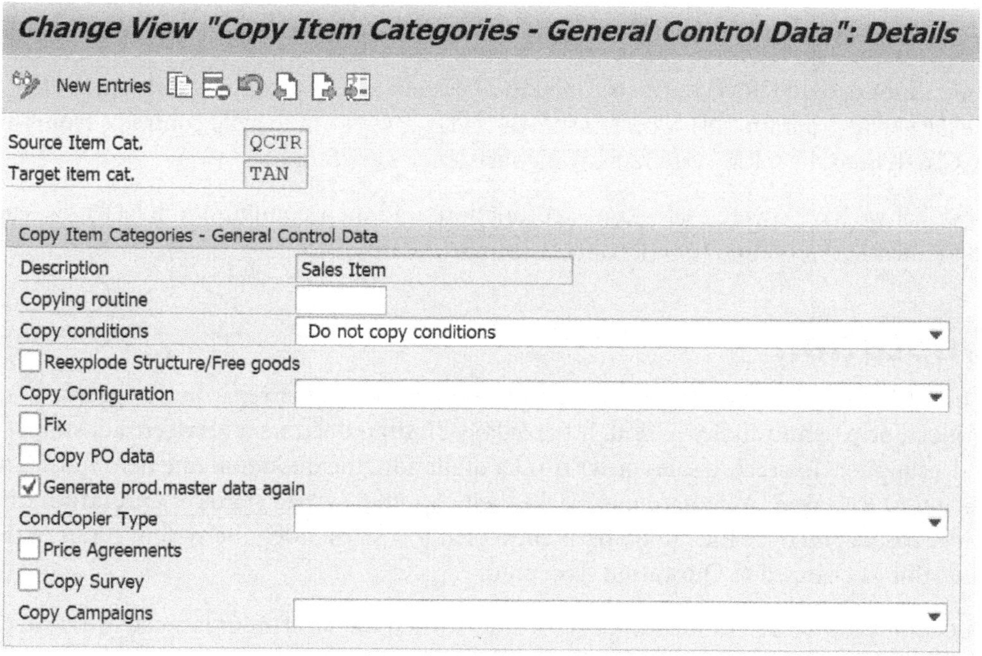

Figure 7.12 – Item category copy control

With this, we have learned about the configuration of copy control settings. Let's now learn about data exchange scenarios.

Data exchange scenarios

If sales contracts are created in the ECC system and contract determination on the sales order happens in the SAP CRM system, then the sales contracts will be replicated from the ECC system to the CRM system.

You can run the initial load with the adapter object named **SALESCONTRACT** to load the contracts from the ECC system to the CRM system. Once the initial load is carried out, the delta change to the sales contract flows automatically to the SAP CRM system. The following are the prerequisites to load a sales contract from the ECC system to the CRM system:

- The same contract type and item categories should exist in both systems.
- The copy control configurations of the sales contract and the sales order should be the same in both ECC and CRM.
- The number ranges should be correctly defined in both systems.
- The same customer and product master data must exist in both systems.
- The same organizational data must exist in both systems.

You cannot upload CRM contracts to the ECC system automatically. SAP has provided the data sync program CRM_CONTRACT_UPDATE_FROM_R3 to sync contracts from the ECC system to the CRM system if any inconsistencies are found.

Now that we have covered sales contract functions and their configuration, let's now learn about the sales quotation functionality within SAP CRM.

Quotation

A quotation is an agreement between a customer and a supplier regarding a specific product, price, and validity period. It is a legally binding document between a customer and a supplier. To create a sales order from a quotation, the quotation line item must have a status of **Released**. A quotation is marked with an item system status of **Quotation** until it is released, and once the quotation is converted to a sales order, the system status of the quotation is changed to **Quotation Accepted**.

Quotations can be determined from sales orders when the sales order is created, or you can create a sales order from a quotation later. The transaction structure of a quotation consists of header and item data, similar to the structure of any other transactions in SAP CRM.

The following are key quotation functions:

- **Sales probability**: The sales probability is the probability of a sales order being created from a quotation. The source of this information is the quotation item category. The success rate of the product can be entered manually in the quotation.

- **Validity**: A quotation has a validity period, similar to a contract. You can configure date management and determine the validity period based on certain rules, or add dates manually based on a customer agreement for a specific product. The quotation price isn't applied to a sales order if the validity period of the quote has expired.

- **Status**: Like any other transaction, a quotation has the system and user statuses at the header and item levels. You configure a status profile and assign it to the transaction type and item category. Whenever a quotation is created, the line item system status is set to **Quotation**. You release the quote item and determine the quote on the sales order. The system status changes to **Quotation Accepted** as soon as the quote is converted into a sales order.

- **Actions**: You can configure an action and assign it to the quotation transaction type as per your business needs. You can trigger a quotation confirmation to the customer or release the quote item based on a certain dollar amount. You can trigger a workflow and send an email to the manager if the quotation amount is beyond a certain value.

- **Availability check**: You can carry out an availability check for a quotation just as you can for a sales order. You have different options with availability checks. The first option is that you can opt out of carrying out an availability check by just not assigning an ATP profile in the quotation item category. Secondly, you have the option of carrying out an availability check by assigning an ATP profile to the quotation item category but not reserving the stock. The availability check, in this case, is checked via simulation, and the configuration of the ATP profile is carried out in APO based on your business needs.

- **Alternative items**: With this, the system provides you with the functionality of selecting a similar product instead of just limiting you to a specific product.

- **Accepting quote**: The item in the business transaction is of the **Quotation** system status. The quotation item can be copied to the sales order item, or it can be converted to the sales order item when you set the status of the item to **Quotation Accepted**. When you set the status of the item to **Quotation Accepted**, the **Quotation** status is removed.

- **Completing quote**: A quotation is deemed complete if the quantity within the quote is consumed by creating the sales order or if the validity of the quote has expired.

- **Approving quote**: SAP has provided a standard workflow template, `10000279` (CRM: Release of Quotations), for quote approval, and this controls the release of quotations. If you want to use the approval process in the transaction type AG (quotation), delivered as standard, you must assign the status profile `CRMQUOTE` to this transaction type.

You can implement the solution based on your business needs; a quotation can be released automatically based on certain conditions, such as "if the quotation net value is less than *$1,000*, then release the quote automatically." In fact, the `WS10001068` (`CRM_O_REL2`) workflow template triggers and releases quotes automatically for any net value less than *$1,000*. Conditions can be configured based on your business requirements to release quotes automatically.

Configuring quotations

Like with sales contracts, the configuration of quotes is done at the header and item levels. The transaction type configuration drives the header data, and the item category configuration drives the item data. *Figure 7.13* shows an example of a quotation (with a transaction type of AG) configuration, displaying the transaction type details and the business transaction categories assigned:

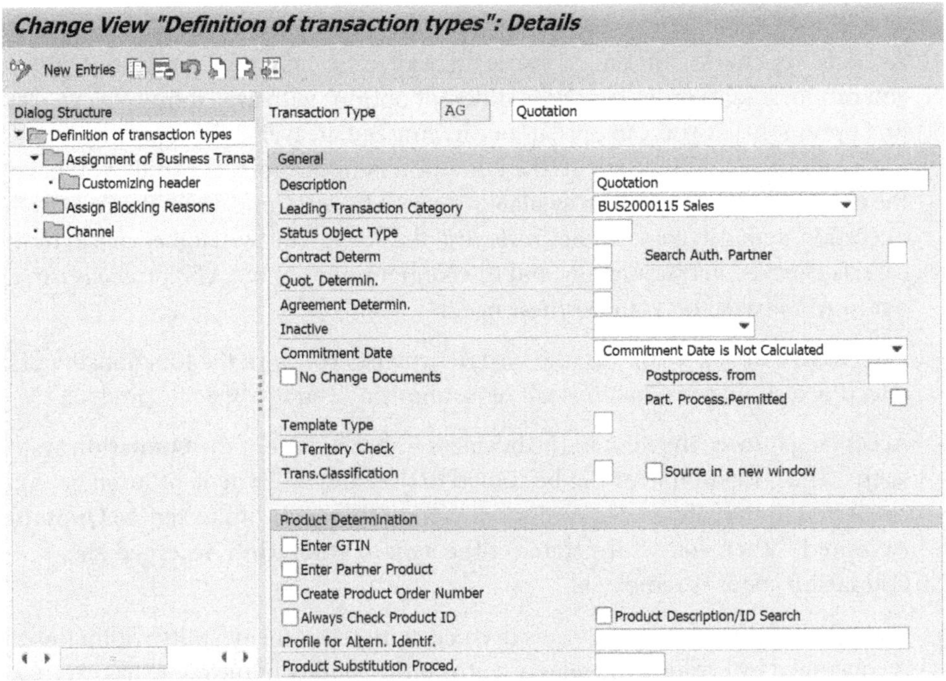

Figure 7.13 – Quotation transaction type definition

The leading business transaction category is assigned as BUS2000115 Sales, and there are various settings that can be configured for product determination, partner determination, date determination, status management, actions, and number range assignment. The configuration details of these profiles were covered in *Chapter 6, Basic Functions in Sales Documents*.

Contract determination, quotation determination, and agreement determination are configured in the sales document to determine contracts, quotations, and agreements when the sales order is created.

The following are a couple more functions within the transaction type configuration:

- **Inactive**: Activating a transaction with the **Inactive** flag blocks the transaction from being created in the CRM system.

- **No Change Document**: Activating the **No Change Document** checkbox will stop logging in the change log for the transaction in the CRM system. It is a good practice to keep this checkbox unflagged so that the change history is logged for any changes made to the document.

Figure 7.14 shows the AG transaction type with its configuration details:

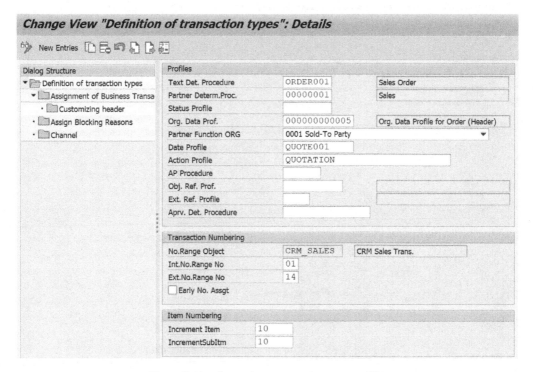

Figure 7.14 – Quotation transaction type profiles

Only certain business transaction categories are assigned to the quotation transaction type. In this case, it is `Sales - BUS2000115` and `Business Activity BUS2000126`. *Figure 7.15* shows the assignment of business transaction categories:

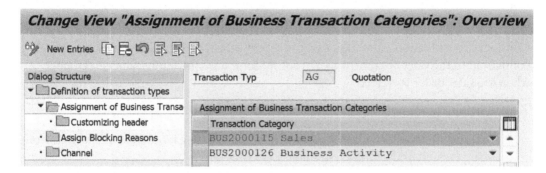

Figure 7.15 – Assignment of business transaction categories

Figure 7.16 shows the header customization details, with configuration options such as **Check PO number**, **Credit Check**, **Rating Profile**, **Propose Order D**, **Text Type**, **Dupl. Check Active**, **Document Pricing Procedure**, and **Payment Data**:

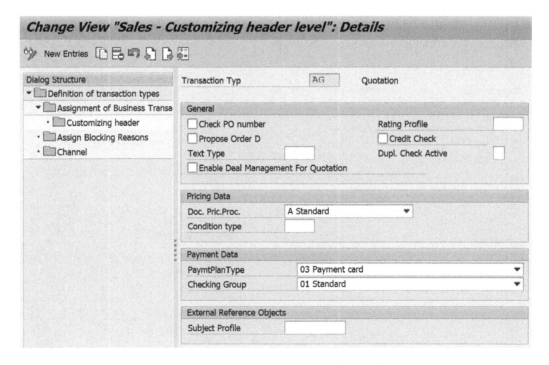

Figure 7.16 – Customizing quotation header data

Configuring item categories

The configuration of the item category level drives the behavior of the item functionality, and the configuration can be different at the header level. You can configure settings such as date profiles, action profiles, partner determination procedures, and much more as per your business needs. The configuration details of these profiles were covered in *Chapter 6, Basic Functions in Sales Documents*.

The object type for the quote item category is the BUS2000131 CRM sales item. Pricing data and quotation data is the most relevant data for quote item configuration.

Figure 7.17 shows the quotation item category configuration details:

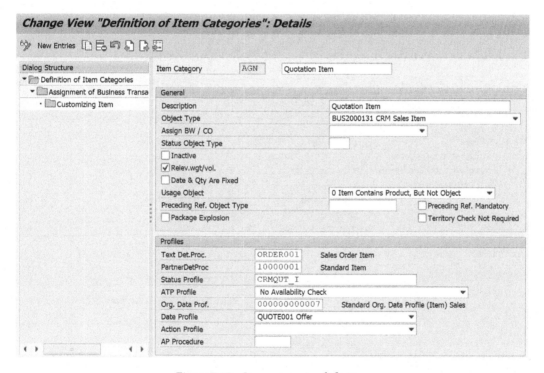

Figure 7.17 – Item categories definition

Figure 7.18 shows the assignment of business transaction categories and the configuration options for sales categories:

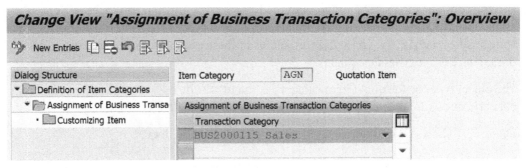

Figure 7.18 – Assignment of business transaction categories

The following screenshot shows the item category configuration details:

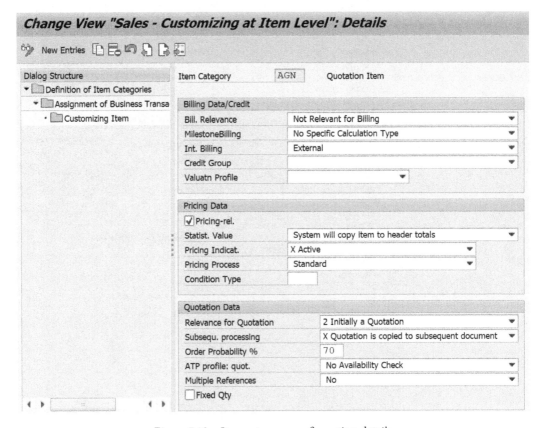

Figure 7.19 – Item category configuration details

The details of the configuration settings are as follows:

- **Pricing-rel**: For pricing to be determined on the quote line item, it is imperative to mark the item category with **Pricing-rel**.

- **Statist. Value**: This provides an option to copy an item's value to the header total; alternatively, you can choose no cumulation based on this configuration option.

- **Pricing Indicator**: Similar to **Pricing-rel**, **Pricing Indicator** needs to be enabled if you want to determine the price on the quotation line item.

- **Pricing Process**: **Pricing Process** helps you to distinguish whether a quotation is free of charge or whether the price is determined on the quotation line item. If it's free of charge, there will automatically be a *100%* discount on the quote line item.

- **Condition Type**: Entering the condition type will allow you to display this condition type in the item **Overview** screen of IC Web Client. This can be edited manually.

- **Relevance for Quotation**: **Relevance for Quotation** determines the system status of the quotation line item, that is, whether it should be a quote item or not. The system status will show **Request for Quotation** if the field is set to **Initially an Inquiry**.

- **Subsequ. processing**: You can control whether the quotation item can be copied to the sales order line item or whether the quotation item can be converted to an order item by resetting the quote status with this configuration option.

- **Multiple References**: This field is to do with whether you will allow multiple orders to refer to one quote or have one order refer to one quote only. If the setting is No, then you can refer only one order to one quote, and if the setting is Yes, you can have multiple orders linked to one quote.

- **Fixed Qty**: If the **Fixed Qty** box is activated, the quantity cannot be changed while the order is created from the quote document via button **create follow-up document** from quote. The configuration option to the multiple reference field is automatically deactivated when the **Fixed Qty** box is activated.

Quotation data exchange

By default, the quotation created in CRM is not transferred to SAP ECC. The document flow of the quotation is not activated. If the quote is transferred from CRM to ECC, the quote is then referenced in ECC and cannot be referenced in CRM. The document flow is updated in both the system and combined business transaction is not supported when transferring the quote from CRM to ECC. To activate the quotation transfer from CRM to ECC, you need to set the middleware parameter QUOTATION_UPLOAD_ACTIVE and a system status (I1055) must be adapted.

Quotation transfer from ECC to CRM

When transferring a quote from ECC to CRM, the quote cannot be changed in SAP CRM and is available for display purposes only.

As we have covered the concepts of quotations and their configuration, let's learn about the concepts of sales orders and their configuration in the following section.

Sales orders

A sales order is a document in SAP CRM that is created for the customer. It shows the customer's interest in buying goods from an organization with a requested sale date specified by the customer. Sales orders are used to track and determine the revenue of a company. You can create sales orders irrespective of sales contracts and quotations, or you can create a sales order that refers to sales contracts or quotations to apply a special price.

Figure 7.20 shows the different places where sales orders can be created in SAP:

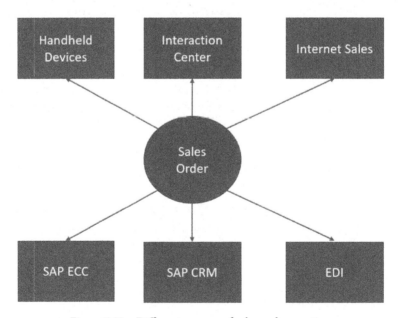

Figure 7.20 – Different sources of sales order creation

These sources are Interaction Center, handheld devices, internet sales, SAP CRM, EDI, and SAP ECC.

The following diagram shows the Quote to Cash process; it states every step, from starting with a quote and converting it to order to finally billing the customer:

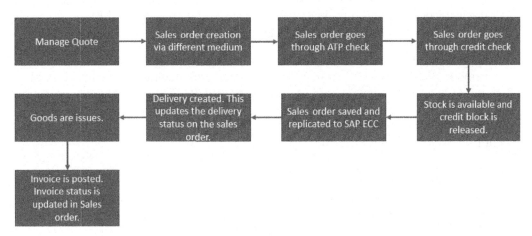

Figure 7.21 – Quote to cash process

When creating a sales order, there are different functionality triggers that are required to fulfill the sales order in a timely manner based on the customer's requested date. Here are the steps that describe the quote to cash process:

1. The quotation is created, and quote prices are determined when the prices are quoted to the customer.

2. The sales order is created through some sort of media, such as EDI, phone, fax, or email. The quote prices are applied to the sales order when the sales order is created.

3. Once the sales order is received, the sales order goes through checks, such as ATP and credit checks.

4. The ATP check looks at whether the product will be available on the date for which the customer has asked for it. The system gives the date back for each line item based on the inventory of that product.

5. The system also goes through a credit check to see whether the customer has paid their dues and whether they have any outstanding dues based on their credit limit. If the customer's credit limit is not sufficient for the sales order value, then the customer sales order goes on credit block and the credit team reviews the order and, if they can, releases the credit block.

6. Once the credit block is removed, the order flows through the downstream process to plan and create delivery and shipments.

7. Once the delivery and shipments are created, the system status of the sales order is updated with the delivery status **Completed**.

8. After the goods are issued and the shipment cost document is created, the customer is invoiced. The invoice document is generated with reference to the delivery document. The invoice status is also updated on the sales order.

Within sales orders, there are several functions. As you may recall, we learned about these functions in *Chapter 6, Basic Functions in Sales Documents*:

- Partner determination
- Organization data determination
- Date management
- Text determination
- Content management
- Status management
- Pricing
- Actions
- Change document
- Archiving
- Incompletion check
- Follow-up documents

These basic functions are also applicable for other CRM transactions, and they can all be configured based on your business needs.

Configuring sales orders

Here is an example of a sales order's (with a transaction type of TA) configuration, showing the transaction type details and the business transaction categories assigned to it. The sales order transaction type definition shown in the screenshot here is similar to any business transaction in SAP CRM:

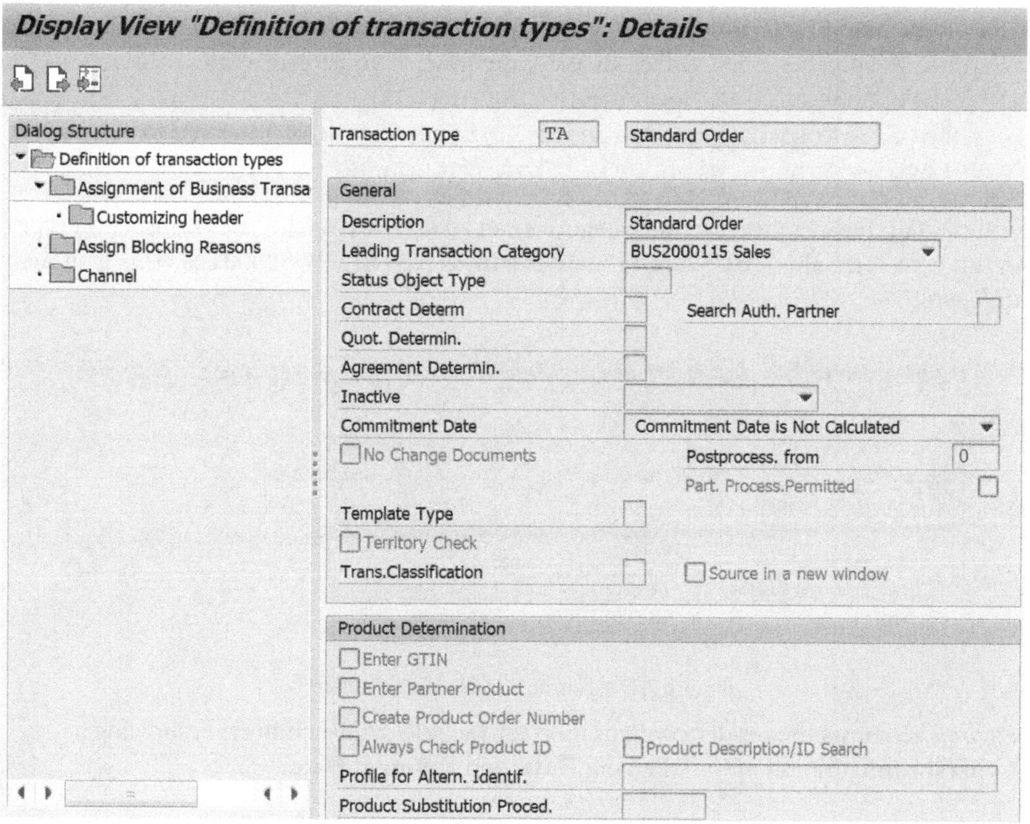

Figure 7.22 – Sales order with a transaction type of TA

Here, the leading business transaction category is set as BUS2000115 Sales. You can configure details such as product determination and number range assignment.

Product determination and the configuration of profiles for a business transaction such as text determination, partner determination, status profiles, org data profiles, date profiles, and action profiles have already been covered in *Chapter 6, Basic Functions in Sales Documents*:

- **Contract Determ**: You can determine contracts based on the settings used for this field. The options are (i) No Contract Determination, (ii) E - Only at Item Level: Assign immediate if Unique, and (iii) F - Only at Item Level: Assign with Selection Option.

- **Quotation Determin.**: Similar to **Contract Determ**, here you can determine the quotation, if one exists. The options are (i) No Quotation Determination, (ii) E - Only at Item Level: Assign immediate if Unique, and (iii) F - Only at Item Level: Assign with Selection Option.

- **Agreement Determin.**: This specifies whether the system should automatically find a sales agreement and makes an assignment when you create a sales transaction. The options are (i) No Agreement Determination, (ii) E - Only at Item Level: Assign immediate if Unique, and (iii) F - Only at Item Level: Assign with Selection Option.

Only certain business transaction categories can be assigned as the sales transaction type; in this case, it is **Sales – BUS2000115** and **Business Activity BUS2000126**. This is shown in *Figure 7.24*:

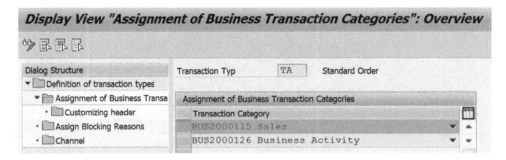

Figure 7.23 – Business transaction categories

Figure 7.25 shows the header configuration for the sales transaction type, showing a **General** configuration option, **Pricing Data**, and **Payment Data**:

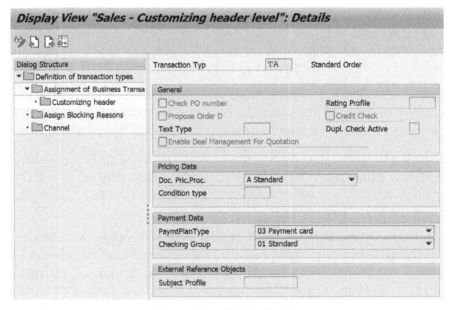

Figure 7.24 – Header details

Here are the header configuration details:

- **Check PO Number**: This check helps to determine whether the same PO number exists for multiple orders. You will receive a warning message on the sales order when the same PO number exists for multiple orders.

- **Propose Order D**: This will set the purchase order date as the order creation date. You can change the date if necessary.

- **Rating Profile**: **Rating Profile** determines the rating procedure assigned to the business partner and checks whether the customer is a high-risk customer while the order is being created. It checks the credit rating of the payer of an order.

- **Credit Check**: If you activate this option, a credit check is performed on the sales order when the order is saved. The credit check functionality works based on the item category settings configuration, that is, Credit Group assignment to the Item category.

- **Duplicate Check Active**: This specifies whether a product can only be entered once in a sales transaction. When the same product is entered several times, you receive a warning message.

- **Enable Deal Management for Quotation**: If you enable this, you can use SAP Price and Margin Management to check existing pricing and agreement data when preparing price quotations for approval.

- **Pricing Data**: A document pricing procedure is used to determine the pricing procedure on a sales order, whereas the condition type field on the pricing data is used when you want to display a specific condition type on the web UI.

- **Payment Data**: If you want to utilize the payment functionality via payment card or cash on delivery, then you need to populate this setting accordingly.

- **Subject Profile**: **Subject Profile** is used to state the reason for a sales order status. For example, if a sales order is rejected, you can state the reason for the rejection status using this.

Now that we've learned about header customization, we'll now look into configuring the item category.

Configuring the item category

Like the transaction type, the sales order item category can be configured to have different behavior at the header level and the item level. This includes settings such as date profiles, action profiles, partner determination procedures, and much more. You can configure item category profiles based on your business needs. The configuration logic and steps were covered in *Chapter 6, Basic Functions in Sales Documents*.

The object type for the sales order item category should be BUS2000131 CRM, with a description of Sales Item. *Figure 7.26* shows the item category configuration details:

Display View "Definition of Item Categories": Details

Dialog Structure		Item Category	TAN	Sales Item

Item Category: TAN — Sales Item

General

Description	Sales Item
Object Type	BUS2000131 CRM Sales Item
Assign BW / CO	
Status Object Type	
☐ Inactive	
☑ Relev.wgt/vol.	
☐ Date & Qty Are Fixed	
Usage Object	0 Item Contains Product, But Not Object
Preceding Ref. Object Type	☐ Preceding Ref. Mandatory
☐ Package Explosion	☐ Territory Check Not Required

Profiles

Text Det.Proc.	ORDER001	Sales Order Item
PartnerDetProc	10000001	Standard Item
Status Profile	CRMORD_I	
ATP Profile	No Availability Check	
Org. Data Prof.	000000000007	Standard Org. Data Profile (Item) Sales
Date Profile		
Action Profile		
AP Procedure		

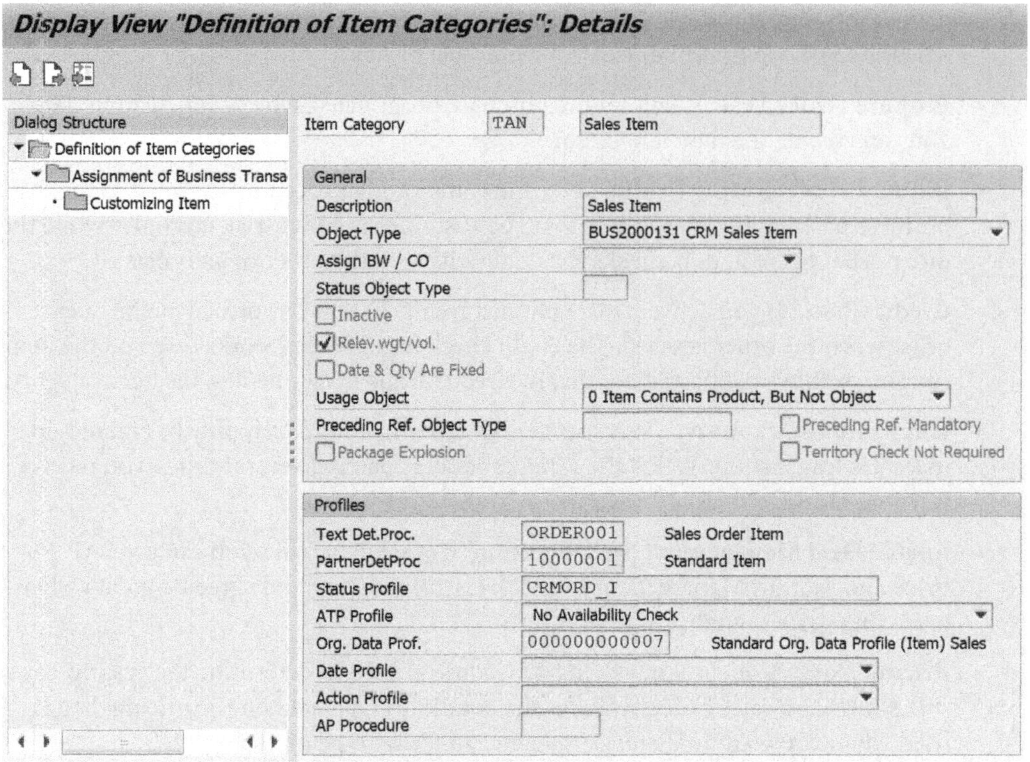

Figure 7.25 – Item category definition

Figure 7.27 shows the item category configuration details with the **Structure** and **Configuration Data** settings required for configurable material:

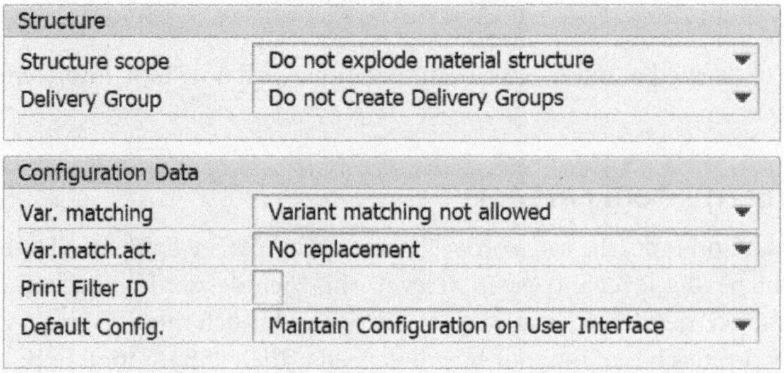

Structure

Structure scope	Do not explode material structure
Delivery Group	Do not Create Delivery Groups

Configuration Data

Var. matching	Variant matching not allowed
Var.match.act.	No replacement
Print Filter ID	
Default Config.	Maintain Configuration on User Interface

Figure 7.26 – Item category definition (2)

Let's review the details of the item category configuration details shown here:

- **Relevant Weight and Volume**: If **Relevant Weight and Volume** is enabled, the system will calculate the weight and volume for each line item from the product master data.

- **Date and Qty are fixed**: Marking **Date and Qty are fixed** keeps the ATP date fixed; so, if you don't want to change the ATP result you got when creating the sales order, mark **Date and Qty are fixed**. For example, if a customer orders a certain product and the ATP result comes back with the available quantity and date and these results are fixed at the schedule line, then the values remain unchanged even after triggering another ATP check. When you run a backorder processing job, these orders won't be picked up to reschedule the line items because they are fixed.

- **ATP Profile**: The way that you configure this decides whether you carry out an availability check. If the ATP check happens in SCM, then the same ATP profile is configured as in the requirement profile in the SAP APO system.

- **Structure Scope**: SAP CRM allows BOM materials to explode, limited to a single-level explosion. There are the following options to choose from: `Do not explode material structure`, `D - Explosion from configuration`, and `A - Single level explosion`. If an item consists of a product with a structure, you can specify whether this structure should be exploded automatically in the business transaction as a main item with one or more sub-items.

- **Delivery Group**: **Delivery Group** helps you to group the main and sub-items in one delivery document.

Figure 7.28 shows the assignment of the business transaction categories. In this case, it is `BUS2000115 Sales`:

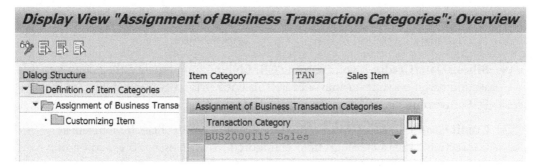

Figure 7.27 – Assignment of business transaction categories

Figure 7.29 shows an item category configuration that includes **Billing Data**, **Pricing Data**, and **Quotation Data** settings:

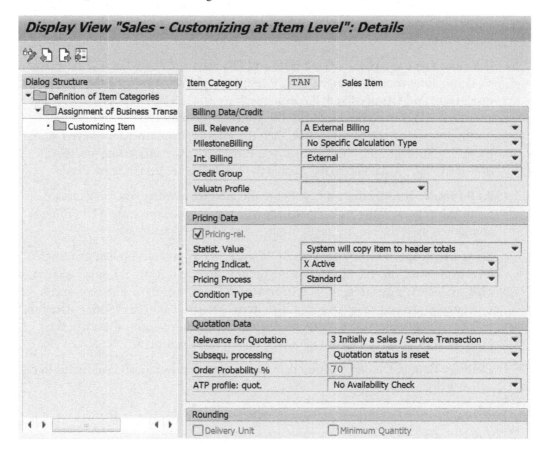

Figure 7.28 – Item category customization

Below is a detailed description of item category customization:

- **Billing Data/Credit**: If you are using CRM billing functionality, then configure this section based on your business needs. This book primarily covers billing in the SAP ECC environment.

- **Credit Group**: **Credit Group** is used to activate a credit check for a business transaction. Once a credit group is configured, you can assign the credit group to the item category.

- **Pricing Data**: **Pricing Data** is used to determine and activate the price in any business transaction.

- **Delivery Unit**: When a quantity is entered at the item level, the system checks whether the quantity is a multiple of the delivery unit. With this indicator, you specify that this quantity should be rounded to the next suitable multiple. The delivery unit for rounding is maintained in the sales area data of the product master data.

- **Minimum Quantity**: If you set the minimum quantity here, the system determines the minimum quantity from the product master. After determining the minimum quantity value from the product master, the system automatically increases the quantity to the minimum quantity on the sales order line item that is given in the product master.

- **Item Category Determination**: This is based on the transaction type, the item category group, and the item category usage. This will determine the main item category, and you can add an alternate item category based on your business needs. Here is the path to use to configure this: **SPRO| Customer Relationship Management| Transactions| Basic Settings| Define Item Category Determination**.

  Here is a screenshot that shows some item category determination configuration details:

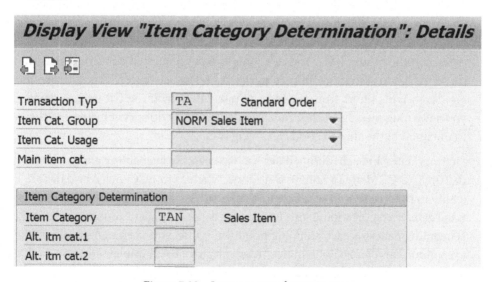

Figure 7.29 – Item category determination

This completes our look at the steps involved in item category configuration. Let's now look at the additional functionality offered by sales orders.

Additional sales order functionality

Here are some details about the additional functionality that can be implemented with sales orders based on business needs:

- **Partner/Product Checks**: Partner product ranges identify the set of products that can be sold to a specific customer for a specific period of time. This can also be set at the sales org level. In addition to this, partner product ranges also allow you to prevent certain products from being sold to certain customers. Exclusion is controlled by the exclusion flag for a partner/product range. The exclusion flag indicates that the products contained therein cannot be sold to the listed business partners during the validity period.

- **Shipping Functions**: Shipping-related functions are functions that are used for delivering goods to the customer. These functions are derived from the sales order fields related to shipping data. They are as follows:

  a). **Proposing Requested Delivery Date**: This value is entered at the sales order header level and is configured within date management as one of the date types. The customer places the sales order and asks for the order to be delivered on a delivery date. The requested delivery date is entered at the header level manually and the confirmed schedule lines are determined based on the requested delivery date entered at the header level. You can configure the requested delivery date within the date type to assign the **Ship-to party** as a reference object. This will take the goods receiving hours from the **Ship-to party** to default the **GR time** and will give you a warning message if the requested delivery date doesn't come within the days maintained in the ship to goods receiving hours.

  Delivery dates and scheduling dates such as material availability and goods issue date in SAP CRM are in Ship to time zone, whereas in ECC, delivery dates are in a Ship to time zone, and schedule line dates such as material availability date, goods issue date, transportation date, and loading date are in plant time zone. To make the scheduling dates for each shipping point time zone, you need to manually make this exception. This can be done in the order exchange BAdI implementation so that the correct time zone is propagated to the downstream process.

  b). **Grouping Sales Order Items for Delivery**: You can group sales order line items for delivery using one delivery document. You can control this functionality based on your customer master data setup. There are two fields in the customer master data (Sold-to party), which are **Delivery Control** and **Delivery Control Item**, where you can set whether you want partial delivery or complete delivery of the sales order for this specific customer.

If the **Delivery Control** field is set to B - Complete delivery and **Delivery Control Item** is set to C - Complete Delivery, then all products in the sales order will be grouped under one delivery and the delivery will be created when all items are available to deliver. The delivery group date is set when the delivery is created and the customer is marked for **Complete Delivery** flag. You can also configure other settings, such as One Time Delivery for **Delivery Control Item**; this will allow you to just create one delivery for the delivery group date that is based on the latest schedule line date on the sales order line item.

c). **Carrier and Means of Transport**: Transportation data on the sales order is determined from the system used for the ATP check. If the ATP check happens from ECC, then the sales order transportation data is derived from ECC, and if the ATP check happens using the SAP APO system, then the transportation data on the CRM sales system is derived from the SAP APO system. The carrier on the sales order can be configured as one of the partner functions. Means of transport options are derived from the ATP calling system. If you enter the means of transport manually, then the sales order ATP check is triggered, which is used to schedule the shipment.

- **Availability Checks**: Availability checks are carried out based on the system middleware parameters that declare whether you want an availability check to be carried out in ECC or SCM. Once that is determined, you need to configure the item category by assigning the ATP profile to call either ECC or SCM to carry out the availability check. More details on availability checks and their configuration are covered in *Chapter 8, Order Fulfillment with SAP APO*.

- **Triggering Third-Party Orders from the Sales Order**: You can configure the item category in CRM to bypass the ATP check, and you can configure the schedule line category assigned to the item category in SAP ECC. This triggers a third-party process and creates purchase requisition and PO from the sales order replicated in SAP ECC. Bypassing the ATP check on the CRM item category can be done by not assigning the ATP profile to the item category in SAP CRM.

Now that we have covered the concepts of the sales order and its configuration, let's learn how data exchange for sales transactions occurs from the CRM system to the ERP system.

Data exchange for sales transactions from CRM to ERP systems

Sales orders created in CRM are replicated to the backend ECC system. Once a sales order is replicated to ECC, it is further processed to execute the delivery, shipment, and invoicing. Once a sales order is delivered and invoiced, the system statuses for delivery and invoicing are also replicated/updated to the CRM system.

The prerequisite for sales order replication is the configuration of the transaction type and item category in the CRM and ECC systems. Once the configuration is complete, the replication between CRM and ECC can occur. We'll now look at different data exchange scenarios.

Standard data exchange scenario

The standard scenario corresponds to the delivered data exchange scenario. If no different scenario is activated in the CRMPAROLTP table, the standard scenario is active by default. The following are some key points to consider if you keep the system settings as they are and do not enter any scenarios in the CRMPAROLTP CRM table:

- You can transfer sales transactions from CRM Enterprise to the ERP system using CRM middleware.

- The orders created in the SAP CRM system are replicated to the ECC system. If you change an order in ECC that was created in SAP CRM, then the changes will not be replicated back to the CRM system. This may cause inconsistency in the transaction data between ECC and CRM.

- You can create sales orders with reference to quotations and trigger subsequent processes for orders in the ERP system.

- You can create quotations and sales orders in the ERP system that are transferred to SAP CRM. The documents are only displayed in the CRM system; they cannot be edited. Any further changes to the orders created in the ERP system are replicated to the CRM system, where they can be viewed but cannot be edited.

- You can use the distribution status of the transaction to check whether the transfer to the ERP system was successful. Error messages regarding the transfer are displayed in the application log.

With that, we have covered the standard data exchange scenario; now let's look into the interdependent change scenario.

Interdependent change scenario

In the interdependent change scenario, you can create, edit, and change orders in both the ERP system and the CRM system. Interdependent changes are also commonly referred to as **scenario A**. This scenario was made available by SAP in ERP release 4.7 and CRM release 4.0.

Here are the settings you need to configure to activate the interdependent change scenario:

Settings in CRM Enterprise: Table SMOFPARSFA

- Key: R3A_SALES
- Parameter name 1: INT_CHANGE_ORDER
- Parameter name 2: <sales document type>, for example, TA
- Parameter value 1: A, for activating the scenario for interdependent changes for <sales document type>
- Parameter value 2: A, for APO activation

Settings in the ERP system: Table CRMPAROLTP

- Parameter name: CRM_SCENARIO
- Parameter name 2: INT_CHANGE_ORDER
- Parameter name 3: <sales document type>, for example, TA
- Parameter value: A, for activating scenario A for <sales document type>

Certain restrictions apply when you activate scenario A. Please consider the following points before activating this functionality:

- Billing is only possible in the ERP system and not with CRM billing.
- The use of rebate conditions is not supported.
- The use of objects is not supported.
- Credit approval and rejection, as well as new credit checks, can only take place in one system. This can be either SAP CRM or the ERP system.
- Availability approval from SAP CRM with SAP APO is not supported. Therefore, a rules-based availability check in SAP APO is not possible either. You can only perform an availability check in the ERP system.
- Maintenance of combined business transactions (that is, where quotations and order items are in one transaction) is not supported by the ERP system. You can only transfer business transactions that contain either only order items or only quotation items.

With that, we have covered the interdependent change scenarios and the parameters required to activate scenario A.

Summary

This chapter covered sales contracts, quotations, and sales order creation in SAP CRM. It covered various functionality around transaction types and item category configurations for these transactions. Each of these transactions covered basic functionality, including partner determination, date determination, status management, action profile configuration, and additional sales order functions. You have learned how business transactions in CRM work and the key functional definition of the quote to cash process. In this chapter, you learned how to create a sales order and learned about all the steps required for successful sales order creation in SAP CRM.

This chapter also provided an overview of the data exchange between CRM and ECC, with coverage of the configuration steps involved. Having an understanding of all these concepts will make it easier for you to understand the next chapter.

Our next chapter covers various scenarios to do with order fulfillment strategy, including basic ATP check methods and advanced ATP check methods. It also covers key features on the backorder processing functions.

Further reading

- Additional information on quotation processing can be found at `https://help.sap.com/viewer/93a1da74776e46c4bae4b5e2cab68bad/7.0.4.15/en-US/aaf2e8539b0e424de10000000a174cb4.html`.

- Additional information on sales order processing can be found at `https://help.sap.com/viewer/93a1da74776e46c4bae4b5e2cab68bad/7.0.4.15/en-US/2dc65b65ad154dc3a8eecc4bb982e9e0.html`.

8
Order Fulfillment with SAP APO

This chapter covers how order fulfillment is executed in SAP **Advanced Planner and Optimizer** (**APO**). When a customer places an order with a customer-requested date, the system should be able to fulfill the customer's demand. This means the product should be available for the date they have requested. To fulfill the order, the system runs an **Available to Promise** (**ATP**) check. This chapter describes the complete functionality around how ATP works to fulfill customer requirements with SAP APO. This chapter also covers understanding the different options of an ATP check when triggering it from a sales order created in SAP CRM. In order to work through order fulfillment, it is important to understand the different options that are available to run an ATP check on a sales order. To confirm the order on the correct date, the planners need to work on getting or reshuffling orders based on the requested date on the sales order.

Here is a list of the topics covered in this chapter:

- Availability check overview
- SAP CRM order integration with global ATP
- General settings to activate an ATP check in SAP APO
- GATP basic methods

- GATP advanced methods
- Transportation and scheduling with GATP
- Backorder processing

By the end of the chapter, you will understand CRM order integration with SAP APO and different options to configure ATP methods to fulfill customer demand.

Availability check overview

An availability check is a very important function within sales order processing. When a customer places an order, the order makes a check to see whether the material is available in stock. Based on the inventory position, the system derives the date when the material can be shipped out. This date is then communicated to the customer as part of the order confirmation. The confirmed delivery date can be the same as the date that the customer asks for or it can be a lead time date of when that product can be produced and shipped. Many times, an organization promises getting the item shipped on time to customers and very often they are unable to get the products to the customer on time because of availability issues.

In an SAP CRM Interaction Center scenario (described in *Chapter 7*, *Sales Document Processing in SAP CRM*), the customer calls a **Customer Service Representative** (**CSR**) to place an order. The CSR enters the product, quantity, and requested delivery date, and as soon as the CSR hits *Enter*, the ATP check is performed and CRM gets the confirmed quantities back from APO. Orders created in the SAP CRM system undergo an ATP check to see whether the ordered products are available and based on the availability check, the requirements are transferred to the availability check leading system (ECC or APO). Once the order is saved in CRM, it is replicated to SAP ECC for further processing. This flow is shown in the following diagram:

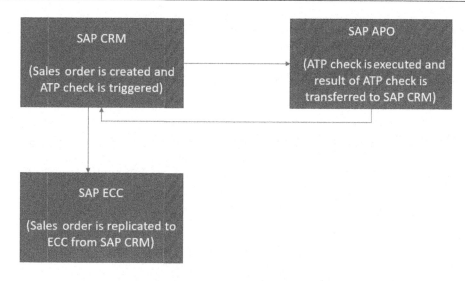

Figure 8.1 – ATP check flow between SAP CRM and SAP APO

By default, the system does the backward scheduling and if the product is not available on the requested material availability date, then the system executes the forward scheduling. *Figure 8.2* shows a depiction of backward scheduling and forward scheduling:

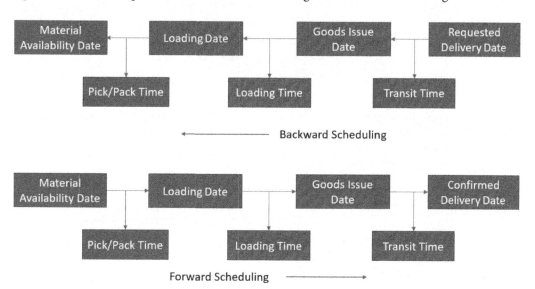

Figure 8.2 – Backward scheduling and forward scheduling

In backward scheduling, the system goes backward from the requested delivery date to the material availability date and checks whether the material is available on that day. If the material is not available on the material availability date, then it checks when the material is available. It then runs the forward scheduling from that day to determine the confirmed delivery date.

SAP CRM order integration with global ATP

Orders created in SAP CRM undergo an ATP check that is based on the configuration in SAP CRM. The configuration within SAP CRM determines which system is the leading system to run the ATP check. This could be the SAP APO or SAP ERP system. *Figure 8.3* shows a diagrammatic representation of an availability check being carried out via the SAP ERP and SAP APO systems:

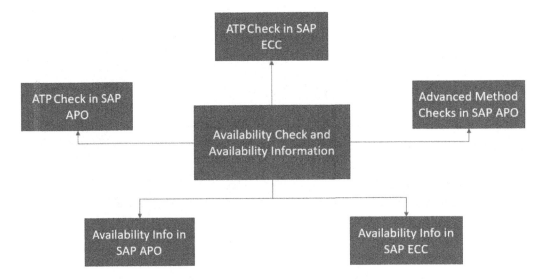

Figure 8.3 – Availability check overview

Let's examine each of these scenarios in detail in the following subsections.

Availability check using APO

A manufacturer or supplier using the SAP APO system would mostly leverage the ATP check functionality on a sales order using **Global Available to Promise (GATP)**. SAP CRM is connected to SAP SCM and BAPI calls are triggered to carry out ATP, shipment scheduling, and transportation scheduling on the sales order line items created from the SAP CRM system.

Using SAP APO compared to SAP ERP for triggering an ATP check has many advantages, one being advanced ATP check methods where you can run different methods to run an ATP check based on your business needs. An APO ATP delivery proposal screen can be called from SAP CRM by manually triggering the availability check button from an SAP CRM sales order.

When working with SAP CRM, there are two possible options provided by SAP for an ATP check from CRM using the SAP APO system, which are availability check and planning with SAP APO and availability check in SAP APO and planning in SAP ERP.

Availability check and planning in APO (direct update scenario)

In this scenario, a sales order is created in the SAP CRM system and ATP and planning are carried out in the APO system. The order is replicated to the ERP system and there is no communication happening between the SAP APO and SAP ERP systems.

Here are the steps for carrying out an ATP check and planning occurrence in APO:

1. Create an order in SAP CRM via the Interaction Center. Enter the requested delivery date with the products and quantity.

2. Once you enter a requested delivery date, products, and quantity, the APO system is called. The quantity ordered resides in temporary quantity assignments in the APO system. The results come back to the CRM system.

3. The order is saved. The transfer of the requirements happens on order save in SAP CRM and the material planning is passed to the APO system. It also releases the temporary quantity assignment in SAP APO.

4. The order is replicated to the ERP system. There is no data transfer happening from the SAP ERP system to the SAP SCM system.

This completes our understanding of the direct scenario. Now, let's understand the triangle scenario.

Availability check in SAP APO and planning in SAP ERP (triangle scenario)

In this scenario, requirements are posted when orders are created from CRM and when an order is replicated to the ECC system, the materials planning is executed from ECC to the SCM system.

Here are the steps to perform an ATP check in APO and planning occurrence in the SAP ECC system:

1. Create an order in SAP CRM via the Interaction Center. Enter the requested delivery date with the products and quantity.

2. Once you enter the requested delivery date, products, and quantity, the APO system is called. The quantity ordered resides in temporary quantity assignments in the APO system. The results come back to the CRM system.

3. The order is saved and replicated in the ERP system.

4. ATP triggers in SAP ECC and the sales order in ECC picks up the results from TQA in SAP APO.

5. The order is saved in ECC and the requirements/material planning is passed to the APO system as soon as the order is saved in the ECC system.

SAP recommends using the direct update scenario rather than the triangle scenario, that is, transferring requirements from SAP CRM to SAP APO, rather than doing it from SAP ECC. One of the reasons why SAP recommends this option is that planning in SAP APO is the most efficient approach. SAP has provided the BADI `CRM_CHANGE_DFLT_SCEN` template for changing the valuation of scenarios/procedures if you want to execute planning in the SAP ERP system after orders are replicated to ECC.

Availability check using ECC

A customer can carry out an availability check in ECC when they don't use the APO system. In this case, the ATP check and material requirements planning happen in ECC.

When you enter a line item in a CRM sales order, an RFC call to ECC happens, an ATP check is performed, and the reservation of stock is performed with transportation and shipping scheduling.

The SAP ERP system transfers the results back to the SAP CRM system. Some of the ATP trigger points are changing the quantity, changing the requested delivery date, changing the schedule line, and removing the cancelation reason code when the order is created from CRM.

Here are the configuration steps required to set up an ATP call from CRM to the ECC system.

In SAP ERP, you must activate the **Business Transaction Events (BTEs)** for the availability check using SAP ERP. To set this flag in SAP ERP, do the following:

1. Enter transaction FIBF.

2. Choose **Settings | Identification | SAP Applications**.

3. Enable the CRMATP application.

In SAP ERP, the material does not need to be relevant for the availability check with SAP APO. The following screenshot shows the BTEs active for an availability check in SAP ECC:

Figure 8.4 – BTE Application Indicator

In the CRM system, the following is the configuration path to activate an ATP call from CRM to ECC: SAP Customer Relationship Management under **Basic Functions | Availability Check | Availability Check Using SAP ECC | Define Middleware Parameters: Availability Check Using SAP ECC**

Enter the middleware parameters as follows:

-   **Key**: R3A_COMMON.

-   **Parameter 1**: CRM_DEFAULT_DESTINATION.

-   **Parameter 2**: CRM_R3MATERIAL_AVAIL.

-   **RFC Destination**: <RFC destination>.

-   **Control Information**: X=R/3<x.yz>; for example, X=R/36.10.<x.yz> stands for the SAP ECC release. In this example, the SAP ECC release is 6.10. If you omit the X in the **Control Information** field, SAP ECC is not activated.

The scheduling dates in an SAP CRM sales order are in ship to time zone whereas the scheduling dates, such as material availability dates, goods issue date, and loading date, are a shipping point time zone.

ATP configuration in SAP CRM with an ATP check in SAP APO

The following are the configurations required to set up an ATP call from SAP CRM to SAP APO for a scenario availability check and planning in APO:

1. Activate the availability check.

2. In this step, you perform an availability check using SAP APO.

    The following screenshot shows the setting to activate an availability check using SAP APO:

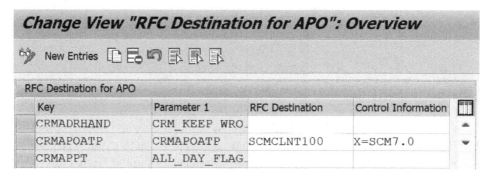

Figure 8.5 – Middleware parameters – availability check using SAP APO

    To configure the settings, go to SAP CRM with the following menu path: **Basic Functions | Availability Check | Availability Check Using SAP APO | Define Middleware Parameters: Availability Check Using SAP APO**

3. Define the ATP profile.

4. The following screenshot shows defining an ATP profile with the **No Availability Check** and **Availability Check in the SAP APO System** options:

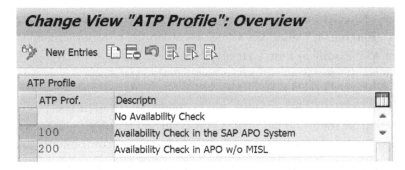

Figure 8.6 – Defining the ATP profile

You define the ATP profile with the following IMG path: **Customer Relationship Management | Basic Functions | Availability Check | Availability Check Using SAP APO | Define ATP Profile**

5. Configure the item category in SAP CRM.

6. In this step, you need to configure the item category to assign the ATP profile configured in the previous step.

    The following screenshot shows the assignment of the ATP profile to the item category:

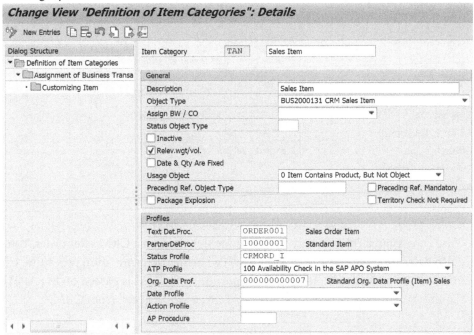

Figure 8.7 – Assigning the ATP profile to the transaction type

You define the item category using the **Customer Relationship Management | Basic Functions | Availability Check | Availability Check Using SAP APO | Assign ATP Profile to Item Category** path.

7. Maintain the requirement profile configuration in SAP APO.

    In this step, you need to configure and maintain the requirements profile in SAP APO using the following path: **SPRO | Advanced Planning and Optimization | General Settings | Requirements Profile | Maintain Requirements Profile**

    The following screenshot shows the ATP requirements profile configuration in SAP APO:

Change View "Maintain Requirements Profile (ATP)": Details

⌕⁷᠈⁷   New Entries 🗋 🗟 🔄 🗋 🗋 🗟

| Reqmts prfl | 100 | CRM ATP Check |

Maintain Requirements Profile (ATP)

Category	BM
Order Header Cat.	
Check Mode	
Business Event	A
Assignment Mode	No assignment ▼
TQA Type	E Write both internal and external temporary objects ▼
Validity TQAs	
Tech. Scenario	
Business Trans.	
RS for Initial Locat.	
Scheduling Ind.	A Execute Scheduling ▼
Preselection Substns	☐
RS for Supplier C.Loc.	

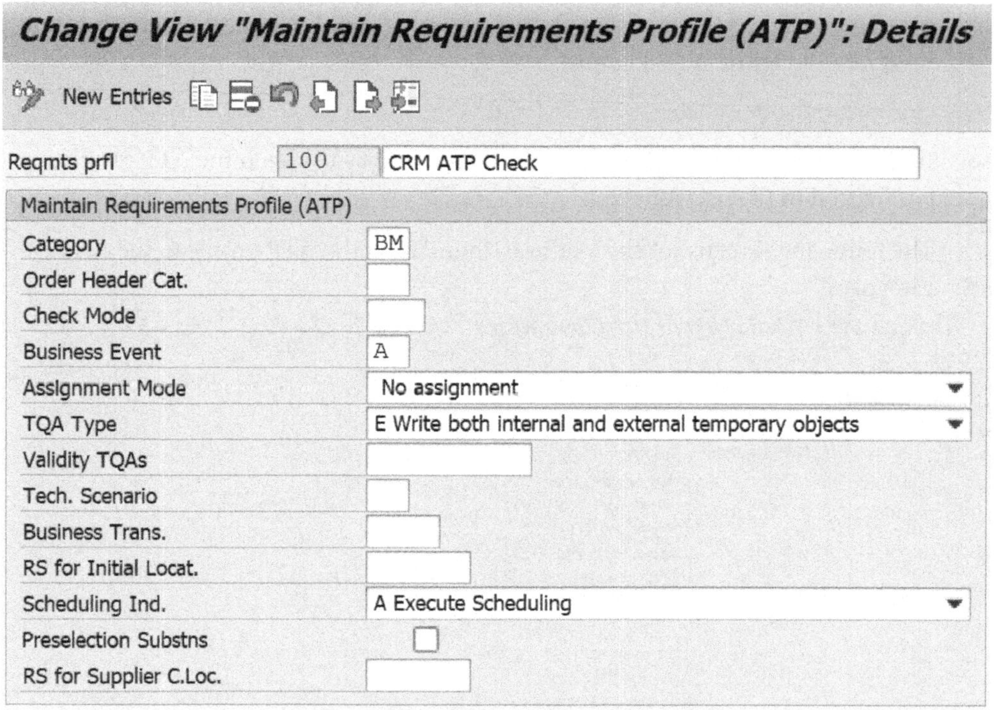

Figure 8.8 – Maintain Requirements Profile

You can assign a rule strategy to determine the plant on a CRM sales order. You can also determine the plant in SAP CRM via a partner determination procedure based on your business needs. The partner determined in CRM is passed on to SAP APO in the ATP field catalog via the BAPI_APOATP_CHECK call from CRM.

Once the aforementioned configuration is completed in SAP CRM and the SAP APO system, the ATP check from the CRM sales order will call SAP APO to get the ATP results from SAP APO.

Additional information around CRM order integration with ATP

To identify which ATP scenario exists in CRM sales order table, the following additional information is useful for you to know. It helps to identify whether the ATP is a direct update scenario or a triangle scenario and whether the order originated in CRM or ECC.

The additional information CRM_SCENARIO_CON identifies 10 possible scenario types based on the different field positions that are shown in the SCENARIO identity of the CRMD_ORDERADM_H table when the order is created in CRM.

The following screenshot shows the SCENARIO field, where you can see what ATP scenario is in the CRMD_ORDERADM_H CRM sales order header table:

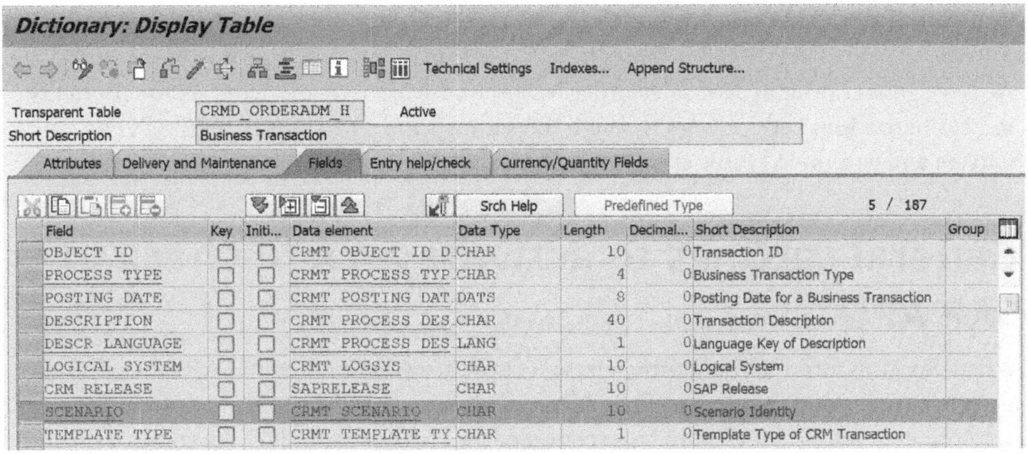

Figure 8.9 – SCENARIO identity in the CRMD_ORDERADM_H table

The next screenshot shows the Business Scenario field for one of the order examples, showing AA in the CRMD_ORDERADM_H CRM sales order header table:

Group description	Cell Content
SAP Release	BBPCRM 713
Business Scenario	AA
Templ. Type	

Figure 8.10 – Business Scenario identity

The `Business Scenario` field in the order header table identifies the ATP scenario and identifies whether the sales order was originally created in SAP CRM or the ECC system. The field length is *10* and the `CRM_SCENARIO_CON` program helps to understand each position definition.

By default, SAP CRM is configured to use a direct update ATP scenario and, based on the standard data exchange scenario, you can create an order either in ECC or CRM.

In *Figure 8.10*, `Business Scenario` has `AA`. The first letter is an indication of the ATP scenario:

- `A` stands for direct update scenario.
- Blank stands for triangle scenario.

The second letter is an indication of where the document originates:

- `A` stands for the document is created in CRM.
- `B` stands for the document is created in SD/FI.
- `C` stands for the document is created in Mobile Client.

We have gone through CRM sales order integration with SAP APO and its functionality and configuration. Let's now go through the settings and functions in SAP APO to activate and run the ATP functionality successfully.

General settings to activate an ATP check in SAP APO

When working through integrating an ATP check from SAP CRM to SAP APO, there are settings required to be set in SAP APO apart from the ATP profile in CRM and the requirements profile in APO. In this section of the chapter, we will cover some of the basic configuration that is mandatory for an ATP check to work from SAP CRM to SAP APO.

Maintaining global settings for an availability check

The first step is to maintain the global settings for an availability check in SAP APO.

Figure 8.11 shows the configuration for both global settings:

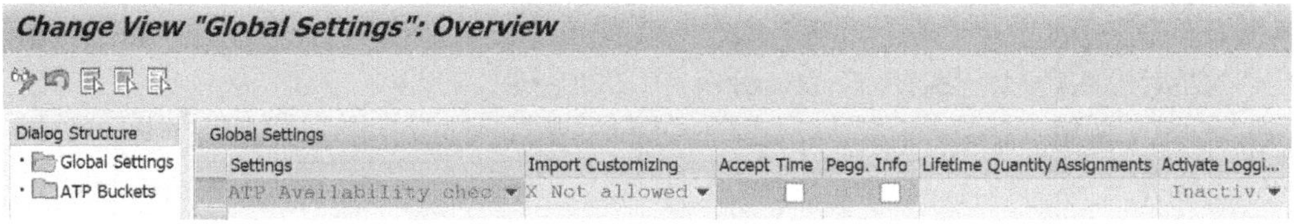

Figure 8.11 – ATP global settings

Here, you maintain the settings to import customizing data using the CIF integration model in the connected ECC system. You have the option of `Allowed/Not allowed`. *Figure 8.12* shows ATP buckets where you define the ATP bucket parameters:

Figure 8.12 – ATP buckets

Here, you specify the ATP buckets created per day. The standard value is 1.

The following is the configuration path to configure the ATP global settings: **SAP - Implementation Guide | Advanced Planning and Optimization | Global Available-to-Promise (Global ATP) | General Settings | Maintain Global Settings for Availability Check**

Maintaining the category

Categories are the scope check considered during ATP checking. Here you configure the category type, which can be **0 Stock**, **1 Receipts**, **2 Requirement**, or **3 Forecast**. These are equivalent to the MRP elements in SAP ECC. You can also see the relevant mapping of **R/3 Object** in this configuration. For non-SAP environments, you can also create non-SAP categories in this configuration. SAP also provides special ATP categories for purchase orders. If you activate any of these special ATP categories, the system uses them instead of the corresponding SAP categories.

Figure 8.13 shows an example of the AA category with the **1 Receipts** category type and **6 Production Order** R/3 object:

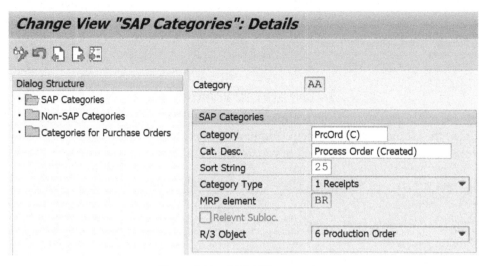

Figure 8.13 – SAP ATP categories

You can configure category settings at the following given path: **SAP - Implementation Guide | Advanced Planning and Optimization | Global Available-to-Promise (Global ATP) | General Settings | Maintain Category**

Business events

A **business event** is used to identify the type of business transaction executed during an ATP check. A business event could be a sales order, delivery, or **Backorder Processing** (**BOP**). This is shown in *Figure 8.14*:

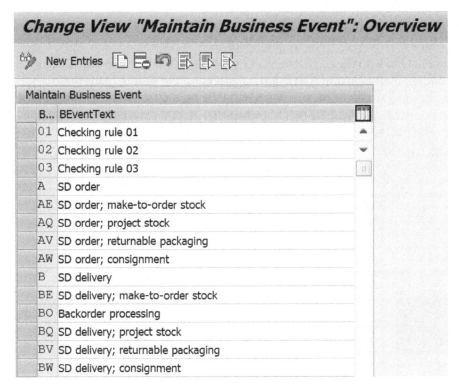

Figure 8.14 – Maintain Business Event

A business event is used during ATP check control and check instructions. Here is the configuration path to define a business event: **SAP - Implementation Guide | Advanced Planning and Optimization | Global Available-to-Promise (Global ATP) | General Settings | Maintain Business Event**

Check mode

Check mode corresponds to the requirement class in the SAP ECC system. The requirement type with the requirement class is transferred from SAP ECC at runtime. The check mode is maintained in the material master and the system reads the check mode from the product master. Check mode can also be used to control whether you want to execute a **Capable-to-Promise (CTP)** or **Multilevel ATP (MATP)** check in production. You can also use check mode to control which procedure the system should use for rounding. *Figure 8.15* shows the requirement class determination in SAP ECC:

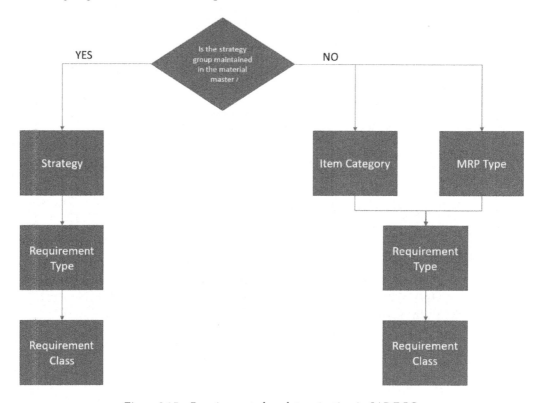

Figure 8.15 – Requirement class determination in SAP ECC

The strategy group is maintained in the material master in ECC. The strategy group is assigned with a requirement type and the requirement type has the requirement class assignment. That is how the requirement type and requirement class are determined in a transaction. If the strategy group is not maintained in the material master in ECC, the requirement type and the relevant requirement class are determined based on the MRP group. If the MRP group is not maintained on the material master, then the requirement type and the relevant requirement class are determined based on the item category and MRP type.

The following screenshot shows the configuration for maintaining check mode:

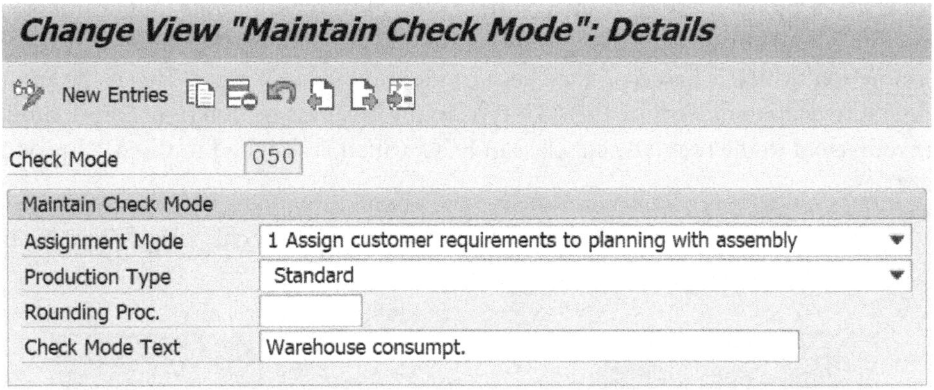

Figure 8.16 – Maintain Check Mode

Figure 8.17 shows the check mode in the APO product master data and this can be accessed via Transaction code /SAPAPO/MAT1 under ATP view:

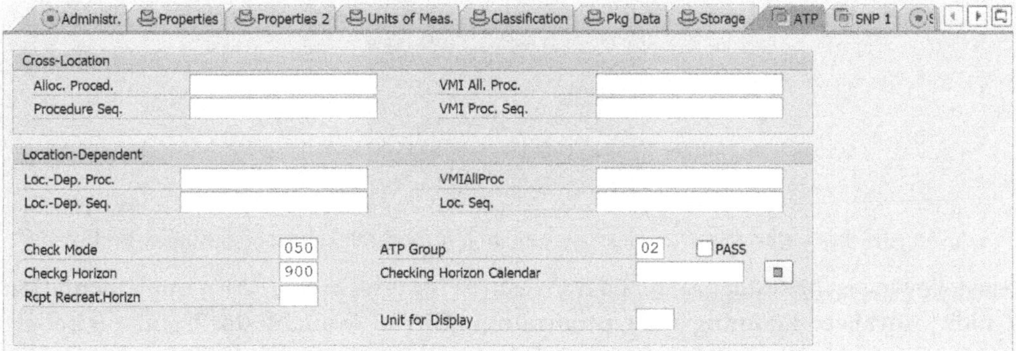

Figure 8.17 – Check mode in APO master data

Here is the path to configure check mode: **SAP - Implementation Guide | Advanced Planning and Optimization | Global Available-to-Promise (Global ATP) | General Settings | Maintain Check Mode**

Check instructions

Check instructions are derived from a combination of the check mode and business events. The complete behavior of the transaction is dependent on the check instructions determination, which is based on the check mode and business event. This is the key configuration step to determine the ATP type in the business transaction. Check mode is the equivalent to the requirement class in ECC, which is assigned in the APO product master.

Figure 8.18 shows the determination of check instructions from check mode and business events:

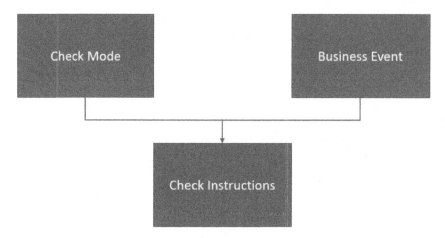

Figure 8.18 – Check instructions determination from check mode and business events

The following is the configuration path to define a business event: **SAP - Implementation Guide | Advanced Planning and Optimization | Global Available-to-Promise (Global ATP) | General Settings | Maintain Check Instructions**

The next screenshot shows the configuration to maintain check instructions:

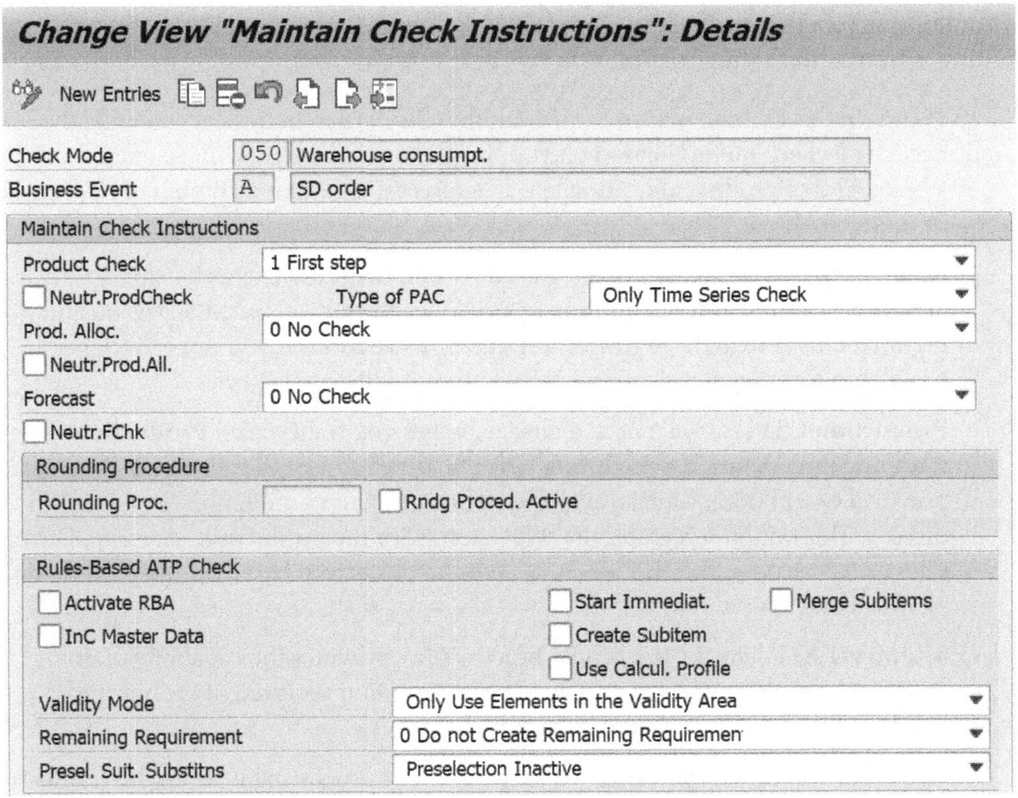

Change View "Maintain Check Instructions": Details

New Entries

| Check Mode | 050 | Warehouse consumpt. |
| Business Event | A | SD order |

Maintain Check Instructions

Product Check	1 First step
☐ Neutr.ProdCheck	Type of PAC	Only Time Series Check
Prod. Alloc.	0 No Check
☐ Neutr.Prod.All.	
Forecast	0 No Check
☐ Neutr.FChk	

Rounding Procedure

| Rounding Proc. | | ☐ Rndg Proced. Active |

Rules-Based ATP Check

☐ Activate RBA   ☐ Start Immediat.   ☐ Merge Subitems
☐ InC Master Data   ☐ Create Subitem
                        ☐ Use Calcul. Profile

Validity Mode	Only Use Elements in the Validity Area
Remaining Requirement	0 Do not Create Remaining Requiremen
Presel. Suit. Substitns	Preselection Inactive

Figure 8.19 – Maintain Check Instructions

The following screenshot shows **Production**, **Multilevel ATP Check**, and **Third-Party Order Processing** in the check instructions configuration:

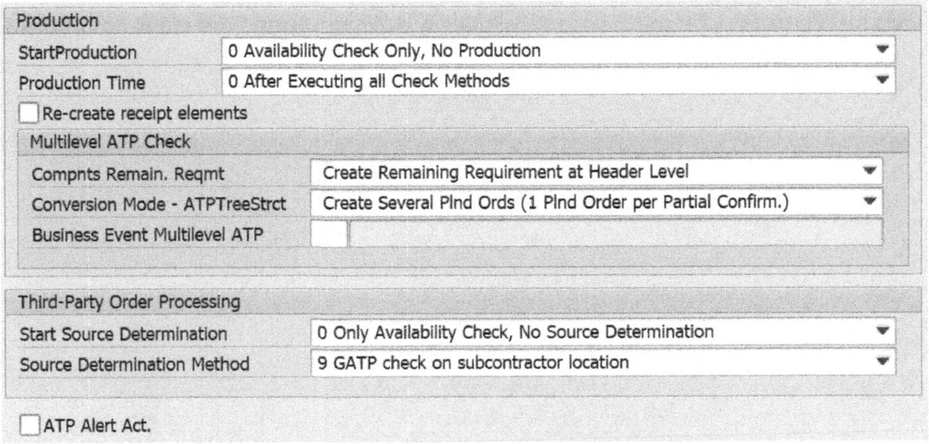

Production

StartProduction	0 Availability Check Only, No Production
Production Time	0 After Executing all Check Methods
☐ Re-create receipt elements	

Multilevel ATP Check

Compnts Remain. Reqmt	Create Remaining Requirement at Header Level
Conversion Mode - ATPTreeStrct	Create Several Plnd Ords (1 Plnd Order per Partial Confirm.)
Business Event Multilevel ATP	

Third-Party Order Processing

| Start Source Determination | 0 Only Availability Check, No Source Determination |
| Source Determination Method | 9 GATP check on subcontractor location |

☐ ATP Alert Act.

Figure 8.20 – Maintaining check instructions

The following provides an overview for each of the key ATP functionality you can control via check instruction configuration:

- **Maintain Check Instructions**: In **Maintain Check Instructions**, you define the basic ATP check method based on your business requirements. You can activate a basic ATP or product allocation check, a forecast check, or a combination of each of these checks.

- **Rules-Based ATP Check**: A **Rule-Based Availability** (**RBA**) check helps determine the location substitution or product substitution based on the business requirements. You activate RBA in the check instructions if you want to trigger product or location substitution based on the condition table rule.

- **Production CTP**: A CTP check defines whether you want to call **Production Planning and Detailed Scheduling** (**PP/DS**) during your ATP check. SAP has provided two options here: an ATP check first and then production or production directly. This option integrates the ATP check with the production planning. During sales order creation, the ATP delivery date can be derived based on the production plan schedule.

- **Multilevel ATP Check**: The MATP functionality provides the capability of doing ATP for the component and proposes a substitution if required. It creates the requirement of the component during an ATP check.

- **Third-Party Order Processing**: Third-party order processing is when the company ships the product out from the vendor location instead of their manufacturing location. The option within the check instructions helps to determine the source of the vendor if the product needs to be sourced out of a vendor location.

As we have gone through the general settings for how to activate ATP in SAP APO, let's understand the basic ATP methods in SAP APO, their function, and their configuration in the next section.

GATP basic methods

SAP APO provides basic and advanced methods to check ATP when a sales order is created. Here, in this section, we will discuss the basic methods. Most companies implement basic ATP methods to find out about availability based on what inventory is on hand plus the total cost. Based on the inventory position, the system proposes a date as to when the product will be available to deliver to the customer. There are three types of basic ATP methods, which are as follows:

- Product availability check
- Product allocation check
- Check against forecast

Let's understand these further in the following subsections.

Product availability check

Product availability check is one of the basic method checks when creating a sales order or stock transport order. A sales order can be created from SAP CRM or SAP ECC, making the call to SAP SCM to run the ATP. This type of check is the same in SAP SCM and SAP ECC. The sales order triggers the ATP check; the ATP quantity is calculated based on the inventory on hand, planned receipts such as the production order, the purchase order, and the planned order, and the planned requirements/demands, such as sales orders, deliveries, and reservations. It also takes into consideration the transit time. The transit time is derived based on the ship from and ship to locations. The scheduling data is maintained in the SAP APO table that is considered during the ATP check. When running the ATP check, some key configurations drive the result of the ATP check, including whether you consider the checking horizon and what the scope of the check is when running the ATP check. These are controlled using ATP group configuration and ATP check control in SAP APO. Based on this configuration, the system gets you the result of the ATP check when creating business transactions.

GATP uses LiveCache and time series to provide the best result of an ATP check. LiveCache enables better performance results during an ATP check. LiveCache manages a large amount of data and increases the speed in processing data while the data is constantly updating and changing. A time series represents incoming and outgoing movements (receipts and issues) for a specific product. Individual time series exist as a combination of product, location, sublocation, and version level. The sublocation corresponds to the storage location in the ERP system. The version corresponds to the batch in the ERP system.

ATP group

An ATP group is equivalent to a checking group in the SAP ERP system. An ATP group controls the behavior of a transaction on how the ATP check should be performed, that is, whether the check should consider cumulated confirmed quantities or requirement quantities when creating or changing a sales order. Having incorrect settings here may lead to over-commitment to the customer. The configuration of an ATP group is transferred using the integration model from ERP to the SAP APO system.

Here is the configuration path to configure an ATP group: **SPRO | Advanced Planning and Optimization | Global Available-to-Promise (Global ATP) | Product Availability Check | Maintain ATP Group**

The following screen shows the configuration details of an ATP group in SAP APO:

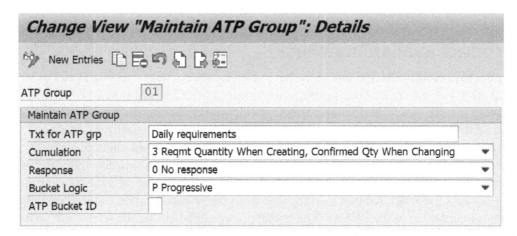

Figure 8.21 – Maintain ATP Group

SAP recommends that you carry out a product availability check, considering the cumulated confirmed quantities or the requirement quantities.

A check considering the cumulated confirmed quantities allows the sales order item to be confirmed on the requested date by comparing the total receipts with the total confirmed quantity.

A check considering the cumulated requirement quantities allows the sales order line item to be confirmed on the requested date by comparing the total receipts with the total requirements quantity.

If you choose no cumulation, the shortage check is not activated.

The ATP group is determined based on the product master settings. The following is a screenshot of the APO product master with ATP group 02 showing in the **ATP** tab:

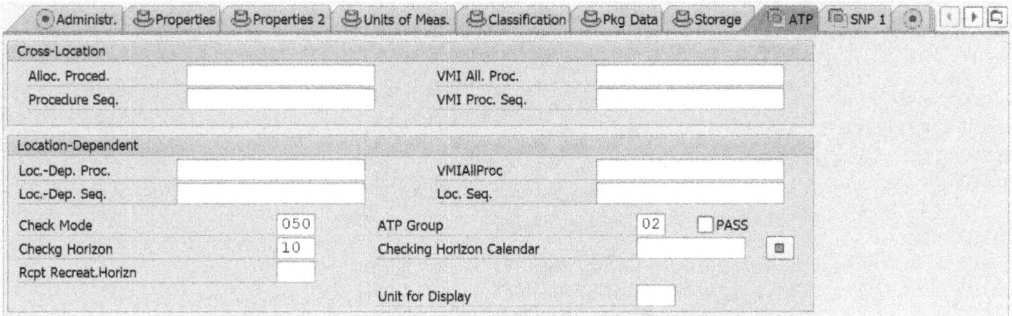

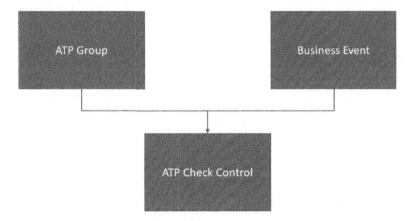

Figure 8.22 – ATP group in the APO product master

The ATP group is assigned to the product master and based on the product master settings, the ATP group configuration is executed during the ATP check.

Check control

A combination of the ATP group and business events derives the ATP check control. The ATP check control decides whether you want to consider the sublocation, version, and characteristics check during ATP. You can also control whether the ATP check should consider the check horizon or not. The check horizon number of days is derived from the product master within the **ATP** tab.

Figure 8.23 shows a diagrammatic representation of the ATP group + business event = ATP check control:

Figure 8.23 – ATP check control determination from an ATP group and business event

Figure 8.24 shows the configuration screen of an ATP check control:

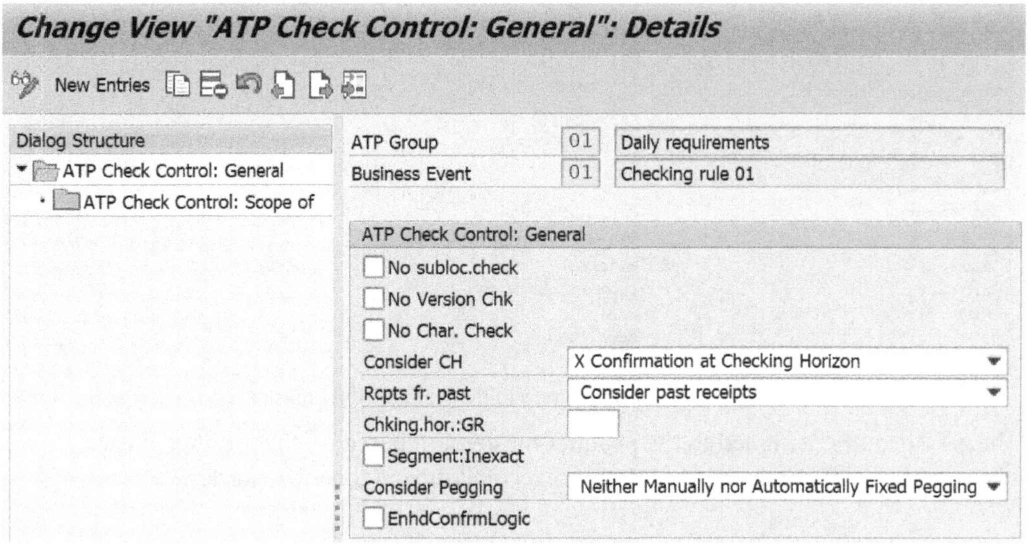

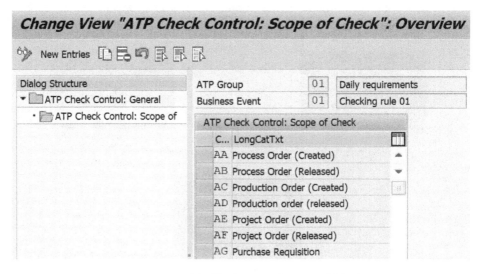

Figure 8.24 – ATP Check Control

The IMG path to configure an ATP check control is stated here: **SPRO | Advanced Planning and Optimization | Global Available-to-Promise (Global ATP) | Product Availability Check | Maintain Check Control**

Figure 8.25 shows an ATP check control scope of check:

Figure 8.25 – ATP Check Control: Scope of Check

It is considered during the ATP check which element should be considered as a receipt or requirement element.

Production allocation

Allocation helps a company to distribute stock based on the customer requirements, meaning if sufficient stock is not available or the company doesn't want to block the stock for one big order for a specific customer, then you can allocate a limited quantity based on distribution channels, geographic region, customer groups, or strategic customers. A situation may arise where the product availability is limited, such as with a seasonal product or a high-demand product with longer lead times. There is a second method of the basic ATP check that allows the business to have better control in situations where they need to avoid customers ordering seasonal **Stock Keeping Units** (**SKUs**) with large quantities, creating disruption in the supply chain for the rest of the customers.

Production allocation integrates with planning tools while executing an ATP check in the SAP APO system. A group of characteristics defined by the product allocation group and product allocation quantities is saved within the product allocation group. An allocation check is executed against the product allocation group and a check is carried out against this time series. The allocation group consists of the characteristics that are the fields with their values from the sales order. The **Characteristics Value Combination** (**CVC**) needs to be created as a prerequisite. The correct characteristics combination maintained here picks up the correct bucket during an ATP check and the system provides the ATP result to the sales order.

When planning, the characteristic values are saved in either planning areas or info structures. This planning data is then transferred to the product allocation group. The constrained quantity, either from ATP or allocation, is confirmed on the sales order line item.

The following is the step-by-step configuration to activate product allocation in SAP APO:

1. Create the planning object structure.

   Figure 8.26 shows the creation of the master planning object structure:

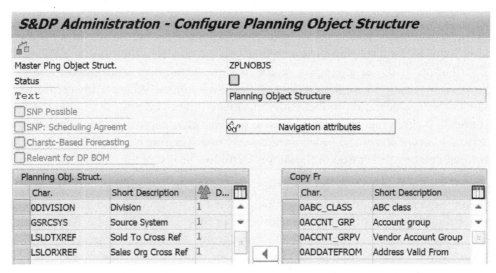

Figure 8.26 – Creation of the master planning object structure

   You create the master planning object structure using the /SAPAPO/MSDP_ADMIN transaction code. Here, you assign the characteristics to the planning object structure. The characteristics are based on what criteria you would like to use to create the allocation bucket based on your business needs. This could be sales org, sold to, division, and so on.

2. Create a new planning area.

   The next step in the process is creating the planning area. You create the planning area in the same transaction, /SAPAPO/MSDP_ADMIN. You assign the planning object structure to the planning and the storage bucket profile, that is, the period defined in the storage bucket up until what period the data will be stored in LiveCache. The data is stored in a time series. Time series data is data that is not linked to the transaction. You define and assign a key figure to the planning area and activate the planning area. Once the planning area is activated, you can create the planning book mentioned in the next step.

3. Define a planning book.

   Once you are done creating the planning object structure and the planning area, the next step in the process is to create the planning book.

Figure 8.27 shows the planning book data view information:

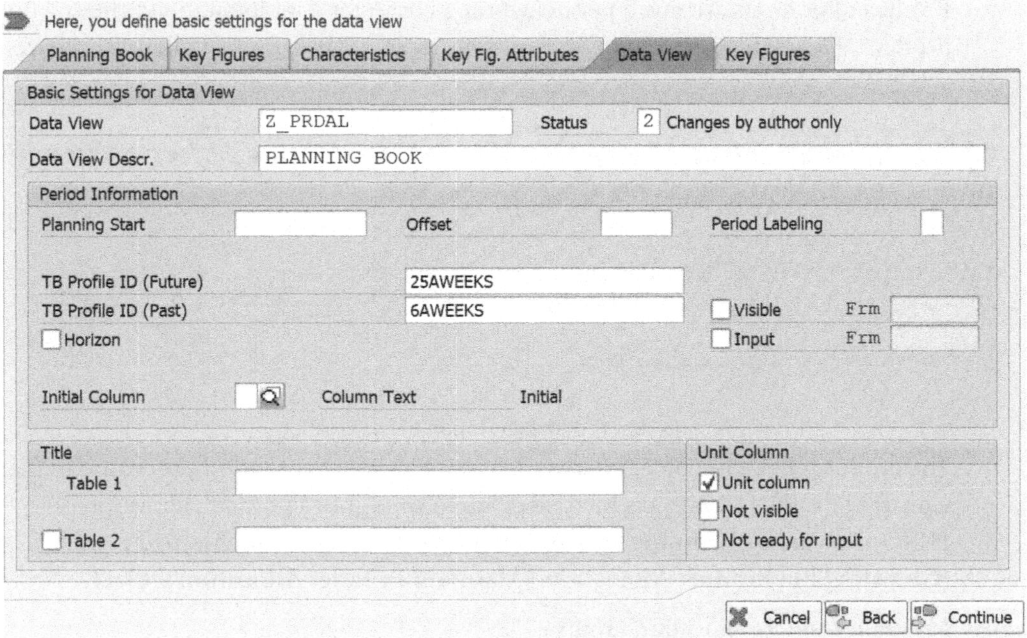

Figure 8.27 – Planning book maintenance

You create a planning book using transaction code `/SAPAPO/SDP8B`. With the planning book, the user can see the allocated quantities to customers easily. This helps them to make a decision if they want to change any of the allocated quantities to a customer. In this step, you assign the planning area to the new planning book you create via `/SAPAPO/SDP8B`. The key figures and characteristics are inherited from the planning object structure and the planning area. There you also define up to how many weeks you want to see the data.

4. Maintain the field catalog.

   In this step, you create the condition fields within the field catalog. SAP GATP has provided standard characteristics that can be used to define the allocation in the field catalog. You assign these characteristics to the product allocation group. The following is the IMG path to configure the field catalog: **SPRO | Advanced Planning and Optimization | Global Available-to-Promise (Global ATP) | Product Allocation | Maintain Field Catalog**

5. Maintain product allocation object.

Product allocations are saved per object for a character's combination in the product allocation group, therefore you have to define the product allocation object.

Figure 8.28 shows the creation of the PRODALLOC product allocation object:

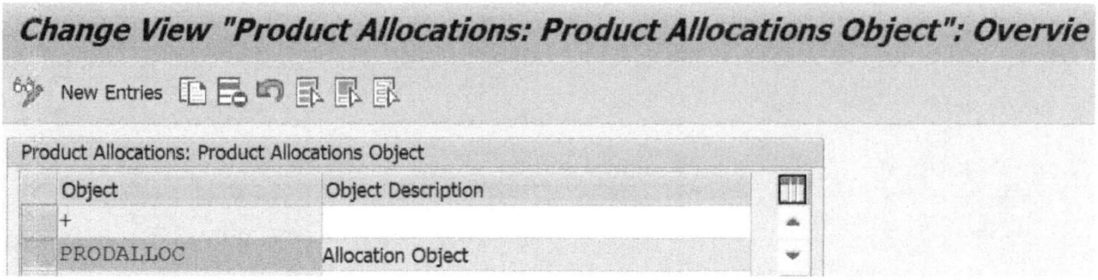

Figure 8.28 – Product allocation object creation

The product allocation object is assigned to the product allocation procedure in the **Control** tab. The following is the IMG path to configure a product allocation object: **SPRO | Advanced Planning and Optimization | Global Available-to-Promise (Global ATP) | Product Allocation | Maintain Product Allocation Object**

6. Maintain product allocation group.

A product allocation group defines a group of characteristics. The characteristics are assigned to the product allocation group that was added to the field catalog. The characteristics combination is maintained based on the business requirements and the allocation buckets are determined while the sales order makes an ATP call to APO. Product allocation quantities and their assignments are saved within the product allocation group. Using a characteristics combination, the ATP check is executed based on the values of characteristics from the sales order line item. A product allocation is a time series against which a check is executed to give the desired ATP results back to the sales order line item. This data is stored in LiveCache.

Here is the IMG path to configure the product allocation group: **SPRO | Advanced Planning and Optimization | Global Available-to-Promise (Global ATP) | Product Allocation | Maintain Product Allocation Group**

Figure 8.29 shows the configuration of the ZPRDALTEST product allocation:

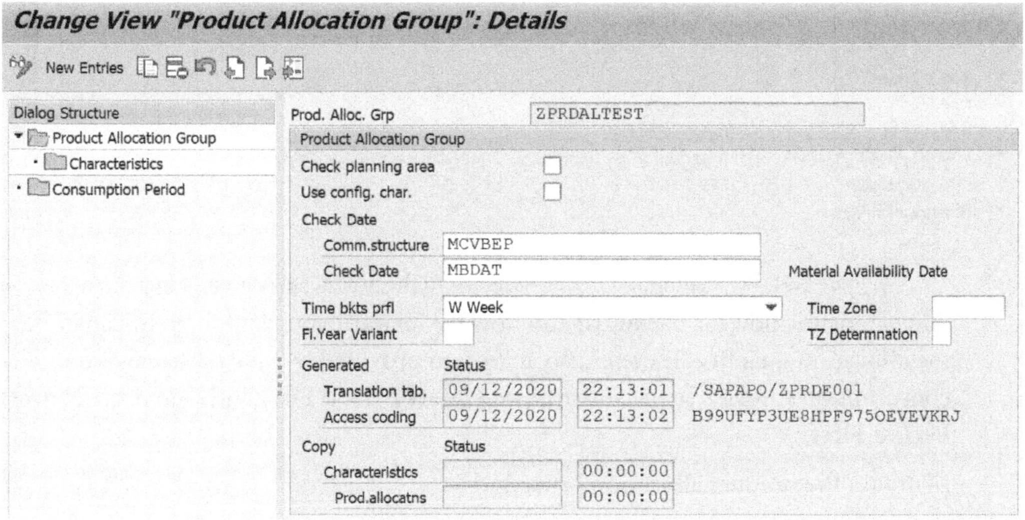

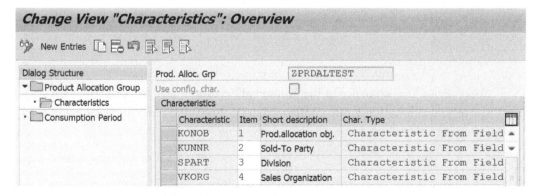

Figure 8.29 – Maintaining a product allocation group

Here you can activate an ATP check against the planning area instead of the product allocation group. If you activate the **Check Planning Area** checkbox, the check happens against the planning area. This option has some limitations due to a locking issue. You also enter the communication structure and time bucket profile, which is whether you want the key figures to be displayed in weekly or monthly buckets.

You assign the characteristics to the product allocation group, which is shown in *Figure 8.30*. Here, the **Sold-To**, **Division**, and **Sales Organization** characteristics are assigned to the ZPRDALTEST product allocation group:

Figure 8.30 – Characteristics assigned to the product allocation group

Figure 8.31 shows the consumption period assigned to the product allocation group:

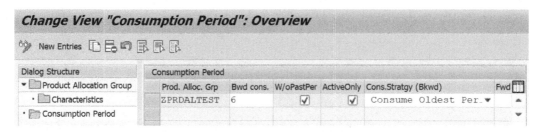

Figure 8.31 – Consumption period assigned to the product allocation group

You can define how far backward and how far forward you want to go to consume the allocation quantity. There is also an option provided by SAP on backward consumption strategy, such as **Consume Oldest Period First** and **Consume Newest Period First**.

7. Maintain the product allocation procedure.

    Once you are done configuring the product allocation group, the next step in the process is to create the product allocation procedure. You configure the product allocation procedure from the IMG path given here: **SPRO | Advanced Planning and Optimization | Global Available-to-Promise (Global ATP) | Product Allocation | Maintain Product Allocation Procedure**

    Figure 8.32 shows the creation of the ZPRDALLPRD product allocation procedure:

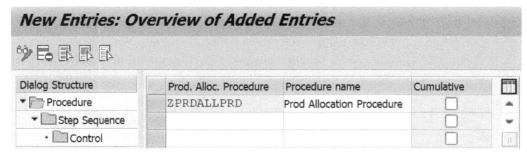

Figure 8.32 – Maintaining the product allocation procedure

You assign a step sequence to the product allocation procedure where you assign the product allocation group configured in the previous step. This is shown in the following screenshot:

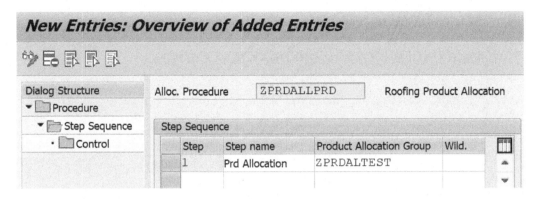

Figure 8.33 – Step sequence assignment to the product allocation procedure

In the **Control** tab, you assign the product allocation object. This is shown in *Figure 8.34*:

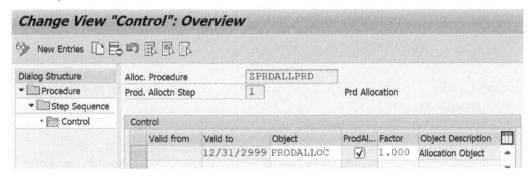

Figure 8.34 – Product allocation object assigned to the product allocation procedure

8. Maintain the sequence of product allocation procedures.

    You can maintain various product allocations procedures that are combined into a specific sequence. The system executes an allocation check going through one allocation procedure to the next if the quantity is not fully confirmed.

    The sequence of product allocation procedures determines several alternative product allocation procedures and their sequence for a product. Once you configure the product allocation sequence, you assign the product allocation procedure sequences to the product master.

    To configure the sequence of product allocation procedures, follow the IMG path given here: **SPRO | Advanced Planning and Optimization | Global Available-to-Promise (Global ATP) | Product Allocation | Maintain Sequence of Product Allocation Procedures**

The following figure shows the sequence of product allocation procedures:

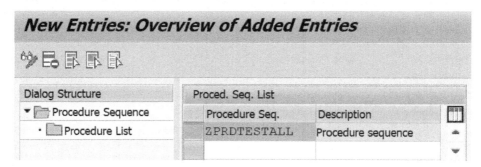

Figure 8.35 – Maintaining the sequence of product allocation procedures

The procedure list consists of a list of the product allocation procedures with the step number, as shown in *Figure 8.36*:

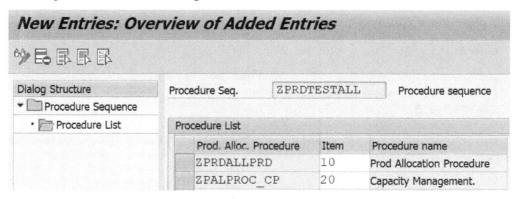

Figure 8.36 – Maintaining the procedure list with the product allocation procedures

9. Maintain a connection to the planning area.

   Once the configuration of the production allocation procedure and product allocation group is completed, the next step is to connect the product allocation group to the planning area. This is the most critical step as this configuration makes the system capable of running a successful allocation check during an ATP trigger from the sales order line item. To configure the connection of the product allocation to the planning area, follow the IMG path given next: **SPRO | Advanced Planning and Optimization | Global Available-to-Promise (Global ATP) | Product Allocation | Maintain Connection to Planning Area**

When you run an ATP check for a sales order line item, the allocation check is executed against the product allocation group table and not the planning area unless you configure the product allocation group to check allocation against the planning area directly. *Figure 8.37* shows the ZPRDALTEST product allocation group mapped to planning area Z_PRD:

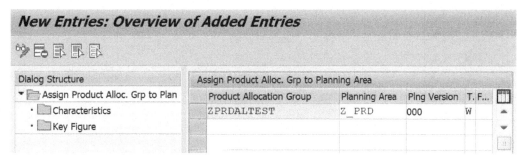

Figure 8.37 – Assignment of the product allocation group to the planning area

You map **Characteristics** from the product allocation group to **InfoObject**, as shown in *Figure 8.38*:

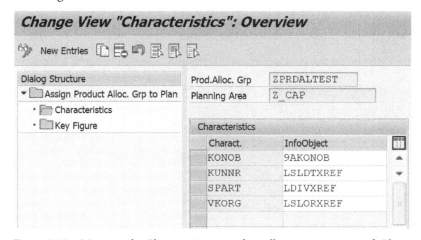

Figure 8.38 – Mapping the Characteristics product allocation group to InfoObject

After **Characteristics**, you map **Key Figure** to **InfoObject**, as shown in *Figure 8.39*:

Change View "Key Figure": Overview

New Entries

Dialog Structure		Prod.Alloc. Grp	ZPRDALTEST
▼ Assign Product Alloc. Grp to Plan		Planning Area	Z_CAP
• Characteristics			
• Key Figure			

Key Figure	
Key figure	InfoObject
AEMENGE	9AADDKF2
KCQTY	9AADDKF1

Figure 8.39 – Mapping the Key Figure product allocation group to InfoObject

10. The final step of product allocation determination is to assign the product allocation procedure to the product master. This is done in the **ATP** tab of the product master. The assignment can be cross-location or location-specific.

Figure 8.40 shows the product master with allocation procedure assignment:

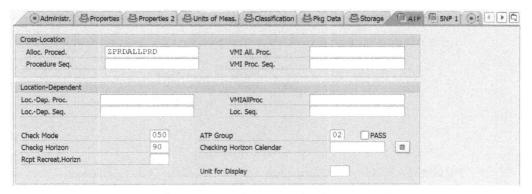

Figure 8.40 – Allocation procedure assigned to the APO product master

Once the configuration is completed and the assignment of the product allocation procedure to the product master is done, the next step is to load the CVCs (characteristics combination) to the planning object structure. You can create CVCs via transaction code /SAPAPO/MC62. You can delete CVCs with the same transaction code. You can load CVCs via different options provided in the /SAPAPO/MC62 transaction. You can load them manually or as a flat file from your local desktop or InfoProvider.

A screenshot of the **Maintain Planning-Relevant Characteristic Combinations** screen is shown next, where you can manage CVCs:

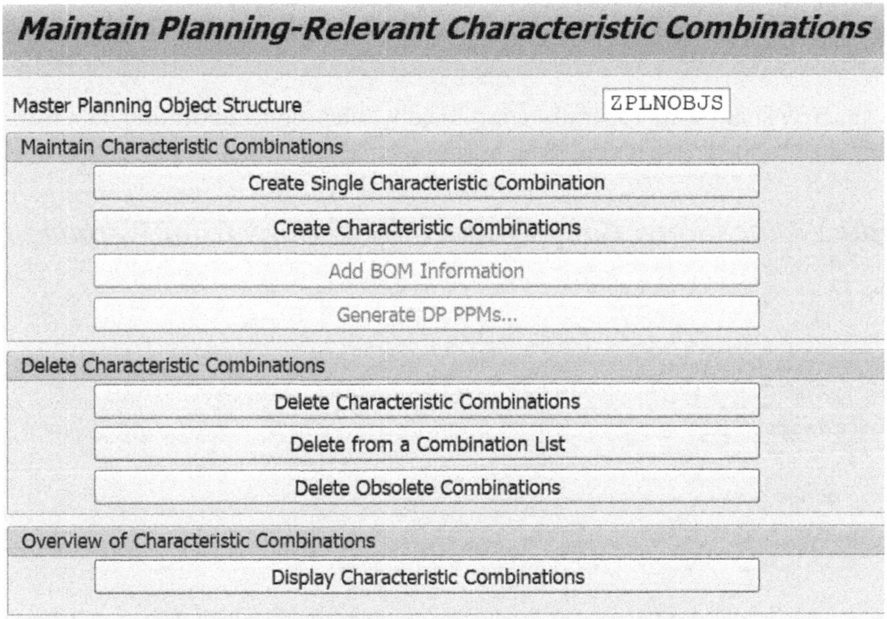

Maintain Planning-Relevant Characteristic Combinations

Master Planning Object Structure	ZPLNOBJS

Maintain Characteristic Combinations

- Create Single Characteristic Combination
- Create Characteristic Combinations
- Add BOM Information
- Generate DP PPMs...

Delete Characteristic Combinations

- Delete Characteristic Combinations
- Delete from a Combination List
- Delete Obsolete Combinations

Overview of Characteristic Combinations

- Display Characteristic Combinations

Figure 8.41 – Maintain Planning-Relevant Characteristic Combinations

Once you have created the CVCs in DP, you can copy the CVCs to the product allocation group via transaction code /SAPAPO/ATPQ_PAREA_K – Copy Characteristics Combination.

The following screenshot shows a transaction that you can run to copy a CVC from the planning area:

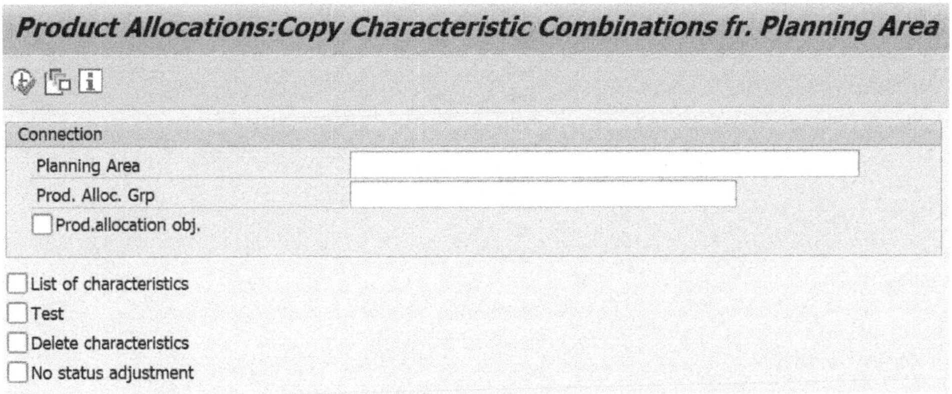

Product Allocations:Copy Characteristic Combinations fr. Planning Area

Connection

Planning Area	
Prod. Alloc. Grp	
☐ Prod.allocation obj.	

☐ List of characteristics
☐ Test
☐ Delete characteristics
☐ No status adjustment

Figure 8.42 – Copy Characteristic Combinations fr. Planning Area

Once this is completed, you create the planning book with transaction code /SAPAPO/ SDP94 to update the allocation quantity for the respective CVC. After maintaining the allocation quantity in DP, you copy the allocation from the DP planning area to the product allocation group via transaction code /SAPAPO/ATPQ_PAREA_R – Copy Data from Planning Area.

The next screenshot shows the transaction to copy the product allocation data from the planning area to the product allocation group:

Product Allocations: Copy Product Allocations from Planning Area

Connection

Planning Area

Planning Version

Prod. Alloc. Grp
☑ Copy product allocation object

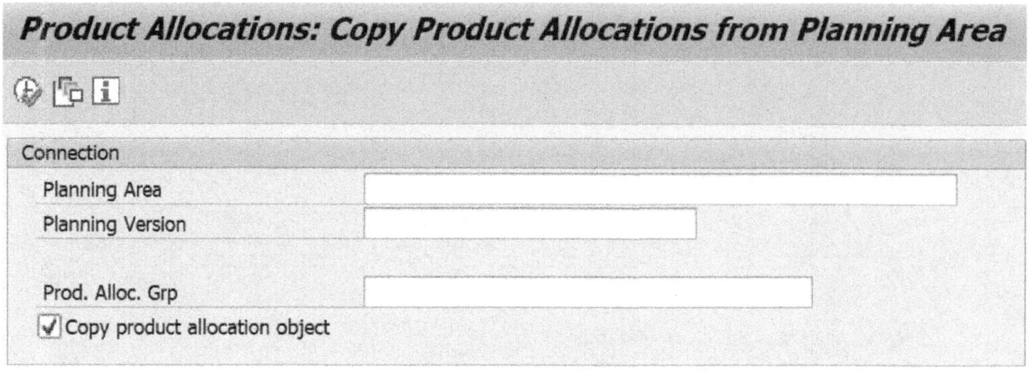

Figure 8.43 – Copy Product Allocations from Planning Area

At any given point in time, DP and the product allocation group should be in sync to avoid any ATP issues or overcommitting to the customer.

For copying the product allocation quantities to the planning area, use transaction code / SAPAPO/ATPQ_PAREA_W – Product Allocations in Plan. Area.

The following screenshot shows the transaction to transfer the product allocation quantity to the planning area:

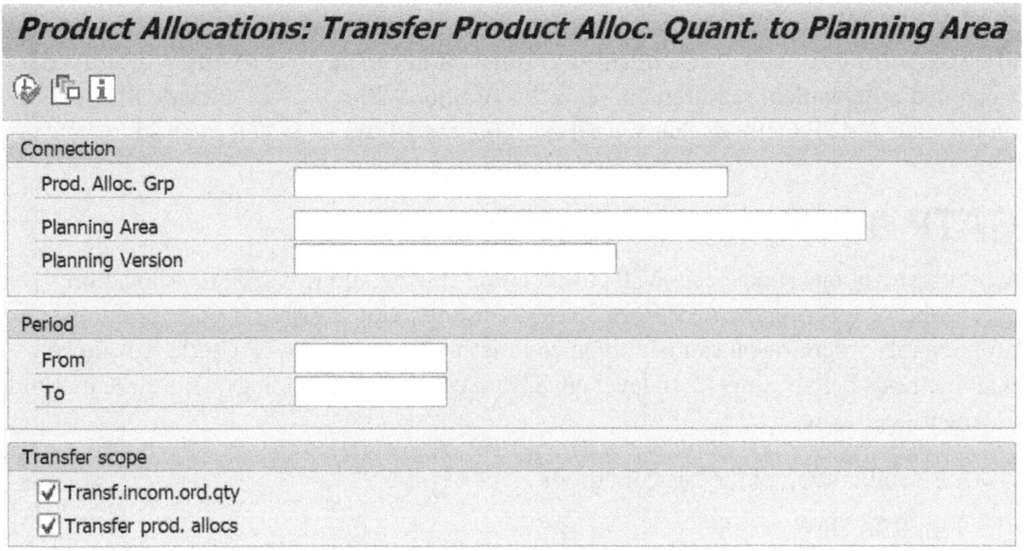

Figure 8.44 – Transfer Product Alloc. Quant. to Planning Area

As we have gone through the product allocation functionality and the steps required to activate it in the SAP APO system, let's now understand ATP checks against a forecast.

Checking against a forecast

SAP provides the option of checking ATP against a forecast in addition to product checks (that is, basic ATP) and product allocation. The configuration is activated in the check instructions, as shown in *Figure 8.45*:

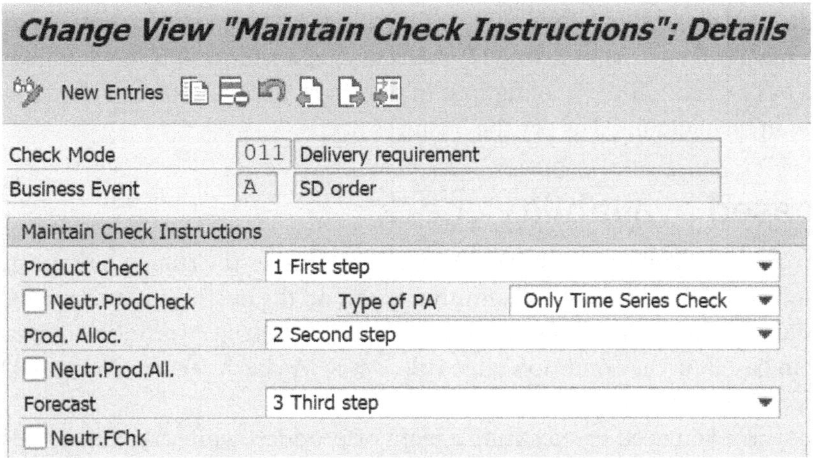

Figure 8.45 – Maintaining a check against a forecast in the check instructions

You can sequence an ATP check call with a product check, product allocation, and forecast. During an ATP check, quantity confirmation can be done against a forecast or a planned independent requirement with this option. With this, we conclude this section on the basic GATP methods. Next, we'll examine the advanced GATP methods.

GATP advanced methods

Most organizations run a basic ATP check, either they would run ATP or Allocation check when triggering the ATP from Sales order line item. However, GATP provides functionality wherein you can use advanced methods to run an ATP check. Advanced ATP methods help businesses to leverage advanced ATP methodology, and these methods are mentioned here:

- A combination of the basic methods
- An RBA check
- **Multi-Item Single Delivery (MISL)**
- CTP
- MATP

Let's understand these further in the following subsections.

A combination of the basic methods

With this option, you can trigger a combination of the basic methods, meaning you can run an ATP check along with an allocation check and a check against a forecast. Based on your business needs, you can configure a sequence as to which check should trigger first when running ATP, such as first an ATP check or first an allocation check followed by the rest of the basic checks. This is configured in the check instructions and the sequence of the check can be maintained as per the business needs.

Rule-based availability check

An Rule-based Availability Check (RBA) check determines the rule to determine the location substitution or product substitution based on the business requirements. You activate RBA in the check instructions if you want to trigger product or location substitution based on the condition table rule. An RBA check is carried out in SAP APO and this is mainly configured in
a scenario where you need to substitute a plant or products while creating a sales order.

The condition techniques for an RBA check are configured in the SAP APO system and the master data for rule maintenance is created in APO. When creating a sales order in SAP CRM, a prerequisite for an RBA check is that the planning is carried out in the SAP APO system and requirements are passed on to the SAP APO system by sales transaction in the SAP CRM system. Some organizations might want to substitute the location if the default location doesn't have the products available, which is termed **location substitution**, and some organizations might like to keep the location and substitute the product based on availability, termed **product substitution**. Some might do both based on their requirements. In each of these cases, an RBA check plays a vital role in achieving this specific functionality.

For an RBA check to take place for an item, it is important to configure the item category, as shown next.

In the SAP CRM system, there are two item category usages:

- `APO1 RBA main item` to determine the item category of the main item

- `APO2 RBA item` to determine the item category of the sub-item

Under item category determination, an entry for the main item and an entry for the sub-item is defined for the transaction type. The standard version of the system includes the following examples:

- Transaction type `TA`, item category usage RBA main item

- Transaction type `TA`, item category usage RBA item

You define item category determination in Customizing for Customer Relationship Management under **Transactions | Basic Settings | Maintain Item Category Determination**.

The following screenshot shows the item category determination configuration with RBA usage:

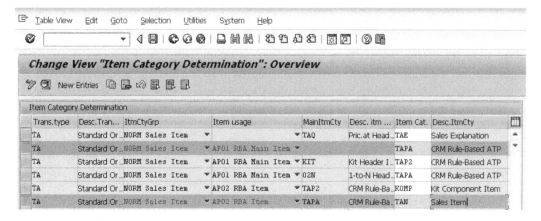

Figure 8.46 – Item category determination

In SAP APO, you define the settings for an RBA check in the IMG of the SAP APO system at the following menu path: **Advanced Planner and Optimizer (APO) | Global Available-to-Promise (Global ATP Check) | Rules-Based Availability Check**

In the requirements profile, which is assigned to an item category as an ATP profile in the CRM system, the following attributes are relevant for an RBA check:

- Technical scenario.

- Business transaction.

- Action type, which is transferred by the CRM online application. Possible values are A (create) and B (change).

Condition records must be created to fulfill the business objective, which serves as the master data and will have the location substitution or product substitution rules assigned. Rule maintenance is carried out in SAP APO and forms the basis of the master data record, which is created in the **SAP Easy Access** screen under **Advanced Planning and Optimization | Master Data | Rule Maintenance**.

Now let's say you want to have an option on a CRM sales order to select the rule criteria, whether it should be location substitution or product substitution. You can control that from the rule criteria, which can be configured from the path stated here: **SAP CRM** under **Customer Relationship Management | Basic Functions | Availability Check | Availability Check Using SAP APO | Rules-Based Availability Check | Define Rule Criterion 1**

RBA checks use a condition technique and must be set up in SAP APO. This includes the following:

- A condition type that uses the **Rule Criterion 1** field (CRMT_ATP_SUBST_EXCL) in its key.

- One or more condition records for this condition type. The condition record has the field value for an ATP exclusion that is entered here in the IMG (for example, A = no product substitution). This condition record should contain a rule that reflects the purpose of this field; for example, in this case, it contains only a location determination procedure.

If you create a sales order with **Rule Criteria 1** set to A and activated on the sales order, an ATP call to APO will look for the location substitution only and will bypass the product substitution.

In this step, you enter the field values that can be used in the **Rule Criterion 1** field in the sales transaction as stated here:

- A (no product substitution)
- B (no location substitution)

The entries that you maintain here are used for input help in the **Rule Criterion 1** field:

- In the business partner master record under **Sales Area Data** on the **ATP** tab
- In the sales transaction header on the **Header Overview** tab in the **ATP** section
- In the sales transaction item on the **Schedule Lines** tab

For a more specific search, you can configure **Rule Criteria 2**, which can be used to determine the product or location at a granular level. The configuration step is similar to **Rule Criteria 1**.

Once you configure the RBA condition techniques in the IMG path mentioned here: **SPRO | Advanced Planning and Optimization | Global Available-to-Promise (Global ATP)| Rules-Based Availability Check**, you then maintain the rule in transaction `/SAPAPO/RBA04` and also maintain the rule determination condition record in transaction code `/SAPCND/AO11 - Create Rule Determination`.

Multi-item single delivery

MISL is also termed complete delivery from a single location for a complete order. This helps an organization to maximize the profit on transportation costs. MISL is an extended function of an RBA check and is automatically activated with the activation of RBA in the check instruction configuration. With this option, you may be able to deliver products quicker than the consolidated scenario. If the stock in the specified location is not available, then the system will partially confirm the item but would stick to one location in this case.

To make use of MISL, you will need to create the rule within integrated rule maintenance master data for the MISL rule type with at least one inclusive rule.

Capable-to-Promise

A production CTP check calls PP/DS during an ATP check. While doing an ATP check, if the quantity requested on the sales order line item is not completely available, then the system calls PP/DS to produce or procure the remaining items. SAP has provided two options here: the ATP check first and then production or production directly. Both of these options integrate the ATP check with the production planning. During sales order creation, the ATP delivery date can be derived based on the production plan schedule.

The activation of the CTP functionality is done via check instruction configuration and RBA, using the IMG path given here: **SAP - Implementation Guide | Advanced Planning and Optimization | Global Available-to-Promise (Global ATP) | General Settings | Maintain Check Instructions**

The following screenshot shows the activation of CTP in the check instructions:

Production	
StartProduction	0 Availability Check Only, No Production ▼
Production Time	0 After Executing all Check Methods ▼
☐ Re-create receipt elements	

Multilevel ATP Check	
Compnts Remain. Reqmt	Create Remaining Requirement at Header Level ▼
Conversion Mode - ATPTreeStrct	Create Several Plnd Ords (1 Plnd Order per Partial Confirm.) ▼
Business Event Multilevel ATP	

Third-Party Order Processing	
Start Source Determination	0 Only Availability Check, No Source Determination ▼
Source Determination Method	9 GATP check on subcontractor location ▼

☐ ATP Alert Act.

Figure 8.47 – Activation of CTP in the check instructions

The basic process steps in CTP are mentioned next:

1. The sales order is created with the requested quantity and date based on the customer's request.

2. When the sales order is created, the ATP check triggers; the result of the ATP check shows the completely confirmed quantity, meaning the requested quantity is available in stock and can be shipped to the customer without calling PP/DS. In situations where the requested quantity is not available or is only partially available, SAP APO calls PP/DS to create a receipt element for the insufficient quantity in stock. The receipt element in this example is the planned order.

3. During ATP checking, a temporary planned order is created for the insufficient stock. The temporary requirement is assigned with the same ATP category as the checked requirement. For a sales order, the system displays the temporary requirement with the BM (Sales Order) ATP category. The temporary requirement is then assigned to the temporary planned order. This assignment cannot be changed.

4. The result of this is displayed on the delivery proposal screen.

5. Customer service accepts the proposal and saves the sales order.

6. Once the sales order is saved, the temporary requirement is deleted, and it is converted into a permanent planned order. The ATP time series is also updated with this information.

With this, we complete the activation of CTP. Now let's understand the MATP functionality.

MATP

The MATP functionality provides the capability of doing ATP for the component and proposes a substitution if required. It creates the requirement of the component during the ATP check, in the scenario when the components are produced and procured before the sales order is placed by the customer. Once the sales order is placed, the components are assembled and the finished goods are shipped to the customer. With an MATP check, the stock availability of the components products is checked whether they are available in stock in addition to the finished product. If the components are not available, the system creates a requirement for these components.

You configure an MATP check with the IMG path given here: **SAP - Implementation Guide | Advanced Planning and Optimization | Global Available-to-Promise (Global ATP) | General Settings | Maintain Check Instructions**

The following screenshot shows the activation of MATP on a check instructions configuration:

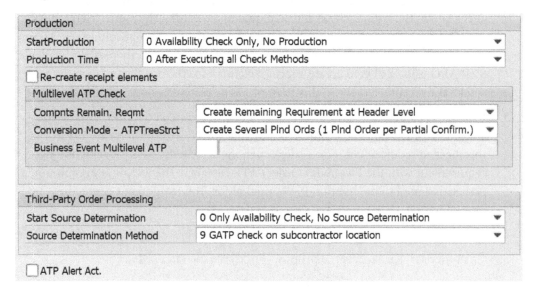

Figure 8.48 – Activation of MATP in check instructions

One of the use cases for an MATP check is for the configurable material. You can trigger an ATP check for the components of configurable items when added to the sales order as a line item. There will be an ATP check for the components based on the customer request date and the sales order will be confirmed if all the components of the configurable material are available. The availability of the components can be seen in the ATP proposal with MATP.

The difference between MATP and CTP is that no receipt elements are created in the SAP APO order network during the MATP check. Instead, the ATP tree structure stores the check results. The ATP tree structure exists in the SAP APO database. The aggregated quantity assignments represent the requirements at the component level. When the conversion of the receipt element takes place, the ATP tree structure and the aggregated quantity assignments are deleted or reduced.

Receipt elements are only generated later when the ATP tree structure is converted in PP/DS.

We have gone through the advanced ATP check methods, covering a combination of the basic methods, an RBA check, MISL, CTP and an MATP function and its setup configuration. Let's now understand the scheduling and transit time determination with SAP APO in the next section.

Transportation and scheduling with GATP

Transportation and scheduling with SAP GATP provides the consistent and automatic scheduling of the sales order, based on the delivery date requested by the customer. Transportation and scheduling in GATP calculates the following dates when the sales order line item runs the ATP check:

- Unloading date
- Delivery date
- Goods issue date
- Loading date
- Transportation planning
- Material availability date

SAP APO has provided the following options to determine these dates, which are mentioned next:

- Scheduling using the condition technique
- Scheduling using SNP master data (transportation lane)
- Configurable process scheduling
- Scheduling with dynamic route determination

The system uses the transportation and scheduling functionality to provide scheduling dates based on configuration done for the different options mentioned previously. If you configure and the prerequisite for configurable process scheduling has been met, then configurable process scheduling is used. If the prerequisites for configurable process scheduling have not been met, but the prerequisites for scheduling based on SNP master data have, then scheduling based on SNP master data is used. If neither of the prerequisites for configurable process scheduling nor those for scheduling based on SNP master data have been met, scheduling takes place using the condition technique.

There is a prerequisite requirement to set up scheduling using a condition technique. When using SAP CRM as the order entry system and utilizing scheduling using a condition technique, you need to configure the requirements profile activating the **A Execute Scheduling** scheduling indicator as shown in *Figure 8.49*:

Change View "Maintain Requirements Profile (ATP)": Details	

New Entries

Reqmts prfl	100	CRM ATP Check

Maintain Requirements Profile (ATP)

Category	BM
Order Header Cat.	
Check Mode	
Business Event	A
Assignment Mode	No assignment
TQA Type	E Write both internal and external temporary objects
Validity TQAs	
Tech. Scenario	
Business Trans.	
RS for Initial Locat.	
Scheduling Ind.	A Execute Scheduling
Preselection Substns	☐
RS for Supplier C.Loc.	

Figure 8.49 – Maintain Requirements Profile

To configure the requirements profile, follow the IMG path given here: The **SAP Easy Access** screen under **SPRO | Advanced Planning and Optimization | General Settings | Requirements Profile | Maintain Requirements Profile**

While running an ATP check from SAP CRM during a sales order entry, SAP fills in the relevant ATP fields to be passed on to SAP APO for running the ATP check in APO. You can add or update the fields that are not part of the standard ATP field catalog in CRM via BAdI CRM_CONFIRM_01 and pass those fields in SAP APO to run the ATP and transportation scheduling.

The following are the steps required to set up scheduling using the condition technique in SAP APO.

Step 1 – defining a condition table for scheduling

You define a combination of fields (keys) that identify an individual condition record. The combination of fields creates a condition table wherein you can create an individual condition record.

Figure 8.50 shows an example of a field catalog with usage scheduling:

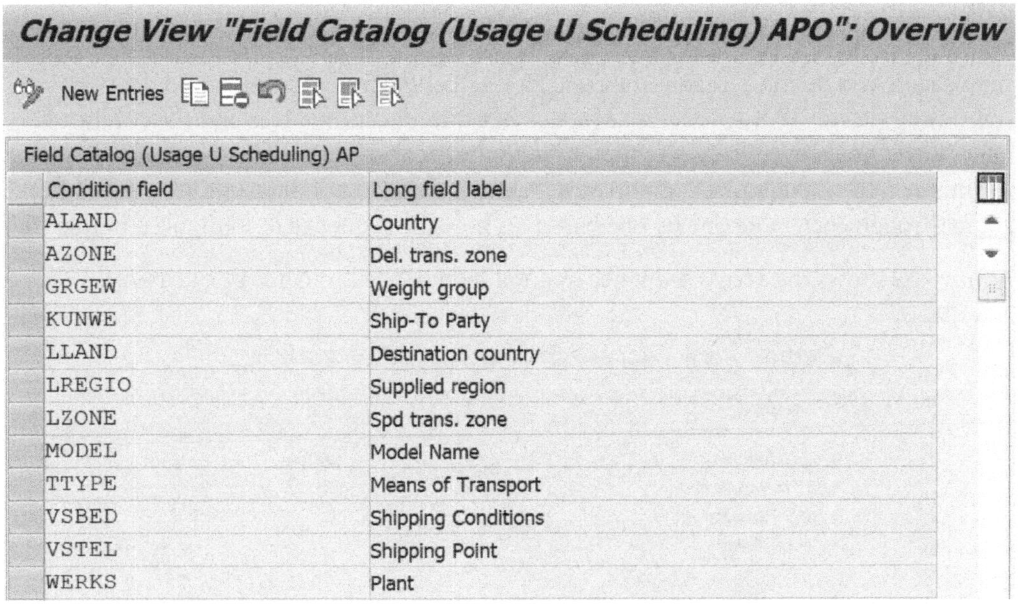

Condition field	Long field label
ALAND	Country
AZONE	Del. trans. zone
GRGEW	Weight group
KUNWE	Ship-To Party
LLAND	Destination country
LREGIO	Supplied region
LZONE	Spd trans. zone
MODEL	Model Name
TTYPE	Means of Transport
VSBED	Shipping Conditions
VSTEL	Shipping Point
WERKS	Plant

Figure 8.50 – Field catalog with usage scheduling

Figure 8.51 shows an example of a table with a field combination:

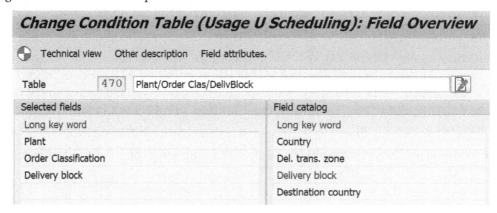

Figure 8.51 – Maintaining a condition table

You configure the fields and the condition table with the IMG path given here: **SPRO | Advanced Planning and Optimization | Global Available-to-Promise (Global ATP) | Transportation and Shipment Scheduling | Scheduling Using the Condition Technique | Define Condition Table for Scheduling**

Step 2 – maintaining access for scheduling

In this step, you define access to the condition tables for transportation and delivery scheduling (usage "U"). An access sequence has the condition tables and the condition tables have the fields with the records. Based on the combination of the records maintained, the system picks up the most relevant record from the condition table after going through each table one by one based on how the sequence is configured in this step.

Figure 8.52 shows the access sequence maintained for LEAD, LOAD, PICK, TRAN, and UNLD:

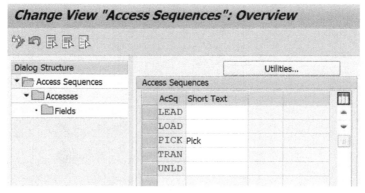

Figure 8.52 – Maintaining access sequence

Mark the table as exclusive for each of the tables maintained in the access sequence. This is shown in *Figure 8.53*:

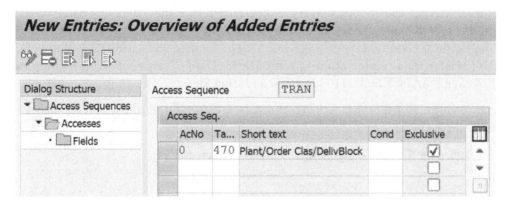

Figure 8.53 – Maintaining access

Step 3 – maintaining control for scheduling

SAP has provided the standard SCHEDL rule strategy scheduling schema for utilizing the condition technique:

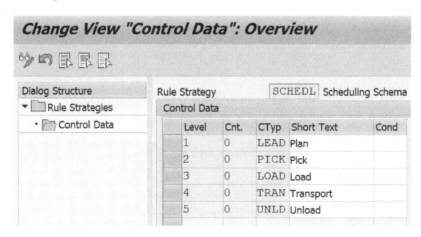

Figure 8.54 – Assignment of the control data to rule strategies

You assign a control to the rule strategy in this step: SAP has provided the LEAD, PICK, LOAD, TRAN, and UNLD condition types assigned as control data.

Step 4 – condition record maintenance

The final step is to maintain the condition record for each of these condition types, which are LEAD, PICK, LOAD, TRAN, and UNLD. The system runs the scheduling based on the condition record maintained in each of these condition types. To maintain the condition record for these condition types, follow the SAP menu path given next: **SAP Menu | SCM Basis | Master Data | Application-Specific Master Data | Transportation and Shipment Scheduling | /SAPCND/AU11 - Create Scheduling Step**

The following screenshot shows the creation of the condition record screen for the Pick condition type:

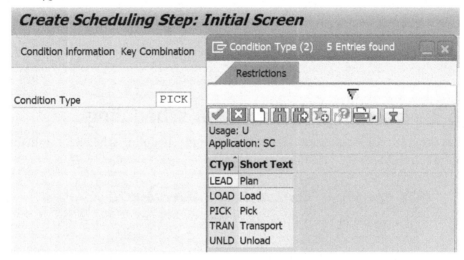

Figure 8.55 – Creating a condition record

Figure 8.56 shows the key combination (tables) for the Pick condition type:

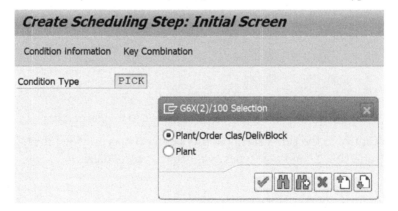

Figure 8.56 – Condition type key combinations

Figure 8.57 shows the screen to enter the duration of the key combination and the `Pick` condition type:

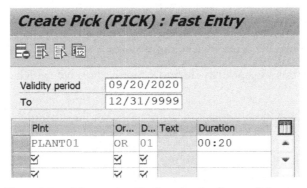

Figure 8.57 – Maintaining the duration for the condition type

> **Note**
>
> If you are using SAP TM and utilizing lane information from TM, then you can customize the duration updates from TM to SCM via a custom program and update the duration in the scheduling conditions mentioned previously.

Backorder processing

BOP allows the business to reconfirm the sales order based on certain priority; for example, if you want to fulfill a priority customer-requested date, the supply chain planner can run a BOP job to move the stock from the order that is assigned to another customer and assign it to the priority customer order. BOP can be executed in ECC or APO system based on your system set up. In BOP, you receive a list for a material with all relevant receipts and dispatches for the availability check and the option of processing shortfall quantities.

You have the following processing options in BOP:

- Open requirements can be re-confirmed, for example, if the stock has increased since the last availability check, another receipt has occurred, and so on.

- Quantities that have already been confirmed can be re-distributed by partly or completely reducing quantities allocated to confirmed requirements, and instead assigning them to other more urgent requirements.

BOP functionality exists both in ECC and SAP APO; BOP functionality with GATP provides more functionality and flexibility when it comes to the filter type and sort criteria. BOP is nothing but re-checking of ATP on the sales order, providing the following benefits:

- Ability to change the product availability dates

- Identifies the business priority during a supply shortage, which leads to customer satisfaction

- Ability to change the product allocation based on the customer and market position.

- Improved stability around availability dates and shipping operations

The following subsections describe the basic configuration required in BOP for the BOP functionality to work. You will need to configure the filter and sort profiles with the activation of the BOP function in GAPT.

Maintaining the filter type

In a filter type, you define which characteristics can be used in a filter for BOP. You configure order categories and the criteria with the filter type in the IMG path given next: **IMG | Advanced Planning and Optimization | Global Available-to-Promise (Global ATP) | Backorder Processing | Maintain Filter Type**

Figure 8.58 shows the SAP_STANDARD standard SAP filter type:

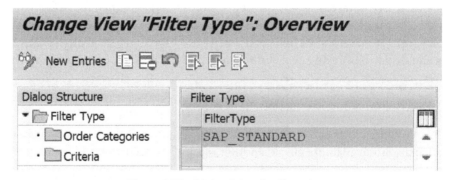

Figure 8.58 – Maintaining the filter type

Order categories are the business object types on which you want to run the BOP, for example, sales order, STO, and scheduling agreement. This is shown in *Figure 8.59*:

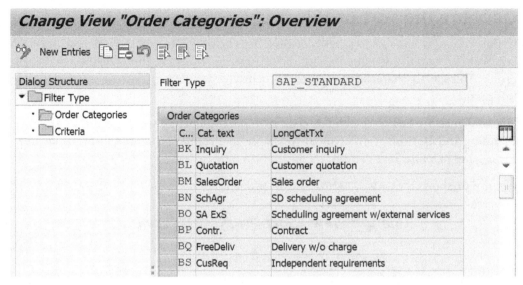

Figure 8.59 – Maintaining order categories under the filter type

Figure 8.60 shows the criteria for which you want to run the BOP for the sales order:

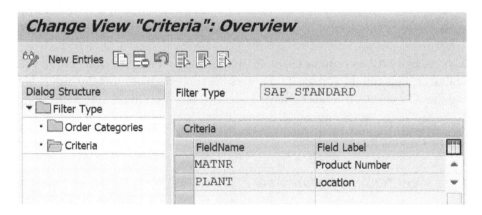

Figure 8.60 – Maintaining criteria

The mentioned criteria in *Figure 8.60* is an example of the filter criteria that can be used to run the BOP for the sales order. Other field criteria can be added based on the business requirements.

Defining the sort profile

In this step, you define a sort profile for BOP. This helps you to sort the orders with certain criteria to process the documents with the processing sequence. This is defined in the sort profile. You specify characteristics, their sequence (or weighting), and the sort order in this profile.

You configure the sort profile and its criteria in the IMG path given next: **IMG | Advanced Planning and Optimization | Global Available-to-Promise (Global ATP) | Backorder Processing | Define Sort Profile**

Figure 8.61 shows the SAP_STANDARD sort profile:

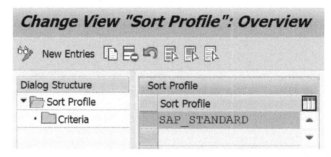

Figure 8.61 – Maintaining the sort profile

This is a standard SAP sort profile example. BOP searches for all the orders to run the ATP and once it gets all the orders, it then uses the sort criteria to sort the orders before running the ATP checks. This sort criteria is defined based on the business priority.

Figure 8.62 shows the field name with the sequence of how the BOP should consider the order while running the ATP check:

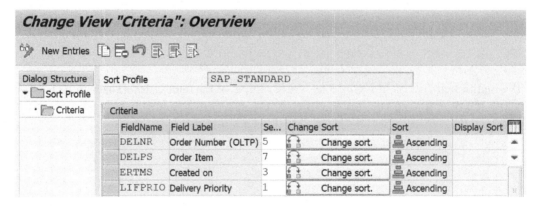

FieldName	Field Label	Se...	Change Sort		Sort	Display Sort
DELNR	Order Number (OLTP)	5		Change sort.	Ascending	
DELPS	Order Item	7		Change sort.	Ascending	
ERTMS	Created on	3		Change sort.	Ascending	
LIFPRIO	Delivery Priority	1		Change sort.	Ascending	

Figure 8.62 – Maintaining criteria under the sort profile

You can sort it in ascending or descending order, sorting results by priority for the documents in BOP.

Running BOP

Once you are done with the filter type and sort profile, you run the BOP with the same criteria. You can run the BOP via the /SAPAPO/BOP transaction.

Figure 8.63 shows the /SAPAPO/BOP transaction screen with the SAP_STANDARD filter type and the SAP_STANDARD sort profile:

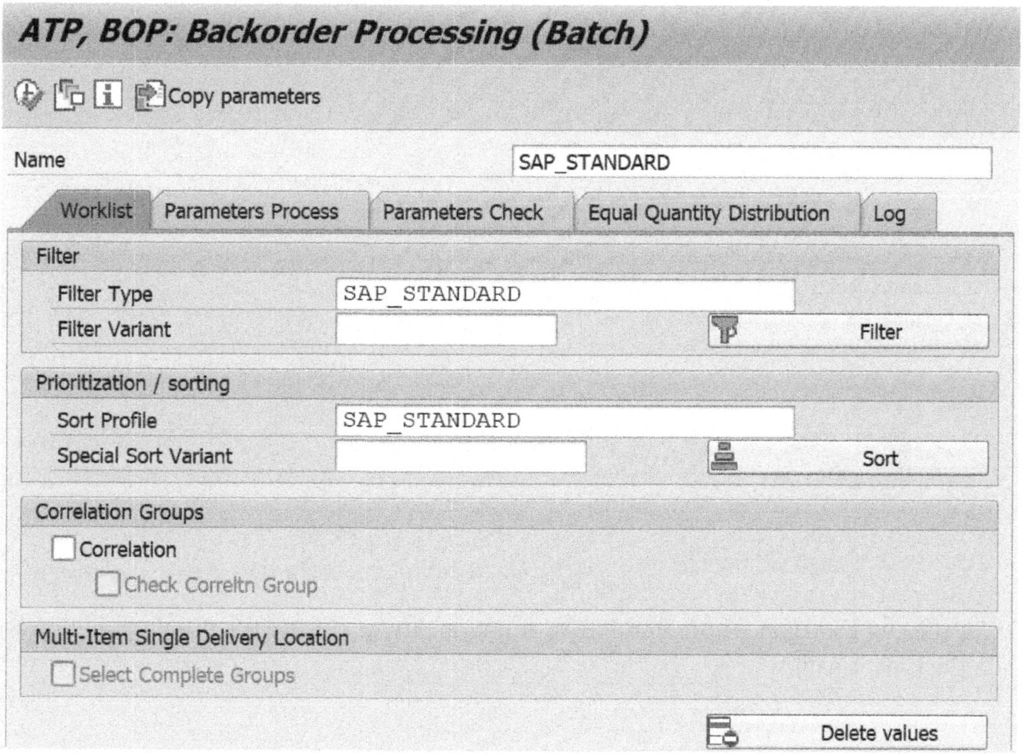

Figure 8.63 – BOP with a filter type and sort profile

Figure 8.64 shows the parameter process, that is, the product ATP/allocation check with the execution mode whether you want to run the simulation BOP or the actual update:

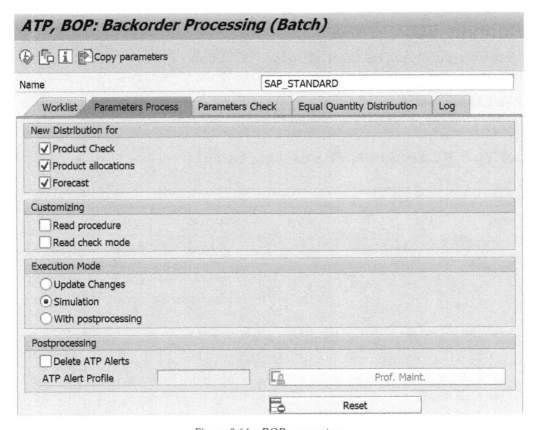

Figure 8.64 – BOP parameters

With this, we have gone through the BOP functionality, setting up the profiles and how to run the functionality.

Summary

With this chapter, you have understood the order fulfillment functionality when working with CRM sales orders. After going through this chapter, you should be well versed in the topics around SAP CRM order integration with GATP and general settings required to set up an ATP check in SAP APO and understand GATP basic methods and advanced methods, as well as how to set up transportation and scheduling with GATP and BOP. Having GATP integrated with a sales order provides basic and advanced ATP check capability to fulfill business needs. This chapter has enabled you to understand the advanced features of SAP APO when it comes to ATP check methods such as ATP plus allocation, RBA checks, MISL, CTP, and MATP. The concept of BOP helps you to understand re-shuffling orders per customer delivery priority.

Once a sales order is created in SAP CRM and fulfilled by running an ATP check with SAP APO, the order is pushed to transportation planning to understand any other constraints on the sales order dates in relation to warehouse or transportation resources. We will understand all this and much more in our next chapter, which is about transportation planning.

Further reading

- Additional information on ATP check methods can be found at `https://help.sap.com/viewer/c95f1f0dcd9549628efa8d7d653da63e/7.0.4/en-US/3643c95360267614e10000000a174cb4.html`.

- Addition information on the scheduling condition techniques can be found at `https://help.sap.com/viewer/c95f1f0dcd9549628efa8d7d653da63e/7.0.4/en-US/4f51c95360267614e10000000a174cb4.html`.

9
Transportation Requirements in SAP TMS

This chapter covers the complete functionality around how transportation requirements are realized in SAP **Transportation Management System** (**TMS**). When a sales order is created, the order replicates in SAP TMS, which creates a transportation requirement in SAP TMS. The transportation process starts with the transportation services being requested, followed by transportation planning, which results in the transportation requirement being consumed. This chapter will cover the different transportation requirement options, including order-based transportation requirements and delivery-based transportation requirements. This chapter will also cover how to record these transportation requirements and the configuration that's required to achieve this.

The following topics will be covered in this chapter:

- Transportation management
- Transportation requirements and sales order processing

By the end of this chapter, you will have learned and understood how to process transportation requirements that have been generated outside the sales orders creation process in SAP CRM. You will have learned about the different options surrounding order-based transportation requirements and delivery-based transportation requirements that are best suited to your business needs, as well as how to configure them.

Transportation management

Transportation management covers the transportation planning phase and the activities related to the carrier picking up the load and shipping the product from the warehouse to the customer's location. Transportation requirements and planning is the key step in the order to cash process as it entails the order being shipped to the customer on time. To be successful in the supply chain, it is essential to understand logistics activities and overcome any hurdles or delays.

Here are the key steps that will be covered in this and the following chapter that will help you understand the transportation requirements, planning, and execution phases in SAP TMS:

1. Integrating a sales order from SAP ECC into SAP TMS

2. Transportation requirements and transportation planning

3. Freight order processing

4. Carrier tendering process

5. Delivery/shipment proposal to SAP ECC

SAP TMS also helps you place the relevant constraints, such as cost or resource availability, to help you efficiently plan your transportation. There are options within SAP TMS that can help save costs and help the system utilize the available resources optimally. Based on the planning outcomes, a transportation service specialist has a better view of how to achieve the customer's requested date and find ways to resolve transportation dates if there are any deviations.

In this chapter, we will cover the **shipper scenario** rather than the LSP scenario. You are already aware that **Logistics Service Provider (LSP)** scenario is the scenario where the company using SAP TMS is a logistics company, such as FedEx, USP, and so on. The other scenario is the shipper scenario, wherein a product manufacturing company manages the freight and subcontracts how goods are transported to the logistics company.

Transportation management functional overview

In this section, we'll gain a detailed understanding of how transportation management is achieved in SAP TMS. The following is a functional overview of transportation management:

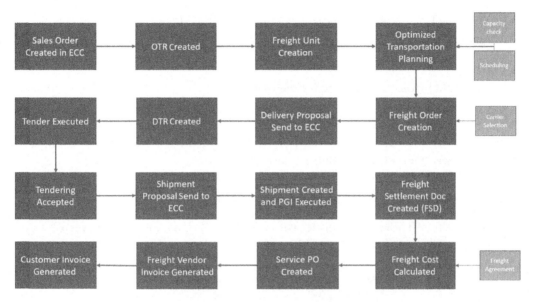

Figure 9.1 – Transportation management flow

The following steps cover the transportation management flow:

1. A sales order is created in SAP CRM, after which it gets replicated to SAP ECC.

2. The sales order in ECC is then replicated to SAP TMS and an **order transportation requirement** (**OTR**) is created in SAP TMS.

3. Based on the freight unit's building rule, a freight unit is created for the OTR in TMS.

4. Transportation planning is executed to run a capacity check, and further scheduling takes place based on the warehouse's capacity.

5. A freight order is created once the transportation planning is completed.

6. A delivery proposal is then sent to SAP ECC.

7. A **delivery transportation requirement** (**DTR**) is created in TMS the system reassigns the freight units from OTRs to DTRs; no further planning is carried out again during this reassignment.

8. The tendering process is executed and accepted.

9. The shipment proposal is sent from TMS to SAP ECC.

10. The shipment is then created in SAP ECC.

11. Pick, Pack, and PGI occurs as the transportation execution steps are initiated.

12. The freight settlement document calculates the freight cost based on the freight agreement with the carrier. It is created in SAP TMS.

13. A service PO is generated in SAP ECC.

14. A freight invoice is generated for the carrier.

15. A customer invoice is generated.

Now that we have understood the transportation management flow, let's have a look at the architecture overview of transportation management.

Technology/architecture overview

Traditionally, SAP TMS communicates with SAP ECC through **SAP Netweaver PI**, as shown in the following architecture diagram:

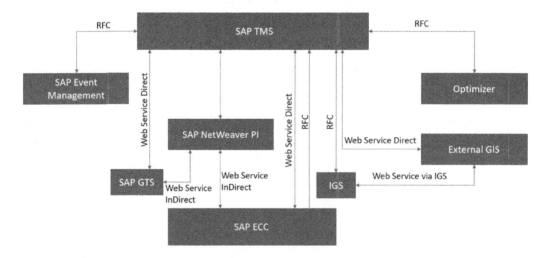

Figure 9.2 – Transportation management architecture overview

The data replicates between SAP TMS and SAP ECC through SAP PI. Geocoordinates are determined from the **external GIS system**, and it can also connect directly to the external GIS system for distance determination between the source location and the destination location. The external GIS system can provide geographical mapping data for transportation routes, and the **Internet Graphics Service (IGS)** uses this data to show the image on the screen. SAP TMS also allows us to make a direct web service call to the external GIS system to determine the geocoordinates and distance between the source location and destination. The call to the IGS is an RFC call, while the call to the external GIS system is a web service call.

SAP Event Management can be installed separately on a new system, or it can be installed as an add-on to another SAP system. Typically, Event Management could be an add-on to your SAP TMS environment and communicate with SAP TMS through an RFC call. Event Management can trigger events for any of the other SAP systems, such as TMS, CRM, and so on.

Like Event Management, you must set up an RFC call to communicate with SAP **Global Trade Service GTS**, as shown in the preceding diagram.

Optimizer is a C++-based application designed to optimize and resolve transportation problems. As shown in the preceding diagram, there is an RFC call to the optimizer during transportation planning. The optimizer runs on different hardware compared to the application server that SAP TMS runs on.

You can run the optimizer connection test via transaction code RCC_CUST. The optimizer provides six different applications, as shown in the following screenshot:

RCCF: Destinations for Engines

Dest. ID	Appl.	Short Text	Status	Ma...	Pri...	Comm. Type	Communication Connection
TSFM01	TSFM	Strategic Freight Management Optimizer	1 Active ▼	10	1	RFC	▼ OPTSERVER_TSFM01
TSPS01	TSPS	Transportation Service Provider	1 Active ▼	10	1	RFC	▼ OPTSERVER_TSPS01
TVRG01	TVRG	Transportation Proposal	1 Active ▼	10	1	RFC	▼ OPTSERVER_TVRG01
TVSO01	TVSO	Load Optimization	1 Active ▼	10	1	RFC	▼ OPTSERVER_TVSO01
TVSR01	TVSR	Vehicle Scheduling and Routing engine	1 Active ▼	12	1	RFC	▼ OPTSERVER_TVSR01
TVSS01	TVSS	Vehicle Scheduling engine	1 Active ▼	10	1	RFC	▼ OPTSERVER_TVSS01

Figure 9.3 – Application call to the optimizer

These applications are stated here:

- TSFM for Strategic Freight Management
- TSPS for Transportation Service Provider
- TVRG for Transportation Proposal

- TVSO for Load Optimization
- TVSR for Vehicle Scheduling and Routing Engine
- TVSS for Vehicle Scheduling Engine

Now that we have gone through the SAP TMS architecture overview and understood its various components, let's understand how the transportation requirements are realized and how sales order processing takes place in SAP TMS.

Transportation requirements and sales order processing

The sales orders and deliveries that are created in SAP ERP are transferred to SAP TMS to facilitate the process of transportation planning and execution. The sales order in SAP ERP is transferred to SAP TMS, which creates an OTR document. A freight unit is created from the OTR and even more transportation planning is executed, thus creating the freight order. The orders and deliveries in SAP TMS are represented as the transportation requirements. The following diagram shows the steps required to activate the order and delivery integration from SAP ERP to SAP TMS:

Figure 9.4 – Steps to activate the order and delivery integration from SAP ERP to SAP TMS

The first step in integrating is to activate the business function, followed by creating the control keys and activating the document transfer in the SAP ERP system.

The following are the business functions that need to be activated to trigger integration with SAP TMS:

- LOG_TM_ORD_INT allows your business to integrate sales orders with sales order scheduling.
- LOG_TM_ORD_INT_TRQ allows your business to integrate sales orders without sales order scheduling.
- The Logistics S&D Simplification (SD_01) or Operations, Enterprise Services (ESOA_OPS01) business function is activated for transferring sales orders to SAP TMS.

- The Operations, Enterprise Services 2 (`LOG_ESOA_OPS_2`) business function in SAP ERP allows you to transfer purchase orders and stock transport orders from SAP ECC to SAP TMS.

> **Note**
>
> Business functions are irreversible once activated, so they should be evaluated before activation.

SAP TMS documents integration with SAP ERP

To integrate SAP TMS documents with SAP ERP, we must understand the following integration scenarios before moving on to transportation planning:

- Integrating an ERP sales order
- Order-based transportation requirement
- Creating ERP deliveries from SAP TMS
- Integrating ERP deliveries
- Delivery-based transportation requirement
- Integrating changed ERP orders and deliveries

Each of these integration scenarios will be discussed in detail in the upcoming subsections.

Integrating an ERP sales order

The prerequisite to transferring a sales order from SAP ERP to SAP TMS is making sure that the relevant master data is transferred to SAP TMS. This includes its location, product, and business partner. Most companies that are not LSPs commonly integrate sales orders from SAP ERP to SAP TMS and run the order-based transportation requirement scenario, wherein the sales orders are transferred to SAP TMS, which creates an OTR in SAP TMS. OTR becomes the parent document for planning the transportation and from there onward, subsequent documents are generated to plan the transportation. We covered the steps to activate the sales order integration shown in the *Figure 9.4*. After activating the business function, the next step is to Configure the key and activate the transfer of orders from SAP ERP to SAP TMS. You can do this in SAP ERP by going to **SAP IMG | Integration with Other SAP Components | Transportation Management | Logistics Integration | Define Control Keys for Document Transfer**.

The following screenshot shows an example of **Ctrl Key** 0001. This has been activated for **SO to TM** and outbound delivery:

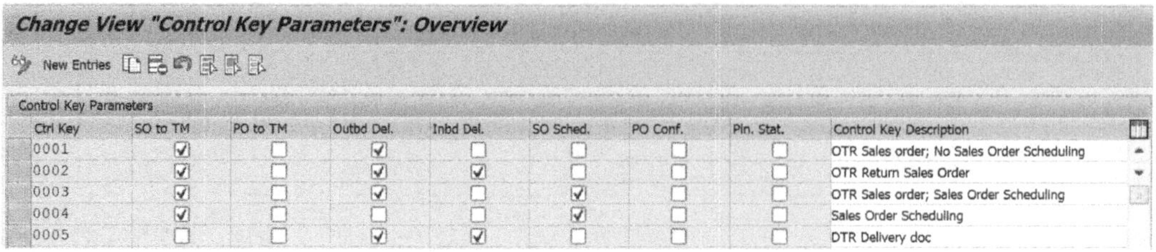

Ctrl Key	SO to TM	PO to TM	Outbd Del.	Inbd Del.	SO Sched.	PO Conf.	Pin. Stat.	Control Key Description
0001	☑	☐	☑	☐	☐	☐	☐	OTR Sales order; No Sales Order Scheduling
0002	☑	☐	☑	☑	☐	☐	☐	OTR Return Sales Order
0003	☑	☐	☑	☐	☑	☐	☐	OTR Sales order; Sales Order Scheduling
0004	☑	☐	☐	☐	☑	☐	☐	Sales Order Scheduling
0005	☐	☐	☑	☑	☐	☐	☐	DTR Delivery doc

Figure 9.5 – Control Key Parameters

Here, you define the control keys that determine which document is to be transferred using the corresponding enterprise services. The next step is to activate the transfer of the sales document. This is done in the SAP ERP IMG path at **SAP IMG | Integration with Other SAP Components | Transportation Management | Logistics Integration | Activate Transfer of Sales Documents**.

The following screenshot shows the sales document being transferred:

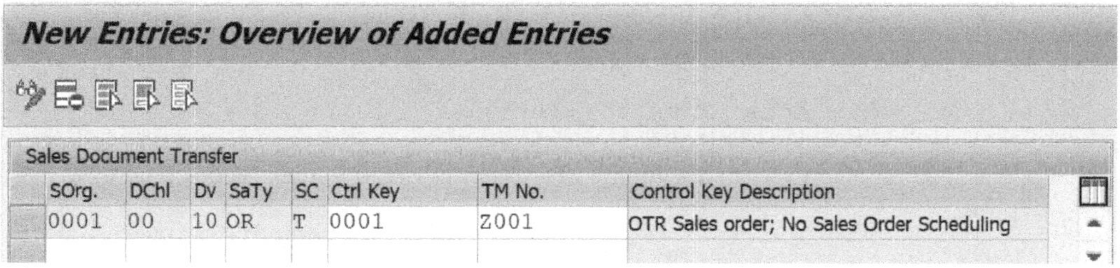

New Entries: Overview of Added Entries

Sales Document Transfer

SOrg.	DChl	Dv	SaTy	SC	Ctrl Key	TM No.	Control Key Description
0001	00	10	OR	T	0001	Z001	OTR Sales order; No Sales Order Scheduling

Figure 9.6 – Sales Document Transfer

In this step, you activate the transfer of sales documents to SAP TMS by assigning a control key to the required sales document types. The control key determines whether a sales document and the corresponding outbound delivery are to be transferred to SAP TMS. It also determines whether sales order scheduling is to be carried out in SAP ERP or in SAP TMS.

When you create a sales document that the transfer has been activated for, the system assigns the control key to the sales document and to all the relevant documents in the document chain, such as outbound delivery. This is a fixed parameter that cannot be changed subsequently in the sales document.

To transfer the sales order from SAP ERP to SAP TMS, you also need to configure the output for the sales order. SAP provides a standard output type of TRS0 and a requirement routine of 27 that needs to be assigned to the output procedure, as shown in the following screenshot:

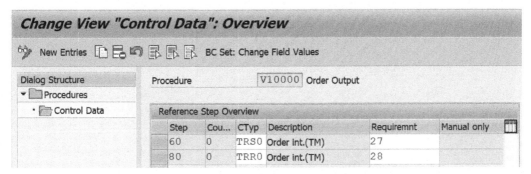

Figure 9.7 – Maintaining the output determination procedure

You configure this in the SAP ERP system by going to **SAP IMG | Sales and Distribution | Basic Functions | Output Control | Output Determination | Output Determination Using the Condition Technique | Maintain Output Determination for Sales Documents | Maintain Output Determination Procedure**.

SAP provides the TRS0 output type. This can be accessed by going to **SAP IMG | Sales and Distribution | Basic Functions | Output Control | Output Determination | Output Determination Using the Condition Technique | Maintain Output Determination for Sales Documents | Maintain Output Types**.

Access Sequence is assigned 0002, as shown in the following screenshot:

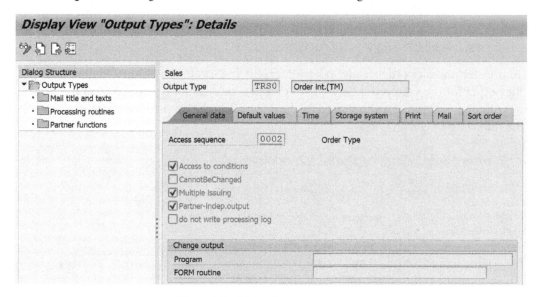

Figure 9.8 – Maintaining output types

The following screenshot shows **Dispatch time** as being immediate. This means that any changes that are made or saved to the ERP sales order will trigger the updates immediately with this output type from SAP ERP to SAP TMS:

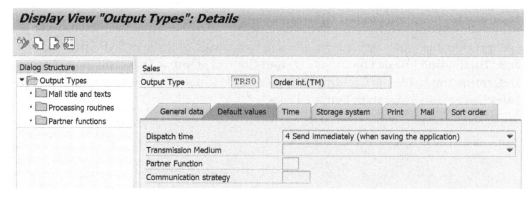

Figure 9.9 – Maintaining output types

The OPS_SE_SOC_SEND_MESSAGE standard SAP service is called when the TRS0 output is called on **order changed** or **order save**. The following screenshot shows how to assign the service to the output type:

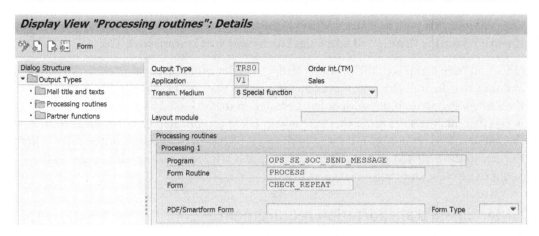

Figure 9.10 – Maintaining output types

Once you are done with configuring the control key and TRS0 output type, you have to create a condition record for each sales document type that is to be transferred to SAP TMS. You do this using TRS0 for sales orders. You can create condition records in the following master data path. Under **SAP Easy Access** screen, choose **Logistics | Sales and Distribution | Master Data | Output | Sales Document | Create**.

For overcoming your business needs and exceptions around integrating sales orders from SAP ERP to SAP TMS, SAP has provided BAdI: Sales Document Integration with TMS with a BAdI name of BADI_LO_TM_SLS, wherein you can add more criteria and filter when you want to transfer the sales order from SAP ECC to SAP TMS.

You can use this BAdI to change the control key and the technical transportation management number that's assigned to the sales document types in the customizing activity. This is activated to transfer sales documents. This BAdI is called when you're saving the sales document.

The following methods are available in the BAdI: Sales Document Integration with TM:

- CHANGE_TM_CTRL_KEY: You can use this BAdI method to change the control key that's assigned to the sales document types.

- CHANGE_LOG_TM_NR: You can use this BAdI method to change the technical transportation management number that's assigned to the sales document types.

The configuration path to BAdI is **SPRO | Integration with Other SAP Components | Business Add-Ins (BAdIs) | BAdI: Sales Document Integration with TM**.

Once you have completed the previous setup, the sales order integration becomes active, and the sales document is transferred as soon as the sales order is created or changed in the SAP ERP system. If the sales order is created in the SAP CRM system, the behavior is no different. The sales order that's created in CRM is replicated to ECC and as soon as the sales order is replicated and saved in the SAP ERP system, the sales order triggers the transfer to the SAP TM system. The TRS0 output is triggered for the CRM order in the SAP ECC system and transfers it to SAP TMS.

Order-based transportation requirement

The order-based transportation requirement uses a sales order to plan the transportation. This is one of the scenarios that is widely used, wherein the sales order is used for transportation planning. Typically, if the client is a manufacturer and if their core business is not transportation, but the business acts as a shipper who wants to ship the product to the customer from their warehouse, they would plan their sales order effectively to optimize this transportation effort.

The following diagram shows the steps of the order-based transportation requirement:

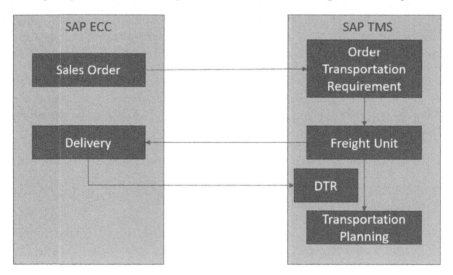

Figure 9.11 – Order-based transportation requirement

Let's look at the steps that are followed here:

1. A sales order is created in the SAP ECC system. The sales order can also be created in SAP CRM and replicated to SAP ECC. The order will contain the material line item, along with its requested date and confirmed schedule line.

2. The sales order from SAP ECC is transferred to SAP TMS and creates the OTR. The dates from the sales order in ECC can also be seen on the OTR. Dates from the sales order in the OTR can be viewed under the schedule line in the OTR.

3. A freight unit is created from the OTR; it can be created automatically or manually. This is based on the OTR document type configuration. You can configure the OTR to create the freight unit automatically, and also determine the freight unit type based on the freight unit building rule. In addition to this, the freight unit can consider requested quantity or confirmed quantity while the freight unit is being created. This is dependent on the settings in the OTR document type.

4. The freight unit then undergoes the transportation planning phase, which then creates the freight order. This further initiates the logistics execution.

5. Once the freight unit has been created, a delivery proposal is sent to SAP ECC. This creates the delivery document in ECC. The delivery document in ECC triggers the creation of DTR; the freight unit is reassigned from the OTR to DTR without executing planning again.

The OTR type is determined based on certain conditions. These conditions are defined under application administration and determine the order-based transportation requirement type. These conditions are created in **SAP NetWeaver Business Client (NWBC)** under the /SCMTMS/OTR_TYPE condition type via **Application Administration | General Settings | Conditions | Create Condition.**

The following screenshot shows an example of an OTR condition with the /SCMTMS/ OTR_TYPE condition type created:

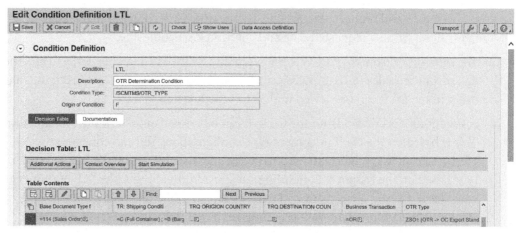

Figure 9.12 – Order-based transportation requirement condition with the /SCMTMS/OTR_TYPE condition type

The OTR represents the sales order from the SAP ERP system. Unlike other documents in SAP TMS, such as freight unit and freight order, that can be edited in SAP TMS, the OTR cannot be edited in SAP TMS. the OTR is a very light document that consists of information such as **General data**, **Business Partner**, **Location & Dates/Times**, **Document Flow**, **Notes**, **Blocking information**, and **Administrative Data**. It also consists of item information, including item data and schedule line. The schedule line shows the dates from the ERP sales order.

Here is a detailed explanation of the information held by the OTR:

- **General data** within the OTR contains some of the key information related to statuses and blocking in information. The statuses are **Lifecycle status**, **Execution status**, and **Consumption status**, as explained here:

  a). **Lifecycle status**: This shows whether the OTR is open, in planning, in execution, or completed. The status changes as the subsequent documents are created and executed.

  b). **Execution status**: This represents whether the execution of the order-based transportation requirement has been completed or it is still open. For execution to complete, all planning documents associated with the order-based transportation requirement should be completed.

c). **Consumption status**: This represents whether all the freight units that were assigned to the order-based transportation requirement have been consumed by a delivery-based transportation requirement.

- Apart from status, general data within the OTR also shows weights and incoterms information. It contains blocking information such as **Planning Block**, **Delivery Block**, and **Execution Block**. Within SAP TMS, you can configure the system to block the transportation planning phase based on a certain type of delivery block. This way, you can restrict further transportation planning until the delivery block is removed.

- **Location & Dates/Times**: This shows the source and destination information of the complete transportation path. The document flow shows the subsequent documents that are created by the OTR, just like in SAP ERP.

To configure the order-based transportation requirement, go to **SAP IMG | SAP Transportation Management | Transportation Management | Integration | ERP Logistics Integration | Order-Based Transportation Requirement | Define Order-Based Transportation Requirement Types**.

The following screenshot shows the OTR type configuration:

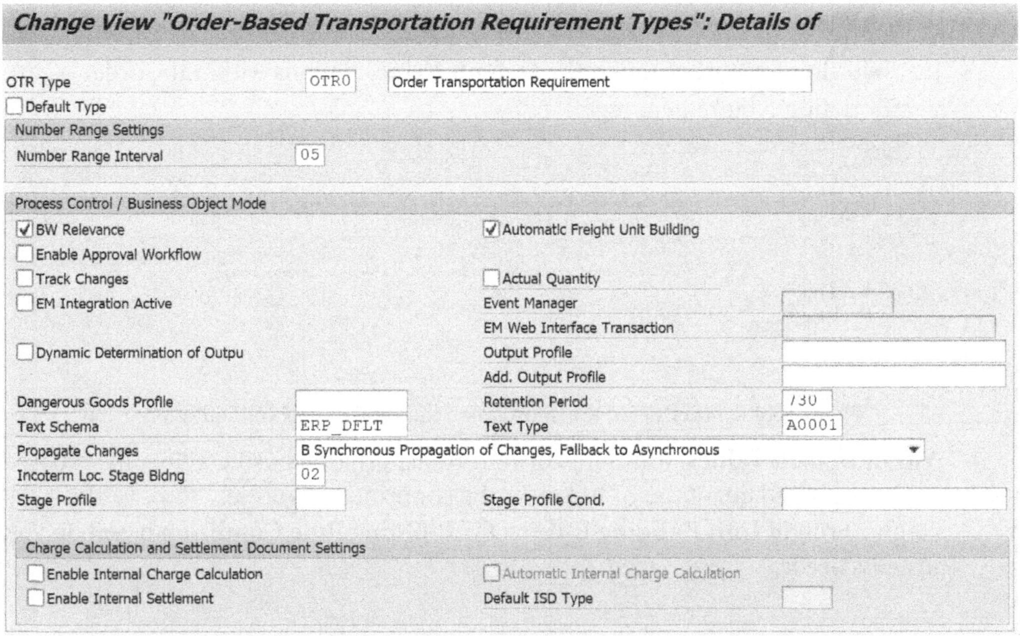

Figure 9.13 – Order-based transportation requirement type configuration

The preceding screenshot depicts certain parameters of the OTR that influence how the system processes the business document. You assign the number range to the OTR document and the configuration option here is divided into **Process Control**, **Charge Calculation**, and **Settlement Document Settings** and **Default Values**.

- **Process Control/Business Object Mode** contains a key configuration option; that is, the flag to create the freight unit automatically using the **Automatic Freight Unit Building rule**, **Track Changes**, activating **EM Integration Active**, assigning **Dangerous Goods Profile**, **Text Schema**, and also enabling stage building based on the Incoterm location (**Incoterm Loc. Stage Bldng**). The stage building rule values define which stages will be built in OTRs if the incoterm location is used for stage building. The system uses the incoterm location for stage building if the incoterm has set the **LOC** flag in the SAP TM system. The **LOC** flag is a flag that indicates that you must enter a location with this incoterm. If no incoterm is specified, the system does not use the incoterm location for stage building and the system creates only one stage from the source to the destination location.

To determine a location from the INCO2 string, you must assign a location to an incoterm location. You can assign the location to the incoterm location in **SAP Easy Access Menu** under **Transportation Management| Master Data| Transportation Network| Assign Location to Incoterm Location (/SCMTMS/INCLOC_MAP)**.

The following screenshot shows the **Default Values** options within the order transportation requirement type:

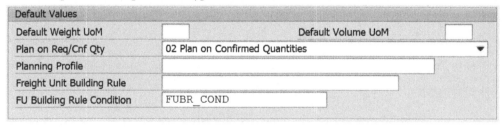

Figure 9.14 – Order-based transportation requirement type configuration

- Within **Default Values**, you can plan your transportation business document based on the requested quantities or based on the confirmed quantities. You can also assign a **Freight Unit Building Rule** or **FU Building Rule Condition** based on your business needs.

You can also map and assign ERP Text Types to TM Text Types for OTRs. The following screenshot shows the ERP text type mapping to the SAP TM text type:

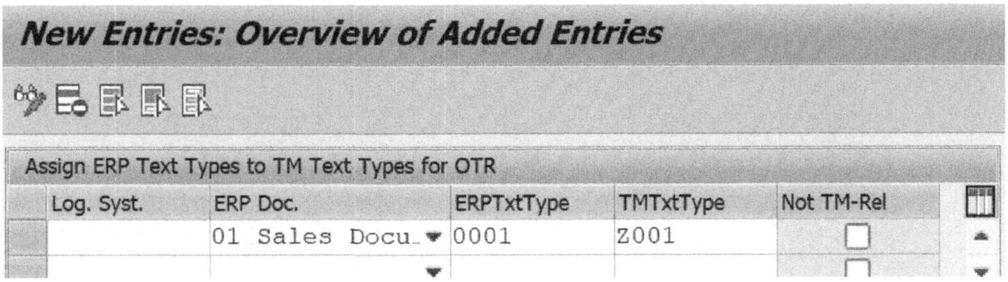

New Entries: Overview of Added Entries

Assign ERP Text Types to TM Text Types for OTR

Log. Syst.	ERP Doc.	ERPTxtType	TMTxtType	Not TM-Rel	
	01 Sales Docu... ▾	0001	Z001	☐	▲
	▾			☐	▾

Figure 9.15 – Mapping ERP Text Types to TM Text Types for an OTR

You can do this by going to **SAP IMG | SAP Transportation Management | Transportation Management | Integration | ERP Logistics Integration | Order-Based Transportation Requirement | Assign ERP Text Types to TM Text Types for OTRs**.

Now that we have understood the order-based transportation requirement, next, we will look at how to create ERP deliveries.

Creating ERP deliveries from SAP TMS

SAP TM allows you to create deliveries through the SAP ERP system. The delivery proposal within SAP TMS can be triggered before or after transportation planning. In general, or in most business use cases, the delivery proposal is based on the result of transportation planning, which considers the resource's availability and the dates/duration for when the freight order is planned and created. To send the delivery proposal, the order-based transportation requirement should not be blocked for delivery and a freight unit should be created.

The following diagram shows the process of sending an ERP delivery to SAP TMS:

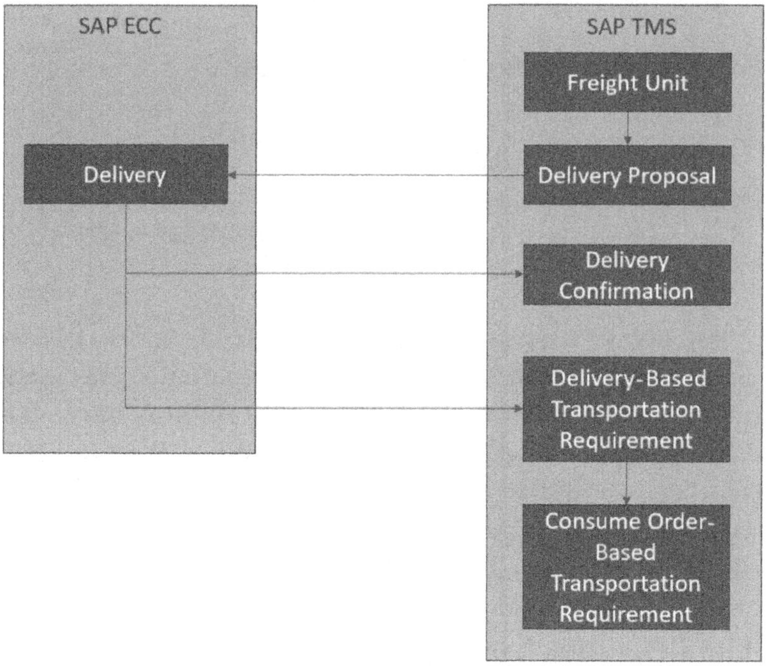

Figure 9.16 – Delivery proposal process steps from SAP TMS

The following steps take place in the delivery proposal process:

1. A freight unit and/or freight order is created in SAP TMS. The delivery can be created using a freight unit or via a freight order.

2. A delivery proposal is initiated from SAP TM. The delivery proposal can be automated using a batch job, though you can manually trigger the delivery from the freight order. The delivery proposal groups the items that need to go on a specific delivery together. A user can also create the delivery proposal interactively through SAP NetWeaver Business Client by going to **ERP Logistics Integration | Delivery Creation | Create Deliveries in ERP**. Here, you can specify the selection profile and then select the relevant document in the list. Once the relevant document has been selected, you can initiate the delivery proposal's creation.

3. You can create delivery proposals for order-based transportation requirements by using a background program such as /SCMTMS/DLV_BATCH. Similar to initiating a delivery proposal interactively, you can enter selection criteria or use selection profiles here. The system selects the documents and creates the delivery proposals. The delivery proposal is then sent automatically to SAP ERP.

4. Once the delivery proposal has been initiated, delivery is created in the SAP ERP system. This delivery sends the delivery confirmation to SAP TMS. Based on the rules in the SAP ERP system, the delivery can further split the SAP ERP system. The dates are taken from the input document that triggers the delivery proposal. It uses dates from the freight order if the delivery proposal is from the freight order. If no freight order has been created for the order-based transportation requirement, then SAP TMS uses dates from the freight units. The quantities come from the freight unit. When the delivery proposal is sent to SAP ERP, the timestamp of when the delivery proposal was initiated is also updated in the freight unit.

5. Once the delivery is created in SAP ERP, the delivery-based transportation requirement is created in SAP TMS. SAP TMS reassigns the freight units from the OTR to the DTR, resulting in the order-based transportation requirement being consumed.

With this, we have learned how to create an ERP delivery. Next, we will examine how to integrate ERP deliveries.

Integrating ERP deliveries

Just like integrating an ERP sales order, there are prerequisites to transferring the deliveries from SAP ERP to SAP TMS. Here is the list of steps involved:

1. First, you need to configure the control key and activate the transfer of deliveries from SAP ERP to SAP TMS. This can be done in SAP ERP by going to **SAP IMG | Integration with Other SAP Components | Transportation Management | Logistics Integration | Define Control Keys for Document Transfer**.

The following screenshot shows an example of **Ctrl Key 0005**, which has been activated for outbound delivery to TMS. Here, you define the control keys that determine which documents are to be transferred using the corresponding enterprise services:

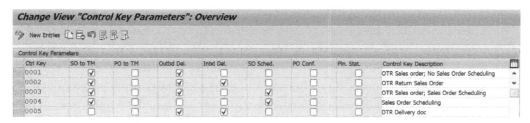

Figure 9.17 – Control key parameters

2. The next step is to activate the process of transferring the sales document. This can be done by going to **SAP IMG | Integration with Other SAP Components | Transportation Management | Logistics Integration | Activate Transfer of Delivery Documents**.

    The following screenshot shows the configuration for activating the process of delivery documents being transferred from SAP ECC to SAP TMS:

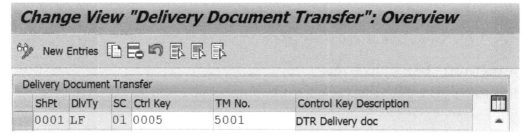

Figure 9.18 – Delivery Document Transfer

    In this step, you activate the delivery document being transferred to SAP TMS by assigning a control key to a combination of the shipping point, delivery type, and shipping condition. The control key determines whether deliveries are to be transferred to SAP TMS.

3. To transfer the deliveries from SAP ERP to SAP TMS, you also need to configure the output for deliveries. SAP provides a standard output type of TRD0 that needs to be assigned to the output procedure. You can configure this in the SAP ERP system by going to **SAP IMG | Logistics Execution | Shipping | Basic Shipping Functions | Output Control | Output Determination | Maintain Output Determination for Outbound Deliveries**.

4. Once you have configured the control key and output type; that is, TRD0, you have to create a condition record for each delivery document type that is to be transferred to SAP TMS, using the TRD0 output type for the delivery document. You can create condition records in the master data path mentioned here. Under the **SAP Easy Access** screen, choose **Logistics | Logistics Execution | Master Data | Output | Shipping | Outbound Deliveries | Create**.

5. To overcome your business needs and exceptions around integrating deliveries from SAP ERP to SAP TMS, SAP has provided BAdI: Delivery Integration with TMS, wherein you can add more criteria when you want to transfer the deliveries from SAP ERP to SAP TMS. Various methods are available in BAdI: Delivery Integration with TM, including CHANGE_TM_CTRL_KEY, which you can use to change the control key that's assigned to the delivery document types, and CHANGE_LOG_TM_NR, which you can use to change the technical transportation management number that's assigned to the delivery document. The configuration path to BAdI can be found at **SPRO | Integration with Other SAP Components | Business Add-Ins (BAdIs) | BAdI: Delivery Integration with TM**.

Once you are done with the aforementioned setup, the delivery integration becomes active and the delivery document would be delivered as soon as the delivery is created or changed in SAP ERP.

Delivery-based transportation requirement

The delivery-based transportation requirement uses SAP ERP delivery to plan the transportation. This is an alternative scenario that can be used to plan the transportation in addition to the order-based transportation requirement. If the ERP sales order is also replicated to SAP TMS and the freight unit is created from the OTR, the transportation demand is passed from the OTR to the DTR, thus reassigning the freight unit to the DTR. This results in the transportation requirement being consumed from the OTR to the DTR.

The following diagram shows the steps involved in the delivery-based transportation requirement:

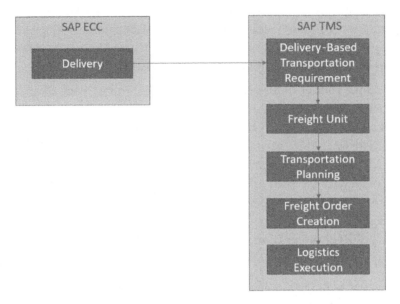

Figure 9.19 – Delivery-based transportation requirement

Here are the steps in detail for the delivery-based transportation requirement:

1. A delivery is created in the SAP ECC system from the sales order in the SAP ERP system. The delivery document contains the material line item, along with the requested date and the confirmed date from the sales order. If you run ATP on delivery, then the delivery document will show the updated ATP dates.

2. Once the DTR is created in TMS, the freight unit is also created, either manually or automatically. This is based on the DTR document type's configuration. You can configure DTR to create the freight unit automatically and determine the freight unit type based on the freight unit building rule.

3. The freight unit then undergoes transportation planning, which then creates the freight order. This further initiates the logistics execution.

To determine the DTR type based on certain conditions, you need to define conditions within the application's administration. Once you've define the condition, you can define which delivery-based transportation requirement type is to be used for delivery. You can do this by creating a condition of the /SCMTMS/DTR_TYPE type in the SAP **NetWeaver Business Client (NWBC)** by choosing **Application Administration | General Settings | Conditions | Create Condition**.

The DTR represents the delivery document from the SAP ERP system. Unlike other documents in SAP TMS such as freight unit and freight order, which can be edited in SAP TMS, a DTR cannot be edited in SAP TMS. Similar to the OTR, the DTR is a document that consists of information such as **General data, Business Partner, Location & Dates/Times, Document Flow, Notes, Blocking information,** and **Administrative Data**. It also consists of item information such as item data, delivery quantities, and weight and document references. Let's take a look at this:

- **General data** within the DTR consists of information related to statuses and blocking information. The statuses are **Lifecycle status, Execution status,** and **Consumption status**:

  a). **Lifecycle status** shows whether the DTR is new, in planning, executing, or completed. The life cycle status changes as the subsequent documents are created and executed.

  b). **Execution status** represents whether the delivery-based transportation requirement has been executed. For the execution to complete, all the planning documents that have been assigned to the delivery-based transportation requirement must be completed.

- Apart from statuses, general data within the DTR also shows weights and incoterms information. It provides blocking information such as **Shipment Planning Block, Planning Block, Delivery Block,** and **Execution Block** data. Within SAP TMS, you can configure the system to execute a planning block or execution block based on the delivery block or shipment block that originated from the SAP ERP system.

- **Location & Dates/Times** shows the source and destination information of the complete transportation path. The document flow shows the subsequent documents that are created from the DTR, just like in the SAP ERP system.

  To configure the delivery-based transportation requirement, go to **SAP IMG | SAP Transportation Management | Transportation Management | Integration | ERP Logistics Integration | Delivery-Based Transportation Requirement | Define Delivery-Based Transportation Requirement Types**.

The following screenshot shows the DTR type configuration. Here, you define certain parameters of the DTR that influence how the system processes the business document:

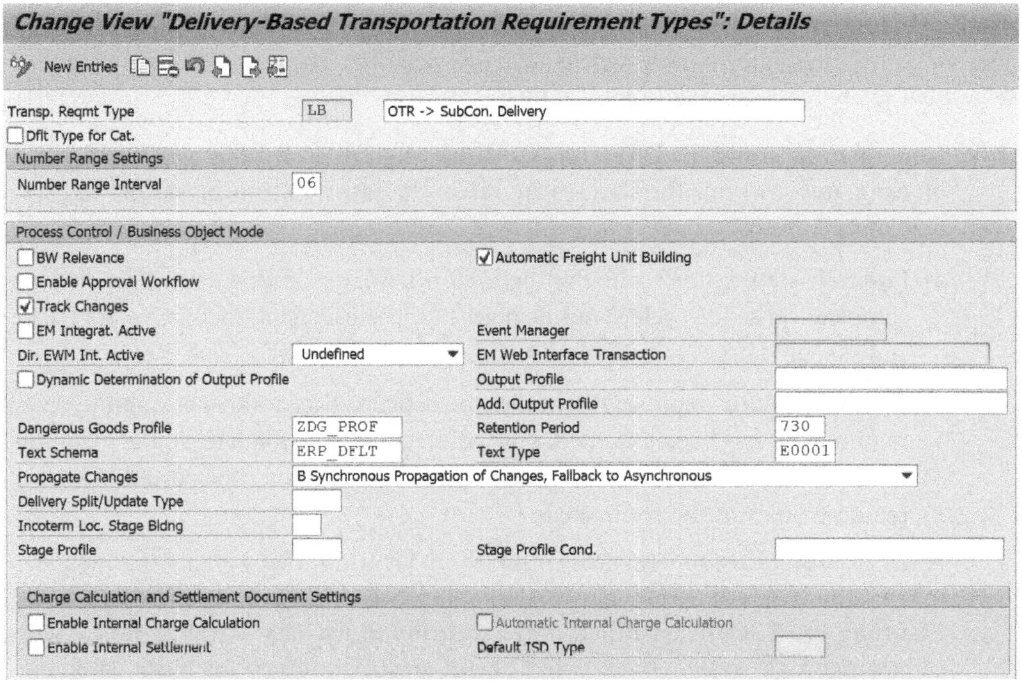

Figure 9.20 – Delivery-based transportation requirement type configuration

You assign the number range to the OTR document. The configuration options here are divided into **Process Control**, **Charge Calculation and Settlement Document Settings**, and **Default values**.

- **Process Control/Business Object Mode** has a key configuration option, which is the flag to create the freight unit automatically through **Freight Unit Building rule**, **Track Changes**, **Activate EM Integration**, **Assigning Dangerous Goods Profile**, and **Text Schema**; it also enables stage building based on the incoterm location. The stage building rule values define which stages will be built in the DTRs if the incoterm location is used for stage building. The system uses the incoterm location for stage building if the incoterm has set the **LOC** (the **INCO2** field in SAP ERP should be filled) flag in the SAP TM system. If no incoterm is specified, the system does not use the incoterm location for stage building; the system only creates one stage from the source to the destination location.

- Within **Default Values**, you assign the **Freight Unit Building Rule** or **FU Building Rule Condition** based on your business needs, as shown in the following screenshot:

Default Values			
Default Weight UoM	LB	Default Volume UoM	
Planning Profile			
Freight Unit Building Rule			
FU Building Rule Condition	FUBR_COND		

Figure 9.21 – Delivery-based transportation requirement type configuration

You can also map and assign ERP Text Types to TM Text Types for DTRs. You can do this by going to **SAP IMG | SAP Transportation Management | Transportation Management | Integration | ERP Logistics Integration | Delivery-Based Transportation Requirement | Assign ERP Text Types to TM Text Types for DTRs**.

Now that we have covered the configuration for the delivery-based requirement type, let's understand the text type mapping between SAP ECC and SAP TM.

The following screenshot shows the ERP text type mapping to SAP TM text type:

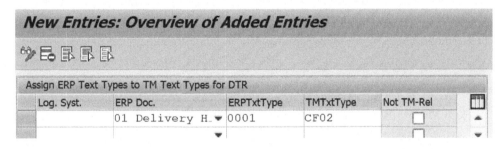

Figure 9.22 – Mapping ERP Text Types to TM Text Types for a DTR

As we can see, the ERP text type is mapped to the TM text type. One of the examples stated is the 0001 text type in ERP, which is mapped to the CF02 text type in SAP TM.

Integrating changed ERP orders and deliveries

The changes that are made to the OTR and DTR are initiated by the SAP ERP orders and SAP ERP deliveries, respectively. You cannot change the OTR or DTR directly in SAP TM. You can integrate the changed documents between SAP ERP and SAP TMS. The concept of the change controller in SAP TM propagates the changes to the transportation documents. This could be the changes to the freight unit or freight order. Based on certain rules and conditions, you can overcome these business requirements based on the changes that have been made to the sales document in the SAP ERP system. For example, changing the sales order may trigger an update to the OTR. The changes are adapted by the freight unit associated with the OTR.

Within the freight unit, the system determines the condition and based on that condition, a change controller strategy is determined and applied. The strategy can be specific to your business requirements. Let's say there is a business requirement that the freight unit should be canceled if the quantity of the sales order is greater than the previous quantity entered. You can create your own strategy and adapt it based on your business needs. The same principle applies if you wish to delete documents.

Typically, a change controller is initiated by making changes to the quantities, dates/times, source locations, and destination locations. SAP has also delivered standard service types for the change controller. You can use a standard SAP change controller strategy or create one per your business needs. If the system can't process a change controller strategy due to a locking issue, then don't worry – SAP provides a background program called /SCMTMS/PROCESS_TRIGGER_BGD to reprocess the strategy.

> **Note**
>
> You can assign the service types to your own strategy, and these service types can be asynchronous or synchronous. For example, TOR_CHACO, TOR_CREATE, and TOR_SAVE are processed asynchronously in a separate task, whereas the strategies of TOR_CHACOS, TOR_CREA_S, and TOR_SAVE_S are processed synchronously.

SAP has also provided change controller settings for the business document types for customizing for SAP TMS, as mentioned here:

- Default change strategy
- Strategy determination condition
- Quantity tolerance determination condition
- Date tolerance determination condition

This is also shown in the following screenshot:

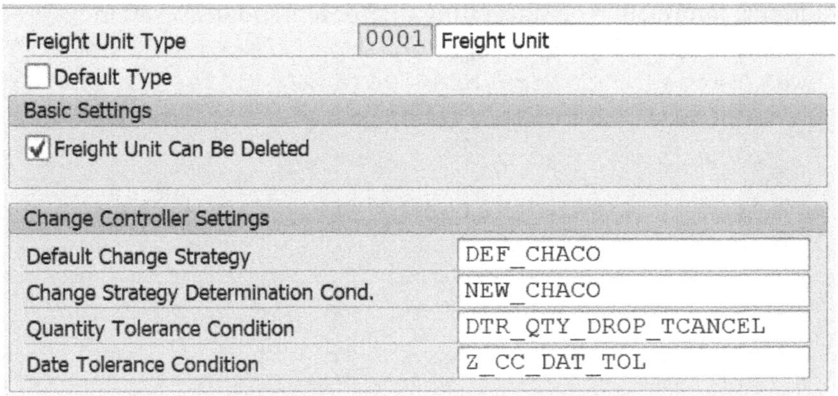

Freight Unit Type	0001	Freight Unit
Default Type		
Basic Settings		
☑ Freight Unit Can Be Deleted		

Change Controller Settings	
Default Change Strategy	DEF_CHACO
Change Strategy Determination Cond.	NEW_CHACO
Quantity Tolerance Condition	DTR_QTY_DROP_TCANCEL
Date Tolerance Condition	Z_CC_DAT_TOL

Figure 9.23 – Freight Unit Type change controller settings

The default change strategy is used when the strategy determination condition is not mentioned in the configuration. If the strategy determination condition is added to the configuration, then the system determines the change strategy based on the condition; otherwise, it takes the default change strategy.

Summary

This chapter provided us with an understanding of the transportation requirements and the configuration required to set up these transportation requirements in SAP TMS. At this point, you should have a good understanding of how the transportation requirement documents are created and the different options you can use, such as an order-based transportation requirement or delivery-based transportation requirement, based on your business needs. You also learned about the key concepts around SAP TMS document integration with SAP ERP, integrating ERP sales orders, and integrating ERP deliveries. These topics are not only beneficial but also act as a prerequisite to the transportation planning topic.

In the next chapter, we will cover transportation planning. Once the transportation requirements have been realized in SAP TMS, the next step is to undergo planning to achieve the most cost-optimal and effective transportation results.

Further reading

- Additional information on integrating ERP orders and deliveries in transportation planning can be found at `https://help.sap.com/viewer/54cf405c9d9e4c96bf091967ea29d6a7/9.6.2/en-US/e50d1242ac58452cbfb50f3f66be7ee8.html`.

10
Transportation Planning and Freight Order Management in SAP TMS

Transportation planning is key when it comes to executing the transportation of goods from one location to another. In order to save money and plan transportation effectively, businesses need to understand their constraints prior to transportation taking place. This chapter talks about those constraints and what options are provided by SAP TMS to overcome those constraints, thereby resulting in the most effective planning.

A freight order document, which results from planning the transportation process, carries transportation information that enables goods to be transported from one location to another. This chapter covers the key concepts regarding the freight order document and its configuration options to effectively utilize the freight order for transportation execution purposes. The chapter also includes different ways to determine carriers and methods for tendering the freight order to these carriers.

Here is a list of the topics that will be covered in this chapter:

- Transportation planning
- Freight order management
- Carrier selection and tendering

By the end of this chapter, you will understand transportation planning and freight order processing, the associated key concepts, and how to configure freight units and freight orders in SAP TMS as per your business requirements. You will also learn the concepts of carrier selection and the tendering process in this chapter.

Transportation planning

In the previous chapter, we covered transportation management architecture and transportation requirements. This chapter covers the key aspects of transportation planning, which, in turn, maximizes logistics activity and brings profit to the organization. In transportation planning, two business documents are created – a freight unit and a freight order. Before these business documents are created, several constraints, including capacities, are considered with a view to optimizing the shipment processing process. Let's start with the freight unit document and understand how this document works and is processed in SAP TMS.

Freight unit

The planning process is broken down into different stages. Transportation requirements initiate the planning process, with a freight unit being the logical unit that groups together the items to be transported. The items in the freight unit stay together and are always transported together from the source to the destination location. The identification of the number of items that go in the freight unit is based on business requirements and can vary from one business to the next.

Transportation planning depends on the freight unit; the larger the freight unit, the simpler the planning activities in the VSR optimizer. The smaller the freight unit, the more complex planning becomes in the VSR optimizer, also resulting in performance issues. There is no exact science here. Identification of the freight unit should be optimal according to the needs of the business. The freight unit should not be too small, nor should it be too big. This will optimize planning further when creating the freight order.

Freight unit configuration is handled in the SAP TMS system under **IMG| SAP Transportation Management | Transportation Management | Planning | Freight Unit | Define Freight Unit Types**.

You assign the number range to the freight unit type. The freight unit document type configuration is divided into several sections. Here is a screenshot of the freight unit configuration, with **Change Controller Settings**, **Execution Settings**, **Event Management Settings**, and **Default MTr Definition** sections:

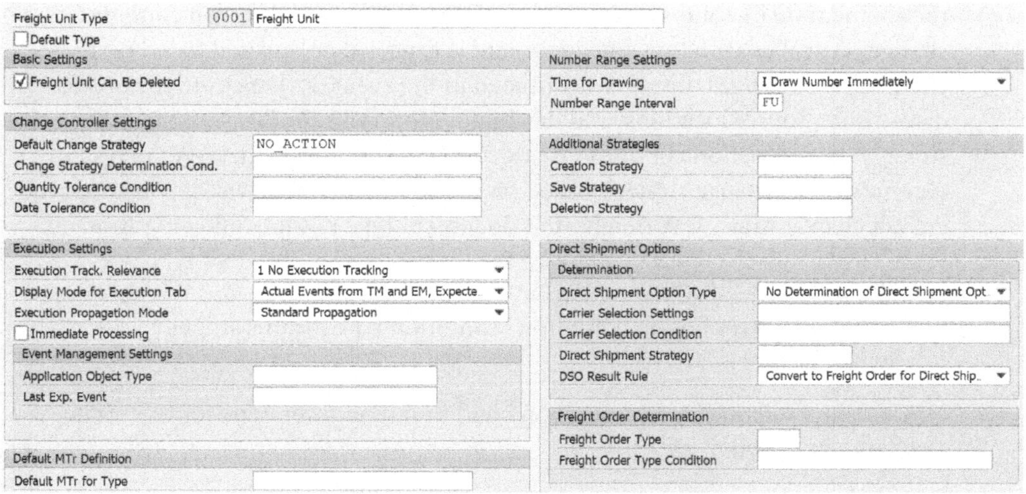

Figure 10.1 – Freight unit type definition (a)

Here is a screenshot showing the remaining sections of the freight unit configuration:

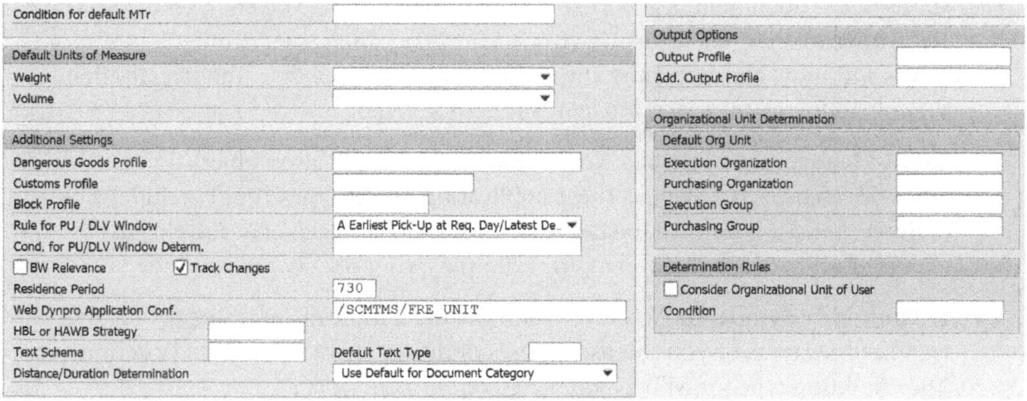

Figure 10.2 – Freight unit type definition (b)

Let's now understand how to configure these settings in detail:

- **Change Controller Settings**: The role of the change controller in SAP TMS is to propagate changes to the transportation document, which is a freight unit in this case. Changes made to the sales order propagate to the order transportation requirement (OTR) and simultaneously to the freight unit. You can configure the change controller as to how the document is canceled or updated based on these changes. The change controller is initiated in the event of changes to the quantities, dates/times, source locations, and destination locations. In this setting, if the strategy determination condition is added to the configuration, then the system determines the change strategy based on the condition, otherwise it will adopt the default change strategy. A freight unit document type has the following strategy:

  a) Default change strategy

  b) A strategy determination condition (condition type for this strategy: /SCMTMS/ CC_TOR_ STRAT)

  c) A quantity tolerance determination condition (condition type for this strategy: / SCMTMS/CC_QUANT_TOL)

  d) A date tolerance determination condition (condition type for this strategy: / SCMTMS/CC_DATE_TOL)

- **Execution Settings**: Execution settings control document tracking. The execution status of the document is governed by the setting here. If you set **Execution Track Relevance** to 1 - No execution tracking, then the document execution status will show **Not Relevant**; if the relevance is set to 2 or 3, the system then sets the initial document execution status to **Not Started**.

- **Event Management Settings**: You can assign the application object type for which you want to track the events. These application object types could include shipment, delivery, handling units of the delivery, and so on. You can also add the last expected event of the document, for example, proof of delivery.

- **Default MTr definition**: You can assign the default means of transport for the freight order type, or you can assign the condition for the default MTr definition. The condition type for MTr is /SCMTMS/TOR_DEF_MTR.

- **Default Unit of Measure**: You can specify the default gross weight and gross volume units for the freight unit type.

- **Direct Shipment option**: SAP has provided three options for direct shipment options. These are as follows: `No determination of Direct Shipment Options`, `Automatic Determination of Direct Shipment Options`, and `Manual Determination of Direct Shipment Options`. You can assign a carrier selection or carrier selection condition to the direct shipment option.

- **Freight Order Determination**: You can assign the freight order type to the freight unit configuration, or you can assign the condition that can determine the freight order type.

- **Organization Unit Determination**: You can assign the execution organization, purchasing organization, execution group, and purchasing group here.

- **Additional Settings**: You activate tracking changes in this configuration. Assignment of the dangerous goods profile, text schema, block profile, customs profile, and rules regarding the pickup and delivery window are configured in the additional settings.

- **Pickup and Delivery Window Determination (PUDL)**: This functionality provides flexibility in terms of how you want to serve your customer. This defines the limit of the requested start and delivery date/time limits. The requested date/time comes from the transportation requirement document, for example, OTR or DTR. These dates can be buffered further based on the PUDL conditions. Pickup and delivery creates four time stamps, which are as follows: `Acceptable date - start`, `Requested date - start`, `Requested date - end`, and `Acceptable date - end`. The requested dates are the desired dates, whereas acceptable dates are buffered dates that the source and destination locations allow. There may be some penalty cost associated with the acceptable dates. The optimizer can plan outside the requested dates window if the other costs outweigh the penalty cost. The condition type for PUDL is `/SCMTMS/TOR_TIMEWIND`. You create this condition in **SAP NetWeaver Business Client (NWBC)** | **Application Administration** | **Create Condition**.

The next step after configuring the freight unit type is to understand how the freight unit is determined for the transportation order requirement using the freight unit building rule.

Freight unit building rule

The **Freight Unit Building Rule (FUBR)** is used to plan the freight unit appropriately and defines how the freight unit should be built. The FUBR is determined based on the transportation requirement document. Freight units can be created manually, or they can be determined automatically using the conditions assigned to the transportation requirement document type. When building freight units; the system groups all the items based on the strategy assigned to the FUBR and creates the freight unit that is transported together from the source location to the destination. The freight unit creates feeds into transportation planning during freight order generation.

Figure 10.3 shows the condition created to determine the FUBR:

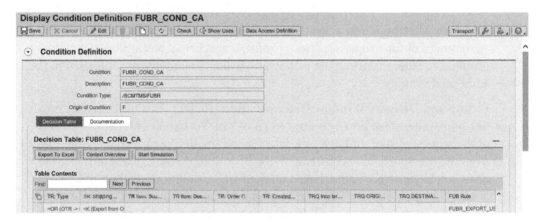

Figure 10.3 – FUBR Condition Definition

You create this condition in **SAP NetWeaver Business Client (NWBC) | Application Administration | Create Condition**.

Figure 10.4 shows the FUBR:

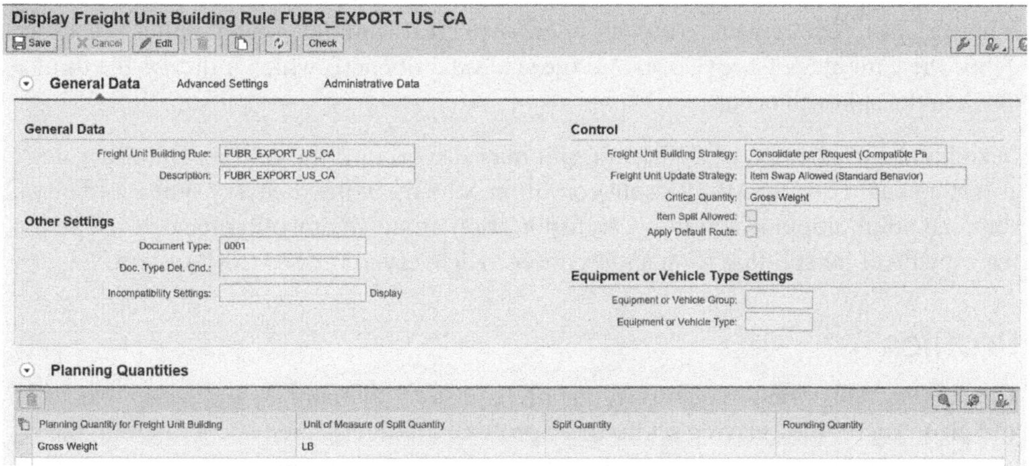

Figure 10.4 – FUBR

The FUBR is configured in **SAP NetWeaver Business Client (NWBC) | Application Administration | Planning | General Settings | Freight Unit Building Rule | Create Freight Unit Building Rule**.

Here, you define the controls in terms of how you want to create the freight unit. When creating the FUBR, you specify the strategy for the freight unit creation. SAP has provided three freight unit rule strategies:

- **Consolidate as much as possible**: This strategy groups all the items in the transportation requirement into a single freight unit, unless there is a resource capacity constraint defined.

- **Consolidate per item**: This strategy creates a separate freight unit for each item in the transportation requirement.

- **Consolidate per request**: This strategy is designed to consolidate each request for compatible parts. The system groups all the items from a business together to form a freight unit.

You must specify the critical quantity when creating the rule. Critical quantities can be a quantity, weight, or volume. This option defines the primary unit of measure for the transportation requirement to be split in order to create multiple freight units. You also define the Unit of Measure (UoM) and the split quantity here, which indicates the limit as to when the split will occur.

In addition to the above, a freight unit split may also occur if the delivery splitting rules are set up based on an SAP ERP split condition, which can be a delivery split based on a shipping point, shipping condition, transportation group, or any other logic developed in the copy BAdI for splitting from a sales order to delivery in the SAP ERP system.

Profiles

To perform transportation planning, one prerequisite is to maintain and set up selection and planning profiles. Having set up these profiles, this allows the system to group the planning-related activities. Once the freight units have been created, the next step in the process is to plan these freight units. Based on the setup of the profiles, the optimizer runs and uses the parameters set up in the profile and creates a freight order. A freight order can be created manually or automatically. The following are the profiles, their sub-profiles, and the settings overview:

1. Selection Profile

    a) Time-related selection attributes

    b) Geographical selection attributes

    c) Additional selection attributes

2. Planning Profile

    a) Capacity selection

    b) Optimizer setting

    c) Load planning setting

    d) Planning costs setting

    e) Carrier selection setting

    f) Incompatibilities setting

Selection Profile

Selection Profile is a user-specific grouping of transportation documents that are required to be considered for transportation planning. Within the Selection Profile, you define sub-profiles such as time-related selection attributes, geographical selection attributes, and additional selection attributes.

Figure 10.5 shows one of the examples of **Selection Profile** with the sub-profile assignment:

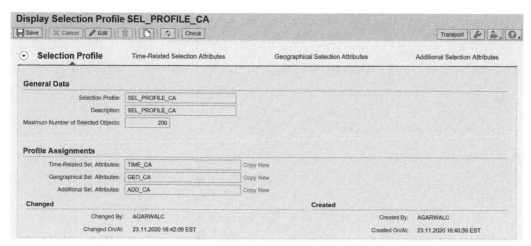

Figure 10.5 – Selection profile (a)

You define Selection Profile in **SAP NetWeaver Business Client (NWBC) | Application Administration | Planning | Selection Profiles | Create Selection Profile**.

Time-related selection attributes

Figure 10.6 shows the time-related selection attributes:

General Data		Pick-Up	
Time-Rel. Sel. Attributes:	TIME_CA	Ignore Pick-Up:	☐
Description:	TIME_CA		
		Pick-Up in Days:	120
		Additional Duration (hh:mm):	
Demand Horizon			
Absolute or Relative Horizon:	Use Relative Horizon	Offset Direction:	Past
		Offset in Days:	5
Round Horizon to Full Days:	☐	Additional Offset (hh:mm):	
Time Zone for Rounding the Horizon:			
		Start Date:	
Factory Cal. for Offs./Dur. Calc.:	01	Start Time:	00:00:00
		End Date:	
Other Settings		End Time:	00:00:00
Use Index Time for Selection:	Use Index Time of Stop		
Comb. of Pick-Up and Delivery Windows:	Combination with OR		
		Delivery	
		Ignore Delivery:	✓
		Delivery in Days:	90
		Additional Duration (hh:mm):	

Figure 10.6 – Selection profile (b)

You define the demand horizon in the time-related selection attributes. **Demand Horizon** can be absolute, or it can relative. Using the absolute option, you can explicitly maintain the pickup and delivery horizons. Using the relative option, you can define a range by specifying the number of days and an additional duration in hours and minutes. Additionally, you can define an offset in days, hours, and minutes, as well as an offset direction – Past or Future. You can select either **Ignore Pick-Up** or **Ignore Delivery** for the documents to be selected for planning.

There is an option to activate the **Round Horizon to Full Days** and assign the factory calendar. The system ignores non-working days based on the factory calendar assigned.

Geographical selection attributes

Geographical selection attributes identify which source and destination location should be considered when selecting the freight unit. These are divided into four sections, which are as follows: source locations; source zones; destination locations; and destination zones. You can choose the inclusive or exclusive option while specifying the locations.

Additional selection attributes

Within additional selection attributes, you can define additional attributes as a selection criterion for database queries. For example, you can have additional document types or business document categories as additional selection attributes during planning.

Planning Profile

Similar to **Selection Profile**, **Planning Profile** is a user-specific grouping of transportation documents that are required to be considered for transportation planning. **Planning Profile** should be created before any manual or automatic planning is executed. The settings implemented in **Planning Profile** act as an input to the optimizer in order to plan transportation efficiently.

Figure 10.7 shows one of the examples of **Planning Profile**, with the sub-profile assignment:

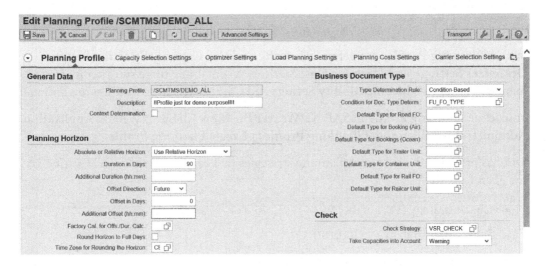

Figure 10.7 – Planning Profile

The following screenshot shows **Profile Assignments**, **Scheduling**, **Parallel Processing Profiles**, and **Loading and Unloading Duration** within the Planning Profile:

Profile Assignments

Selection Profile for Transportation Units:		Copy New
Selection Profile for Freight Orders:	/SCMTMS/DEMO_ALL	Copy New
Selection Profile for Freight Bookings:		Copy New
Capacity Selection Settings:	/SCMTMS/DEMO_ALL	Copy New
Optimizer Settings:	/SCMTMS/DEMO_ALL	Copy New
Load Planning Settings:		Copy New
Planning Costs Settings:	PLANNING_COST_SETTIN(	Copy New
Incompatibility Settings:		Copy New
Carrier Selection Settings:	/SCMTMS/DEMO_ALL	Copy New
Manual Planning Settings:	/SCMTMS/DEMO_ALL	Copy New

Scheduling

Scheduling Strategy:	VSS_DEF
Scheduling Direction:	Backward
Consider Freight Unit Dates:	Consider Freight Unit Dates as So

Loading and Unloading Duration

Dependence:	Freight Unit and MTr Dependent
* Condition for Loading/Unloading Duration:	LOADTIME

Parallel Processing Profiles

Input Data Selection:	
Lane Determination:	
Distance and Duration Determination:	

Figure 10.8 – Planning Profile

Within **Planning Profile**, you define sub-profiles such as **Capacity Selection Settings**, **Optimizer Settings**, and **Planning Cost Settings**. Maintaining these sub-profiles is mandatory, whereas **Incompatibility Setings** and **Carrier Selection Settings** are optional.

You define **Planning Profile** in **SAP NetWeaver Business Client (NWBC)** | **Application Administration** | **Planning** | **Planning Profiles** | **Create Planning Profile**.

SAP has provided the following planning strategies that can be assigned while setting up the Planning Profile:

- Check strategy (VSR_CHECK)
- Scheduling strategy (VSS_DEF)
- Standard planning strategies (VSR_DEF and VSR_1STEP)
- Planning for transportation proposals (VSR_DEF and VSR_1STEP)
- Load planning strategy (ALP_DEF)

Here is the manual planning strategy (also termed interactive planning) provided by SAP that can be assigned to the Planning Profile:

- Interactive planning and carrier selection (VSRI_1STEP)
- Interactive planning and automatic load planning (VSRI_ALP)

- Interactive planning strategy and check (VSRI_CHK)

- Default interactive planning strategy (VSRI_DEF)

- Interactive planning and scheduling (VSRI_SCH)

The following section includes a description of the Planning Profile configurations, together with their functionalities:

- **Planning Horizon**: The planning horizon option defines the possible period during which the system plans the freight unit and schedules transportation activities in relation to the freight orders. You can only view those freight units in the transportation cockpit with transportation dates that fall within the days mentioned in this setting. The planning horizon can be absolute or it can be relative. Using the absolute option, you can maintain the planning horizon explicitly. Using the relative option, you can define a range by specifying the number of days and an additional duration in hours and minutes. Additionally, you can define an offset in days, hours, and minutes, and an offset direction, such as Past or Future. There is an option to activate the **Round Horizon to Full Days** and assign the factory calendar. The system ignores non-working days based on the factory calendar assigned.

- **Business Document Type**: The business document type option determines which document type should be created when planning the freight order. You can assign a condition for document type determination. The condition type for document type determination is SCMTMS/TOR_TYPE.

- **Check Strategy**: SAP has provided a standard check strategy, VSR_CHECK, that verifies capacities, incompatibilities, and multi-resource assignments, and also performs a dangerous goods check. You can also stipulate whether the system should raise a warning or error message if the vehicle load capacity goes beyond the specified limits.

- **Scheduling Strategy**: SAP has provided a standard check strategy, VSS_DEF. This defines whether the system should consider the dates from the freight unit as a constraint and whether backward or forward scheduling should be used.

- **Loading and Unloading Duration**: You determine the duration for loading and unloading through **Planning Profile**. The condition type regarding the duration for loading and unloading is assigned to **Planning Profile**, which helps the system to determine the load and unload durations automatically during manual or automatic planning. Based on your business needs, you can create your own attributes using data access definitions and determine the loading and unloading durations based on these attributes. This could be a combination of source location, means of transport, destination location, and so on. The condition type regarding the duration for loading and unloading is /SCMTMS/FU_LOAD_DURA and is maintained using **SAP NetWeaver Business Client (NWBC) | Application Administration | General Settings | Conditions | Create Condition**.

- **Parallel Processing Profile**: The parallel processing profile option allows you to define the profile to control parallel processing to determine the optimizer's input data selection, transportation lane/distance, and duration. You can create the profile under **Application Administration | General Settings | Define Parallel Processing Profile**. Parallelization reduces the overall runtime and helps to improve performance.

- **Capacity Selection Settings**: The Capacity Selection Profile defines the vehicle capacity during transportation planning. *Figure 10.9* shows a screenshot of the Capacity Selection Profile:

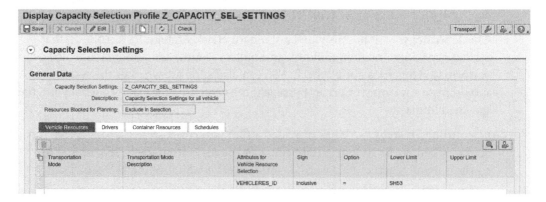

Figure 10.9 – Capacity Selection Profile

It determines the optimal use of resources based on vehicle resource capacity. You maintain the vehicle resource master and list all the vehicle resources that are going to be used for the stated Capacity Selection Profile. Both active and passive resources should be added to the **Vehicle Resources** tab.

Next, we look at Optimizer Settings.

Optimizer Settings

The Optimizer Settings option consists of a planning strategy that calls a VSR optimizer to implement transportation planning. This is a mandatory setting and is required to optimize transportation scheduling and route determination. Within **Optimizer Settings**, you also define the planning strategy for transportation proposal. Internally, it calls the transportation proposal optimizer. You can define whether you want VSR_DEF, which is to execute just the VSR optimizer, or assign VSR_1STEP, which also considers the carrier selection to be executed in a single step following VSR optimization. The optimizer checks all the constraints and minimizes the total cost. As a result of the planning run, VSR optimization optimizes the request and returns the optimal solution identified. You can generate multiple alternative transportation proposals for each freight unit.

The following are some of the constraints that the VSR optimizer takes into consideration:

- Handling resources
- Opening hours of the location
- Minimum/maximum storage time
- Loading/unloading duration
- Distance limits, duration stopover
- Conditions
- Incompatibilities
- Vehicle capacity
- Pickup delivery window
- Wait time and stay time
- Schedules of vehicle types

Figure 10.10 shows one of the optimizer's example settings:

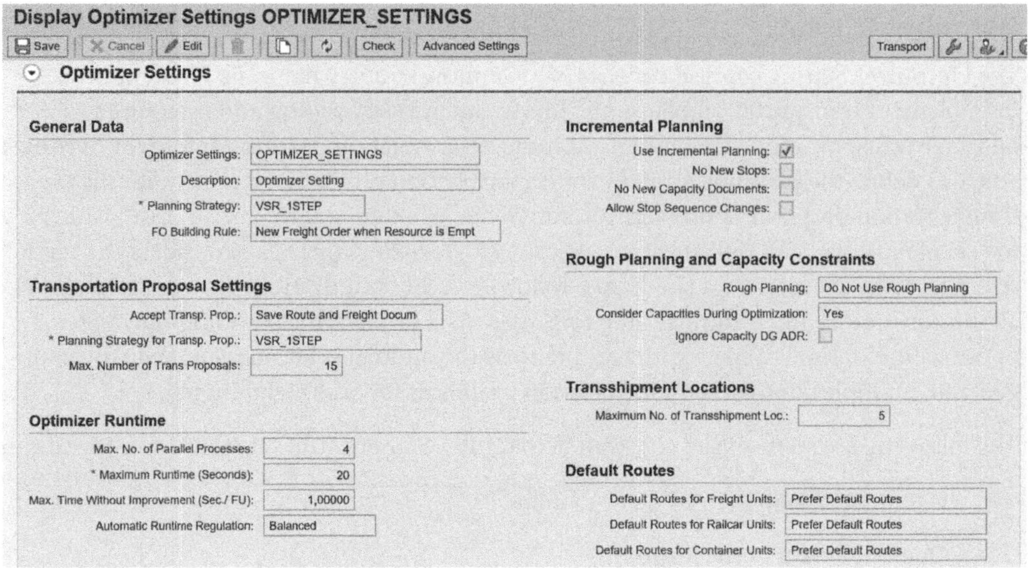

Figure 10.10 – Optimizer Settings

You can define **Max. No. of Parallel Processes**, which allows you to define how many parallel processes can be started on the part of the VSR optimizer. You can choose **Rough Planning** and **Consider Capacities During Optimization** with the Optimizer Settings.

The **Maximum No. of Transshipment Loc.** field defines the number of transshipment locations any freight unit can be routed through between the source and destination.

Load Planning Settings

Load distribution within a truck is one of the most important factors when it comes to safety and regulations. It depends on the nature of the goods being transported between locations. SAP has provided a load planning strategy, ALP_DEF, that helps to establish the suitable assignment of pallets with a truck that satisfies all hard constraints. A failure to load all pallets may result in significant penalties. These are the things taken into consideration by the load planning strategy. The following screenshot shows one example of **Load Planning Settings**:

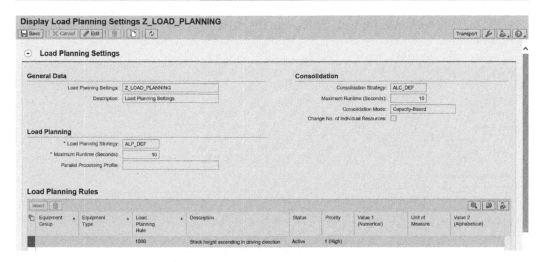

Figure 10.11 – Load Planning Settings

You can assign the load planning rule to the load planning profile. It helps you to prioritize loads. For example, in *Figure 10.11*, the load should be stacked based on ascending height in the direction of travel.

Planning Costs Profile

Planning Costs Profile is one of the mandatory settings required in the Planning Profile. The VSR optimizer considers the fixed costs associated with each capacity, in other words, vehicle resources and scheduling. In addition to fixed costs, the planning cost profile allows variable costs to be taken into consideration. These variable costs are penalty costs, distance and duration costs, basic quantity costs, and costs for each additional intermediate stops. You can also consider the distance costs from the transportation lane. You configure these for each of the means of transport that are added to the planning cost profile under the means of transport setting. The following penalty costs are defined in the Planning Profile and can be used to control the decisions made by VSR optimization:

- Premature pickup
- Delayed pickup
- Premature delivery
- Delayed delivery

You assign the conditions for penalty costs to the planning cost profile as shown in *Figure 10.12*:

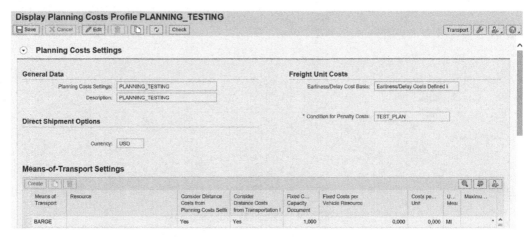

Figure 10.12 – Planning Costs Profile

Carrier selection settings

Carrier selection is used to determine the perfect combination of carrier assignment-based costs, priority, equipment availability, and business shares selection. The following screenshot shows **Carrier Selection Settings**:

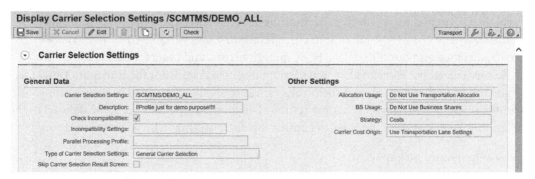

Figure 10.13 – Carrier Selection Settings (a)

A carrier is assigned to the freight order once the planning run is executed. The planning run can be executed manually or automatically. SAP has provided a planning strategy, TSPS_DEF, for the carrier selection profile. You assign this strategy as shown in the following screenshot:

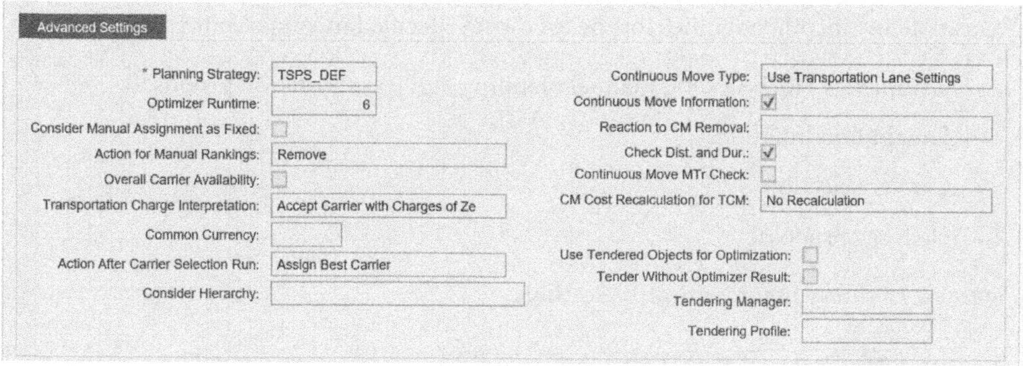

Figure 10.14 – Carrier Selection Settings (b)

You can activate incompatibilities for the carrier selection if there are any. The carrier selection profile considers other settings that are important when setting up the carrier selection profile, and these are listed here:

- **Cost and Priority**: A carrier can be determined based on transportation charge management costs or planning costs. The strategy options are `costs`, `priority`, `cost+priority`, and `cost*priority`.

- **Business shares**: If you allocate a certain fixed percentage of freight business to a specific carrier, then that is considered to be a business share.

- **Transportation allocation**: You use transportation allocation if you want to restrict how much business you wish to engage in with a specific carrier in a certain region for a certain means of transport.

The carrier selection profile also considers **Continuous Move Type**, which stipulates whether the profile involves a simple continuous move, a round-trip continuous move, or whether you can use transportation lane settings. Under **Advanced Settings**, you can choose options for **Transportation Charge Interpretation**, which accepts the cheapest or most expensive carrier.

Incompatibilities

Incompatibilities are limitations that you can set to effectively plan your transportation. Let's say that you don't want two freight units involving different types of products to go together in a single freight order, then those can be set up as incompatibilities. Another example could be a freight unit with two different incoterms or a certain Means of Transport (MTr) cannot be unloaded at a specific unloading location due to insufficient space and suchlike.

You can define incompatibilities for the following specified incompatibility areas:

- Complete VSR (VSR Opt, manual planning and transportation proposal)
- Freight unit building
- Carrier selection
- Delivery proposal

Figure 10.15 shows **Incompatibility Settings**:

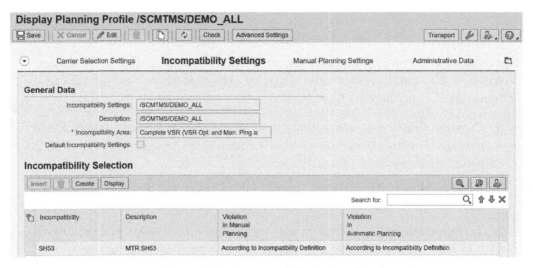

Figure 10.15 – Incompatibility Settings (a)

You can set the incompatibility determination method either on the basis of conditions or through external determination settings:

- **Conditions**: You can define conditions in relation to the incompatibilities as shown in *Figure 10.16*. There can be two attributes of the two business nodes where you can define incompatibilities. You can define two conditions and specify the relevant results. If those results match, then the two business object instances are incompatible. The other option is that you can enter only one condition and select the **Identical Values Only** checkbox. With this option, you have the same business object in relation to which you are defining an incompatibility between two instances, for example, freight units. VSR optimization regards incompatibilities as hard constraints.

- **Reaction**: You have the option to configure manual and automatic violation here. You can also set incompatibility reaction here if you wish to ignore the error, or make it a warning or an error:

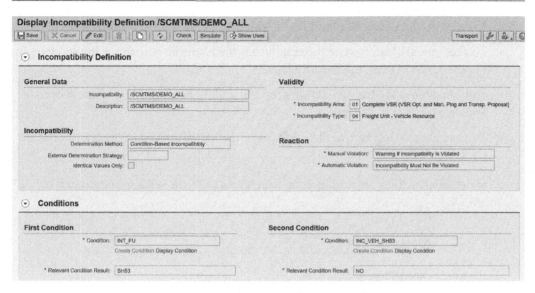

Figure 10.16 – Incompatibility Settings (b)

- **Incompatibility**: SAP has provided different incompatibility types that define the object where the rule is to be executed. Examples of incompatibility types include the following:

a) `Freight unit - Freight unit`

b) `Freight unit - Vehicle`

c) `Freight unit - Transshipment location`

d) `Carrier - Transportation Order`

Interactive planning with the transportation cockpit

Most planning activities are executed using the transportation cockpit. Transportation planning, including freight order creation, is executed in the transportation cockpit. A prerequisite for executing transportation planning is to create the profile and layout settings, wherein you select the relevant selection and planning profiles. Manual planning allows you to manually create or change the transportation plan. Interactive planning with the transportation cockpit allows you to perform the following actions:

- You can create the freight order directly from the freight unit.

- You can drag and drop the freight unit to resources in order to create the freight order.

- You can assign an existing freight unit to the freight order created.

- You can perform various planning activities using the drag and drop capability.

- You can manually overwrite the result from the planning run; for example, changing the carrier or MTr on the freight order.

- You can choose the transportation proposal and then select one of these proposals to create the freight order.

- You can execute interactive planning from the map displayed in the transportation cockpit.

You can personalize the transportation cockpit layout with the settings mentioned in *Figure 10.17*:

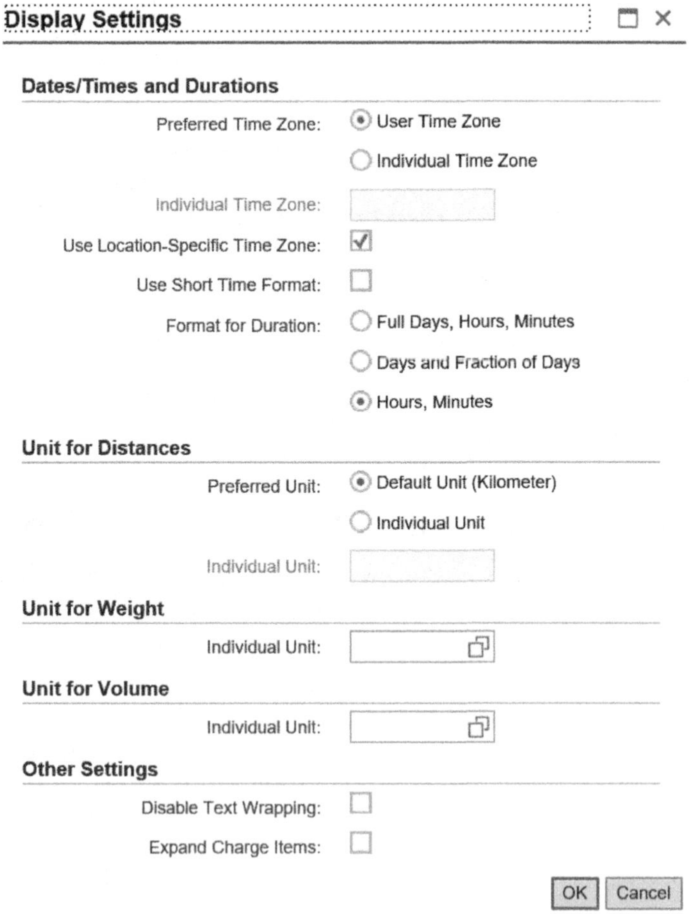

Figure 10.17 – Transportation cockpit personalization

Here are the options regarding transportation cockpit personalization:

- The time zone in which to present the time-related information

- Units for distance

- Units for weight

- Units for volume

- The position and width of the tabs on screen

- Visibility of the tabs

- The sequence and number of rows and columns visible

The following screenshot shows the transportation cockpit page layout settings that you can configure. Here, you can choose which push buttons you want to appear on the application toolbar:

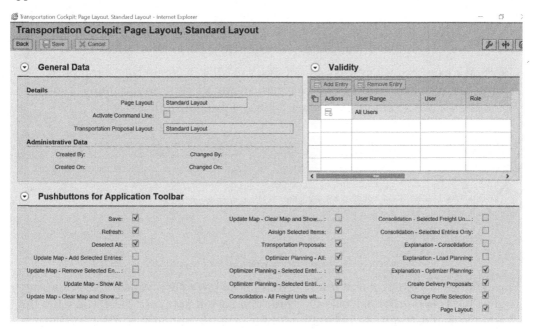

Figure 10.18 – Transportation cockpit: page layout, standard layout (a)

Additionally, you can configure what you want to see in the top left and top right areas, as well as in the bottom left and bottom right areas, as shown in the following screenshot:

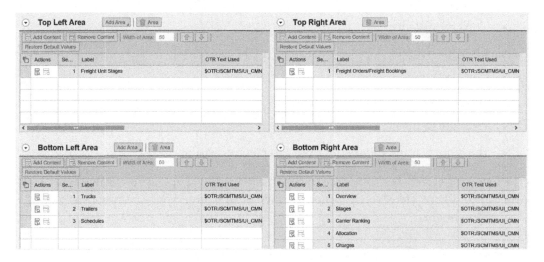

Figure 10.19 – Transportation cockpit: page layout, standard layout (b)

Once you are finished with the layout settings, you will need to update your profile settings. The mandatory settings in this regard are the selection and planning profiles. *Figure 10.20* shows an example of the selection and planning profiles:

Figure 10.20 – Transportation Cockpit: Profile and Layout Sets

Once you select the freight unit from the transportation requirements worklist, you land on the **Transportation Cockpit: Profile and Layout Sets** page. Here, you select the relevant **Selection Profile** and **Planning Profile** fields to continue on to the standard layout, showing the freight unit that you need in order to plan transportation interactively.

The following screenshot shows the transportation cockpit, standard layout, with the **Freight Unit Stages**, **Freight Orders**, and means of transport views:

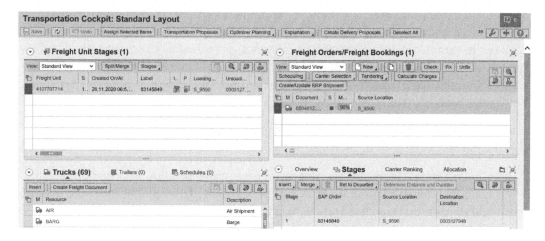

Figure 10.21 – Transportation Cockpit: Standard Layout

Automatic planning

Automatic planning allows you to automate the planning process in TMS, meaning the automatic creation of order-based transportation requirements, automatic freight unit creation, automatic freight order creation, automatic carrier selection, and automatic freight order tendering.

Within automatic planning, a freight unit is created using the FUBR. A freight order is created automatically for the order-based transportation requirement once the freight unit has been created. This can be done by scheduling background job to create the freight order. Carrier selection is also triggered automatically by using the VSR_1STEP planning strategy in the Optimizer Settings assigned to the Planning Profile. You can assign the tendering profile to the carrier selection profile. The tendering profile is used to define the tendering plan. Setting up this information helps to execute tendering automatically; the carrier is tendered, and the tender is then accepted or rejected.

We have covered the transportation planning steps, including an understanding of automatic and interactive planning. Let's now move on to freight order management within SAP TMS.

Freight order management

Freight orders are created after the freight units have been organized. Based on the selection and planning profiles, the system undergoes transportation planning using the optimizer and freight orders are created. The freight order includes the information required to execute the transportation process that is planned by the carrier. The freight order includes information such as products, the date and time of departure, the vehicle, the freight units that need to be loaded, and execution data. Freight orders are used for land transportation, that is, road freight orders and rail transportation.

The following is an overview of the structure of a freight order and the key information that it contains:

- **General Data**: **General Data** contains general transportation information, including transportation mode, means of transport, driver and license information, and much more. **General Data** is structured into the following sub-sections: **Transportation**, **Resource Capacity**, **Organization Data**, **Cargo Information**, and, most importantly, the source and destination information, including departure and arrival dates and times. Transportation information includes information pertaining to the carrier, the total distance to be covered, duration, dates, and the number of stops:

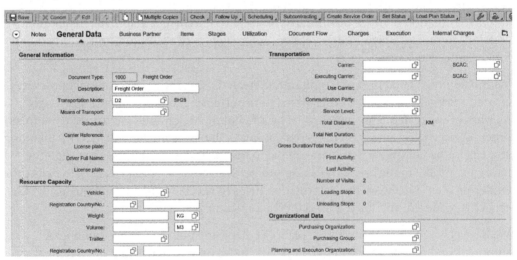

Figure 10.22 – Freight order: General Data view

- **Business Partner**: This tab contains information regarding business partners, for example, the carrier, the party responsible for shipping, and the consignee.

- **Items**: This tab contains product-related information, including the quantity, weight, and volume. It also contains other information, such as the product freight group, the transportation group, information concerning dangerous goods, the commodity code, and customs-related information.

- **Stages**: This tab displays logistical information pertaining to the freight order. For each stage, the distance, duration, planned dates and times, and the source/ destination information is shown in stages. Stage-dependent block statuses, in other words, one for planning and one for execution, are also shown here.

- **Charges**: The freight charges that are required to be paid to the carrier are captured on this tab. The charges are determined on the basis of the rates and the freight agreement between the shipper and the carrier.

- **Execution Data**: This tab includes information relating to the expected and the actual dates and times of events concerning the freight order.

- **Statuses**: The freight order shows statuses, such as **Life Cycle Status**, **Subcontracting Status**, **Planning**, and **Execution**, as shown in *Figure 10.23*:

	Output Management	Customs	**Statuses**	Terms and Conditions		Subcontracting	Attachments		Blocking Information

General

Life Cycle Status:	New	Changed By:	AGARWALC	Changed On:	17.12.2...	12:14:44	EST
Fixing Status:	🔓						
Archiving Status:	Not Archived						
		Changed By:		Changed On:		00:00:00	EST
Delivery Cost Transfer Status:	Not Initiated						
Goods Movement Status:	Not Initiated	Changed By:		Changed On:		00:00:00	EST

Subcontracting

Subcontracting Status:	No Subcontracting Result	Changed By:	AGARWALC	Changed On:	17.12.2...	12:14:44	EST
Confirmation Status:	No Confirmation Yet	Changed By:	AGARWALC	Changed On:	17.12.2...	12:14:44	EST
Dispute Case Status:	No Dispute						
Invoicing Status:	Not Invoiced	Changed By:		Changed On:		00:00:00	

Planning

Load Plan Status (Stop):	( ) Not Planned

Execution

Execution Status:	Not Relevant
Logistical Execution Status:	

Figure 10.23 – Freight order: Statuses

- **Subcontracting**: This tab shows information about the subcontracting processes, including carrier information, an overview of the tendering process, carrier ranking, and continuous move documents.

- **Attachments**: Here, you can insert and attach any transportation-related documents.

- **Map**: This tab shows the source and destination information related to the shipment. You can display the utilization of a freight order for each stage and each relevant dimension.

- **Change documents**: Here, you can view all the changes that are made to the freight order, in the same way as any other change documents in any other SAP transactions.

- **Notes**: This tab includes specific notes and information that needs to be printed on the transportation document. This information can be added in the notes section of the freight order.

- **Output Management**: Output processes print documents or electronic messages, and these can be viewed in the output management tab of the freight order. Output actions can be generated and triggered from here.

- **Document Flow**: This tab lists all business documents that have a direct or indirect relationship to the freight order. These documents could be freight units, OTR, DTR, deliveries, and shipments. The freight settlement document is also tagged to the document flow.

Freight orders can be planned manually or automatically. As we have gone through some of the key document structure functions, let's now look into the configuration aspect of the freight order type. The freight order types are configured in the configuration path mentioned here.

This is handled in the SAP TMS system under **IMG | SAP Transportation Management | Transportation Management | Freight Order Management | Freight Order | Define Freight Order Types**.

You assign the number range to the **Freight Order Type** field. The freight order type configuration is shown in *Figure 10.24*:

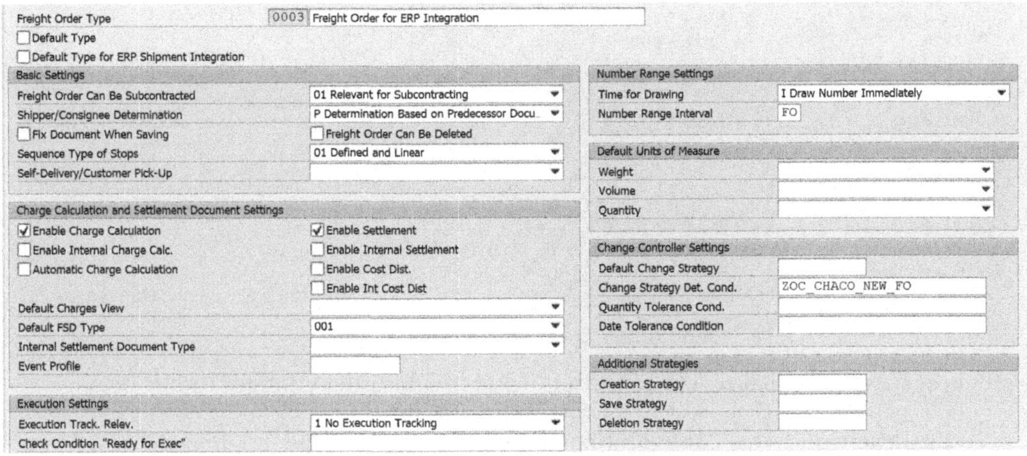

Figure 10.24 – Freight order type definition (a)

The following screenshot shows the freight order type configuration for **Event Management Settings**, **Tendering Settings**, **Additional Settings**, **Service Definition**, **Default MTr Determination**, **Output Options**, and **Organization Unit Determination**:

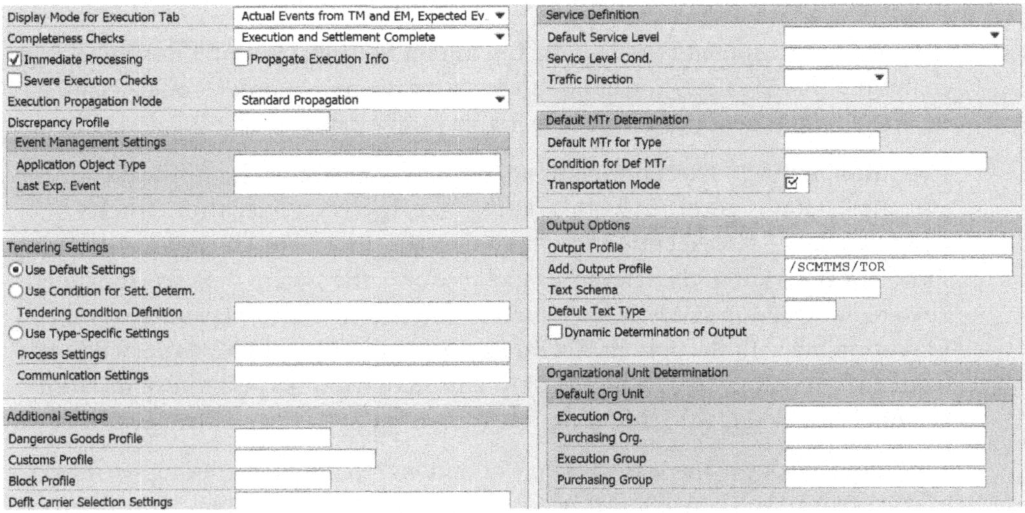

Figure 10.25 – Freight order type definition (b)

The following screenshot shows the freight order type configuration for **Driver Settings**:

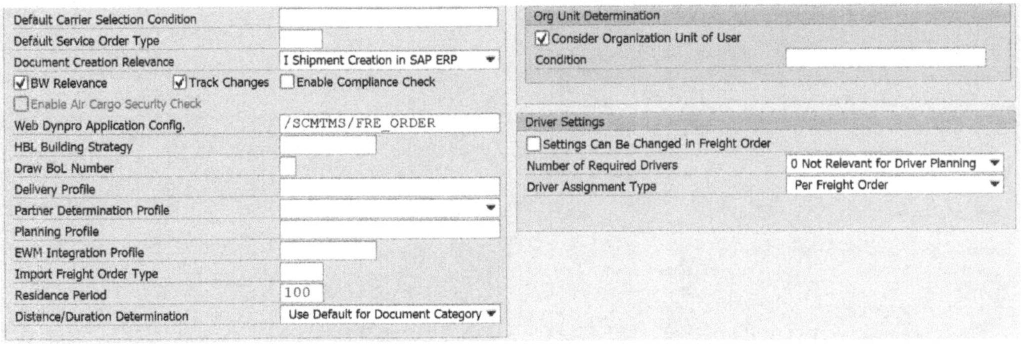

Figure 10.26 – Freight order type definition (c)

Let's now have a detailed review of the following freight order configurations:

- **Basic Settings**: This configuration enables the option if the freight order is relevant for subcontracting. It consists of the shipper/consignee determination options, such as determination based on the predecessor document or based on the first and last locations. **Sequence Type of Stops** specifies the type of structure used to link stages to one another. The **Defined** and **Linear** types can be used in all the usual processing functions. Within this configuration, you can also specify whether the freight order is to be used for customer self-delivery or pickup.

- **Charge Calculation and Settlement Document Settings**: Within this setting, you enable the charge calculation and settlement for the freight order. You determine the freight settlement document type in this configuration.

- **Execution Settings**: Execution settings control document tracking. The document execution status is governed by this setting here. If you set **Execution Track Relevance** to **1 – No execution tracking**, then the document execution status will show **Not Relevant**; if the relevance is set to **2** or **3**, the system then sets the initial document execution status as **Not Started**. You also set the display mode for the **Execution** tab with the options **Actual Events from TM and EM, Expected Event from EM, Actual Events from TM only, and Actual and Expected Events from EM only**. You define the settings for integration with SAP Event Management.

- **Tendering Settings**: There are a couple of options relating to tendering settings, in other words, you can define process and communication settings, or you can define a condition to determine these settings. With these settings, the system can automatically create a tendering plan.

- **Additional Settings**: This option allows you to define the changes that are tracked for freight orders of this type, activate settings for freight orders relevant to BW integration, and whether and how freight orders of this type relate to SAP ERP shipments. You can also assign a dangerous goods profile, a planning profile, a delivery profile, and a customs profile here.

- **Change Controller Settings**: The concept of the change controller in SAP TMS propagates changes to the transportation document, which is a freight order in this case. Changes made to the sales order propagate to the OTR and simultaneously to the freight unit. You can configure the change controller as to how the documents react to these changes. The change controller is initiated as a result of changes to the quantities, dates/times, and the source and destination locations. If you indicate a strategy determination condition in this configuration, the system uses the change strategy identified via the condition. If you do not indicate a condition, or if the condition does not return a strategy, the system automatically uses the default change strategy. The freight order document type has the following strategy:

  a) Default change strategy

  b) Strategy determination condition (condition type for this strategy: /SCMTMS/ CC_TOR_ STRAT)

  c) Quantity tolerance determination condition (condition type for this strategy: / SCMTMS/CC_QUANT_TOL)

  d) Date tolerance determination condition (condition type for this strategy: / SCMTMS/CC_DATE_TOL)

- **Event Management Settings**: You can assign the application object type for which you want to track the events. These application object types may be the shipment, delivery, handling unit of the delivery, and so on. You can also add the last expected event of the document, for example, proof of delivery.

- **Default MTr definition**: You assign the default means of transport type for the freight order type, or you can assign the condition for the default MTr. The condition type for MTr is /SCMTMS/TOR_DEF_MTR.

- **Default Unit of Measure**: Here, you can specify the default gross weight and gross volume unit for the freight unit type.

- **Organization Unit Determination**: Here, you assign the execution organization, purchasing organization, execution group, and purchasing group.

- **Output Options**: Here, you define the possible outputs that are required to be triggered from the freight order document. Possible outputs include forms, print documents and EDI messages. You can trigger the actions for B2B messages related to the transportation order.

- **Freight Order Type Determination**: The system determines the freight order type using one of the following methods.

    a) The freight order created from the freight unit when the **Direct Shipment Option (DSO)** is determined. The system determines the freight order type that is specified for the DSO in the freight unit type.

    b) Freight orders are determined via planning profiles, wherein you specify the freight order type or the condition to determine the freight order under the business document type section of the planning profile.

As we have gone through the freight order functionality, its configuration, and its determination from the freight unit or planning profile, let's now understand how carrier selection and tendering takes place in the freight order.

Carrier selection and tendering

Carrier selection is used to determine the perfect combination of carrier assignment-based costs, priority, equipment availability, and business share selection. This is also covered in the *Profiles* section of this chapter. The carrier is assigned to the freight order once the planning run is executed. The planning run can be executed manually or automatically. SAP has provided a planning strategy, **TSPS_DEF**, for the carrier selection profile. You assign this strategy as shown in *Figure 10.27*:

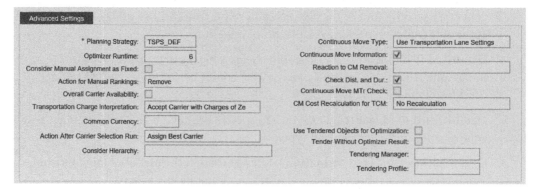

Figure 10.27 – Carrier selection profile

You can activate the incompatibilities for the carrier selection, if there are any. The carrier selection profile considers other settings that are important when setting up the carrier selection profile, and these are listed here:

- **Cost and Priority**: The carrier can be determined on the basis of costs arising from transportation charge management or planning costs. The strategy options are `costs`, `priority`, `cost+priority`, and `cost*priority`.

- **Business shares**: If you allocate a certain fixed percentage of freight business to a specific carrier, then that is considered to be a business share.

You define business shares under **SAP NetWeaver Business Client via Planning| Business Share | Create Business Shares**.

When creating business shares, you have the option to create a business share with a transportation lane reference. You create trade lane business shares and define tolerances and penalty costs that are incurred when an excess or shortfall occurs in these tolerances. You define actual business shares within the target share.

Transportation allocation: You use transportation allocation when you want to restrict how much business you wish to engage in with a specific carrier in a certain region for a certain means of transport.

The following are the prerequisites required to set up transportation allocations:

1. Activate the use of transportation allocations. This is done in the IMG path: **SPRO | SAP Transportation Management | Planning | General Settings | Define Transportation Allocation Settings**.

2. Define the transportation allocation types. This is done in the IMG path: **SPRO | SAP Transportation Management | Planning | General Settings | Define Transportation Allocation Types**.

3. Define the carrier selection allocations. This is executed in **SAP NetWeaver Business Client** by choosing **Planning | Allocation | Create Allocation**.

4. In the carrier selection profile settings, you can define whether you want to use transportation allocations or whether the system ought to consider the settings from the transportation lane. This is shown in *Figure 10.28*:

Display Carrier Selection Settings /SCMTMS/DEMO_ALL

Save   Cancel   Edit   Check   Transport

Carrier Selection Settings

General Data

Carrier Selection Settings:	/SCMTMS/DEMO_ALL
Description:	!!Profile just for demo purpose!!!!
Check Incompatibilities:	✓
Incompatibility Settings:	
Parallel Processing Profile:	
Type of Carrier Selection Settings:	General Carrier Selection
Skip Carrier Selection Result Screen:	☐

Other Settings

Allocation Usage:	Do Not Use Transportation Allocation
BS Usage:	Do Not Use Business Shares
Strategy:	Costs
Carrier Cost Origin:	Use Transportation Lane Settings

Figure 10.28 – Carrier Selection Settings (a)

The carrier selection profile also considers **Continuous Move Type**, which stipulates whether the profile involves a simple continuous move, a round-trip continuous move, or whether you can use transportation lane settings. Under **Advanced Settings**, you can choose options for **Transportation Charge Interpretation**, which accepts the cheapest or most expensive carrier. This is shown in *Figure 10.29*:

Advanced Settings

* Planning Strategy:	TSPS_DEF
Optimizer Runtime:	6
Consider Manual Assignment as Fixed:	☐
Action for Manual Rankings:	Remove
Overall Carrier Availability:	☐
Transportation Charge Interpretation:	Accept Carrier with Charges of Ze
Common Currency:	
Action After Carrier Selection Run:	Assign Best Carrier
Consider Hierarchy:	

Continuous Move Type:	Use Transportation Lane Settings
Continuous Move Information:	✓
Reaction to CM Removal:	
Check Dist. and Dur.:	✓
Continuous Move MTr Check:	☐
CM Cost Recalculation for TCM:	No Recalculation
Use Tendered Objects for Optimization:	☐
Tender Without Optimizer Result:	☐
Tendering Manager:	
Tendering Profile:	

Figure 10.29 – Carrier Selection Settings (b)

You can assign a carrier manually or automatically to the freight order via the transportation cockpit. You can also run the carrier selection report, `/SCMTMS/VSR_OPT_BGD`, or `/SCMTMS/TSPS_OPT_BGD`, to assign a carrier to the freight order automatically, based on the aforementioned settings.

Tendering

Once the carrier is selected, the next step involves tendering the freight order to one or more carriers. You can configure the tender profile by selecting the tendering process, which can be freight RFQ-based or direct tendering, to tender the freight order to the carrier. RFQ-based tendering can be initiated manually or automatically. Let's now look at both these tendering processes in detail:

- **RFQ-based tendering process**: In this process, the tendering manager sends the freight RFQ to the carrier. You can define the tendering type rules in the tendering profile, wherein you can select the option of peer-to-peer tendering or broadcast tendering. Once the freight RFQ is received by the carrier, they may accept or reject the freight RFQ. If accepted, the carrier will respond with a freight quotation. The tendering manager will either award or reject the freight quotation following an evaluation. Once the tendering manager has awarded the freight order, the system sends the updated freight order to the carrier.

  The following screenshot shows the RFQ-based tendering process:

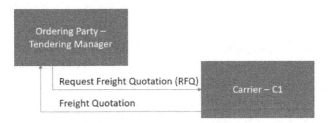

Figure 10.30 – RFQ-based tendering process

- **Direct Tendering**: In this process, the freight order is sent directly to the carrier without creating the freight RFQ. Carriers can confirm or reject freight orders. Unlike the freight RFQ process, the system generally awards a carrier if the carrier does not reject the freight order within a given time limit:

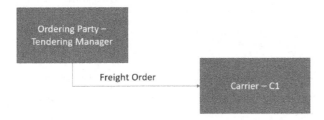

Figure 10.31 – Direct tendering process

Let's now look at the steps that are required to be configured in order to activate freight tendering.

Step 1 – Defining general settings for tendering

You can configure the general settings for tendering in the IMG path mentioned here: **IMG | SAP Transportation Management | Transportation Management | Freight Order Management | Tendering | Define General Settings for Tendering**.

In this step, you configure the standard settings for tendering. You can configure the tendering communication and process settings, which can be assigned to the freight order type configuration.

The general settings are divided into seven dialog structures, and these are stated here:

- **01 – Visibility Settings**: This option allows you to determine the visibility level of a price limit, the price submitted, and the stop dates in a tendering process.

- **02 – Rejection Reason Codes**: Here, you define the rejection reason **code identifiers** (**IDs**) and descriptions to classify the reasons for rejecting freight quotation requests.

- **03 – E-mail and SMS Content**: Email and SMS is one of the communication options for communicating with carriers. You can configure separate contents for the email subject field, email body text, and SMS text content. These options are available for the complete tendering cycle: Published Request for Quotation, Canceled Tendering, Awarded Quotation, and Rejected Quotation.

  You can schedule the sending of emails and SMS messages in a batch report. With this, the contact person for the carrier receives emails or SMS messages only when running the batch report. The emails or SMS messages contain information about all the new events that have taken place since the last bundle of emails or SMS messages were sent. This means that the carrier does not receive multiple separate emails for new freight RFQs, but only one email containing information on all new freight RFQs.

  The general settings allow you to specify the default communication language and time zone. You can also specify the email address that the system uses for inbound emails, including the configuration option to send an automatic status confirmation by email. There is also the option to mark email as encrypted and to sign emails for security purposes.

The following screenshot shows the **E-mail and SMS Content** document for notifications with the email body and subject for each function of **Canceled Tendering, Published Request for Quotation**, and **Awarded Quotation**:

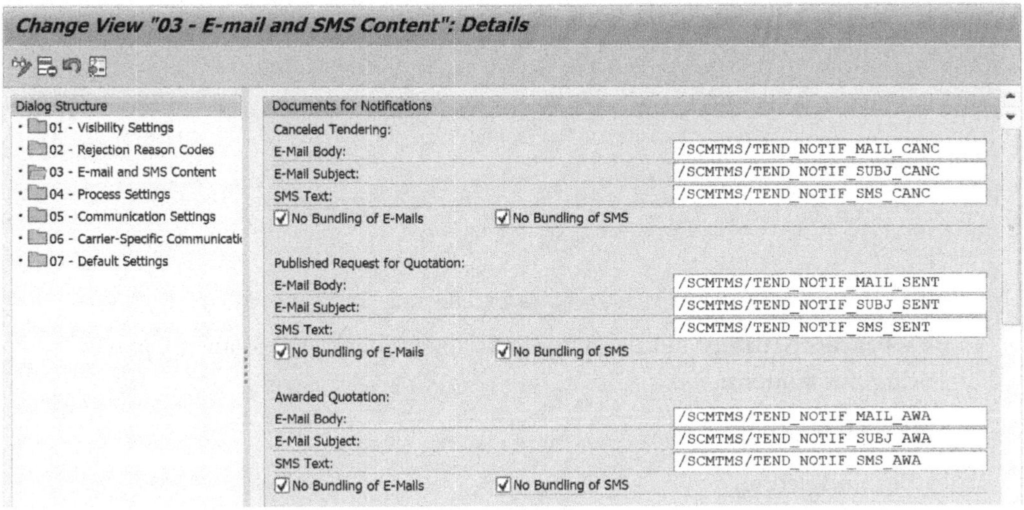

Figure 10.32 – General settings for tendering: Email and SMS (a)

The following screenshot shows the **E-mail and SMS Content** document for notifications with the email body and subject for each function of **Rejected Quotation, Documents for Tendering by E-Mail**, and **Documents for Inbound Error Notification**:

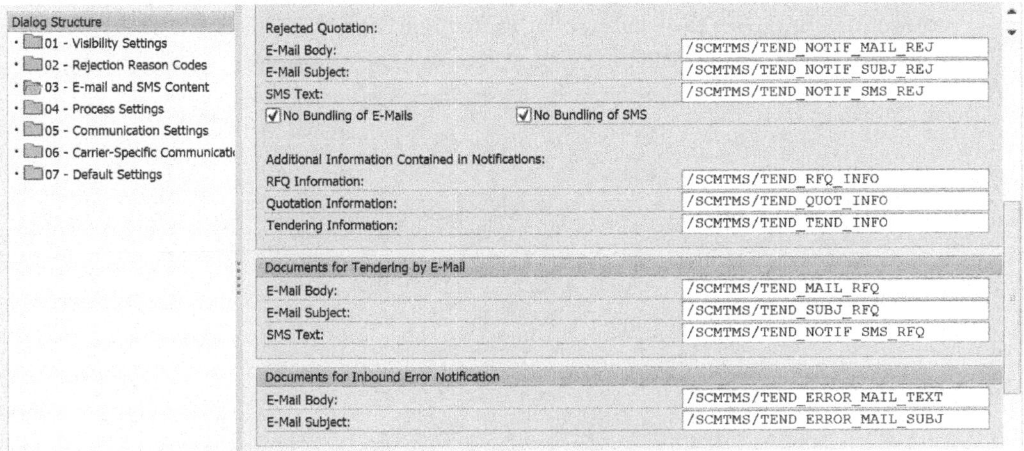

Figure 10.33 – General settings for tendering: Email and SMS (b)

The following screenshot shows the **E-mail and SMS Content** document for **General Settings** and **E-Mail Security Settings**:

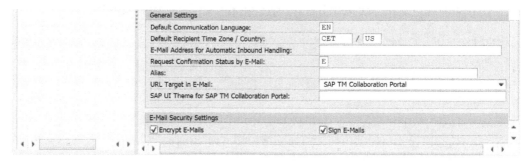

Figure 10.34 – General settings for tendering: Email and SMS (c)

- **04 – Process Settings**: In this configuration, you specify the following process settings for tendering:

a) Default tendering manager

b) Visibility settings

c) Tendering profile

d) Carrier selection settings: the maximum response duration and consideration of the calling hours of a business partner

Process settings defined in this step can be assigned to the freight order type.

- **05 – Communication Settings**: Here, you can configure the methods for communicating with the carrier, be it EDI, email, or SMS. This is shown in *Figure 10.35*:

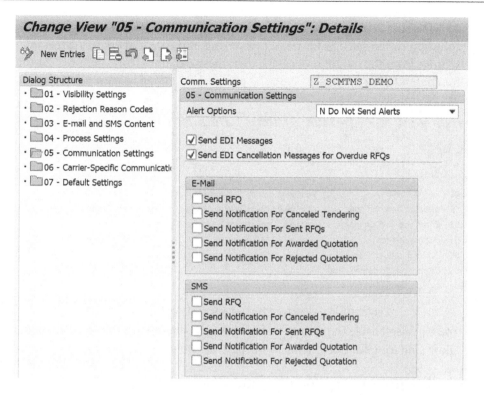

Figure 10.35 – General settings for tendering: Communication Settings

You can also configure the sending of alerts to tendering managers if these managers have subscribed to a tendering alert category.

- **06 – Carrier-Specific Communication Settings**: Here, you have the option to configure specific means of communication for a specific carrier. The communication setting for the carrier can be different to the general communication settings defined in the **Communication Settings** view.

- **07 – Default Settings**: You can specify a default set of process settings and communication settings for freight tendering. If the system doesn't determine these settings from the freight order type, then these default settings are used for the freight tendering process:

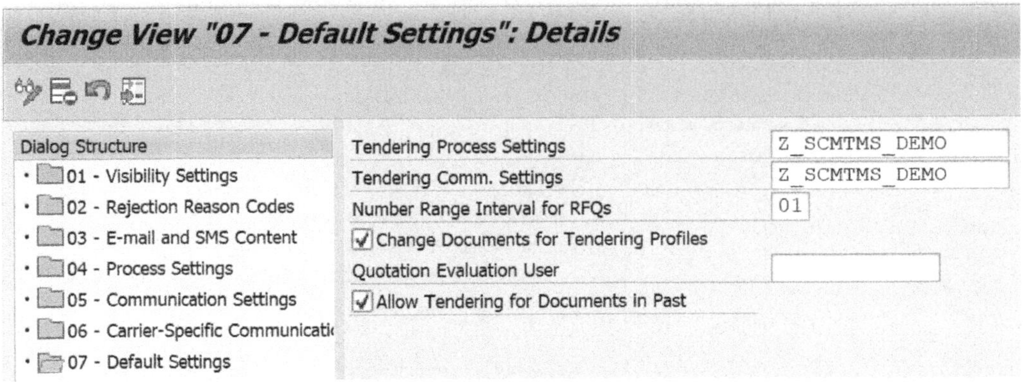

Figure 10.36 – General settings for tendering: Default Settings

You can also enable the system to create change documents to record changes and allow tendering for documents in the past, as shown in the preceding *Figure 10.36*.

Step 2 – Freight order type configuration

The freight order type should be relevant for subcontracting. You also assign process and communication settings to the freight order type once you configure the general settings for tendering. The following is the IMG path to activate subcontracting for the freight order: **IMG | SAP Transportation Management | Transportation Management | Freight Order Management | Freight Order | Define Freight Order Types**.

Step 3 – Setting up a tendering profile

The tendering profile contains tendering data that is used for automatic tendering. Tender profiles are set up in **NetWeaver Business Client | Application Administration | Tendering | Tendering profiles | Create Tendering Profiles**.

Figure 10.37 shows an example of the tendering profile:

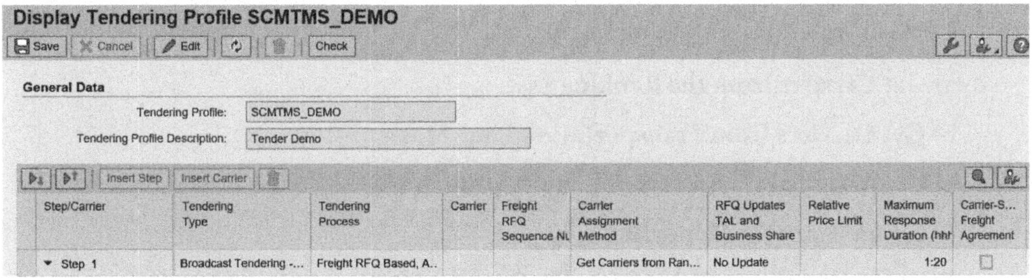

Figure 10.37 – Tendering profile

The tendering profile is divided into the following configuration options:

- **Step/Carrier**: This option is used when you want to plan tendering in multiple steps, meaning that if the carrier in step 1 doesn't accept freight tendering, then the system goes to the next step and sends the tender to the next carrier. This is based on the business rule and business requirements.

- **Tendering Type**: The following are the different types of tendering provided by SAP:

  a) **Peer-to-Peer Tendering – Response Required**

  b) **Peer-to-Peer Tendering – No Response Required**

  c) **Broadcast Tendering – Best Offer**

  d) **Broadcast Tendering – First Acceptable Offer**

- **Tendering Process**: The following are the different tendering process types. You can either choose the RFQ-based tendering process or direct tendering based on your business needs:

  a) **RFQ – Based. Award Manually**

  b) **RFQ – Based. Award Automatically**

  c) **Direct Tendering. Send Freight Order Directly**

- **Carrier Assignment Method**: You can assign a carrier in the tendering profile with the methods provided with SAP TMS. You can choose one of the options provided based on your business requirements:

  a) **Get Carriers from the Ranking List**

  b) **Get Carriers from Transportation Lane Master Data**

  c) **Get Assigned Carrier from Freight Order**

  d) **Assign Carriers Manually**

- **RFQ Updates TAL and Business Shares**: You can configure RFQ updates to TAL and Business Shares. You can free up TAL or Business Shares upon rejection and SAP has provided the following stated options:

  a) **No Update**

  b) **Update TAL; Do not Free Up TAL Upon Rejection**

  c) **Update All; Free up TAL and Business Share Upon Rejection**

  d) **Update All; Do Not Free Up TAL but Free Up BS Upon Rejection**

- **Relative Price Limit**: The relative price limit acts as a threshold to avoid awarding the freight order based on a price quotation that is too high.

- **Maximum Response Duration**: This is the longest period within which a carrier should respond. If the response is not received, then the next step in the profile is executed.

- **Carrier-Specific Freight Agreement**: If this checkbox is selected, the price limit is calculated per carrier on the basis of their specific freight agreement.

The tendering process can be initiated interactively using a freight order or from the transportation cockpit. Additionally, you can run the batch report program, `/SCMTMS/TOR_TENDERING_BATCH`, to execute the tendering process.

The following screenshot shows the report program for background processing for tendering:

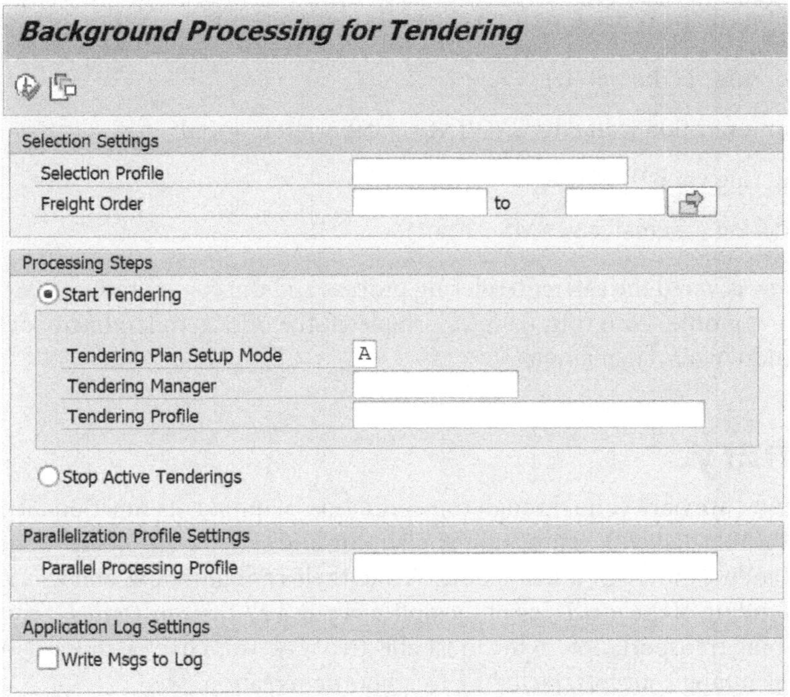

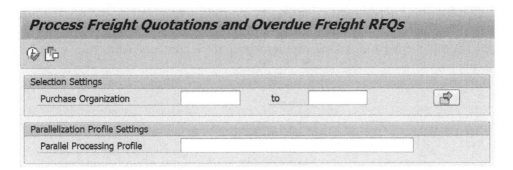

Figure 10.38 – Background Processing for Tendering

The report /SCMTMS/TEND_CONT_PROCESS evaluates the responses received from the carriers. This is shown in *Figure 10.39*:

Figure 10.39 – Process Freight Quotations and Overdue Freight RFQs

The following are the communication channels mentioned in the tendering process:

- Tendering via the web UI

- Communication using the SAP TMS collaboration portal

- Tendering via B2B messages

- Tendering via email and SMS

We have now covered the carrier tendering process and the configuration to set up the tendering profile. With this, we have completed the critical functionality of the transportation management system.

Summary

In this chapter, we have gone through transportation planning, its functionality, and the constraints associated with setting up the planning and selection profiles. We now have an understanding of freight unit documents and their configurations and use, along with an understanding of the functions of the optimizer and all the constraints it considers while planning transportation in the most effective way. This chapter covered manual and automatic planning concepts, including freight order creation.

We have also gone through freight order document configuration and its usage. The key concepts regarding carrier selection and freight order tendering processes/plans were also covered. The chapter included different ways to determine carriers and the methods to tender the freight order to these carriers. Before we deep dive into the execution of transportation, it is imperative to understand transportation planning and slot shipments effectively by running the optimizer and planning these shipments. This is what we have learned in this chapter and it is important to grasp these concepts before moving on to the next chapter.

In our next chapter, we will cover all the basics in terms of initiating logistics execution in SAP LES.

Further reading

- Additional information on transportation planning can be found at `https://help.sap.com/ viewer/54cf405c9d9e4c96bf091967ea29d6a7/9.6.2/en-US/ceb2c9 9144e84056a9a707798aa9a0db.html`.

- Additional information on freight order management can be found at `https://help.sap.com/ viewer/54cf405c9d9e4c96bf091967ea29d6a7/9.6.2/en-US/ ff8bbbea9bd0421b9f833793d8d52b3d.html`.

11
Logistics Execution in SAP LES

Once the freight order is planned, a carrier assigned, and the tendering process has been executed, the next step in the order to cash cycle is to initiate **Logistics Execution** (**LE**). LE is processed in the warehouse where the goods are picked, packed, and shipped out to deliver to the customer. We covered ERP delivery creation in *Chapter 9, Transportation Requirements in SAP TMS*, where we saw that the delivery proposal is sent to SAP ERP from the SAP TMS system. This delivery proposal can be automated via a batch job or you can manually trigger the delivery from the freight order. The delivery proposal groups the items together that need to go in a specific delivery.

In this chapter, you will learn how, once a delivery is created in the SAP ERP system, the shipment creation process is initiated to start LE. You will see that as the goods are delivered to the customer, the carrier invoice related to the freight charges and freight settlement is processed thereafter.

Here is a list of the topics covered in this chapter:

- Freight order integration with shipment and shipment processing
- Picking
- Packing

- Post goods issue
- Freight settlement and carrier invoicing processing

By the end of this chapter, you will understand freight order integration with a shipment and how to process a shipment document in the SAP ECC system. You will learn the key concepts around picking, packing, and shipping products from the warehouse, covering the configuration aspects of shipping products. You will also learn the concept of transportation charge management and how to settle freight with the carrier.

Freight order integration with shipment and shipment processing

SAP TM provides two options for integrating ERP shipments, which are shipment-based freight orders and freight order-based shipments. In shipment-based freight orders, transportation planning occurs in the SAP ERP system. The delivery and shipment in the case of shipment-based freight orders are created in the SAP ERP system and the SAP ERP shipment document triggers the creation of the freight order. The freight order is then tendered and further performs freight cost settlement. This scenario is adopted when customers want to plan transportation in the SAP ERP system but would like to utilize SAP TM for tendering functions, freight costing, and rate purposes. This scenario is also called **shipment integration inbound**.

The other option to integrate with SAP ERP shipments is freight order-based shipment. In this option, the transportation planning is initiated and executed in the SAP TM system. Freight order planning in SAP TM triggers the creation of an SAP ERP shipments document. This scenario is also called **shipment integration outbound**.

In this chapter, we will consider a freight order-based shipment scenario. *Figure 11.1* shows a freight order-based shipment scenario:

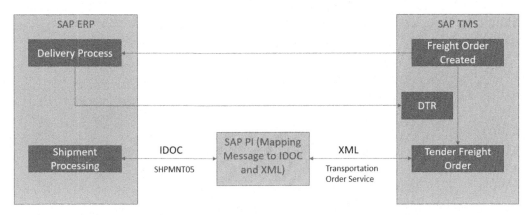

Figure 11.1 – ERP shipment integration flow

Here are the process steps for freight order-based shipments:

1. A sales order created in the SAP ERP system creates an **order transportation requirement(OTR)** in the SAP TM system. A freight unit is created from the OTR document.

2. The system initiates the transportation planning to create the freight order. Once the freight order is created, the delivery proposal is sent to the SAP ERP system. A delivery document is created in the SAP ERP system.

3. The delivery document creates the **delivery transportation requirement (DTR)** in SAP TM and consumes the OTR requirement.

4. A carrier is assigned, and tendering is executed in SAP TM. At the same time, the shipment document is created in the SAP ERP system. This is initiated from the freight order.

5. Once the shipment document is created in the SAP ERP system, confirmation from the ERP system is sent to SAP TM. Any update to the shipment status in the SAP ERP system is also sent to the freight order in SAP TM. Thereafter, LE is initiated with the shipment document.

The following screenshot shows the process flow of a freight order-based shipment scenario:

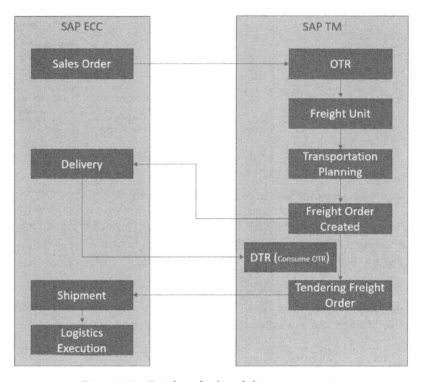

Figure 11.2 – Freight order-based shipment scenario

You can create the shipment from the freight order using the freight order UI as a follow-up function, or you can trigger the shipment creation via the /SCMTMS/TOR_ FO_PROCESS batch job report.

SAP ERP creates an ERP shipment for each freight order received from SAP TM. There is an *n-to-one* relationship between DTRs and a freight order. Any update to or deletion of the freight order in SAP TM is updated in the shipment document in the SAP ERP system.

The following settings are required to activate freight order-based shipment integration:

1. Maintain the output profile in the freight order type and mark the freight order type for shipment relevance. This is done by going to SAP TM, then selecting **IMG | SAP Transportation Management | Transportation Management | Freight Order Management | Freight Order | Define Freight Order Types**.

2. The freight order should have an in-process status and shouldn't be marked as **blocked** or **cancellation**.

3. Set the relevant shipment document type in the SAP ERP system and maintain the external number range for the shipment document type.

4. Set up a transportation planning point in the SAP ERP system.

5. In SAP ERP, configure the output type for the confirmation and status update to SAP TM. Configure the partner profile for the `SHPMNT05` message type with the `CRE`, `CNF`, `STA`, and `UPD` message codes.

6. Create the output record in SAP ERP for the shipment document.

7. You also need to set up a configuration scenario for the `TM_ERPShipmentIntegration_Out` outbound integration scenario in SAP NetWeaver **Process Integration** (**PI**). SAP PI must be set up to process and map `SHPMNT05` to the appropriate message for SAP TM.

Now that we have understood the steps for integrating a freight order-based shipment, next we will understand the message flow that happens between SAP TM and SAP ERP.

Message flow between freight orders in SAP TM and shipment documents in the SAP ERP system

SAP TM creates the freight order; then the freight order triggers to create the shipment in the SAP ERP system. It triggers the `TransportationOrderSCMExecutionRequest_Out` service, which is mapped to `SHPMNT05` in SAP PI, which then creates the shipment document in the SAP ERP system. The acknowledgment is then received via `TransportationOrderSCMExecutionConfirmation_In`.

Figure 11.3 shows the freight order and shipment message flow between the SAP TMS and SAP ERP systems:

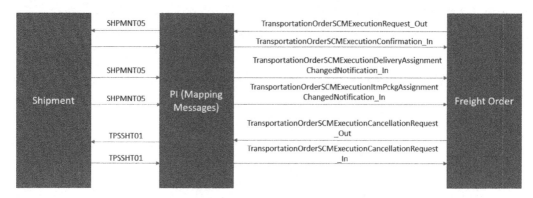

Figure 11.3 – Message flow between the freight order and shipment document

The `TransportationOrderSCMExecutionStatusNotification_ ln` service is used to perform status updates from SAP ERP in SAP TM. The `TransportationOrderSCMExecutionDeliveryAssignmentChanged Notification_ln` service is used to send information for any deliveries that are added or deleted from the shipment in ERP.

Similarly, updates to the item packaging assignment are received through the `TransportationOrderSCMExecutionItmPckgAssignmentChanged Notification_ln` service. IDOC `TPSSHT01` is used in SAP ERP for shipment cancellation. The cancellation can be triggered from either the freight order or the shipment document in the SAP ERP system. The services used in SAP TM are `TransportationOrderSCMExecutionCancellationRequest_Out` and `TransportationOrderSCMExecutionCancellationRequest_In`.

For any additional enhancements for shipment integration required per business rules, you can follow the IMG path provided next and implement the Business Add-In (BAdI) as per your business requirements: **IMG | SAP Transportation Management | Transportation Management | Business Add-Ins (BAdIs) for Transportation Management | Integration | ERP Logistics Integration | ERP Shipment Integration**

The following screenshot shows the BADI implementations for outbound and inbound integration of ERP shipments:

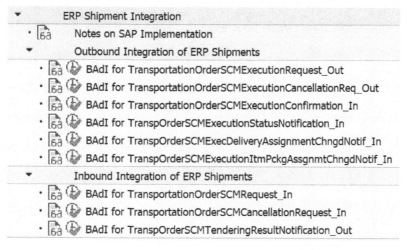

Figure 11.4 – ERP shipment integration BADI implementations

We have covered the message flow of the shipment document between SAP ECC and TMS; let's now understand how to integrate the text types between freight orders and shipment documents.

Integrating text types between freight orders and shipment documents

Some of the key communication around shipping instructions or carrier instructions is important to print on the paperwork, which could be captured through text on the freight order or the shipment document. This type of information can be supported by text management. The text should be flexible and should be easily tailored to business needs.

Here are the steps to configure the text type and text schema in a freight order and its mapping to the shipment document. The following configuration is executed in the SAP TMS environment:

1. In this step, you can define text types and text schemas and assign text types to text schemas. A text schema can be assigned for a given hosting **Business Object (BO)** node that uses dependent object text collection. You can also specify an access sequence that enables you to determine the source of the text, that is, to copy text from a preceding document or a master record.

Figure 11.5 shows the **Text Schema** configuration screen:

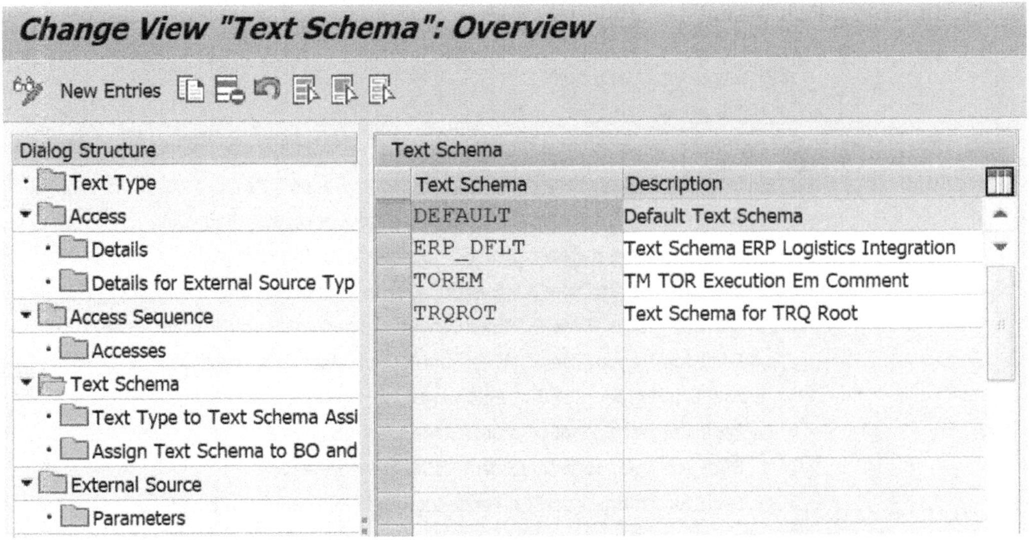

Change View "Text Schema": Overview

New Entries

Dialog Structure	Text Schema	
• Text Type	**Text Schema**	**Description**
▼ Access	DEFAULT	Default Text Schema
• Details	ERP_DFLT	Text Schema ERP Logistics Integration
• Details for External Source Typ	TOREM	TM TOR Execution Em Comment
▼ Access Sequence	TRQROT	Text Schema for TRQ Root
• Accesses		
▼ Text Schema		
• Text Type to Text Schema Assi		
• Assign Text Schema to BO and		
▼ External Source		
• Parameters		

Figure 11.5 – Maintaining the text schema

It is configured under the IMG path given here: **IMG | Cross-Application Components | Processes and Tools for Enterprise Applications | Reusable Objects and Functions for BOPF Environment | Dependent Object Text Collection | Maintain Text Schema**

2. You can define and describe the text type based on your business requirements, for example, shipping instructions, carrier instructions, or sales text. This is also shown in *Figure 11.6*:

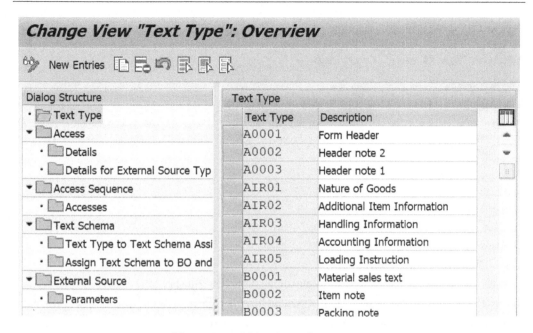

Figure 11.6 – Maintaining the text type

3. In this step, you define the access sequence where the accesses are assigned. Defining the access sequence allows you to identify and describe an access sequence for each text type. This is shown in *Figure 11.7*:

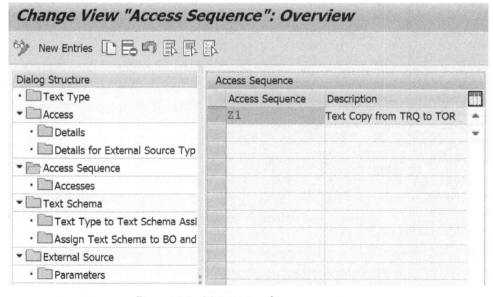

Figure 11.7 – Maintaining the access sequence

Figure 11.8 shows the access assigned to an access sequence:

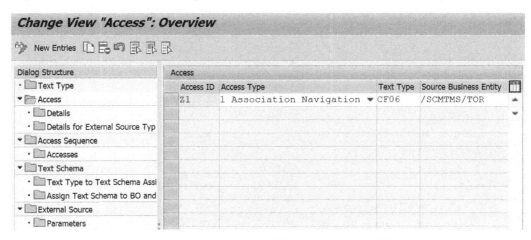

Figure 11.8 – Maintaining the access sequence (2)

There are four types of access: **Association Navigation**, **Association Navigation with Node attribute**, **External BO**, and **External Source**.

4. Once you are done with the text type and access sequence configuration, the next step is to assign the text type to the text schema and then assign the text schema to the BO and node. This is shown in *Figure 11.9*:

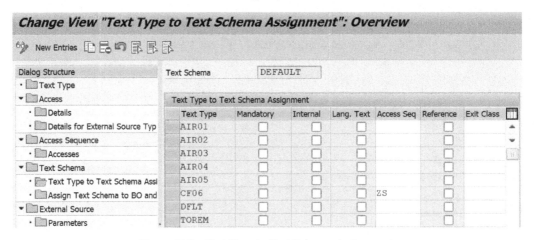

Figure 11.9 – Text Type to Text Schema Assignment

The following screenshot shows the assignment of the text type to the text schema:

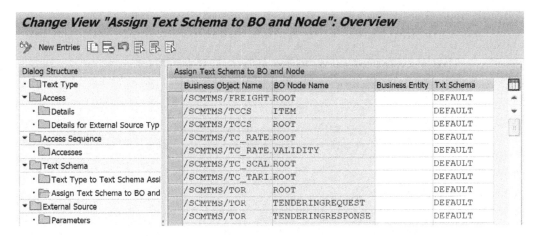

Figure 11.10 – Text type to text schema assignment (2)

5. After configuring the text schema, it is then assigned to the freight order type. The text type configured in the text schema will appear in the freight order once this step of assigning the text schema to the freight order type is completed. This is shown in *Figure 11.11*:

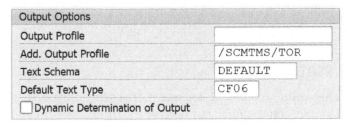

Figure 11.11 – Text schema to freight order type assignment

6. The final step is the mapping of the ERP text type to the freight order text type.

The following screenshot shows the assignment of ERP text types to the TM text types for the freight order:

New Entries: Overview of Added Entries

	Assign ERP Text Types to TM Text Types for Freight Orders				
	Log. Syst.	ERPTxtType	TMTxtType	Not TM-Rel	
	TMSCLNT100	Z001	CF06	☐	▲
				☐	▼
				☐	

Figure 11.12 – Assigning ERP text types to TM text types for freight orders

This is done through the configuration path given here: **SPRO | SAP Transportation Management | Transportation Management | Integration | ERP Logistics Integration | Shipment Integration | Assign ERP Text Types to TM Text Types for Freight Orders**

We have gone through the text schema functionality and configuration in SAP TMS and its mapping with the shipment document in the SAP ECC environment; let's now understand different shipment statuses in the next section.

Shipment statuses

The shipment status within a shipment document drives the initiation of LE process. These statuses are important to understand before the truck checks in and the loading starts. A shipment document has planning dates and execution dates for each of the statuses mentioned next. Let's go through the definition of each of these statuses:

- **Check-In**: The check-in date is updated when the carrier arrives at the shipper's facility. In cases where empty trailers are brought into the shipper's yard, this event occurs as soon as the trailer is ready for loading.

- **Loading Start** and **Loading End**: There are two types of loading events: loading start and loading end. The loading starts when the goods are being loaded; the loading end occurs when the loading of the goods is completed in the truck, as an example. No more loading activities are carried out after the loading end status is updated.

- **Shipment Completion**: This occurs when all the necessary paperwork is completed. This includes the BOL, packing slip, and much more.

- **Shipment Start**: This occurs once the carrier departs from the loading facility. The shipment is considered in transit at this time.

- **Shipment End**: This occurs after the carrier completes the unloading of all items and the co-signee signs the proof of delivery.

As soon as the check-in starts, the SAP TM freight order status is set to `In Execution`. Depending on the integration scenario, the freight order can be rendered as display only per shipment status. This also includes assigning carriers, changing vehicle resources, changing partners, and so on. This behavior can further be enhanced by implementing a custom enhancement.

Additionally, when the freight order has the `In Execution` status, control is managed by the execution system as soon as the shipment is in the `Check-In` status.

Defining and assigning activity profiles

When working with shipment statuses on the shipment document, you can trigger subsequent actions with each of these statuses. For example, if you are working with a warehouse-managed inventory and would like to create the transfer order automatically with the `Check-In` status, you can trigger the transfer order creation at the `Check-In` status. Similarly, if you want to print the paperwork on shipment completion, you can do so when updating the shipment completion status. Another example is posting a goods issue on shipment start or shipment completion. This can be done by configuring the activity profile. Specific actions can be executed via the activity profiles based on the shipment status.

You define a selection variant in the `RV56ABST` program, which is assigned to a shipment type. In this way, the shipment activities that are to be carried out are defined for the shipment type as soon as the corresponding status is set. *Figure 11.13* shows the activity profiles assignment for the shipment types at different shipment statuses:

Change View "Activity Profiles for Shipment Types": Overview

Maintain

ShTy	Description	For planning	At check-in	At load. start	At load.finish	At completion	At shpmt begin	At shpmt. end
0001	Indiv.Shipmt - Road		ZPICK				ZPGI	
0002	Collct.Shipmt - Road							
0003	Collective Shipment							
0004	Prelim. leg by road							

Figure 11.13 – Assigning activity profiles to the shipment types

You configure the activity profiles under configuration in the SAP ERP system. The configuration path is as follows: **IMG | Logistics Execution | Transportation | Shipments | Define and Assign Activity Profiles**

Figure 11.14 shows the selection variant in the RV56ABST program – **Control of Activities when Setting a Status in the Shipment**:

Control of Activities when Setting a Status in the Shipment

Dialog box for fast entry during setting of status

☑ Dialog box for fast entry during setting of status   [Fld Selectn]

   Identification of handling unit to which data is to refer

     Packaging mat. type   [   ]

     Packaging materials   [   ]

Issue log during save of shipment

◯ Do not issue log (even if there are errors or warnings)

◉ Issue log if errors or warnings occur

◯ Always issue log after save

   ☐ Save Log (Display Using Transaction VT05)

Post goods issue for deliveries of shipment

◯ No goods issue posting

◉ Carry out goods issue posting during save

◯ Carry out goods issue posting in background

   Background proc.variant   [   ]   [Maintain]

☑ GI for non-mvmnt-rlvnt dlvrs

Further functions when saving shipment

☐ Carry out billing

☐ Generate delivery item for HUs

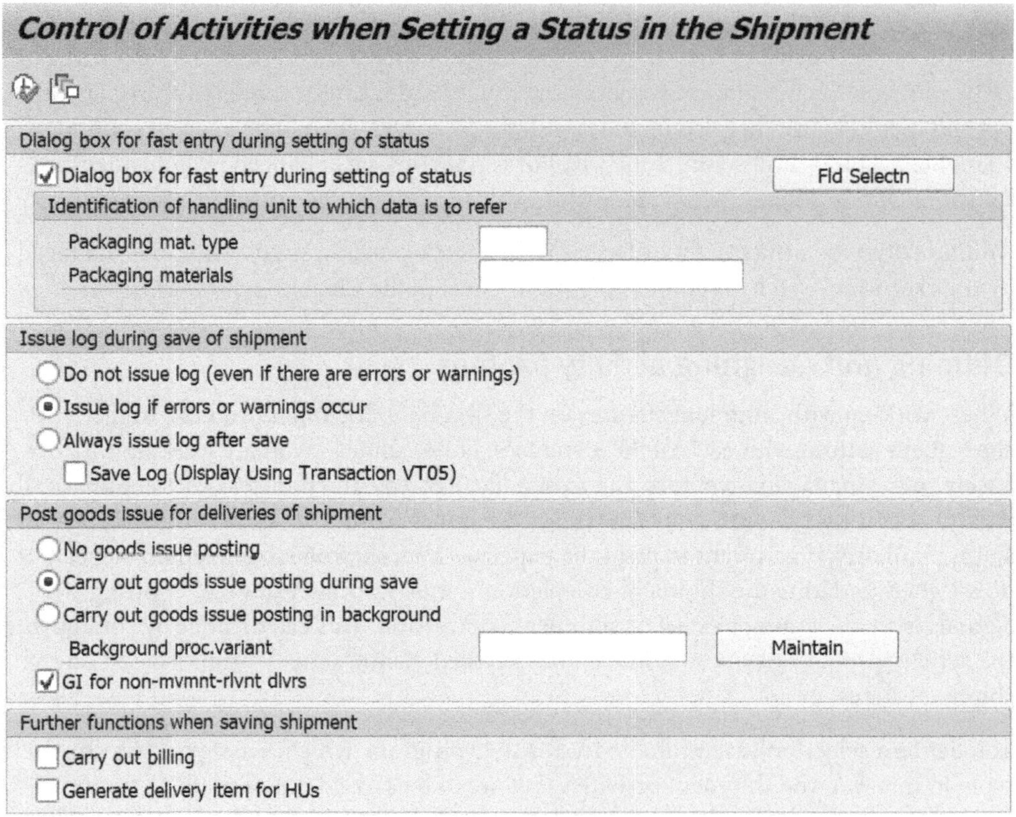

Figure 11.14 – Control of Activities when Setting a Status in the Shipment document

The following screenshot shows the print output after saving the options with the RV56ABST program:

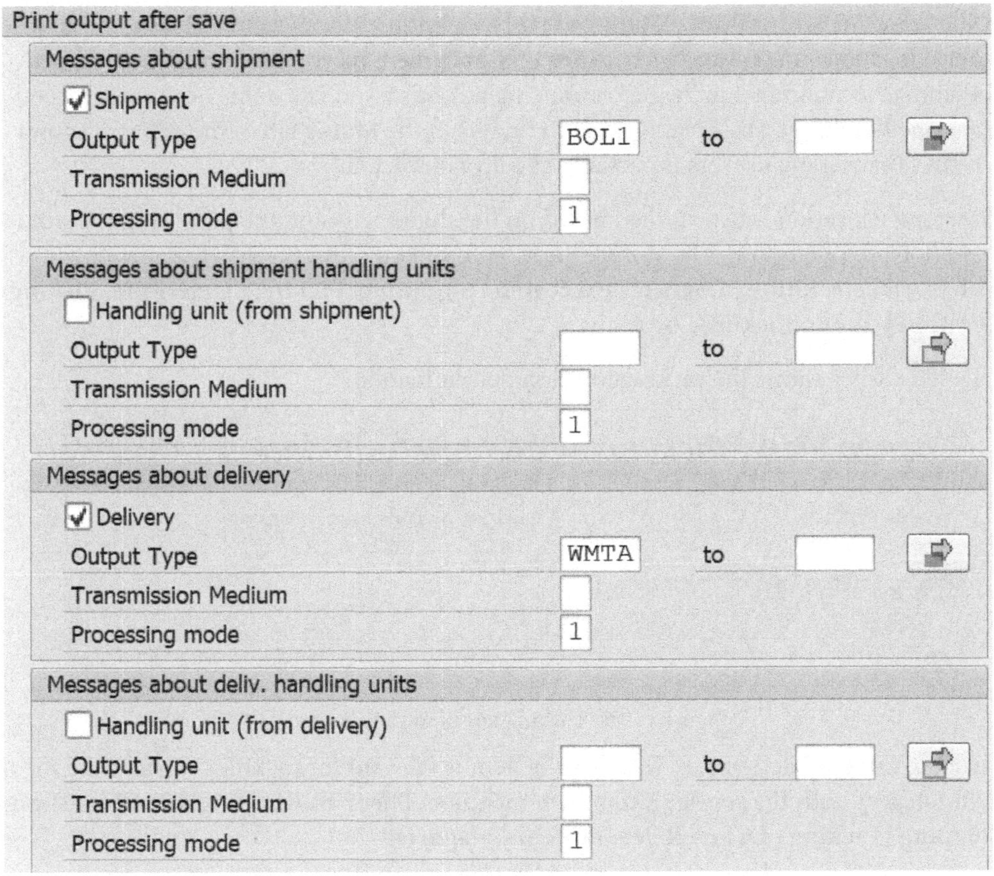

Print output after save

Messages about shipment

☑ Shipment
Output Type   BOL1   to
Transmission Medium
Processing mode   1

Messages about shipment handling units

☐ Handling unit (from shipment)
Output Type   to
Transmission Medium
Processing mode   1

Messages about delivery

☑ Delivery
Output Type   WMTA   to
Transmission Medium
Processing mode   1

Messages about deliv. handling units

☐ Handling unit (from delivery)
Output Type   to
Transmission Medium
Processing mode   1

Figure 11.15 – Control of Activities when Setting a Status in the Shipment document (2)

In this section, we covered the shipment integration option and its creation in the SAP ERP system. The shipment document is created in the SAP ERP system. This initiates the check-in process; then the carrier arrives at the shipping facility and the picking process is initiated, which is discussed in the next section.

Picking

Picking is the process of taking goods from a storage location and moving them to an interim or staging area where the goods can be packed and shipped out to the customer. Companies can perform picking based on how they are set up, meaning whether their warehouse is inventory-managed or warehouse-managed or whether they are using **Handling Units (HUs)** to track the material.

If you are using an **Inventory Managed** (**IM**) warehouse, the system can determine the storage location automatically in the delivery document or you have added or changed the storage location manually. Before posting a goods issue, the items need to be picked and staged in the staging area. Picking the status in the **Status** tab of the delivery shows whether the picking process is partially or fully completed.

The storage location is determined based on the shipping point, the plant, and the storage condition. You determine the storage location for picking in LES with the customizing path given here: **SPRO | Logistics Execution | Shipping | Picking | Determine Picking Location | Assign Picking Locations**

This screenshot shows the picking location determination:

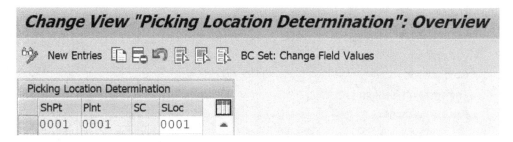

Figure 11.16 – Picking Location Determination

The item category determines whether the item is relevant for picking. You activate the item category with the configuration path mentioned here: **SPRO | Logistics Execution | Shipping | Picking | Define Relevant Item Categories**

The next screenshot shows the delivery item categories relevant for picking:

Change View "Deliveries: Item categories - picking": Overview

BC Set: Change Field Values

Deliveries: Item categories - picking

ItCa	Description	Relevant for picking
ADP1	Ret.Pack. Pickup	☐
ADP2	Ret. Pack. Shipment	☑
ADP3	Ret.Pack. Sales	☐
AEBT	Indep. Payt Process	☑
ALEN	ALE Standard Order	☑

Figure 11.17 – Delivery item categories relevant for picking

If you are using a **Warehouse Managed (WM)** warehouse, the **Warehouse Management System (WMS)** module is fully integrated with LE. You can create a WM transfer order directly from the outbound delivery. The status of the warehouse management process can also be monitored from the delivery.

Note

This chapter does not include any configuration related to warehouse management or HU management as they are outside the scope of this book.

Warehouse management provides automated and flexible processes for all goods movements and managing stocks efficiently in a complex warehouse environment.

HU management helps you to track the movement of the goods associated with the HU in its entirety. The HU associated with the finished goods and packaging material tracks all transactions, right from the procurement, production, and selling of the goods.

This chapter covers some parts of the processes, touching on both warehouse management and HUs related to outbound delivery.

Picking with warehouse management

Picking with warehouse management allows you to create the transfer order as you initiate the picking process. With the `Check-In` status of the shipment document, you can trigger creating the transfer order through a variant in the `RV56ABST` program, which is also mentioned in the activity profiles in the *Shipment statuses* section of this chapter. The transfer order is created with reference to the outbound delivery document; before creating the transfer order, the system checks whether the warehouse number is assigned to a combination of the plant and storage location in the `T320` table. If so, it assigns the same warehouse number and updates the overall WM status indicator to the delivery document. This indicator indicates that a transfer order is required for the material to be picked from its storage bin in the warehouse and moved to the area where materials are staged for delivery.

In standard SAP, storage type `916` is assigned for picking for deliveries. In addition to the creation of the transfer order, a picking slip can be generated for the warehouse personnel to physically pick up the goods and move them to the interim storage location or staging area. The transfer order has information regarding the source storage bin and the destination storage bin with the material and quantity information. You can also create the transfer order manually via transaction code `LT03`.

Once the goods have been picked and are moved to the staging area, the transfer order is confirmed. You can confirm the transfer order via transaction code LT10. Confirming the transfer order moves the stock from the source to the destination storage bin and the same is reflected in the system. You can see the quantity information with the updated destination bin and the quantity associated with the movement.

The following figure shows the picking and **Post Goods Issue (PGI)** process:

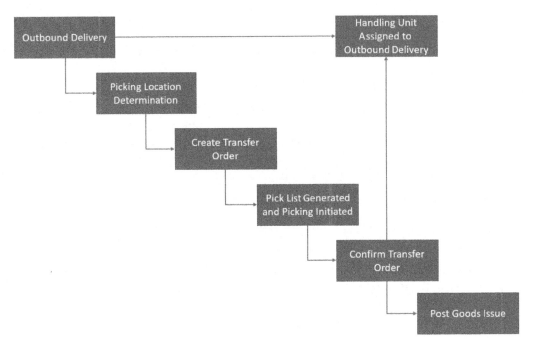

Figure 11.18 – Picking and post goods issue process

Here is the process flow of the goods being picked and the PGI for outbound delivery using WMS:

1. The outbound delivery and shipment documents are created via the proposal sent by SAP TMS.

2. With WMS, the system determines which items are relevant for stock removal based on the stock removal strategies. This is where the correct location is determined to pick the quantities for the specific delivery items.

3. Once the pick location is determined, the transfer order is created. The transfer order has all the information relating to the source storage bin and the destination storage bin.

4. At the same time, the pick list can be generated and physical picking by warehouse personnel is initiated.

5. The transfer order is confirmed as soon as the material is staged in the staging area to be loaded onto the truck or the trailer. The system reduces the stock in the source storage bin by the quantity of the material that has been picked and posts this material quantity to the destination storage bin.

6. At the same time, the HU is generated and is associated with the delivery document if you are working with HUs for tracking purposes.

7. Once the transfer order is confirmed, the PGI can be initiated. With the shipment document, you can configure the activity profile to trigger the PGI at a certain status, for example, `Shipment Start Date`.

Strategies

In WMS (**LE-WM**), you can define strategies in order to receive proposals from the SAP system of which storage bin goods are to be picked and which storage bins the goods are to be put away in. Therefore, SAP has provided two strategies in the system: a **picking strategy** and a **putaway strategy**. These strategies help you to use the available transfer and warehouse capacity optimally and efficiently.

Picking strategy

A picking strategy is a process of determining a source bin during the stock removal process. This strategy could be based on your business needs, meaning the strategy could be to pick materials by their remaining shelf life or by the sequence in which they are added to stock.

The warehouse personnel doesn't need to know which material needs to be picked as the system determines this with the configured picking strategy. This reduces the burden on the warehouse personnel as to which bin, location, and material to choose from manually. This also reduces the picking time and the picking process becomes more efficient. Manual changes should be kept to a minimum and reviewed periodically to ensure that the picking strategy still follows the most effective configuration.

The strategy of picking means what material is to be picked when delivering it to the customer. SAP has provided several picking strategies that can be used, which are listed here:

- **First In, First Out (FIFO)**
- **Last In, First Out (LIFO)**

- Fixed storage bin
- Shelf life expiration
- Partial quantities
- Quantity relevant

You need to complete several steps to configure the picking strategies before they can be applied to materials. This configuration is executed in the configuration path given here: **SPRO | Logistics Execution | Warehouse Management | Strategies**

You activate the storage type search and the related configuration in this step and you assign the storage type to the material master under the warehouse management view so that the system searches the storage bin for the storage type assigned to the material master. You determine the search sequence in the storage type search configuration.

Figure 11.19 shows the stock removal control configuration, where you can configure the strategies mentioned based on your business needs:

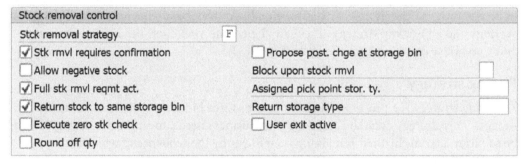

Figure 11.19 – Stock removal control

Although the FIFO and fixed bin strategies are widely used, some companies may go with other strategies depending on how their stock is valued. Here is the configuration path to configure the picking strategies: **SPRO | Logistics Execution | Warehouse Management | Strategies | Stock Removal Strategies**

Putaway strategy

Like the picking strategy, the putaway strategy, or stock placement strategy, helps you to decide where to store material received in the warehouse. The putaway strategy is used by WM to determine the storage bin during the creation of the transfer order during the putaway process. In this process, the system determines the putaway location so that warehouse personnel don't need to determine it manually. Although the system determines the putaway location, the warehouse personnel can manually change the location based on any kind of business rule exceptions. Using the storage type configuration, you can always overwrite the putaway bin determined by SAP so that a new bin has a different storage type.

SAP has provided putaway strategies that can be reviewed and adopted by companies to efficiently place materials in their warehouses. Once the putaway strategy has been adopted, the system uses it to assign the appropriate storage bin to store the material. A putaway strategy relieves the warehouse staff of one more responsibility and effectively speeds up material putaway.

Here are the different putaway strategies provided by SAP:

- Fixed bin storage
- Open storage section
- Next empty storage bin
- Bulk storage
- Near picking bin

Figure 11.20 shows the stock placement control configuration where you can configure the strategies mentioned based on your business needs:

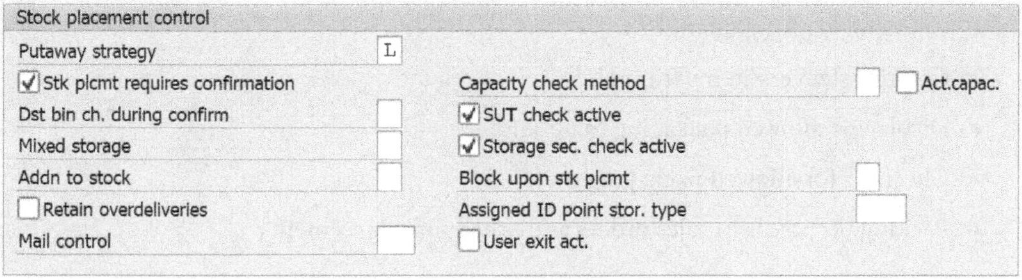

Figure 11.20 – Stock placement control

The process of putaway strategies should be reviewed carefully as not moving the picked material to the right place in the warehouse causes delays to the shipping material. The putaway strategies are important for the efficient flow of goods within the warehouse.

Here is the configuration path to configure the putaway strategies: **SPRO | Logistics Execution | Warehouse Management | Strategies | Putaway Strategies**

Once the picking process is completed, the next step is to pack the goods and ship them, which is explained in the next section.

Packing

The packing process is a part of delivery and shipment; you can execute the packing process from the delivery document. The items selected for packing can be assigned to the HU while packing.

Packing can be single-level or multi-level packing. Packing materials can be a box, carton, pallet, or container. Here are some of the different key functions that are available when packing with the SAP system:

- Packing delivery items in HUs and allocating individual items to several HUs
- Multi-level packing
- Unpacking items that were already packed
- Responses to exceeding weight or volume
- Deleting HUs
- Emptying HUs
- HU single entry
- Changing packing quantities
- Creating delivery items from HUs
- Displaying allowed packaging materials
- Checking for allowed packaging materials
- Packing proposals in sales orders and scheduling agreements

To carry out packing successfully, you need to go through the configuration steps stated here:

1. You activate packing in the item category at the following path: **SPRO | Logistics Execution | Shipping | Packing | Packing Control by Item Category**

   The following screenshot shows the configuration of the packing control for the item categories:

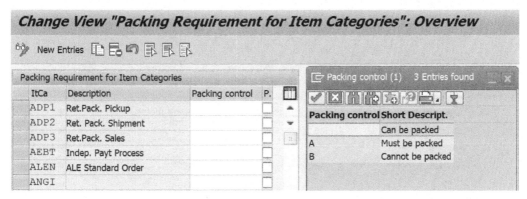

Figure 11.21 – Packing Requirement for Item Categories

2. You can define your own requirements for packing delivery items and for any business rule exception; you can implement the requirements routine for packing items in delivery.

   You configure the requirements routine from **SPRO | Logistics Execution | Shipping | Packing | Define Requirements for Packing in the Delivery**.

3. Packaging materials are combined into groups by the packaging material type and contain essential control features that apply to the corresponding shipping materials. The **VERP** material type is the most widely used packaging material type and is a standard material type for packaging material.

   The packaging material type controls the following functions:

   a) Output determination procedure and output type

   b) Sorting sequence

   c) Plant determination

   d) Number assignment

   e) HU category for SSCC18

You configure the packaging material types from **SPRO | Logistics Execution | Shipping | Packing | Define Packaging Material Types**.

The following screenshot shows the configuration of packaging material types:

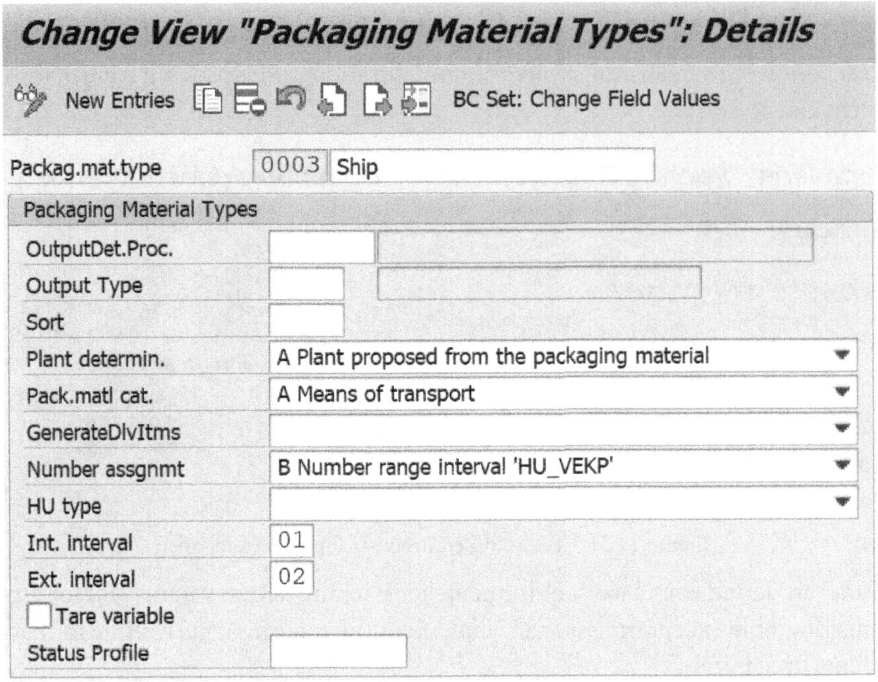

Change View "Packaging Material Types": Details
New Entries
BC Set: Change Field Values
Packag.mat.type
0003
Ship
Packaging Material Types
OutputDet.Proc.
Output Type
Sort
Plant determin.
A Plant proposed from the packaging material
Pack.matl cat.
A Means of transport
GenerateDlvItms
Number assgnmt
B Number range interval 'HU_VEKP'
HU type
Int. interval
01
Ext. interval
02
Tare variable
Status Profile

Figure 11.22 – Defining packaging material types

4. Materials that are to be packed into similar packaging materials are grouped together and therefore you need to create a material grouping for the packaging material as you define other material groups. The material grouping for packaging materials is entered in the material master record of the shipping material.

   You configure the material group for packaging materials from **SPRO | Logistics Execution | Shipping | Packing | Define Material Group for Packaging Materials**.

   The following screenshot shows the configuration for defining a material group for packaging materials:

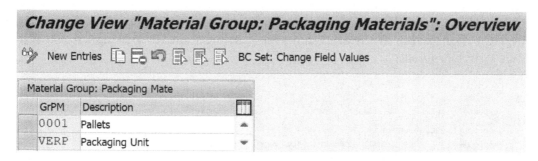

Figure 11.23 – Defining a material group for packaging materials

5. In this step, you create a mapping of the material group packaging material and packaging material type. Whether the packing is allowed or not for the packaging material pertaining to the HU is controlled via **Define Allowed Packaging Materials**.

    You configure the allowed packaging materials from **SPRO | Logistics Execution | Shipping | Packing | Define Allowed Packaging Materials**.

    The next screenshot shows the configuration for defining allowed packaging materials:

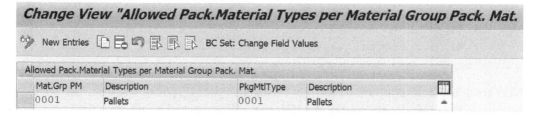

Figure 11.24 – Defining allowed packaging materials

6. Finally, you assign the packaging material type and material group for the packaging material in the packaging material master.

Once you are done with the preceding configuration, you can pack the materials from the HU packing screen. *Figure 11.25* shows the structure of the HU packing screen that is used to pack materials:

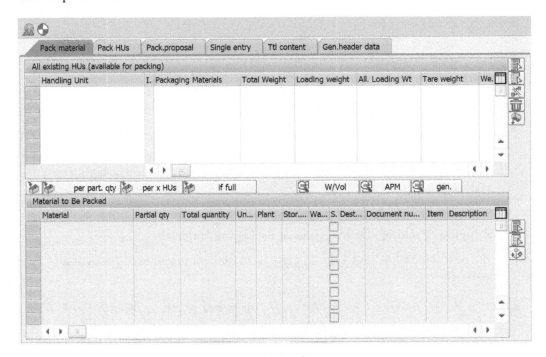

Figure 11.25 – HU packing screen

Next are detailed descriptions for each of the tabs on the HU packing screen. The upper portion of the screen consists of all the HUs that can be packed in, whereas the lower portion of the screen shows the materials that are to be packed:

- **Pack material**: The **Pack material** tab shows the materials packed into HUs. You can delete HUs or empty HUs on this screen.

- **Pack HUs**: The **Pack HUs** tab provides an overview for packing HUs. You can execute functions such as delete HUs or assign HUs for processing. You can also access a detailed display of the HUs.

- **Pack.proposal**: **Pack.proposal** shows an overview of the packaging materials and HUs. You can use previously defined packing instructions or manually defined packing proposals.

- **Single entry**: Here you can pack one material per activity with a specific quantity or you can pack one HU into another HU.

- **Ttl content**: You can display a total overview of all the HUs with the corresponding hierarchy levels in this tab.

Now that we have covered the packing functionality and configuration required for packaging materials, let's cover the PGI functionality in the next section.

Post goods issue

After the transfer order has been confirmed and completed, HUs have been assigned, and transportation documents have been printed, the material is now ready for shipment. The material that is moved to the staging area is packed and loaded onto a truck or trailer. The activity profile on the shipment document can drive the PGI based on the shipment start status. Once the warehouse personnel triggers the update of the shipment start status, the PGI is also initiated, assuming that the shipment status is set to the PGI in the activity profile. With this, the outbound delivery document is ready to be closed and the movement of the material out of the warehouse is completed in the system by posting the goods issue.

The movement type is 601 for a goods issue for delivery. If, for any reason, the delivery cannot be posted, an error log will be displayed to identify the problems that are preventing the goods issue for the line items on the document. Posting the goods issue moves the material from the warehouse and the inventory value is also removed from the plant.

Transportation charge management

Once the PGI is initiated, the carrier will deliver the goods to the customer and will send proof of delivery to the shipper/manufacturer. This information can be updated on the shipment document with the shipment end date. The next step in the process is to pay the carrier for the shipment and settle the charges. Before executing this step, SAP TMS determines these carrier charges on the freight order. Let's understand the master data required to determine these transportation charges that need to be paid to the carrier and how these charges are determined on the freight order.

The diagram here shows the master data required to set up the transportation charge that is reflected on the freight order:

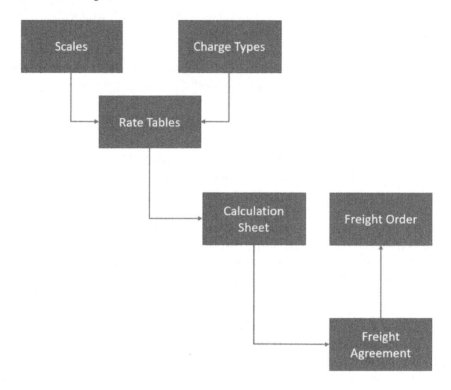

Figure 11.26 – Transportation charge management – master data

You maintain scales, rate tables, charge types, a charge calculation sheet, and a freight agreement as prerequisite master data before determining the freight agreement on the freight order. As shown in *Figure 11.26*, you assign scales to the rates when creating the rate table.

You then create a charge type and assign the charge type to the rate table. The charge type is then added to the calculation sheet. Within the calculation sheet, you can either assign the rate table or add rate table determination, which determines the rate table through a rate table determination rule. You maintain the condition for the rate table determination rule with the TCM_Rate condition type. Similarly, you can determine the calculation charge sheet and freight agreement through a condition with the TCM_TCCS_DET and TCM_FAGDET condition types, respectively. You maintain **Calculation Profiles** and **Charge Profiles**; assign the charge profile to the org unit to determine the freight agreement.

Scales

The scale forms the basis for the rate. Let's say the rate is dependent upon distance and weight; a separate scale is defined for both distance and weight. Once you define the scale, this is then used to define the rate. A scale can be used in multiple rate tables.

Figure 11.27 shows a scale master record with the **General Data** and **Items** tabs:

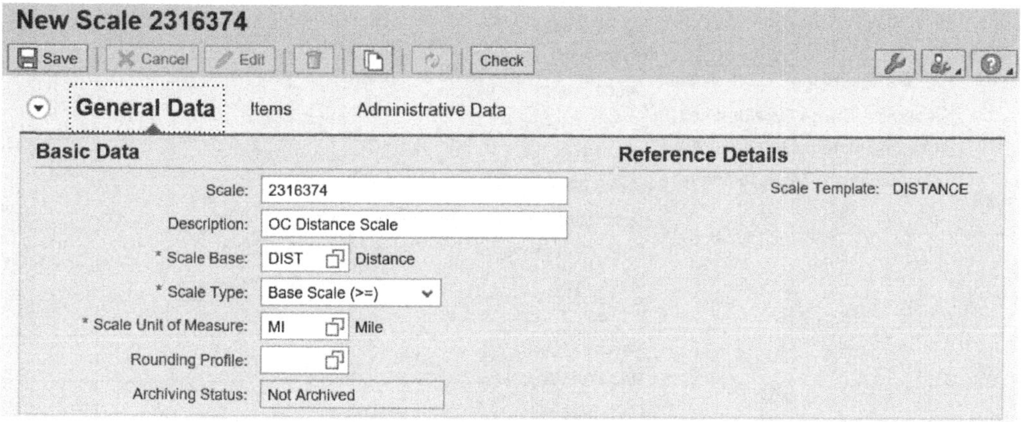

Figure 11.27 – Defining the scale

General Data contains information such as **Scale Base**, **Scale Type**, and **Scale Unit of Measure**. In the **Items** tab, you can assign a calculation type, which defines how the system should calculate the charges with the scale item.

You define the scale base with the configuration path given here: **SPRO | SAP Transportation Management | Basic Functions | Charge Calculation | Data Source Binding | Define Scale Bases**

Charge types

The charge type is created and assigned to calculation sheets and rate tables. The charge type plays an important role in determining the transportation charges for a specific line. You configure the charge type in the configuration path given here: **SPRO | SAP Transportation Management | Transportation Management | Basic Functions | Charge Calculation | Basic Settings | Define Charge Types**

Figure 11.28 shows an example of a charge type; here you configure the charge type with **Charge Category**, **Charge Subcategory**, whether the charge type is positive or negative, and whether the charge type is absolute or a percentage:

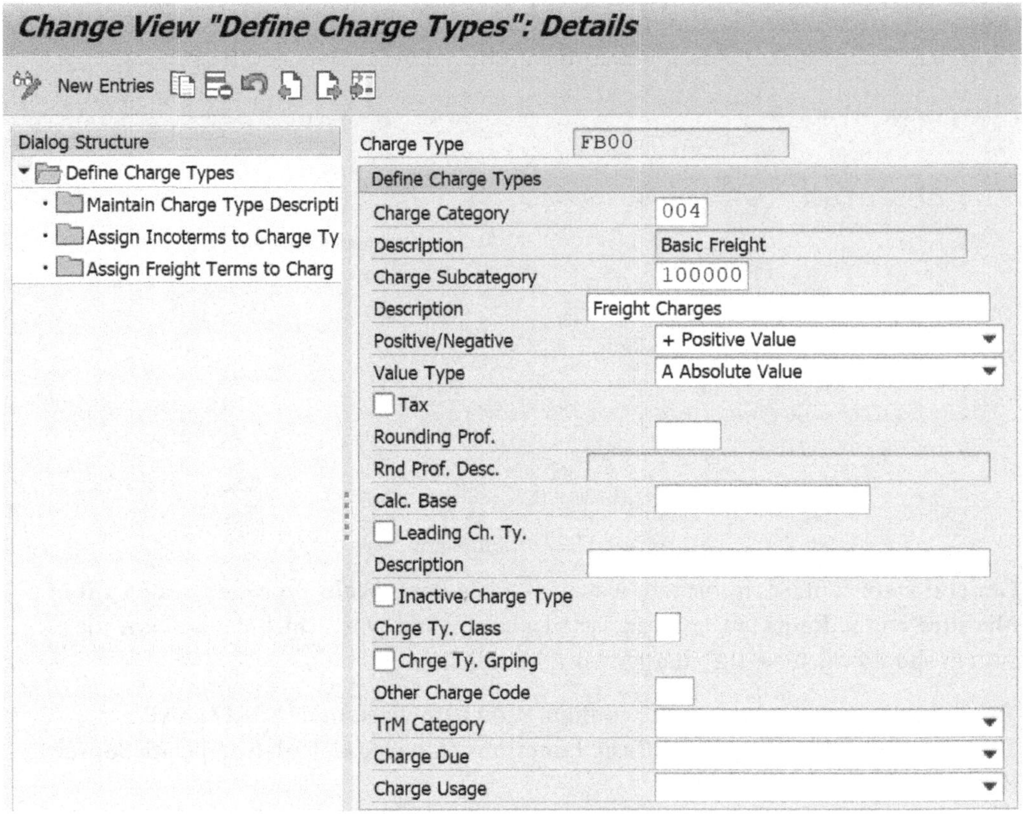

Figure 11.28 – Defining charge types

You define the charge category with the following configuration path: **SPRO | SAP Transportation Management | Transportation Management | Basic Functions | Charge Calculation | Basic Settings | Define Charge Categories**

You can define the charge subcategory with the following configuration path: **SPRO | SAP Transportation Management | Transportation Management | Basic Functions | Charge Calculation | Basic Settings | Define Charge Subcategories**

Charge categories and subcategories can be used to determine the ERP condition type during billing or ERP service material during settlement.

Rate tables

Within the rate table, you define the prices with the validity period of the transportation services. You can maintain the rate table manually or automatically through a rate table template. *Figure 11.29* shows the structure of the rate table master:

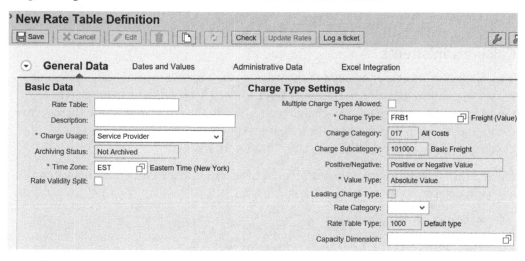

Figure 11.29 – Defining the rate table

The **General Data** tab shows the **Charge Usage** and **Charge Type** values assigned to the rate table. *Figure 11.30* also shows the scale assigned to the rate table:

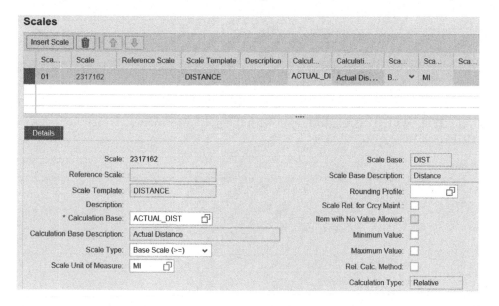

Figure 11.30 – Defining the rate table (2)

You cannot directly reuse the reference scale in the rate table, but you can copy a reference scale into the rate table. You can also create new scales for the rate table with or without a scale template.

To load a large amount of rate data, you can upload or download Microsoft Excel sheets to speed up data maintenance.

Calculation sheets

The calculation sheet is equivalent to the pricing procedure in the SAP ERP system. It is used to calculate the transportation charges and consists of different charge types. Based on the rates set up and the charge type added to the calculation sheet, the system determines the sequence for how these charge types should be considered in the document and how to calculate the transportation charges.

Figure 11.31 shows the structure of the calculation sheet divided into basic data, items, and item details:

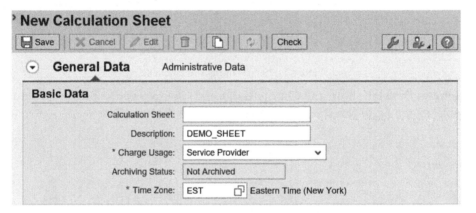

Figure 11.31 – Defining the calculation sheet

Figure 11.32 shows the calculation sheet with the item information, which includes the charge type:

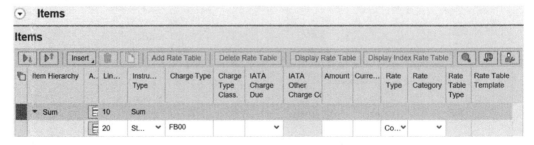

Figure 11.32 – Defining the calculation sheet (2)

Figure 11.33 shows the calculation sheet with the item details, which includes basic data, rate, classification, notes, and calculation bases:

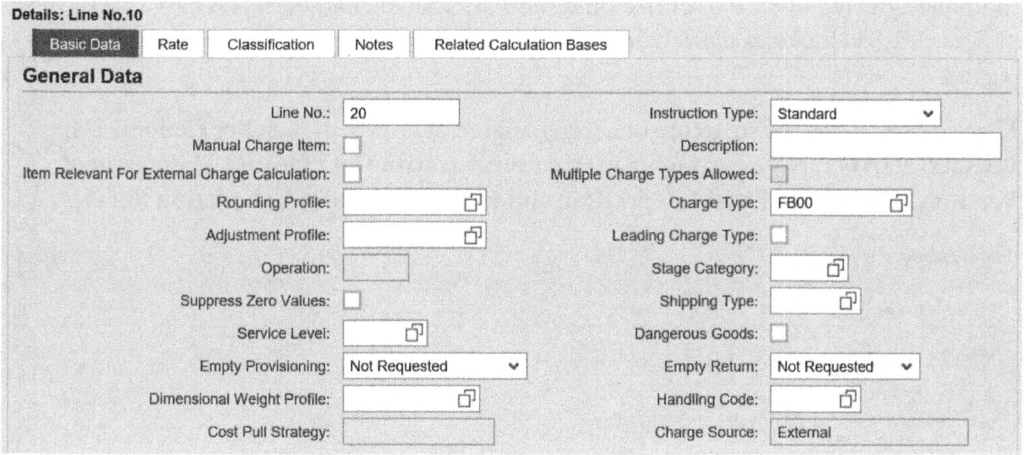

Figure 11.33 – Defining the calculation sheet (3)

Figure 11.34 shows the calculation sheet with the item information, which includes the validity period, calculation method, and resolution base:

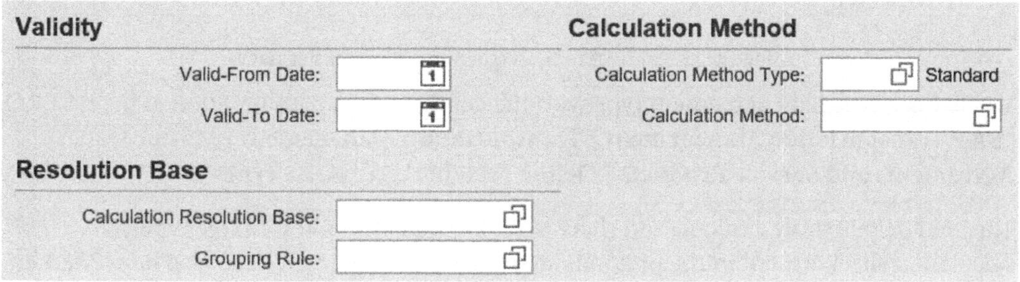

Figure 11.34 – Defining the calculation sheet (4)

General Data contains general information, such as **Description**, **Charge Usage**, **Archiving Status**, and **Time Zone**. The item data includes all the charge types you want to add based on the prices agreed with the carrier per different charge types.

As shown in *Figure 11.32*, **Items** general data includes **Charge Type**, **Instruction Type**, **Dimensional Weight Profile**, **Valid-From Date**, **Valid-To Date**, and so on and so forth. You can assign **Calculation Method** and **Calculation Resolution Base** to determine the charges per business requirements. The **Rate** tab page contains details of the rate table for each standard charge item. You can also create scales for each rate table. You can also assign a precondition rule to the calculation sheet item. You can update the calculation sheet charges on mass via the /SCMTMS/TCCS_MASS_UPDATE program.

Freight agreements

A freight agreement is a legally binding contract between the shipper and the carrier mutually agreeing upon the services and their associated charges. It can have one or more parties and also includes data such as organization units, terms of payment, and validity period.

Figure 11.35 shows the structure of a freight agreement, which includes **General Data**, **Business Partner**, **Notes**, **Attachments**, **Administrative Data Output Management**, **Versions**, **Capacities**, **Excel Integration**, and **Items containing Calculation Sheets**:

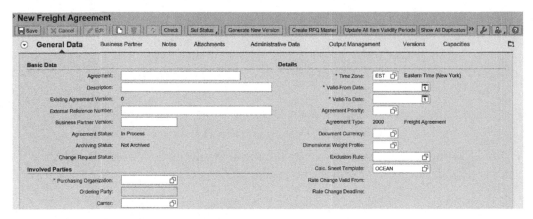

Figure 11.35 – Defining freight agreement master data

You define the freight agreement type with the configuration path mentioned here: **SPRO | SAP Transportation Management | Transportation Management | Master Data | Agreements and Service Products | Define Freight Agreement Types**

The item details show a calculation sheet overview containing the charge types; the calculation sheet created in the previous step with the charge types can also be viewed in the agreement when the calculation sheet is added as an item to the agreement.

Next is a screenshot of the freight agreement item:

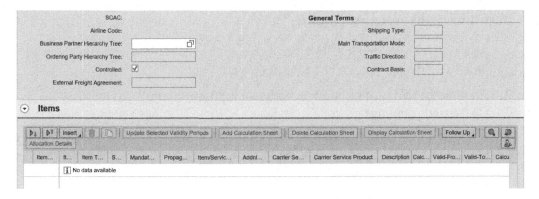

Figure 11.36 – Defining freight agreement master data (2)

You can maintain the freight agreement manually and use a Microsoft Excel file to update the details when you create a new freight agreement or edit an existing freight agreement.

As we have now gone through the transportation charge management setup, including the master data required to set up and and understood how to determine the freight charges, let's now continue the flow where we left off by executing the PGI in the next section.

Freight settlement and carrier invoicing processing

Once the PGI is initiated, the carrier will deliver the goods to the customer and will send the proof of delivery to the shipper/manufacturer. The next step in the process is to pay the carrier for the shipment and settle the charges. *Figure 11.37* shows the freight settlement and carrier invoice process:

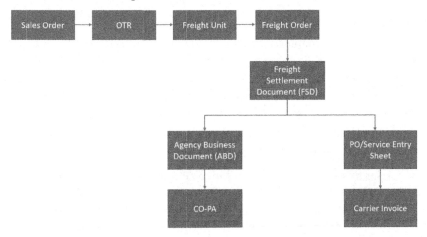

Figure 11.37 – Freight settlement and carrier invoicing process

Let's go through this process step by step:

1. A sales order is created in CRM; it replicates to the SAP ERP system. The same sales order is then replicated to the SAP TM system.

2. An order-based transportation requirement is generated (process considering OTR-based planning).

3. A freight unit is generated from the OTR document and the freight order is planned thereafter.

4. Once the delivery and shipment are processed from the freight order and the transportation charges are calculated appropriately in the freight order, a **Freight Settlement Document** (**FSD**) is generated, which carries the transportation cost from the freight order.

5. An FSD is created in SAP TMS to transfer the price to the SAP ERP system. The cost distribution takes place in the FSD based on business rules and conditions, for example, weight, volume, or any other customer-specific rules.

6. All freight costs, including the distributed cost from FSD, are sent to the SAP ERP system. Once this is done, two steps happen in the SAP ERP system. First, the overall freight cost is posted to SAP Material Management where the service **Purchase Order** (**PO**) is created, and a **Service Entry Sheet** (**SES**) is generated. The vendor (carrier) posts the incoming invoice, which matches the vendor invoice generated in the SAP ERP system. Once the invoice verification process is executed successfully, the carrier payment is processed. Second, the distributed cost from the FSD is transferred to the **Agency Business Document** (**ABD**). The ABD distributes the cost to the appropriate cost object in controlling (CO-PA). It takes the reference of the sales order line item to determine the account assignment details in the ABD.

Within this section of the chapter, it is also important to understand three key aspects, stated next:

- How the cost distribution takes place in the FSD and the configuration steps required to set up the cost distribution.

- How FSD is created and how the settlement takes place. These are the configuration steps required to set up the FSD.

- How carrier invoices are created and invoice verification takes place for the carrier invoices.

Let's go through these points and review the setup. We'll get to understand cost distribution, as well as its functionality and configuration, in the next section.

Cost distribution

Cost distribution is working out an accurate freight cost distribution across the order and line items based on the business rules, such as weight or quantity, for material valuation and order profitability analysis. Cost distribution can take place in a freight order, freight booking, or FSD. There are two important things to be considered when running through the cost distribution process. First, the cost distribution of the sales order item executes in SAP TMS, whereas the processing of this distributed cost happens in the SAP ERP system. The outbound delivery line item is posted to the costing objects, meaning CO-PA posting to determine the sales order profitability and this posting can be done through the ABD. SAP TMS uses SAP ERP's Agency Business module for freight cost posting. SAP TMS uses the Agency Business module posting engine to hand over the distributed freight cost to the SAP ERP system for processing.

Agency Business provides functionality with native integration to FI functions, which are financial accounting and controlling, CO-PA analysis, material ledger, and material valuation. The following are the steps required to configure cost distribution in both SAP TMS and the SAP ERP system:

1. Define the cost distribution methods: You define the cost distribution methods in **SPRO | SAP Transportation Management | Transportation Management | Basic Functions | Cost Distribution | Define Cost Distribution Methods**.

2. Define the cost distribution profile: You define the cost distribution profile in **SPRO | SAP Transportation Management | Transportation Management | Basic Functions | Cost Distribution | Define Cost Distribution Profile**.

3. Assign a cost distribution profile to the charge profile: You assign the cost distribution profile to the charge profile in **SPRO | SAP Transportation Management | Transportation Management | Basic Functions | Charge Calculation | Basic Settings | Define Charges Profiles**.

4. Assign the charge profile to the purchasing org unit (transaction code PPOME).

5. Enable cost distribution in the document types, which are the freight order type and FSD type: You enable cost distribution in the document types in **SPRO | SAP Transportation Management | Transportation Management | Freight Order Management | Freight Order | Define Freight Order Types**.

   Following is the configuration path to define and enable the cost distribution in the Freight Settlement Document Type: **SPRO | SAP Transportation Management | Transportation Management | Settlement | Freight Settlement | Define Freight Settlement Document Types**

You activate the `ISR_APPL_AGENCY_4` business function to enable ABD functionality in SAP ERP and you also need to configure the ABD in **SPRO | Logistics General | Agency Business**.

Freight settlement document

An FSD is a business document created to capture the freight cost that is created in SAP TMS and sent to the SAP ERP system for accruals requesting the creation of service PO and SES. It is also used for the verification of the invoice received from the supplier or carrier. When an invoice is received from the carrier, SAP ERP checks the data against the FSD.

The transportation charges are calculated in the FSD based on a freight order or freight booking. The invoice verification message is sent using an SAP NetWeaver **Exchange Infrastructure** (**XI**) message from SAP TMS to SAP ERP and the actual invoice verification takes place in SAP ERP.

The following are the steps executed during freight settlement:

1. The FSD created in SAP TMS runs through the cost distribution process. FSD creation triggers a service that processes the FSD to create the PO and SES. This also posts accruals via SES posting to accounting.

2. Once the PO and SES are created, the confirmation is sent back from the SAP ERP system to SAP TMS.

3. The carrier will send the invoice, which is then verified with the FSD in SAP TMS. Once the verification is successful, the carrier is paid with the amount invoiced.

The following are the background jobs used to create the FSD and transfer the FSD to the ERP system, respectively:

*   `/SCMTMS/SFIR_CREATE`: Creation of the FSD
*   `/SCMTMS/SFIR_ TRANSFER`: Transfer of the FSD to the ERP

Next are the steps required to configure the freight settlement both in SAP TMS and the SAP ERP system:

1. Define the settlement profile: You define the cost distribution method in **SPRO | SAP Transportation Management | Transportation Management | Settlement | Define Settlement Profile**.

2. Assign a settlement profile to the charge profile in the **Define Charges Profiles** configuration and also assign the settlement profile to the carrier business partner under **Vendor Org** data tab.

3. You assign the settlement profile to the charge profile in **SPRO | SAP Transportation Management | Transportation Management | Basic Functions | Charge Calculation | Basic Settings | Define Charges Profiles**.

4. Define the FSD type: You can define the FSD type in the path **SPRO | SAP Transportation Management | Transportation Management | Settlement | Freight Settlement | Define Freight Settlement Document Types**

Figure 11.38 shows the FSD configuration:

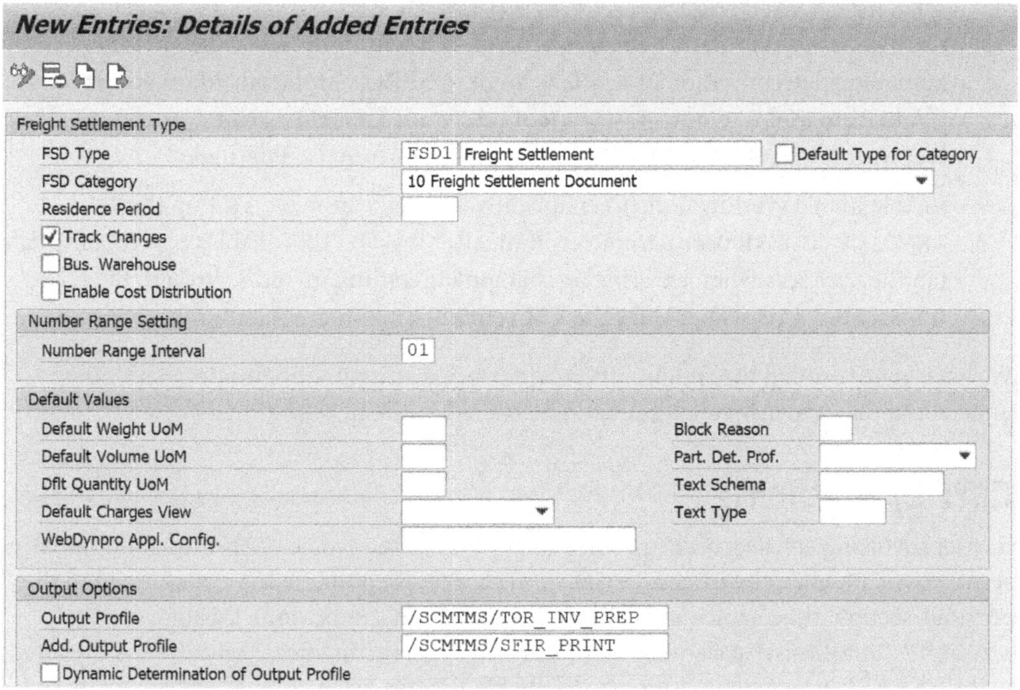

Figure 11.38 – Defining the FSD type

5. Assign an FSD to the freight order: You assign the FSD to the freight order in **SPRO | SAP Transportation Management | Transportation Management | Freight Order Management | Freight Order**.

The following are the steps for freight settlement configuration in SAP ERP:

1. Map the organization in SAP TMS to the organization in the SAP ERP system: You map the organization in SAP TMS to the organization in the SAP ERP system in **SPRO | Integration with other SAP Components | Transportation Management | Invoice Integration | Invoicing | Mapping of Organizational Units | Assign Organizational Units for Purchasing**.

2. Map the charge transportation charges to the service master: You map the organization in SAP TMS to the organization in the SAP ERP system in **SPRO | Integration with other SAP Components | Transportation Management | Invoice Integration | Invoicing | Assignment of Transportation Charge Types | Assign Service Master Record and Account Assignment Category**.

3. Configure the automatic determination of a G/L account: You configure the automatic determination of a G/L account in **SPRO | Materials Management | Valuation and Account Assignment | Account Determination | Account Determination Without Wizard | Configure Automatic Postings**.

4. Enable invoice verification: To enable invoice verification, you set up the `TM_INVOICE_CLERK` user parameter in the user master. This enables control of which tab the user sees when entering or changing incoming invoices through the `MIRO` transaction. This also enables the **TM reference** tab in the `MIRO` transaction.

We have gone through the freight settlement process and its configuration; let's now understand the carrier invoicing function, covered in the next section.

Carrier invoicing

Carrier invoicing consists of the process steps, which are invoice verification and initiating actual payment when the invoice verification process is completed. As mentioned in the previous section, the enablement of invoice verification can be done through the `TM_INVOICE_CLERK` user parameter in the user master. The invoice verification is executed in the SAP ERP system with reference to the FSD. If this verification is successful, then the SAP ERP system sends the information back to SAP TMS. With this, the FSD is updated with the invoice number and the actual amount. SAP TMS also updates the status of the FSD to **Invoice Verified**.

Summary

In this chapter, we have gone through LE, freight settlement, the carrier invoicing process, and the configuration required to set up these processes. We learned about key topics such as the shipment integration between SAP TMS and the SAP ERP system, picking with and without warehouse management, packing with HUs, post goods issues, master data around transportation charge management, freight settlement, and carrier invoices. These are very crucial processes that play an important role in executing the order to cash cycle. If these processes are not run effectively, it will cause delays to the shipment, resulting, in turn, in the loss of customers and business.

We are at the tail end of the order to cash process; our next and last step in the whole order to cash process is customer billing. Customer billing is a critical process where payments are received from the customer. Let's review the billing process and the configuration required to support processes in the next chapter.

Further reading

- Additional information on picking, packing, and goods issues can be found at `https://help.sap.com/viewer/072e1e902dfa4546970c7966a47c42da/6.18.15/en-US/ca34ba53422bb54ce10000000a174cb4.html`.

- Additional information on transportation charge management can be found at `https://help.sap.com/viewer/54cf405c9d9e4c96bf091967ea29d6a7/9.6.2/en-US/a1d8bc8e5bbe474c846c30cff4244646.html`.

12
Customer Billing

Customer billing is the last and the most important step in the Order to Cash cycle. We have gone through the complete Order to Cash cycle right from creating the sales order, fulfilling the sales order, and planning transportation, to picking and posting goods issues in the warehouse in the last few chapters. In this chapter, we will continue with the Order to Cash cycle by describing the billing process. We will cover the different billing document types and their functions. We will also understand how the billing documents are processed once the freight settlement process is completed. As you may recall, the freight settlement process was covered in *Chapter 11, Logistics Execution in SAP LES.*

The following topics will be covered in this chapter:

- Billing process
- Billing document type processing
- Methods of billing
- Billing document type configuration

By the end of this chapter, you will have learned how to set up the billing document types in a SAP ECC system, including billing functionality and different methods of billing.

Billing process

Customer billing is processed once you've create the delivery and shipment. In *Chapter 11, Logistics Execution in SAP LES*, we covered the steps and the process of picking and shipping the goods to the customer. The billing document is generated as soon as the goods are issued to the customer. The billing can be order-related or delivery-related. Within order-related billing, you create a billing document that references the order, whereas with delivery-related billing, you create a billing document that references the delivery document. Once the order has been billed, the delivery shows the billing status as completed. Once the billing document has been generated and saved, the billing data is then transferred to financial accounting so that the account receivables can be processed.

Billing document type processing

The billing document type controls the features of the billing document's functionality. Like any other SAP transactions, the billing document type contains the basic configuration you need, which includes the number range assignment, general billing control data that's relevant for billing, billing category, account assignment data, output, and partner and text configuration.

SAP provides different billing types to process billing documents. Let's go through each of these billing document types and understand the concept behind when these billing documents types are used in which business scenarios.

Customer billing

Customer billing type F2 is generated when the goods are sent to the customer. When you create this type of customer billing, the billing document is referenced in terms of when you want to bill the customer for the goods that have been shipped. If you want to bill the customer and receive money before the goods are shipped out, then you can bill the customer by creating a billing document that references the sales order. You can define the billing document's relevance by going to **SPRO | Sales and Distribution | Sales | Sales Documents | Sales Document Item | Define Item Categories**.

The following screenshot shows the **Billing Relevance** configuration, wherein H stands for delivery-related billing and F stands for order-related billing:

Change View "Maintain Item Categories": Details

New Entries BC Set: Change Field Values

| Item category | TAN | Standard Item |

Business Data

Item Type		☑ Business Item
Completion Rule		☑ Sched.Line Allowed
Special Stock		☐ Item Relev.for Dlv
Billing Relevance	H	☐ Returns
Billing Plan Type		☑ Wght/Vol.Relevant
Billing Block		☑ Credit active
Pricing	X	☑ Determine Cost
Statistical value		
Revenue Recognition		
Delimit. Start Date		

Figure 12.1 – Billing relevance configuration

SAP has provided various options for billing relevance; you can configure these options based on your business needs. Now, let's review some other billing document types.

Credit memo

Like customer billing, another type of billing document is the **credit memo**. This billing document type is used when you want to give the customer their money back, such as when they have returned goods. This is generally used in complaint scenarios. Customers may call to complain about the goods that have been delivered. This may be due to delivery, quality, or any other product-related issue. In this case, you will create a credit memo document that's of the CR billing document type. There are two types of such document: one where how the goods were transported is involved and you want to give the customer their money back, while the other is where you simply want to refund the customer without them needing to return the goods. The billing document type that's used for returning goods is RE - Credit on Return, whereas the billing document type that's used where this is not involved is G2 - Credit. You can create a credit memo request or returns document by using the reference to the sales order, a customer billing document, or no reference. For returns, an inbound delivery is created, and a **Post Goods Receipt (PGR)** is posted. Once the PGR has been posted, the credit on returns billing document type is created and credit is given to the customer. For credit without goods movement, a credit memo request is created with reference to the invoice document and a CR credit memo billing document is generated.

Debit memo

Debit memo is another billing document type that can be created when you want to charge customers more than what were supposed to be charged when generating customer bill. You may wish to do this when it costs more to deliver the item, an incorrect price is shown on the customer billing document, and so on. SAP provides the L2 – Debit Memo standard billing document type for creating a debit memo. In the case of a debit memo, the supplier receives money, which increases the receivables in their financial account. Like a credit memo, a debit memo request is created with reference to the customer invoice or sales order, or is created without a reference. Referencing a document such as a customer invoice or sales order copies all the data from this document to the debit memo request document. Once the debit memo request has been generated, the debit memo billing document is posted to the customer so that they can send the funds they owe the supplier. In the case of a debit memo, the goods don't need to be returned.

Pro forma invoice

Pro forma invoice is a type of billing document that can be used for export scenarios or when the customer needs a replica of the invoice for authority approval. The pro forma invoice is not posted to financial accounting, so the pro forma data is not passed on to the **Financial Accounting (FI)** module for receivables to be processed. SAP provides two billing document types for the pro forma invoice: **F5 - Pro Forma** for order and the **F8 - Pro Forma** invoice for delivery. A pro forma invoice consists of the data that matches the actual billing document so that it can be shown to customs authorities to prove the cost of the goods that have been sold.

Intercompany billing

Intercompany billing is a type of billing that can be used when the sales company is shipping goods that don't belong to the same company code of the sales company. For example, if there are two different lines of products and both are produced in different plants that fall under different sales structures (SO1 and SO2), they are assigned different company codes (C1 and C2). If Sales Org SO1 sells a product that is produced in the plant and is assigned sales structure SO2 and company code C2, then this triggers the intercompany sales transaction between company code C1 and company code C2. As a result, intercompany billing takes place between the two company codes. SAP has provided standard intercompany **billing type IV - Intercompany Billing**, which can be used for this purpose. Intracompany sales are within the same company code and don't involve two company codes. Intracompany sales are mostly where stock transfer occurs between the two plants that fall under the same company code.

Cancellation invoice

SAP has provided the S1 - Cancellation Invoice billing document type so that we can process a customer invoice being canceled. Based on your business needs, you can configure and process this billing document type. This can be used when an error has been found in the customer billing document.

Now that we have covered the different types of billing document, let's understand the different methods of billing that can be used to bill the customer.

Methods of billing

SAP has provided different methods we can use to bill customers. Based on your business needs, you may want to consider billing a customer for every delivery when you ship the products out to the customer, or when the shipping volume is more but the volume of the goods of each delivery is partial or less than a truckload; at this point, you may want to club multiple deliveries together and bill the customer in one go.

This depends on the type of business you are in and for this reason, SAP has provided options such as individual billing and collective billing.

One another option that SAP has provided is an invoice split. You can have different business rules to split the invoice into multiple invoices for a single delivery. For example, if the payment terms are different on different line items on the sales order, you may want to split the invoice, even though all the items have been shipped out in one delivery.

Let's go through each of these options and understand their capabilities.

Individual billing

Individual billing is defined by creating each invoice for each delivery that's been created for the sales order. The following diagram shows a couple of examples of individual billing. For example, a sales order with one delivery has one invoice, whereas a sales order with multiple deliveries has an equal number of invoices:

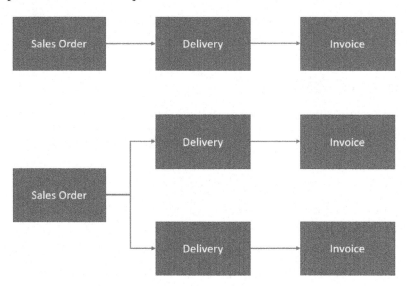

Figure 12.2 – Individual billing

In a business scenario where you are working with a full truckload and the volume isn't that big, most businesses would go for individual invoices. Again, this is based on specific business requirements and determined through copy control settings.

The copy control settings are where you define a single invoice. You can do this by going to **SPRO | Sales and Distribution | Billing | Billing Documents | Maintain Copying Control for Billing Documents**.

The following screenshot shows the copy control setting, from delivery to invoice:

Change View "Item": Details

New Entries   [icons]   BC Set: Change Field Values

Dialog Structure		
▼ Header		
• Item		

Target		Source	
Target Bill. Type	F2	From Delivery Type	LF
	Invoice		Outbound Delivery
		Item Category	TAN
			Standard Item

Copy

Copying requirements	004	Deliv-related item	Billing quantity	B
Data VBRK/VBRP	003	Single invoice	Pos./neg. quantity	+
			Pricing type	G
			PricingExchRate type	
			☐ Cumulate cost	
			Price source	F

Figure 12.3 – Copy control setting from delivery to invoice

In the preceding screenshot, **Data VBRK/VBRP** for the item category has a routine of `003 Single Invoice`, which drives the creation of individual billing for a specific delivery document.

We'll review collective billing in the next section and understand how that is set up in a SAP ECC system.

Collective billing

Combining multiple sales orders and multiple delivery costs into one billing document is known as **collective billing**. The following diagram shows how one sales order with multiple deliveries can be used to create one invoice:

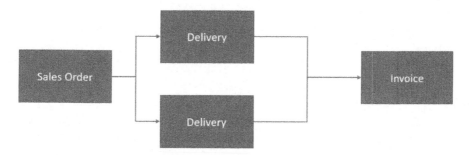

Figure 12.4 – Collective billing (1)

Another example is shown in the following diagram. This shows that multiple sales orders have their corresponding deliveries and that combining all these deliveries creates one invoice document:

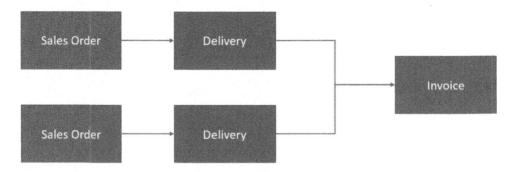

Figure 12.5 – Collective billing (2)

To create collective billing, you need to process the billing due list, which can be accessed with transaction code VF04. With collective billing, the system combines multiple delivery documents that have the same customer number, and they contain customer data and sales org data. This can be seen in the following screenshot:

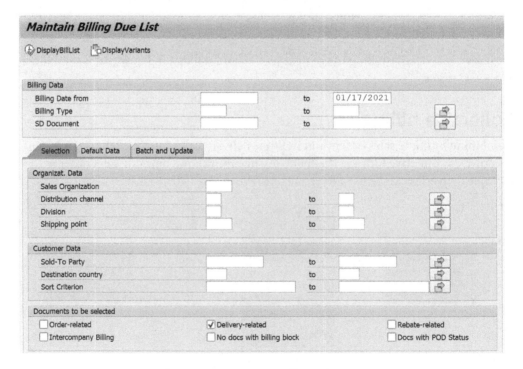

Figure 12.6 – Maintain Billing Due List

Now, let's jump into another method, known as invoice split.

Invoice split

Invoice split is the process of creating multiple invoices for one sales order or delivery, as shown in the following diagram:

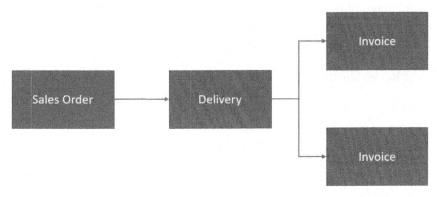

Figure 12.7 – Invoice split

An invoice split is done based on line item fields, and you can add more rules to the copy control to split the invoices. SAP has provided standard routine 001 for this, which you can leverage to add your own business rules and additional fields to split the invoices into multiple invoices.

You can configure the copy control routine by going to **SPRO | Sales and Distribution | Billing | Billing Documents | Maintain Copying Control for Billing Documents**.

One example of an invoice split is concerned with payment terms. The payment terms are at the header and the line item in the sales order, whereas the payment term is on the header in the invoice document. Therefore, if you have different payment terms on the header and the item in the sales order, then the invoice will be split based on the payment terms. This is because the payment terms are in the header of the invoice document.

Now that we have covered different methods of billing, let's look at billing type configuration and the options available.

Billing document type configuration

To create a billing document once an item has been delivered, you must configure the billing document type based on your business needs. The configuration path you can use to configure the billing document type is **SPRO | Sales and Distribution | Billing | Billing Documents | Define Billing Types**.

The following screenshot shows the **General Control** data billing type, which controls the number range assignment and signifies which type of document it is. The invoice document category is M, whereas the delivery document category is J:

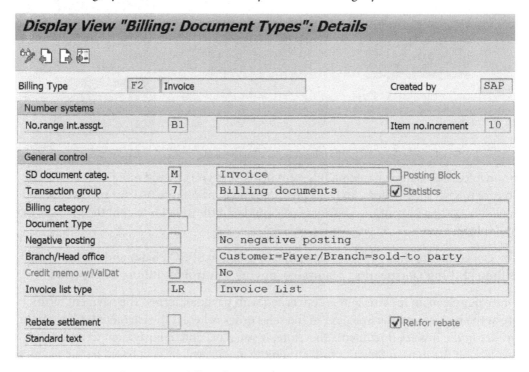

Figure 12.8 – Billing document type – General control data

You can also control if you can execute negative posting and if the invoice is relevant for rebate processing. Posting a block checkbox prevents the billing document from being automatically posted to accounting.

The following screenshot shows the cancellation and account assignment/pricing configuration within the billing document type:

Cancellation		
Cancell.billing type	S1	Cancel. Invoice (S1)
Copying requirements	0	
Reference number		
Assignment Number	E	

Account assignment/pricing		
AcctDetermProc.	KOFI00	Account determination
Doc. pric. procedure	A	Standard
Acc. det. rec. acc.		
Acc. det. cash. set.		
Acc. det. pay. cards	A00001	Standard

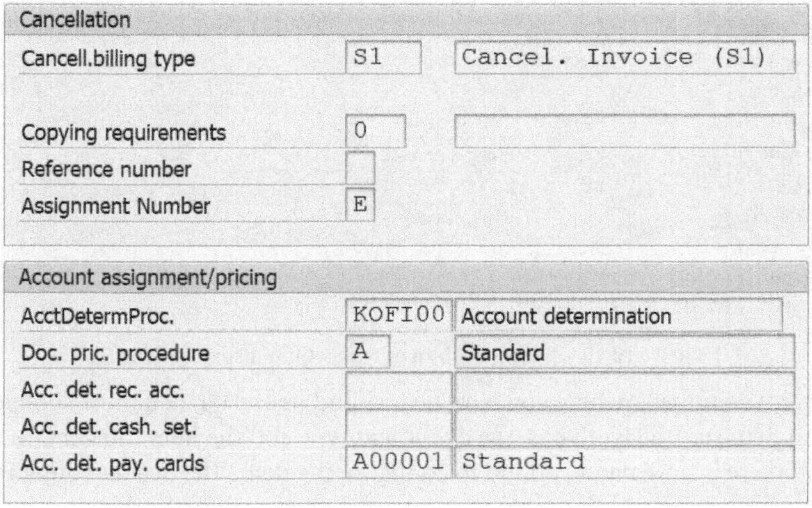

Figure 12.9 – Billing document type – Cancellation and account assignment/pricing

SAP has provided a standard cancellation billing type S1 for customer billing document F2. In most business scenarios, the best practice is to create a credit or debit memo, so canceling an F2 customer invoice is very unusual. Once you've canceled the customer invoice, the system automatically uses an S1 cancellation invoice, as well as the copy requirement that's been configured in the billing document type.

Within account assignment/pricing, the account's assignment and pricing is determined based on the settings that have been configured in the billing document type. The account determination procedure determines the correct general ledger accounts for entry posting. To determine the pricing procedure, a document pricing procedure indicator is used. Price procedure determination is also based on the sales area and the customer pricing procedure.

The following screenshot shows the **Output/partners/texts** options, which you can also configure with the billing document type:

Output/partners/texts				
Output determ.proc.	V10000	Billing Output	Application	V3
Item output proc.				
Output Type	RD00	Invoice		
Header partners	FK	Billing document		
Item partners	FP	Billing Item		
TextDetermProcedure	03	Billing Header		
Text determ.proc.itm	04	Billing Item		
☐ Delivery text				

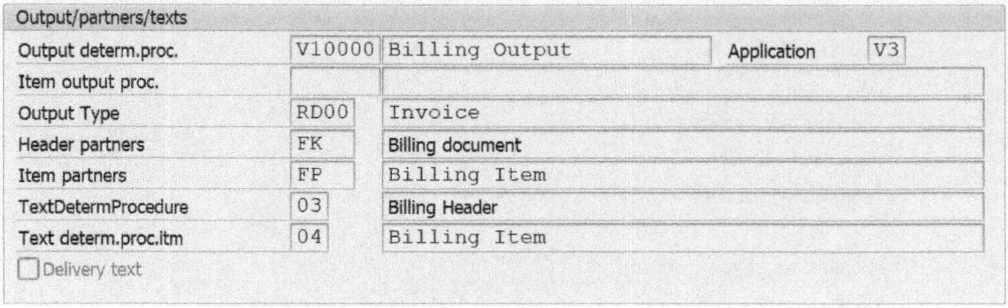

Figure 12.10 – Billing document type – Output/partners/texts

Unlike a sales document, where you have header and item data, you must configure the header and item separately; that is, the document type and the item category. In a billing document, there is no separate option to configure the item. The header configuration drives both the header and the item.

You can define and assign the header and item procedure for output, partners, and text in the billing document type configuration.

Additionally, SAP has provided the RV60SBAT program, which you can run as a background job to create a billing document at regular intervals.

Now that we have reviewed the billing document type configuration, let's go through the copy control setting, for which you need to copy the data from a delivery or order billing to the invoice. To configure the copy control, go to **SPRO | Sales and Distribution | Billing | Billing Documents | Maintain Copying Control for Billing Documents**.

Figure 12.11 shows the **Copy Control – Header data** configuration, where you enter the source document type that you want to copy the data from and the target document type to create the invoice document for:

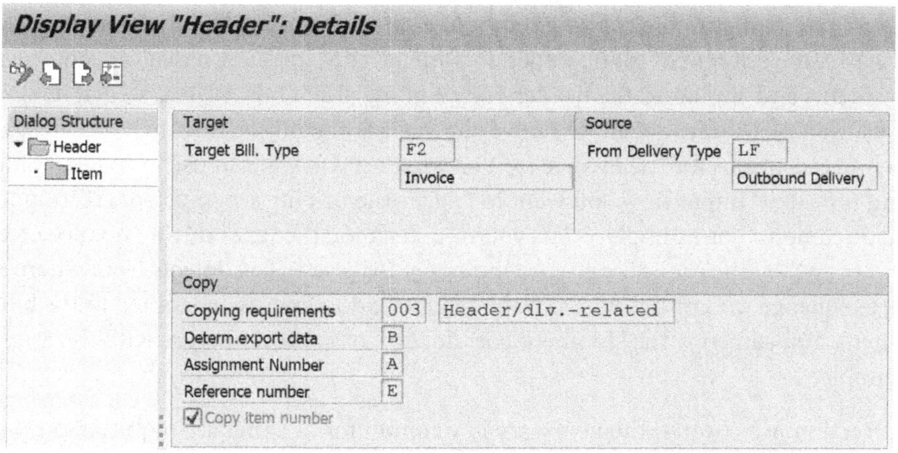

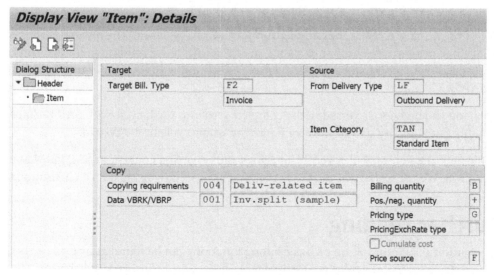

Figure 12.11 – Copy control – Header configuration

SAP has provided three options for the copy control: a sales document, a billing document, and a delivery document. In the header, SAP has provided the copying requirements that you can implement to copy the data from the source to the target document. Based on your business rules, you can implement an exception here. You can transfer the assignment number and the reference number from **Sales and Distribution** (**SD**) module to FI based on the options you've selected in this configuration option. Similar to the header, you can select the item category and configure the item-specific requirements for the copy control at the item level. The following screenshot shows an example of the item category's TAN copy control configuration:

Figure 12.12 – Copy control – Item configuration

Here, you can configure the copying requirement based on the data that you would copy from the source document to the target document. This, again, is based on your business requirements and similar to the header copy routine. The **Data VBRK/VBRP** field signifies what method you want to use while creating the billing document; that is, you can define exceptions for the invoice split or whether you want to use individual billing. **Pricing type** determines how you want to trigger the pricing when you're creating the billing document. For example, G lets you re-determine the taxes during invoice creation, thus keeping the other condition types the same. **Price source** controls from where and in what sequence the conditions from the reference documents are copied to the billing document. You can copy the shipment cost document condition types with the F option, for example.

In this section, we covered the necessary key configurations that are required to set up a billing document type and learned how to use the copy control to successfully create a billing document. With this, we have covered all the important aspects of billing documents. Now, let's review the topics we've covered in this chapter.

Summary

In this chapter, we covered the billing process and billing document type processing, including customer invoicing, credit memos, debit memos, pro forma invoices, intercompany invoices, and cancellation invoices. With this, you should have a good understanding of the customer billing document. We also covered the methods of billing, including individual billing, collective billing, and invoice split. Additionally, we understood how to configure the billing document type with the copy control.

With this, we have covered the complete Order to Cash cycle with the mySAP Business Suite. This includes sales order processing in SAP CRM, order fulfillment in SAP APO, transportation planning in SAP TMS, logistics execution with SAP LES, and finally billing in SAP ECC.

Now, you should be well-versed in the complete Order to Cash cycle with SAP Business Suite, its functionality, and how to configure the whole cycle in the system.

In the next chapter, we will cover the analytics and reporting concept in SAP CRM and SAP TMS. We will also cover the HANA Sidecar approach by using a SAP environment.

Further reading

- Additional information on basic billing functions can be found at `https://help.sap.com/viewer/a2d139d094f04ad6812f613fa64640d4/6.18.15/en-US/d46fb6535fe6b74ce10000000a174cb4.html`.

13
Analytics

This is the last chapter of this book. Now that we have gone through the complete Order to Cash cycle, including master data, it is vital to understand some of the reporting capabilities and measure the accuracy of the Order to Cash cycle. Understanding sales analytics provides insight into sales forecasting and helps us plan for production based on historical data. Two things are key when it comes to analytics: how analytics improves the existing processes and how it helps us plan future sales efficiently. In this chapter, we will focus on reporting related to sales and transportation and understand some of the key reporting capabilities that are available.

Here is the list of topics that will be covered in this chapter:

- Analytics overview
- CRM analytics
- TMS analytics
- Analytics powered by HANA

By the end of this chapter, you will have learned about the concepts of analytics and reporting in SAP CRM and SAP TM. You will have also understood the concept of the HANA Sidecar approach in a SAP environment and how to leverage the reporting capabilities with HANA Sidecar.

Analytics overview

Analytics helps you measure, predict, and optimize the overall Order to Cash cycle, which results in customer satisfaction. In analytics, data that's gathered via operational transactions is analyzed in terms of how customers are being serviced. This can help us identify the key customers and help with cross-selling and up-selling potential. Analytics helps forecast the organization's needs and determine the customer's behavior. Data collection and analysis is an ongoing and iterative process. With effective analytics, companies can reduce their unnecessary inventories, thereby reducing overall inventory costs.

Analytics provides organizations with real-time insights into key customer information, such as their identity, behavior, activity, and much more. This helps organizations plan their manufacturing processes and accomplish on-time delivery. Sales and accurate transportation data helps customers and transportation service specialists provide effective customer interaction, which results in strategic and effective selling.

This chapter will focus on the master data and transactional reporting aspect, which is essentially all about the reports in the SAP CRM and SAP TMS systems. The reporting functionality within these systems covers analytics processes that help organizations understand their customers' behavior and provide timely delivery. Sales analytics provides information about the sales data so that we can analyze company performance, whereas freight analytics helps us effectively plan transportation and strategic processes. Combining these analytics processes provides companies with a competitive edge. **Business Intelligence (BI)**, on the other hand, offers a comprehensive reporting functionality as separate application software.

Let's deep dive into some of the reporting capabilities in SAP CRM.

CRM analytics

SAP NetWeaver Building Block consists of BI, which allows companies to work through the **Business Warehouse (BW)** reporting functionalities within SAP CRM. Additional BI content within SAP CRM also allows an organization to work through Interactive reporting, which helps companies meet their ad hoc reporting requirements.

Generally, SAP BW's reporting functionality is used, which is a separate system connected to SAP CRM. This concept of historical reporting driven by SAP BW is true for many SAP systems, such as SAP TMS, SAP ECC, and so on. SAP CRM transaction data is loaded into the business data warehousing system using standard or custom data sources. SAP has provided standard data sources for each transaction object, such as sales orders, contracts, and quotations. Once the data has been extracted from the data sources, and then transformed and loaded into the BW system, it is stored in the operational data stores or OLAP cubes in the BW system.

Based on your organization's reporting requirements, the BW reports are then launched from the CRM system and can be role-specific.

The following diagram shows a breakdown of SAP CRM Analytics. It shows the specific areas in which SAP CRM provides sales reporting capabilities:

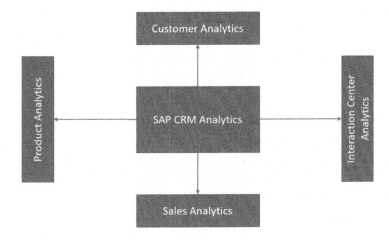

Figure 13.1 – SAP CRM Analytics reporting capabilities

The following are the capabilities of SAP CRM Analytics reporting:

- Sales analytics
- Customer analytics
- Product analytics
- Interaction center analytics

Now, let's examine each of these in more detail.

Sales analytics

With **sales analytics**, an organization can understand market trends regarding which product sells the best and the sales pipeline. This helps organizations plan the customer's delivery and improve on sales planning. The following are some of the sales analytics reporting capabilities that are useful for an organization:

- Sales Planning
- Sales Pipeline Analysis
- Activity Analysis
- Opportunity Planning and Analysis
- Contract Analysis
- Sales Quotation and Order Analysis
- Sales Analysis

SAP CRM Analytics also provides sales order and sales contract analysis capabilities, which drive many of the organization's key selling decisions.

Customer analytics

It is imperative for any organization to understand the customer buying behavior. **Customer analytics** helps organizations gather customer-related information and that way, an organization can predict their customer's behavior. Here are some of the customer analytics reporting capabilities you can use:

- Customer Satisfaction and Loyalty Analysis
- Customer Segmentation with Clustering
- Account and Fact Sheet Analysis
- Customer Profitability Analysis
- BP Marketing Attributes Analysis

In addition to customer behavior, organizations are also interested in understanding their prime customers so that they can bring more business to the organization. This is also known as **customer value analysis**.

Product analytics

Product analytics helps organizations understand the associated products that can be sold to customers. Some examples of product analytics reporting are listed here:

- My Top 10 Products
- Product Profitability
- Cross Selling Analysis
- Complaints by Product
- Competitor Analysis

Making the right decision regarding cross-selling analysis helps organizations increase their sales and, in turn, generate more revenue.

Interaction center analytics

SAP CRM Analytics provides reporting capabilities that capture interactions between the customers and the customer service representative. Understanding the average wait time for calls to be received, the percentage of the calls that are answered, customer feedback, and so on is important to know, and improving on customer service results in customer satisfaction. The following are some examples of Interaction center reports:

- Interaction center Analytics
- Helpdesk Analytics
- Interactive Scripting Analytics
- E-Mail Response Management System Analytics
- Interaction Statistics

The following screenshot shows some of the reports that are available from the Analytics Professional Business Role:

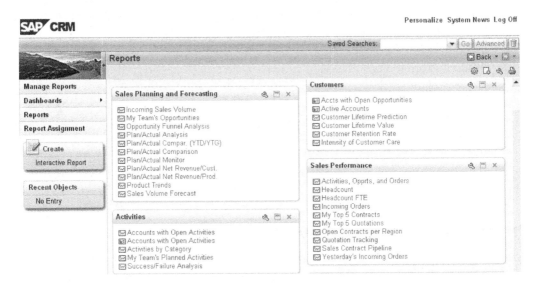

Figure 13.2 – SAP CRM Analytics Professional Business Role

This includes **Sales Planning and Forecasting, Customers, Activities,** and **Sales Performance**.

Report assignment function

SAP CRM's Analytics Professional Business Role allows us to assign the reports from SAP NetWeaver BW to the selected Business Role and their work centers. You can also select and assign interactive reports to the Business Role and their work centers.

The following screenshot shows how to assign reports to the Business Role view from
ANALYTICSPRO – Analytics Professional:

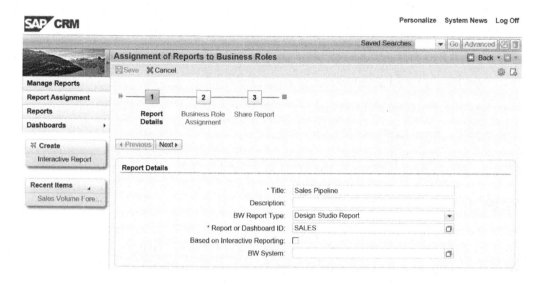

Figure 13.3 – Assigning reports to a Business Role

The following report types can be imported using the wizard:

- BW Enterprise Report 7.x

- BW Info Provider 7.x

- BW Query7.x

- BW QueryViews7.x, 3.x

- BW Template 7.x, 3.x

- Xcelsius dashboards

- Crystal Reports

- SAP BusinessObjectsEnterprise reports (for example, Web Intelligence)

CRM Analytics provides different options based on the user experience. This means that the appropriate reporting tool should be available for the right user group. There are different reporting tool options available, as follows:

- Xcelsius
- Crystal Reports
- Web Intelligence/CRM Interactive reporting
- SAP BusinessObjects Explorer
- SAP **Business Explorer** (**BEX**)

Now, let's learn how Interactive reporting works in SAP CRM.

Interactive reporting

SAP CRM also provides real-time reporting as part of its Interactive reporting for data modeling. It is also helpful for an organization that is not dependent on separate SAP BW systems and provides functionality for creating ad hoc reports based on their specific needs. For Interactive reporting, you don't need a separate SAP NetWeaver BW system. BI content within SAP CRM is used to run Interactive reporting, and you need to create a separate client within SAP CRM to access Interactive reporting. Interactive reporting is a self-service reporting and analysis process that is simple to use and is designed for all types of users.

The following interactive reports are available in each of the CRM Sales areas:

- Sales Analytics
- Opportunities
- Activities
- Sales Quotation
- Sales Order
- Sales Contracts

SAP has a CRM **Interactive Reporting Configuration Wizard** transaction code of -/CRMBW/CONFIG_WIZARD, which consists of the configuration steps to activate Interactive reporting. To use the interactive reporting configuration wizard, you need to activate the SAP Business Objects Integration and CRM Interactive Reporting business function (CRM_ANA_BOB).

Now that we have looked at some of the key reporting capabilities in SAP CRM, let's review the reporting and analytics capabilities in SAP TMS.

TMS analytics

Like SAP CRM Analytics, SAP TMS Analytics allows you to collect and merge different data elements across different operational areas, thus imparting insight and transparency into the transportation processes. Reporting in SAP TMS can lead you to effectively understanding the most profitable transportation and shipping routes. Having reporting capabilities in this area can improve the overall cost of the product, and that can lead to you maximizing your profit.

The following diagram shows the typical layout you'll come across when working with a SAP NetWeaver BW environment:

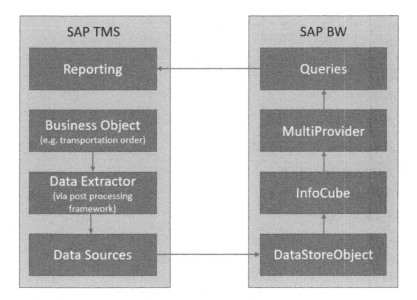

Figure 13.4 – SAP TMS reporting integration with SAP NetWeaver BW

SAP provides delivered contents within SAP NetWeaver BW and the standard extractors that extract data from SAP TMS. You can use this to transfer data to SAP BW, wherein the data from different objects and systems can be merged to show it on the reporting application in the SAP TM system.

The business object is associated with the extractors that extract the data from the business object. Before you execute any kind of reporting work, the pre-requisite is to connect SAP TMS to the SAP NetWeaver BW system so that the extractors can extract the data and transfer it to SAP BW. Transaction code RSA5 in SAP TM consists of all the data sources for the master data and the transactional data.

The data extractor is the method program that extracts the data and loads the data source tables. You execute these extractors to load the data in the data sources. The data in the data sources is then transferred to the SAP NetWeaver BW. Within SAP NetWeaver BW, the data is stored in the datastore objects.

The data that's stored in the datastore objects are placed in InfoCube, which is then used by the MultiProviders, which use the data from various sources. Once the data is made available in the MultiProviders, this data is used in different queries. You can also combine this data with other information to perform further analysis in SAP NetWeaver BW. This reporting information can then be accessed in SAP TMS for the user to view.

SAP provides many standard MultiProviders, as well as the relevant queries:

- Transportation Request
- Transportation Order
- Transportation Cost Analysis
- Transportation Revenue Analysis
- Transportation Allocation
- Business Share
- Trade Lane Analysis
- Transportation Order Execution

In this section, we reviewed the reporting capabilities within SAP TMS and its integration with SAP NetWeaver BW. Both SAP CRM and SAP TMS can be powered by HANA as a sidecar and leverage key real-time reporting. We'll look at this next.

Analytics powered by HANA

SAP Business Suite is powered by **SAP HANA**, which allows us to use in-memory computing. This means that a large amount of data can be stored in the main memory of the database system, which reduces how long it takes to fetch the data and run the logic on SAP Business Suite. This improves the business processes in one aspect and reduces the round trip to the database system. In-memory computing can be used to message and analyze massive amounts of data and gives you the result without any delay. This helps organizations make key decisions quickly, thereby increasing the organization's overall efficiency.

In simple terms, SAP HANA is a modern platform that leverages the power of in-memory computing. SAP HANA provides real-time analytics capabilities because of massive data being accommodated in memory. It also gives the information back to the source system. With the transaction data and analytical data stored, operational analytics can be executed in real time, which helps organizations make decisions on key issues quickly.

SAP HANA can be used in conjunction with SAP Business Suite; that is, SAP CRM, SAP TMS, and SAP ERP. Here, the data flows from SAP Business Suite to SAP HANA in real time. The data within SAP HANA is fed into SAP BI or SAP Business Suite.

The following diagram shows SAP HANA on a sidecar with a new application:

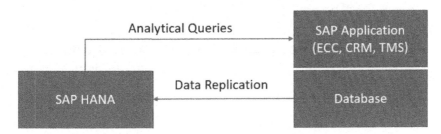

Figure 13.5 – SAP HANA in a sidecar approach with a new application

In the sidecar approach, you can implement SAP HANA without changing your existing system setup. Operational information can be transferred to SAP HANA in real time so that it can be used for real-time analytics.

SAP CRM and SAP TMS, when powered by SAP HANA, also provides key insights into the complete Order to Cash cycle in real time. This helps us quickly improve any process gaps that have been identified through reporting.

Summary

This chapter provided an overview of SAP CRM Analytics and SAP TMS Analytics, along with some of its key reporting functions. We looked at the areas where SAP CRM and SAP TMS Analytics have provided reporting capabilities that can help your organization get the required information to make key decisions, once the Order to Cash process has been reviewed. Some of the reporting capabilities we covered included those surrounding products, customer, sales, Interaction center, and transportation analytics. In addition to these reports, you learned about Interactive reporting, which acts as an ad hoc report that provides real-time information about operational analytics. You also learned about the basic functions of SAP CRM and SAP TMS Analytics, both of which are powered by SAP HANA.

At this point, you have a good understanding of the analytics and reporting concepts in SAP CRM and SAP TM. With this chapter, we have covered the complete O2C cycle including master data, transaction data, and its integration touchpoints to SAP business suites and analytics.

Further reading

- Additional information on SAP CRM Analytics can be found at `https://help.sap.com/viewer/e90618c412754f38bcf6776fe9c1c64e/7.0.4.15/en-US/4582ba557e9a40bfe10000000a1553f7.html`.

- Additional information on SAP TMS Analytics can be found at `https://help.sap.com/viewer/54cf405c9d9e4c96bf091967ea29d6a7/9.6.2/en-US/629c30be88ce47d5ab247d37e533c6e0.html`.

`Packt.com`

Subscribe to our online digital library for full access to over 7,000 books and videos, as well as industry leading tools to help you plan your personal development and advance your career. For more information, please visit our website.

Why subscribe?

- Spend less time learning and more time coding with practical eBooks and Videos from over 4,000 industry professionals

- Improve your learning with Skill Plans built especially for you

- Get a free eBook or video every month

- Fully searchable for easy access to vital information

- Copy and paste, print, and bookmark content

Did you know that Packt offers eBook versions of every book published, with PDF and ePub files available? You can upgrade to the eBook version at packt.com and as a print book customer, you are entitled to a discount on the eBook copy. Get in touch with us at customercare@packtpub.com for more details.

At www.packt.com, you can also read a collection of free technical articles, sign up for a range of free newsletters, and receive exclusive discounts and offers on Packt books and eBooks.

Other Books You May Enjoy

If you enjoyed this book, you may be interested in this other book by Packt:

SAP on Azure Implementation Guide

Nick Morgan and Bartosz Jarkowski

ISBN: 978-1-83898-398-7

- Successfully migrate your SAP infrastructure to Azure
- Understand the security benefits of Azure
- See how Azure can scale to meet the most demanding of business needs
- Ensure your SAP infrastructure maintains high availability
- Increase business agility through cloud capabilities
- Leverage cloud-native capabilities to enhance SAP

Mastering SAP ABAP

Paweł Grześkowiak, Wojciech Ciesielski, and Wojciech Ćwik

ISBN: 978-1-78728-894-2

- Create stable and error-free ABAP programs
- Leverage new ABAP concepts including object-oriented programming(OOP) and Model-View-Controller (MVC)
- Learn to add custom code to your existing SAP program
- Speed up your ABAP programs by spotting bottlenecks
- Understand techniques such as performance tuning and optimization
- Develop modern and beautiful user interfaces (UIs) in an ABAP environment
- Build multiple classes with any nesting level

Packt is searching for authors like you

If you're interested in becoming an author for Packt, please visit `authors.packtpub.com` and apply today. We have worked with thousands of developers and tech professionals, just like you, to help them share their insight with the global tech community. You can make a general application, apply for a specific hot topic that we are recruiting an author for, or submit your own idea.

Leave a review - let other readers know what you think

Please share your thoughts on this book with others by leaving a review on the site that you bought it from. If you purchased the book from Amazon, please leave us an honest review on this book's Amazon page. This is vital so that other potential readers can see and use your unbiased opinion to make purchasing decisions, we can understand what our customers think about our products, and our authors can see your feedback on the title that they have worked with Packt to create. It will only take a few minutes of your time, but is valuable to other potential customers, our authors, and Packt. Thank you!

Index

S

Made in the USA
Coppell, TX
25 March 2022